Routledge Revivals

Realism in Alexandrian Poetry

The poetry of Alexandria under the first three Ptolemies represents a second golden age of Greek literature. The eminence grise of poetic circles was Callimachus, whose poetic manifesto in favour of small scale, meticulously detailed and mannered works was to be of great influence on Augustan poetry in Rome. The stylistic aims of the Alexandrian poets have been much discussed, as has their reliance on literary tradition.

First published in 1987, *Realism in Alexandrian Poetry* covers less familiar ground. Taking the whole canon of Alexandrian poetry as his starting point, Dr Zanker surveys the use of the realistic mode in works like *The Idylls of Theocritus* (were these real shepherds?), including such matters as the humorous elements of Callimachus Hymns, the love-story in Apollonius' 'Argonautica', and the low-life sketches of epyllia like Hecale as well as the *Mimes of Herodas*. The striving for realism and minute detail is set in the context of the admiration of pictorialism in the plastic arts, the new valuation of science as a measure of human experience, and the deliberate mingling of high and low genres. All this is in turn placed in the cultural context of early Alexandria. Few books take the whole of Alexandrian poetry as their canvas. This one which does will be as valuable a study of the Alexandrian poets as it will be a forceful contribution to literary criticism.

Realism in Alexandrian Poetry
A Literature and its Audience

Graham Zanker

First published in 1987
by Croom Helm Ltd

This edition first published in 2024 by Routledge
4 Park Square, Milton Park, Abingdon, Oxon, OX14 4RN

and by Routledge
605 Third Avenue, New York, NY 10017

Routledge is an imprint of the Taylor & Francis Group, an informa business

© G. Zanker 1987

All rights reserved. No part of this book may be reprinted or reproduced or utilised in any form or by any electronic, mechanical, or other means, now known or hereafter invented, including photocopying and recording, or in any information storage or retrieval system, without permission in writing from the publishers.

Publisher's Note
The publisher has gone to great lengths to ensure the quality of this reprint but points out that some imperfections in the original copies may be apparent.

Disclaimer
The publisher has made every effort to trace copyright holders and welcomes correspondence from those they have been unable to contact.

A Library of Congress record exists under LCCN: 86023994

ISBN: 978-1-032-85806-7 (hbk)
ISBN: 978-1-003-51992-8 (ebk)
ISBN: 978-1-032-85807-4 (pbk)

Book DOI 10.4324/9781003519928

REALISM IN ALEXANDRIAN POETRY:
A LITERATURE AND ITS AUDIENCE

G. Zanker

CROOM HELM
London • Sydney • Wolfeboro, New Hampshire

© G. Zanker 1987
Croom Helm, Provident House, Burrell Row,
Beckenham, Kent BR3 1AT
Croom Helm Australia Pty Ltd, Suite 4, 6th Floor,
64–76 Kippax Street, Surry Hills, NSW 2010, Australia

British Library Cataloguing in Publication Data
Zanker, Graham
  Realism in Alexandrain poetry: a
  literature and its audience.
  1. Greek poetry — History and criticism
  2. Realism in literature
  I. Title
  881'.01'0912   PA3014.R4
  ISBN 0–7099–3005–4

Croom Helm US, 27 South Main Street,
Wolfeboro, New Hampshire 03894-2069

Library of Congress Cataloging-in-Publication Data

Zanker, Graham, 1947-
  Realism in Alexandrian poetry.
  Bibliography:p.
  1. Greek poetry, Hellenistic — History and criticism.
  2. Greek poetry, Hellenistic — Egypt — Alexandria — History
  and criticism. 3. Realism in literature. 4. Callimachus
  — History and criticism. 5. Callimachus — Influence.
  I. Title.
  PA3014.R4Z36   1986   881'.01'09   86-23994
  ISBN 0-7099-3005-4

For Ruth

Printed and bound in Great Britain by Mackays of Chatham Ltd, Kent

Contents

Acknowledgements
Abbreviations
1. Definitions and a Sample   1
2. The Hellenistic Theory of Pictorial Realism   39
3. The Practice of Pictorial Realism   55
4. The Appeal to Science   113
5. The Ancient Theory and Pre-Alexandrian Practice of
   Everyday and Low Realism   133
6. The Everyday and the Low in Alexandrian Poetry   155
Conclusion   229
Bibliography   233
Index   243

Acknowledgements

I have received generous help in writing this book. I must first thank institutions: the University of Canterbury for a number of research grants; the Institute of Classical Studies at the University of London for awarding me the 1985 Commonwealth Study Grant which enabled me to work on the final draft in ideal conditions; and the Deutscher Akademischer Austauschdienst for financing an invaluable sojourn in Tübingen in autumn, 1985. Then there are the friends. Miss F. Muecke and Dr R.L. Hunter read through the penultimate draft in its entirety, Professor K.H. Lee, Dr P.J. Tremewan, Professor C. Collard and Mrs P.E. Easterling in part. Their comments have led to a major re-shaping of the book, and the reader should be as grateful to them as I am. Professor P. Bing, Dr N. Hopkinson and Professor E.A. Schmidt read and criticised parts of the final draft, which has in consequence been improved in many places. I have benefited from the reactions of audiences in Cambridge, Durham, Heidelberg, Tübingen, the Canberra Humanities Research Centre and Berkeley who have patiently listened to some of my thoughts on the Alexandrians. Sadly, I cannot thank Mr L.P. Wilkinson, who died a year ago to the day. Patrick was my doctoral supervisor at Cambridge and introduced me to Hellenistic poetry with characteristic sensitivity and ribaldry; my debt to him as a scholar and a friend is deep and perennial. My first personal debt, however, is to my wife, Ruth. As my *advocata diabolae* she has never failed to make me see the humour of it all.

G.Z.
23 April 1986
Christchurch, New Zealand

Abbreviations

A.A.	*Archäologischer Anzeiger*
A.u.A.	*Antike und Abendland*
A.C.	*Antiquité classique*
A.J.P.	*American Journal of Philology*
B.E.F.A.R.	*Bibliothèque des Écoles françaises d'Athenes et de Rome*
B.I.C.S.	*Bulletin of the Institute of Classical Studies of the University of London*
Buc. Gr.	A.S.F. Gow, *Bucolici Graeci* (Oxford, 1958)
C.L.	*Comparative Literature*
C.P.	*Classical Philology*
C.Q.	*Classical Quarterly*
C.R.	*Classical Review*
E.P.R.O.	*Études préliminaires aux religions orientales dans l'empire romain*
F.G.H.	F. Jacoby, *Die Fragmente der griechischen Historiker* (Berlin, 1923–30 and Leiden, 1940–58)
G.L.P.	D. L. Page, *Select Papyri III: Literary Papyri, Poetry* (London and Cambridge, Mass., 1941)
Gött. Nachr.	*Nachrichten der Gesellschaft der Wissenschaften zu Göttingen, philologisch-historische Klasse*
G. & R.	*Greece and Rome*
G.R.B.S.	*Greek Roman and Byzantine Studies*
H.	*Hermes*
H.D.	U. von Wilamowitz-Moellendorff, *Hellenistische Dichtung in der Zeit des Kallimachos*, 2 vols. (Berlin, 1924)
H.E.	A. S. F. Gow and D. L. Page, *The Greek Anthology: Hellenistic Epigrams*, 2 vols. (Cambridge, 1965)
H.S.C.P.	*Harvard Studies in Classical Philology*
J.H.S.	*Journal of Hellenic Studies*

J.R.S.	Journal of Roman Sudies
M.H.	Museum Helveticum
Mnem.	Mnemosyne
N.Jb.	Neue Jahrbücher für das klassische Altertum
Philol.	Philologus
Pow.	J. U. Powell, *Collectanea Alexandrina: Reliquiae minores Poetarum Graecorum Aetatis Ptolemaicae 323–146 A.C. Epicorum, Elegiacorum, Lyricorum, Ethicorum* (Oxford, 1925)
P.Oxy.	B. P. Grenfell *et al.*, *The Oxyrhynchus Papyri* (London, 1898–)
P.P.	Parola del passato
Q.U.C.C.	Quaderni Urbinati di cultura classica
R.F.I.C.	Rivista di filologia e di istruzione classica
Rh.M.	Rheinisches Museum
R.I.E.	Revue internationale de l'enseignement
Σ	Scholia
S.B.A.W.	Sitzungsberichte der bayerischen Akademie der Wissenschaften
S.H.	H. Lloyd-Jones and P. Parsons, *Supplementum Hellenisticum, Texte und Kommentare* 11 (Berlin and New York, 1983)
S.I.F.C.	Studi italiani di filologia classica
T.A.P.A.	Transactions of the American Philological Association
T.R.S.L.	Transactions of the Royal Society of Literature
T.W.A.S.	Twayne's World Authors Series
V.S.W.G.	Vierteljahrschrift für Sozial- und Wirtschaftsgeschichte
W.d.F. 296	A. D. Skiadas (ed.), *Kallimachos, Wege der Forschung* 296 (Darmstadt, 1975)
W.S.	Wiener Studien
Y.C.S.	Yale Classical Studies
Z.P.E.	Zeitschrift für Papyrologie und Epigraphik

The numbering of the fragments of Callimachus is that of Pfeiffer except where otherwise specified.

1 Definitions and a Sample

This book sets out to discuss a neglected aspect of Alexandrian poetry, its realism. Both 'Alexandrian' and 'realism' call for definition.

Until the 1920s, scholars appeared on fairly safe ground when they used 'Alexandrian' to describe the literary period falling between the death of Alexander and the principate of Augustus; it was, moreover, generally held that the most distinguished, important and 'characteristically Alexandrian' poetry was written at the beginning of the period, under the first three Ptolemies, and that the succeeding two centuries saw the sporadic appearance of poets who possessed remarkable but minor talents; in the Augustan era, the spirit of Alexandrian poetry continued to flourish, but it was then almost exclusively the Latin poets who evoked it.[1] The assumptions underlying this definition were challenged in 1934 when K. Ziegler published *Das hellenistische Epos: ein vergessenes Kapitel griechischer Dichtung*.[2] Ziegler demonstrated that in fact the main bulk of poetry produced in the period consisted of epic written in a manner entirely opposed to that of the poets of Alexandria centred around Callimachus. There were histories of kings and patrons like those told by Choerilus of Iasus, who celebrated the achievements of Alexander, there were historical epics like Rhianus' *Messeniaca* and mythological epics like the same poet's *Heraclea* in fourteen books, though Ziegler perhaps overestimated the interest in epics on legendary themes in the wider Hellenistic context.[3] Ziegler also attempted to show that it is only by historical accident that we possess so little of these works; in particular, audiences at Rome had little interest in the epics on the Hellenistic Greek monarchs, leagues and states once the Hellenistic world had been turned into mere provinces of the Roman empire.[4] Furthermore, our assumption that Hellenistic epos was bad poetry is largely conditioned by the *cantores Euphorionis* in the Sullan period who re-discovered Callimachus. The Augustan elegists, too, have nourished our prejudice, for they shared Callimachus' distaste for contemporary epic and used his aesthetic preferences as a means of excusing themselves from the

2 Definitions and a Sample

political activity of writing epics in praise of influential men in Rome.[5] I think we must take Ziegler's point[6] and accept Alexandrian poetry in its proper perspective, as a movement of comparatively short duration, with only intermittent reappearances in later Greek poetry, and one unrepresentative of the great mass of poetry written at the same time.[7]

For that reason, when I use the term 'Alexandrian', I shall be referring to a literary movement rather than a historical period or a body of literature bound physically, as it were, to the city of Alexandria by the fact that it was written there.[8] The central figure of the movement, as I intend to define it, is Alexandria's greatest poet, Callimachus. 'Alexandrian' will, therefore, first denote poetry composed by older contemporaries of Callimachus who exerted a direct and, in certain cases, a personal influence on his poetry, even where we have evidence that he fell out with them. Aratus of Soli and Philetas of Cos, for example, seem to have remained formative influences on his poetic taste,[9] while he is recorded as having quarrelled with other older poets to whom he is indebted, notably Asclepiades of Samos and Posidippus of Pella.[10] Secondly, the movement will include poets whom Callimachus appears to have influenced, as in the case of Apollonius of Rhodes, said to be his pupil,[11] Theocritus of Syracuse,[12] Eratosthenes,[13] Euphorion of Chalcis and, in the next century, Moschus of Syracuse,[14] Bion of Smyrna and Nicander of Colophon.[15] Thirdly, even where evidence for direct influence is disputed or lacking and where, moreover, even contact with Alexandria is unverifiable or non-existent, we may include in the movement those poets of the period who demonstrably share Callimachus' precepts; Herodas, for example, experimented with language, metre, form and subject-matter in a way strikingly analogous to Callimachus' stance on those issues;[16] Philicus of Corcyra's *Iambe* bears interesting resemblances to the *Hecale*, though perhaps we cannot talk of actual influence,[17] and Philicus, too, plainly experimented with form and subject-matter along Callimachean lines;[18] epigrammatists like Leonidas of Tarentum,[19] Hedylus and Meleager share some of Callimachus' literary tastes even if they do not borrow from him.[20] Poets of the period who either arguably had nothing to do with the movement or to whom it would have been openly hostile, including Erinna (who is a marginal case for actual membership of the movement, for she was admired by Asclepiades[21] and has affinities with Theocritus),[22] Rhinthon of Syracuse, Lycophron, Machon,

Dioscorides, Rhianus and various anonymous composers will be discussed where they provide a perspective on the 'realist' tendency within the movement which is the subject of this book. The definition I am proposing covers types of poetry like Theocritus' pastoral *Idylls*, which a narrowly geographical definition probably precludes;[23] in any case it would be irrational to omit Theocritus, whose works would easily be recognised from their form as sharing Callimachean poetic ideals, even if we did not possess *Idyll* 7 which explicitly places Theocritus' poetry in the Alexandrian manner.[24]

Other poetry composed in the Hellenistic period need not be examined in this book, except fragments which shed light on the Alexandrian movement as I have defined it. Nor do the Roman Alexandrians, the *cantores Euphorionis*, the young Virgil or the Augustans, fall within the scope of my inquiry. Now there are many aspects of Alexandrian poetry which mark it out as a movement, its esoteric erudition, its learned imitation and variation in its handling of poetic language as inherited from the canonical classics, its allusiveness and its irony. But what I hope will emerge from my study of it is that it can be viewed as united not only by these characteristics and by the impetus of its central figure, Callimachus, but also by a repeatedly observable desire to bring poetry into the closest possible contact with sensory, intellectual and emotional experience, in short, by its *realism*, although I do not wish to suggest that that is the key to the whole of Alexandrian poetry. If I am successful in that aim, my definition of the movement will be further substantiated.

And now the second term central to our inquiry, 'realism', must be defined. The kind of realism which chiefly concerns us here is the realism which J. P. Stern calls a 'perennial mode',[25] observable in all periods of literature and art. As Stern says, 'Every age — at all events since "the Greek revolution" — has its own realism. It is the representative mode of that age in the sense that it re-presents — makes and matches in words — the reality, the system that works in that age.'[26] There is, of course, evidence of the mode right at the beginning of European literature, in Homer, whether in the poet's approving assessment of the verisimilitude of works of art like the scenes on Achilles' shield (*Il.* 18.548f., 561ff., 574ff.) or the animal-figures on Odysseus' brooch (*Od.* 19.226–31), or in Odysseus' praise for the historical accuracy of Demodocus the minstrel's account of the wooden horse at Troy (*Od.* 8.487–91).

4 Definitions and a Sample

The mode is, therefore, discernible well before the fourth-century Greek achievements in illusionism and realism that Stern refers to, which in fact bears out what he says about every age having its own realism. This is realism in the wide sense defined by the *Oxford English Dictionary* as 'Close resemblance to what is real; fidelity of representation, rendering the precise details of the real thing or scene.'

This eternal realism must be differentiated from the realism which perhaps most colours our view of the concept, that of the nineteenth-century Realist movement either as its protagonists and their contemporaries perceived it or as more recent literary critics understand it (the two perceptions are not the same thing).[27] Alexandrian poetry will indeed be found to share some of its subjects, preoccupations and conventions, but to define the realism of the Alexandrians starting from the Realists would lead and has led to intolerable misapprehensions and distortions.[28]

Nineteenth-century European Realism is a particular, historically determined subset of the category of eternal realism described by the *Oxford English Dictionary*. The Alexandrians' realism will be a similar subset. We must, therefore, arrive at an abstract definition of the perennial mode which will help us to identify the ways in which it manifests itself in Alexandrian poetry and hence to define Alexandrian realism.

First, a caveat. We must be aware of the role of convention referred to in Stern's statement that 'Every age . . . has its own realism'. The importance of convention is easy to understand, for every age has its own reality. The witches in *Macbeth*, for example, would have been real to an Elizabethan audience in a way that we find it hard to recapture. So, too, if we find Alexandrian poetry depicting a Medea or a Simaetha, we should be chary of dismissing such characters as bizarre and therefore 'non-realistic'. And then there is the convention involved in the manner in which each age represents its reality. If Lysippus, Myron or Praxiteles in the fourth century were shown the objets d'art of which Homer admired their 'close resemblance to what is real', they would probably have felt that this was all pretty stylised stuff indeed. In fact, even the fourth-century artists' advances in realism were only achieved by the introduction of a new set of conventions. The function of convention in the history of 'making and matching' has been interestingly explored by scholars like E. H. Gombrich in *Art and Illusion*.[29] If, therefore, we are ever inclined to rule any notion of realism out of court when we encounter a product like Callimachus' *Hecale* on the grounds that it has a sophistication of poetic style in the starkest possible contrast with the flatness which the Realists demanded of their media,[30] then we must again exercise caution: Callimachus and his contemporaries may well have felt that his hexameters lent the lowly old figure of Hecale a remarkable dignity, which would actually bring the Alexandrian back into line with the Realists who, while preferring the 'flat style', demanded the serious study, if not the heroisation, of the lower classes, as we shall see.

Inherent in realism is the insistence on detail referred to by the *Oxford English Dictionary*. Detailed descriptive writing was one of the means by which the eighteenth-century novelists attempted to achieve a most cherished aim, illusion.[31] The case of Diderot is instructive. In his *Éloge de Richardson* he defends Richardson's descriptions against the charge of being mere 'longueurs' and says 'Sachez que c'est à cette multitude de petites choses que tient l'illusion.'[32] This statement, I think, illustrates one means by which realism aims at verisimilitude, the attention to precise, minute and even insignificant detail. It is a technique which the Alexandrians used as no one before them.

Moreover, the detail which realism characteristically embraces tends to be of a certain kind, namely that which is drawn from common and familiar experience. As Diderot says to Richardson's detractors, 'Ils [ces détails] sont communs, dites vous; c'est ce qu'on voit tous les jours! Vous vous trompez; c'est ce qui passe tous les jours sous vos yeux, et que vous ne voyez jamais.'[33] This appeal to the familiar and the everyday was felt by the French novelists to be another vital means of securing the illusion of reality. In the following century the Realists take up the everyday, and also the lowly, and raise it to the level of material worthy of serious depiction and contemplation. Here we think immediately of painters like Millet with *The Sower*, but especially of Gustave Courbet with *The Stone-breakers*.[34] The movement's great champion, Champfleury, wrote of Courbet 'M. Courbet est un factieux pour avoir représenté de bonne foi des bourgeois, des paysans, des femmes de village de grandeur naturelle.'[35] The question of the tone that this and other types of realism achieve is something to which we shall return presently.

Realism is characterised by its fidelity to what is perceived as nature or reality. As such, of course, it points up the paradox of most *mimēsis* in that it pretends, as no other artistic mode does, to present reality while remaining art. But what actually happens when a writer tries to describe a fictional scene or event realistically? The short and obvious answer is that he takes care to remain faithful to our experience of nature or reality and avoids offending our sense of what is credible. This, again, is exemplified by the eighteenth-century French novelists, who, following the lead of English writers like Richardson, exhibit an increasing preoccupation with the standards of probability and plausibility.[36] The approach can be seen in the Alexandrians as well, especially in their evocation of myth. We shall find Apollonius, for example, again and again trying to reconcile variant versions of a myth to make a plausible unity: the final, reconciled version shows that a unity can be constructed from an at times discrepant tradition and thus vindicates its credibility. Naturally, such a procedure entails vast and scholarly erudition in mythology, but contemporary science is also invoked to bring myth into line with documented reality. Callimachus' statements 'When I tell fiction, let it persuade the listener's hearing' (*H*. 1.65: ψευδοίμην, ἀίοντος ἅ κεν πεπίθοιεν ἀκουήν) and 'I sing nothing unattested' (*Fr.* 612: ἀμάρτυρον οὐδὲν ἀείδω) nicely express this aspect of realism.

Realism constantly tries to relate its object to the observable present. In order to illustrate the fact that the mode of realism is both 'perennial' and bound to its times, 'courting as though deliberately the oblivion of passing circumstance, in need of "historical context" and explanatory information',[37] Stern adduces the *Eumenides* of Aeschylus, a play in which, he argues, the dramatist builds, through his depiction of the foundation of the Areopagus, a bridge from the visible landmark on which the lawcourt was situated and the institutions it preserved, reaching right back to the invisible world of myth in which it was supposed to have been established: the mythical account is verified by the tangible evidence of the present (and, of course, the present-day institution is ennobled by its alleged origin in mythical times). A similar impulse seems to stimulate several of the Alexandrians' aitia as well. And, before we object that their main interest was in aitia that are to us 'bizarre' or 'out of the way', we should reflect on the factor of convention in what men believe, reminding ourselves of, for example, Theocritus', Apollonius' and Shakespeare's witches: antiquarianism may indeed incline to the bizarre and grotesque, but often cultural issues are at stake, like the recuperation of a former world, a national or regional identity or popular, if quaint, customs in danger of extinction, and such matters are not necessarily to be dismissed as learned playfulness or the like.[38] Here again we perhaps have an example of the part played by convention in realism. But my real point is realism's concern to *relate*. It may try to relate in order either to achieve realistic ends, as happens in the *Eumenides*, or for the purposes of irony, of even, for example, actually drawing attention to the rift between the world evoked by past poetry and that of the present. In both procedures, however, there is often a common cultural element, namely the desire to come to terms with the phenomenon depicted, whether enhancing its believability or shattering it through laughter. This, too, is of crucial importance to the Alexandrians in their approach to traditional, mainstream Greek culture, especially its myths.

Up till now my remarks have been confined to the forms and techniques of the eternal realism. The final aspect of the mode to which I wish to draw attention is its characteristic function. The insistence on detail, the familiar, credibility and observable 'traces' of the world of myth can obviously be used for different tones, ranging from the serious to the comic, and I have already had occasion to notice this flexibility. In fact, if there is a tendency nowadays to associate realism with some degree of seriousness, that is probably mainly the result of the nineteenth-century movement. The Realists' elevation of the everyday and the low is the pivotal point in Western literature as analysed in Auerbach's *Mimesis*,[39] for, as Auerbach teaches us, it was the achievement of Realism to break with 'the rule of the separation of styles which was later [after Homer] almost universally accepted and which specified that the realistic depiction of daily life was incompatible with the sublime and had a place only in comedy or, carefully stylised, in idyl',[40] a statement which we shall find to be of key significance to the argument of this book. This central facet of modern Realism must be taken into account in any discussion of it. So, for example, René Wellek in his succinct description of the phenomenon proposes as a working definition of it the 'objective representation of contemporary social reality'.[41] But, although our knowledge of modern Realism has alerted us to realism's links with the familiar, we should not for a moment assume that the Alexandrians, for example, always put such material to serious use. Actually, they most commonly use it for comic and ironic purposes. Theocritus' bucolic and urban. *Idylls* and Herodas' *Mimiambi* spring to mind as the most obvious examples of this: these pieces may be realistic in subject-matter but they are far from serious in conception or effect. Their subject-matter is a source of humour, so they are the absolute antithesis of nineteenth-century Realism in tone. More complex effects are produced when the Greek deities are presented in a context of almost banal domesticity, Callimachus' *Hymn to Artemis* being a case in point. Familiar, everyday motifs on such occasions make comic figures of the Olympians. Yet Greek religion from Homer onwards had made fun of its gods and the humour in Callimachus' depiction of Artemis' childhood is not necessarily preclusive of the poet's genuine belief in them.[42] This peculiar mixture of irony and veneration is a special achievement of the Greeks' and in particular the Alexandrians' use of realism, conditioned as it is by Greek religious attitudes, and it will claim our special attention. On the other hand, there are works like the *Hecale* which I shall argue do indeed quite strikingly approximate to the subject-matter *and* tone demanded by the nineteenth-century Realists.

We must, therefore, assess each use of realistic material in its own context. And we shall find that Alexandrian poetry was at an interesting crossroads in its attitude to Auerbach's 'separation of styles'. But central to these different functions is the impulse to *relate*, an impulse which we have already observed in the use of aetiology. Laughing at what is emotionally, intellectually or culturally real to you can be as much a way of coming to terms with it as trying to verify it by some serious means at your disposal.

So realism, as a universal mode, can be observed principally, as far as literature is concerned, in a style which emphasises detail, in a subject-matter which tends towards the everyday and familiar, or in an intellectual approach which pays especial attention to probability and plausibility. These three main types of realism may work independently or in concert but they share the same aims and functions. They may aim at tonal effects ranging from irony to solemnity and they may perform cultural or social functions which include the destruction or the authentification of a nation's cultural heritage and the ridicule or the ennoblement of the everyday. Common to these opposing aims and functions is the desire to relate the objects of literature to the audience's experience of nearby reality.

We have now arrived at the nucleus of a working definition of the perennial mode and we are in a position to ask in what ways it manifests itself in Alexandrian poetry. Theocritus' fifteenth *Idyll*, *The Syracusan Women at the Adonis-Festival*, will be a useful proving-ground.

Idyll 15 is a mime which deals with two Syracusan women living in Alexandria. They may be said to be members of the *petite bourgeoisie*.⁴³ It begins with a scene at Praxinoa's house (1– 43). Her friend, Gorgo, is at the door asking the servants whether her mistress is at home. Praxinoa answers the call herself and expresses surprise over the visit. Gorgo complains about the distance they live apart and Praxinoa blames it on her husband, Dinon (ταῦθ' ὁ πάραρος τῆνος:8); Gorgo notices the baby looking at Praxinoa, and tells her not to talk like that about her husband in front of the child. Praxinoa is horrified to see that the little boy understands (14). Gorgo tries to gloss it over for him (14),⁴⁴ but Praxinoa, undaunted, resumes her complaints about Dinon, and Gorgo joins in by moaning about *her* husband, though she cuts herself short to ask Praxinoa to come and see the Adonis-festival put on at the palace by Queen Arsinoe. Praxinoa answers with a gruff proverb ('every day's a holiday for the idle':26) and makes a show of being busy, but gets ready for going out, tells the servant to pick up the spinning and not to let it lie around, for 'pet weasels like soft beds' (28), asks her to bring soap and water and complains about her service. Gorgo comments on her dress and asks what it cost and Praxinoa expresses her annoyance at the amount of money and work she put into it. She then asks for her wrap and sun-hat. She decides to leave the baby at home, though he starts crying, and orders the servant to play with him, call in the dog and lock the front door.

The scene changes to the street (44–77) where Praxinoa complains about the crowd and thanks Ptolemy Philadelphus for ridding the streets of Egyptian molesters. She grows frightened at the approach of the king's chargers, one of which rears; at this, she remarks how lucky she was to have left her child at home. While Gorgo tries to calm her, she says she has been afraid of horses and snakes from childhood. Just outside the palace the crowd grows again and Gorgo asks an old woman whether it is easy to get inside; she replies with the equivalent of the proverb 'nothing ventured, nothing gained'⁴⁵ and leaves the girls to find the palace doors crowded. Praxinoa is once again frightened and urges the party to hold hands so that they don't get separated. Her shawl gets torn and she begs a man not to tear her wrap; he replies that he is being jostled, too, and helps them as best he can, for which Praxinoa thanks him. She calls to her slave to push her way through the crowd to rejoin her and, apparently with another proverb from her (77),[46] they get into the palace.

The scene is now inside the palace (78 to the end). Gorgo immediately calls Praxinoa's attention to the tapestries and the latter praises the workers who made them; her criterion is truth to life — the figures are so lifelike that she calls them 'alive, not woven'; she also expresses her admiration for a representation of Adonis on the tapestries (separate, it seems,[47] from the tableau, which is described in the hymn they are shortly to hear), speaking of Adonis as if he were alive and not a mere icon (84f.). At this point, a man in the crowd gets angry at their chattering and their Syracusan accent. Praxinoa answers in kind, asking him to mind his own business, vehemently proclaims her Syracusan citizenship and Corinthian descent and says that it's quite natural for them, as Dorians, to speak Doric. She has time to have the last word ('don't waste your breath on me')[48] before Gorgo tells her to be quiet, for the singer is about to perform: she is just clearing her throat. After the hymn, which we shall examine in detail presently, Gorgo praises the singer for her erudition (ὀλβία ὅσσα ἴσατι:146) and for her voice, but remembers that she must get home to cook her husband's dinner, for he gets bad-tempered when he's hungry. The poem ends with her farewell to Adonis and her prayer for happiness.

Before discussing the hymn, let us take stock of our findings so far. Gorgo and Praxinoa are members of the lower middle class. Their lack of sophistication is again and again emphasised: for example, they express naïve wonder at the lifelikeness[49] of the tapestries, stand in awe of the singer's erudition and can over-react when they feel they are being 'got at'. They are set firmly within the context of their age and the ordinary life of Alexandria: witness Praxinoa's reference to Egyptian rough-necks and her brush with the stranger over her dialect.[50] In his choice of subject-matter, therefore, we are surely justified in calling Theocritus realistic. The characterisation of the two girls is probably indebted to mime,[51] a genre always felt to be in contact with the lower classes and with the humbler areas of human life,[52] and they are examples of what becomes from the fourth century onwards a preoccupation in the comedians like Menander, *mimēsis biou*, the representation of everyday life.⁵³ Moreover, their conversation, consisting largely of complaints about their husbands and of comments on domestic life and continually punctuated by humble proverbs, seems calculated to characterise them as folk we would meet in ordinary life. And yet there is an astonishing fact about their chatter which requires an effort of imagination on our part to comprehend fully. They are represented as speaking in the hexameter, of which Aristotle less than a century before Theocritus wrote his poem had said

τῶν δὲ ῥυθμῶν ὁ μὲν ἡρῷος σεμνὸς καὶ λεκτικῆς ἁρμονίας δεόμενος . . .
(*Rh.* 3.8.4 1408ᵇ32f.)

Of the metres the heroic is grand and lacks the rhythmical structure of ordinary speech⁵⁴ [in contrast with iambics] . . .

and

τὸ γὰρ ἡρωικὸν στασιμώτατον καὶ ὀγκωδέστατον τῶν μέτρων ἐστίν . . .
(*Poet.* 59ᵇ34f.)

The heroic metre is the stateliest and most weighty of the metres . . .

The hexameter would thus appear the most unlikely — and the most unrealistic — vehicle for a mime. Moreover, it was inextricably associated in Greek literary thought with the genre of heroic poetry, which had at least by Aristotle's time become a genre in which to represent *hoi spoudaioi*, 'our betters' (the term will be discussed in detail later); Aristotle had written, for example,

ἡ μὲν οὖν ἐπιποιία τῇ τραγῳδίᾳ μέχρι μὲν τοῦ μετὰ μέτρου λόγῳ μίμησις εἶναι σπουδαίων ἠκολούθησεν. (*Poet.* 49ᵇ9f.)

Epic followed tragedy inasmuch as it was a metrical representation of superior people.

It is obvious, therefore, that in the Hellenistic period the metre had an association of grandeur.⁵⁵ Theocritus is deliberately aiming at an incongruous clash between the realism of the subject-matter of his poem and the non-realism and artificiality of its metre; the incongruity must have seemed strikingly humorous to his contemporaries.[56] That he was interested in the humour derived from the incongruity of form and content appears to be confirmed in an interesting way by a clash of the two components when the man in the palace complains about the girls' Doric accent, but, in accordance with the literary dialect of the poem, he expresses himself in the same broad Doric with the same broad [a] vowels.[57] Gow calls this 'indifference to realism'[58] but, as I shall suggest in Chapter 6, it is more probably that Theocritus is amusing himself and his readers with the incongruity. What we have in Theocritus' juxtaposition of form and content is an instance of the 'crossing of genres'.[59] We must attempt to understand the range of tonal effects which can be achieved by the process. An examination of this aspect of the *Idyll*'s realism appears to add a new dimension to our appreciation and understanding of the poem.

But what precisely is this realism? It is the realism of subject-matter in the sense defined above, that of the everyday, where people are depicted with an intentional emphasis on their homeliness and domesticity. It approaches the 'kitchen sink' of modern Realism, but, significantly, we are meant, not least because of the playful and ironic contrast of form and subject-matter, to smile at Gorgo and Praxinoa (except, presumably, when they eulogise Ptolemy Philadelphus and Queen Arsinoe), whereas 'kitchen sink' realism often aims to expose the serious tensions in everyday modern life. This ironically undercut realism is a most important aspect of Alexandrian poetry, though we shall find that the realistic depiction of humble folk is not by any means always humorously ironic but can be quite serious in tone.

But in what ways can realism be descried in the hymn to Adonis? A hymn, after all, may seem an unlikely place to look for realism. Its structure is simple and may be outlined briefly. The singer announces to Aphrodite the return of Adonis from the dead and tells her that Queen Arsinoe has prepared a welcome for him out of gratitude for Aphrodite's deification of Berenice, the Queen's mother; the gifts to Adonis are described, as are the tableau depicting the reunion of Aphrodite and Adonis and the scene of the lament to follow on the next day by the sea; Adonis is addressed and contrasted with the heroes of old because he alone may yearly revisit the earth; his favour is invoked for the next year.

Three aspects of the hymn may be called realistic: its pictorialism, its deployment of that most human of human experiences, love, and its intellectual approach to myth. Its pictorialism results from the way in which, through the medium of words, Theocritus has drawn as precise and graphic a series of pictures as possible; the reader may visualise in his mind's eye the objects which Theocritus describes. There are three descriptions of this kind in the hymn. The first is that of the gifts for Adonis (111–27); fruits, miniature gardens in silver baskets, perfumes, wheat-cakes of different colours and honey-cakes made with olive oil are detailed with remarkable sensuousness; birds and animals are also present in the scene, but Theocritus directs our attention to the figures of Eros which flit above the verdant and scented bowers and which he compares with young nightingales flitting from branch to branch as they try out their wings, a simile which 'fixes' their *putti*-like movement in our minds; next are mentioned the ebony, gold and white ivory used in a representation of the rape of Ganymede and the soft, crimson coverlets for Adonis and Aphrodite. Throughout the description of the gifts Theocritus has been concerned to recapture the richness of the colours in particular, though of course all the other senses are appealed to. He has been setting the scene for the second description, that of the union of the lovers (128–30); the tableau is described briefly but with a deftly erotic visual appeal; Adonis is 'rosy-armed' for Aphrodite's embrace, a youth of eighteen or nineteen years, whose golden down has not yet left his lips and whose kisses are thus not rough.[60] The singer bids Aphrodite farewell as she embraces her lover, a prelude to the final picture of the hymn (131–5); the singer describes the women who will bear Adonis on the morrow in the dew of dawn to the waves, beating upon the shore; they will let down their hair and loosen their tunics so that their breasts are bare and their tunics trail down to their ankles and will begin their dirge. This is a fairly traditional picture of ritual lamentation[61] but the visual images of the early morning and the surf lend the scene an atmosphere of haunting sadness.

It is clear that in these passages Theocritus has intended to make the visual richness of the different scenes vivid and immediate to us; this he has effected by the precision and careful selection of detail with which he has drawn his verbal picture. Another consequence of his pictorial realism is emotional, for by means of it he has tried to invest the Adonis-rite at Alexandria with all the sensuousness, eroticism and pathos it will have held.

14 *Definitions and a Sample*

This leads us directly into my assertion that the hymn uses love for realistic purposes, a notion which will certainly need some explanation for those who come to Alexandrian realism directly from the viewpoint of the nineteenth and twentieth centuries. The basic rationale of some of the Alexandrian poets in their deployment of love seems to have been that love is the emotion which everybody can experience — and wants to — and that the judicious use of it will interest people and help them to relate to the world of poetry from their own experience of life. This is illustrated by the way Praxinoa is engaged when she views the tapestries of Adonis: a principal ingredient in her rapt attention to them, besides her admiration for their lifelike quality, is undoubtedly their erotic appeal (84–6). In this respect, love can be regarded, with due reservations, as comparable with the familiar matter of the everday. So in the hymn Theocritus uses the deified Berenice's allegedly close association with Aphrodite (106–8) and the sensuousness of the tableau to demonstrate the relevance of the Ptolemies' dynastic and religious programme to the people of Alexandria. He adopts this approach even more clearly in the *Encomium for Ptolemy*, where he emphasises the close, loving family bonds between Berenice and Soter and says that one of the cult-functions of Berenice in Aphrodite's precinct is to ease the path of people's love (*Id.* 17.34–52). This is intended to highlight the relevance of the new myths to everyman. But elsewhere love is used for the verification of the world of traditional myth. For example, in his treatment of the love of Medea, Apollonius may indeed be concerned primarily with dramatic impact, but he also explores her love in a realistic manner, and to verificatory realistic ends: he seems to have hoped that by showing her in a pre-eminently human situation he might help us assent to the mythical barbarian princess, a contention which I shall support in detail later. *Idyll* 15 thus introduces us to a vital component of Alexandrian realism.

We may now pass on to the third type of realism that I think can be discerned, though perhaps only faintly, in the hymn's treatment of myth. The singer displays some erudition in matters of cult-lore. In her address to Aphrodite, she names cult-places of the goddess on Cyprus and Sicily, Golgi, Idalium and Mt Eryx; she calls her 'Aphrodite playing with gold', thus making a variation on the traditional epithet 'golden' and at the same time possibly alluding to a detail of Aphrodite's iconography, for she is often represented in statues as playing with a pendant which hangs from her necklace;[62] she addresses her as Dionaean Cypris, thus associating her with Dione as was traditional for the Cyprian Aphrodite. Apart from this, the singer makes repeated allusions to mythology; Arsinoe is compared with Helen (110); she has occasion, as we have seen, to mention the Ganymede myth, though with characteristically Alexandrian fastidiousness she forbears from stating the obvious and naming him (124); she contrasts Adonis with other heroes who have not, for all their greatness, been granted the privilege of re-visiting earth, Agamemnon, Ajax, Hector, Patroclus,[63] Pyrrhus, the Lapiths, Deucalion, the house of Pelops and the Pelasgian chieftains of Argos (136ff.). It is this knowledge of myth which causes Gorgo to exclaim 'The woman's so clever; how happy to know so much' (145f.).

Now this particular display of erudition cannot in itself be called realistic. Nor does it even seem especially erudite, and we are left wondering whether Gorgo's comment isn't yet another part of Theocritus' irony at her expense.[64] But it will serve as an introduction to certain other manifestations of erudition in Alexandrian poetry which definitely can be termed realistic in a sense that we have already touched upon. There is, first, the mythical erudition exercised in order to harmonise divergent traditions of a myth and thus to confer upon it coherence and plausibility. Secondly, there is the appeal to modern science. Geographical erudition, for example, is utilised for realistic purposes in the evocation of myth, to refer the audience to landmarks which are associated with a myth and can still be observed, and thus to 'prove' the truth of a poet's account of it. We shall even find instances where contemporary medical research is drawn upon to give a more credible presentation of myth. This kind of realism seeks to make the world of myth accord with what the audience knows of reality from the criterion of probability and the empirical standard of science. We have seen explicit adherence to this approach in the two comments of Callimachus, 'When I tell fiction, let it persuade the listener's hearing' and 'I sing nothing unattested'. Realism of this type is particularly characteristic of the early poets of the movement like Callimachus and Apollonius, a fact which, it will be argued, can be attributed to the sociological make-up of the city of Alexandria in its first generation. With later poets of the movement, however, erudition is aired apparently for its own sake; this is probably the case with Euphorion, for instance.

16 Definitions and a Sample

There is another aspect of the hymn's treatment of myth which has yet to be discussed. Immediately after her invocation of Aphrodite, the singer describes the origin of Arsinoe Philadelphus' personal sponsorship of the Adonis-cult at Alexandria (106–11): Aphrodite, men say, immortalised the Queen Mother, Berenice, upon her death; in thanks to the goddess, Arsinoe has prepared the lavish reception-ritual for Adonis. This aition is of a particularly instructive type. As a literary subject, the aition enjoyed an extraordinary vogue among the Alexandrian poets (one need only call to mind the *Aetia* of Callimachus himself to gauge its popularity). Normally, an aition describes something which occurred in mythical times and which was the cause of a ritual so that the latter can be observed 'even to this day' — εἰσέτι νῦν περ is a typical formula[65] — and this observability is sometimes construed as a 'proof' of the historicity of the mythical occurrence, at which point we can call an aition realistic as we saw it was possible to do in the case of Aeschylus' *Eumenides*. To be sure, many, perhaps even the majority of Alexandrian aitia are vehicles for the display of recondite knowledge and recherché wit and exhibit a distinct preference for the obscure, the bizarre and the fantastic. It has become a cliché of modern scholarship to comment on this aspect of the Alexandrians' aetiology. But there is in fact a more serious side to the age's interest in aitia, local myths and the like. F. Cairns has drawn a balanced picture of the true situation in a statement well worth quoting in this context:

> One area of learning prominent in Hellenistic poetry must be the result of political developments. It is antiquarian interest. Citizens of now powerless cities fostered their local identity through scholarship: their foundations and histories, their idiosyncratic variant legends and customs, their local festivals, rites and deities, their petty notables and heroes, all these become sources of immense pride as links between the city and its splendid past.[66]

Moreover, there are some *aitia*, and the singer's in *Idyll* 15 is an instance, which are demonstrably realistic, and these are the ones to which I wish to draw particular attention. They also constitute further evidence for the age's interest in the heritage of Greek culture, correctly discerned by Cairns, which is of great significance for our inquiry. To return to Theocritus' poem, the singer's aition plainly shares the structure of other aitia in Alexandrian poets, but it differs from the normal format in that the origin of Arsinoe's special patronage of the cult occurred in recent history, at the deification of Berenice.[67] For that reason, the aition would have seemed to an Alexandrian audience doubly realistic; the actual *raison d'être* of the festival (if not of the cult itself), the deification of Berenice, would have gained credibility because they could observe the ritual sponsored by Arsinoe, and the mythical story of Adonis would have done likewise because of its association with a recent historical event. We may call this procedure realistic, however unreal the myth involved might appear to us, for the myth was part of the context of life in Alexandria and Theocritus has tried to close the gap between the visible and the invisible in something like the way J. P. Stern interpreted Aeschylus as having done with the Areopagus.[68]

The hymn, therefore, exhibits three main types of realism. The first is its realistic pictorialism which will had added immediacy and credibility to the mythical subject-matter on the reasoning that, as Heraclitus put it, ὀφθαλμοὶ τῶν ὤτων ἀκριβέστεροι μάρτυρες — 'seeing's believing'.[69] This is a realism of style. The second is a realism of subject-matter. Love is used, like other subjects drawn from familiar experience, to lend a sensual immediacy to the remote world of myth and to put a human face on certain aspects of the Ptolemies' ruler-cult. The third has to do with an intellectual approach and is what we may term the appeal to learning in the singer's account of the Adonis-myth and of Berenice's deification. We have noted that the hymn incorporates much erudite cult-lore. Now though the use of cult-lore in the hymn cannot in itself be called realistic, it may have introduced us to the demonstrably realistic appeal to scholarship and science which we shall see was a common preoccupation among the Alexandrians in their presentation of myth and seems to have been used by them, at least in the early period, to bolster the credibility of their accounts. In general, it should be remarked, Theocritus seems not to have been as interested in this kind of realism as his contemporaries Callimachus and Apollonius. We may, however, with full justification describe the singer's use of aetiology as realistic, and we shall find that the Alexandrians made aitia the subject of serious, even scientific research, to a greater extent, indeed, than is witnessed in the hymn. *Idyll* 15 may thus serve to draw to our attention the Alexandrians' realistic employment of science and erudition in mythological matters, though it is admittedly not the most representative example of all aspects of the phenomenon.

If we now view *Idyll* 15 as a whole, we can make some rather striking observations. The first concerns Theocritus' use of the hexameter. Though I suggested that in the rest of the piece the poet is playing on the incongruity of depicting realistic, everyday matter in the grand metre, in the case of the hymn he employs it to totally contrasting ends, for there it is in harmony with the heightened diction and material. It thus performs one of its traditional roles in Greek poetry and elevates the tone of the song.[70] The actual Adonis-song at Alexandria would probably have been composed in a lyric metre, and Theocritus' hexameters might well have had the effect of placing it in a novel and noble framework. In the hymn, secondly, Theocritus' realism seems calculated to lend a seriousness to it which constrasts starkly with the tone of the rest of the poem. These two factors are crucial to the contrast between frame and inset in the *Idyll* and to its principal charm. Thirdly, the poem incorporates and deploys to a concerted artistic end what this work attempts to show are the three most important forms of realism in Alexandrian poetry, pictorialism, the appeal to science and the representation of the everyday, low and familiar, including love. An examination of the piece in terms of its realism has, therefore, led us to a perhaps greater understanding of its subtlety and vividness, and has also introduced us to the realism of Alexandrian poetry as a whole. This realism is, I submit, unique in Greek literature because it is present in Alexandrian poetry to a degree unprecedented in earlier poetry and unparalleled in what we know of contemporary poetry written outside the movement.

Idyll 15 also points to an important fact about the audience for which the poets of the early Alexandrian movement were writing. It is inconceivable that it was composed for the urban masses of Alexandria. The view of the *petite bourgeoisie* in the poem is one from above. The full irony of the treatment of Gorgo and Praxinoa could only be appreciated by members of a social and intellectual class considerably higher than theirs. Theocritus and the other early Alexandrians were court-poets writing for what must have been small audiences of highly cultivated patrons, including the royal house itself.

Are there, we may ask, any elements in the social make-up of the population of Alexandria, especially the upper classes and the intelligentsia, under Soter and Philadelphus from, say, 305 to 247 BC, which might have had bearing on the forms of realism that I have described? If there are and if we can identify them, we would be in a better position to determine the function and effects of the realism of *Idyll* 15 and of Alexandrian poetry in general.[71]

Most importantly for our purposes, it appears that the early Greek population of the city, whether those immigrants who were offered Alexandrian citizenship and accepted it or the important group who resided in the city without ever becoming citizens, felt a deep psychological need for a sense of unity with mainstream Greek culture, cut off from it geographically as they were in a new city which had not yet developed its own identity.

This feeling is evidenced by the history of social and religious institutions at Alexandria. The example of marriage is instructive.[72] The Alexandrians maintained a civil marriage (συγχώρησις) and a religious marriage (συγγραφὴ συνοικισίου) which continued the traditional Greek customs of *ekdosis* and *engyēsis* and even reinforced their continued existence by putting them under the control of the city, whether represented by its magistrates or priests. Thus the marriage-customs of Alexandria remained strikingly Greek and conservative, especially when compared with what happened to them in the *chōra*, where they had become disassociated from traditional Greek practice.[73]

The feeling is also evidenced by the fact that we again and again find Greeks living in Alexandria but maintaining their association with their cities of origin. As P. M. Fraser has expressed it, '. . . in the earlier third century . . . the citizen-body must have been composed largely of Greeks who had not lost the centripetal links with their mother-cities'.[74] We remember, for example, how Callimachus' host at a party, Pollis, resident in Alexandria, is described as keeping up the festivals of his native Athens (*Fr.* 178.1–2). And we have seen with what fierce pride the women of Theocritus' fifteenth *Idyll*, resident in Alexandria in its first generation, proclaim their Syracusan origins: the memory of their old city remains fresh and is clearly represented as providing them with a sense of identity in their brush with the man in the crowd who carps at their Doric accent. It is pertinent, too, to note the large number of Greek residents in Alexandria who were merchants and soldiers and held administrative offices of considerable power in the city and its government, but who retained their city-ethnics and never took up Alexandrian citizenship. There is evidence demonstrating that these immigrants kept up their links with their original Greek cities.[75] The poets of the period themselves are also instances of this tendency. They will naturally have felt the same sense of cultural isolation as the rest of the immigrant Greek population of the city, perhaps, as poets, even more keenly. With the exception of Apollonius, who was born in the city,[76] the Alexandrian poets of the early period never became Alexandrian citizens. Thus, for example, Philetas of Cos, Callimachus of Cyrene,[77] Theocritus of Syracuse and Eratosthenes of Cyrene all retained their ethnics. Moreover, this is true of the intelligentsia in general: for instance, the Librarians of the third century, Zenodotus of Ephesus, Eratosthenes and Aristophanes of Byzantium never became Alexandrians, though Apollonius is of course again the exception.[78] All these men were apparently free to take up citizenship, though they were under no obligation to do so.[79]

Further evidence of these groups' need for cultural continuity may be found in the discomfort that they felt in an alien land[80] and the way in which they tried to safeguard their Greekness by excluding the native Egyptians from Greek society, especially in the capital. The Greeks' discomfiture over residence in Alexandria is illustrated, first, by an almost total absence of reference to the native Egyptians in the early Alexandrian poets; Praxinoa's reference at *Idyll* 15.47–50 to street-thieves who rob people 'Egyptian-style' is solitary and disparaging.[81] Secondly, it is significant that there is no evidence as yet for intermarriage between Greeks of whatever class and Egyptians in Alexandria at this period.[82] Thirdly, there is the fact that the Egyptian population in Alexandria was discriminated against and excluded from key institutions of the city. Thus it seems that in our period Egyptians were not admitted to the city's Greek gymnasia.[83] The main gymnasium at Alexandria must, therefore, have been a special focus of Egyptian resentment, for its imposing buildings occupied a position in the very centre of the city.[84] Most importantly, perhaps, the Egyptian population of Alexandria suffered from a total lack of constitutional status in the city.[85] This discrimination led to the momentous eruption of interracial tension after the Battle of Raphia in 217 when the 20,000 Egyptian troops, whom Ptolemy Philopator had armed to defend his kingdom against the invasion of Palestine in 219/18 by Antiochus III and who played a dominant role in the victory, started a sporadic revolt which lasted for some years.[86] Morover, there may have been previous revolts.[87] For their part, therefore, it is clear that the native Egyptian population in this period resented Macedonian rule.[88] Thus racial tension will have been a considerable factor in the immigrant Greeks' failure to assimilate into the life of their new city.[89]

Another factor which may explain their persistence in maintaining contact with their cities of origin is that the young capital, with its Macedonian overlords, was unable to provide them with a sense of cultural continuity, even though we see the Ptolemies addressing themselves to the problem, for example in Soter's establishment of the cult of Sarapis, which is most convincingly construed as an attempt to supply Alexandria with a city-god and hence to fill a need felt by the large Greek immigrant population who had left their own city-deities behind. As Fraser has put it, the Sarapis-cult was motivated by Soter's awareness of the 'centrifugal element in the life of the new capital'.[90] Moreover, it seems to me entirely reasonable to regard early Ptolemaic patronage of poets and intellectuals, almost all of whom come from the older Greek centres outside Alexandria and retain the citizenship of their home-cities, as another method of filling the 'cultural vacuum' of the young Alexandria. This must also be at least part of the reason for the establishment of the Museum and the Libraries, although patronage was a common feature of the Hellenistic monarchs.[91] The overriding concern of the Ptolemies, especially Soter, will no doubt have been to provide their city with an institution comparable with those in Greece proper, particularly the Lyceum at Athens, in which, of course, Demetrius of Phaleron was Soter's chief adviser.[92] Indeed, the Ptolemies seem to have aimed at reconstituting Athens in Alexandria. It should be added, finally, that, although traditional Olympian religion maintained its vigour in the early period,[93] it was under threat from the 'atheist' philosophers, the most important of whom was Euhemerus, who certainly resided in Alexandria for a time. His rationalistic account of the gods is in fact violently opposed by Callimachus in his first *Iambus*, where he is called an 'old babbling scribbler of impious scriptures who fabricated the ancient Panchaean Zeus' (*Fr.* 191.10–11). That Callimachus feels the necessity to attack him shows that Euhemerus' doctrine had some impact on traditional belief among early Alexandrians and hence on their sense of cultural identity, even if we have little evidence as to its real extent other than that provided by Callimachus.[94]

In some ways the picture that I have drawn of the 'culture shock' of the Greeks living in early Alexandria is generally true of the Greek colonies of the Hellenistic world as a whole: so, presumably, the problem of cultural identity will have been just as great for recent immigrants from Greek lands to Antioch or Seleuceia.[95] But the Greeks' experience of Egypt at this period is likely to have been even more disturbing for them than that of the other areas of colonisation in the East. For, whereas the Persian empire would have confronted the Greeks with a multinational, incohesive and diffuse society and Ionia would have presented a social milieu containing elements of long-standing Greco-Asiatic symbiosis, the Greeks who founded and colonised Alexandria would have been in stark confrontation with a culture, the Pharaonic, which was remarkably ancient, conservative, articulated and coherently uniform; the fact that the Greeks found the cult of Isis in Egypt so impenetrable is only one illustration of this.[96] It is thus probable that the Greeks of Alexandria would have found Egyptian life and culture as strikingly contrary to their own as Herodotus had done two centuries before.[97]

I suggest, therefore, that the poets employed realism in a manner unique in Greek poetry as a means of relating mainstream Greek culture to life as experienced by the expatriate Greeks, especially the educated elite, in their new capital in Egypt, thus helping them come to terms with the sense of cultural dislocation which they apparently felt. But *Idyll* 15 teaches us the complex means by which they intended their realism to fulfil this function and the effects that they wanted it to achieve in the process. Irony, the role of which in realism's concern to relate has already been explained, must have been a considerable factor. Gorgo and Praxinoa must have presented the court-audiences with a hilarious view of Greek commoners coping with life in Alexandria, but there was also the ironical humour arising from the portrayal of such a subject in the grand metre of traditional epic: here the poet is drawing attention to the distance between the form of past poetry and the subject-matter treated by the Hellenistic 'new wave'. At the same time, the aetiological realism of the hymn would have helped to 'verify' and ennoble the new Adonis-cult of the city, conferring upon it an authentic Greekness,[98] while the hexameters now elevate the content with their traditional solemnity and sonority; no irony can possibly have been intended in the presentation of an aspect of the Ptolemies' ruler-cult like the deification of Berenice. Nor is there an overriding concern with irony in the attempts made by certain of the other Alexandrians to bolster the credibility of Greek myth for their sophisticated listeners, as seems likely in the case of Apollonius' *Argonautica*, where, it will be argued, the poet may on occasion use one or another of all the forms of realism that I have described to bring the saga into contact with contemporary experience of the world and thus breathe new life into it: here we have a poet apparently bent at certain junctures on satisfying a nostalgia for the hallowed Greek tradition, a πόθος Ἑλλάδος, to use one of his own phrases (3.262). Moreover, between the two poles of irony and verification there are many degrees, and the Alexandrian elite must have sensed a piquant mixture of the two in, say, the picture in the *Encomium for Ptolemy* of the deified Soter hobnobbing on Olympus with his ancestor, Heracles (*Id*. 17.13–33). If these are the likely responses to the realism of *Idyll* 15 and other poems employing realism of one sort or another, then it is likely that the court-poets intended their realism to elicit them. In that case, we can indeed conclude that the Alexandrians at least partly intended their realism to reflect and possibly even, by reassurance or irony, to answer their original audience's need to come to terms with their traditional cultural heritage in the context of the new reality of colonial life away from Greece itself, a need which, it may reasonably be supposed, was also felt at least to some degree by the poets themselves.

The reaction to this social and cultural impulse was in fact, I suggest, the chief concern of Alexandrian realism. Alexandrian realism may of course be viewed simply as a consequence of certain tendencies observable already in early literature. Thus the pictorial realism of the Alexandrians can be construed as an extension of a characteristic of earlier poetry, in particular epic. Again, the increase in interest in realistic subject-matter can be seen as a continuation of a trend observable in Euripides and the Middle and the New Comedy and the occurrence of such material in grand genres, in particular epic, can be put down to a desire to flout the rigid categorisations of literature discernible in Aristotle's *Poetics* and elsewhere. This is undeniably the source of much of our poets' literary achievement. However, given the changes in literary tastes and expectations, we may legitimately ask what caused *them*, for they do not explain, but are rather the symptoms of a fundamentally new world view, particularly, as we have seen, as regards the cultural heritage of traditional myth. And here is the relevance of the social and cultural factors to which I have drawn attention. Moreover, if all the different forms of Alexandrian realism are at least in part ways of responding to the original audience's feelings of cultural rift, they are intrinsically connected by their common purpose, and it cannot fairly be objected that this book is dealing with unrelated entities. Furthermore, the claim can be made that the complexity of Alexandrian realism's function and effects is another feature which makes the phenomenon unique in Greek literature.

In their use of the various forms of realism, therefore, the Alexandrian poets were operating in a way comparable with their patrons, the Ptolemies: the early sovereigns of Alexandria tried to reinforce their city's contact with Greek culture by the establishment of the Museum and Libraries, which were designed to preserve no less than the πᾶσα παιδεία, the entire culture and learning of Greece.[99] But were the activities of the Ptolemies and their poets simply comparable? Is it possible to discern actual Ptolemaic encouragement of the realism of their court-poets? Were the poets in fact catering for Ptolemaic taste, or indeed, policy?

To answer these questions we must first try to establish Ptolemaic preferences in poetry. The most obvious place in which to look for traces of these is the encomiastic poetry of the Alexandrians.[100] *Idyll* 17 of Theocritus, the *Encomium for Ptolemy*, is particularly informative, especially lines 13–76 on the lineage of Philadelphus. It there exhibits among other things a desire to put the Ptolemaic ruler-cult within the context of Olympian religion, and its methods include vividly picturing Soter rubbing shoulders with the sated Heracles, his ancestor, whose traditional grandeur is lowered a little to make Soter's new relationship with him on Olympus appear quite in the normal run of things (13–33). It is manifest from this scene and others in the encomium that the Ptolemies liked to see themselves presented as if absolutely at home in the realm of traditional Greek religion, indeed emphatically 'at home'. We have already considered the likelihood that the sophisticated audiences at Alexandria will have sensed some admixture of irony in such low-brow accounts of Olympus and its new inhabitants and protégés, but evidently the royal house did not regard this irony as at all obnoxious. The context of tradition in which they were now being placed seems to have been paramount for them.

The same preoccupations can be seen, for example, in *Idyll* 15, with its aition describing the reason for a cult-festival of

Alexandria itself. The recent deification of Berenice and Arsinoe's sponsorship of the cult as an act of gratitude to Aphrodite are hallowed by the association with the ancient myth of Adonis. Moreover, we have seen that Theocritus is by no means frightened of setting his encomiastic aition in an everyday framework, for *Idyll* 15 is a mime and Gorgo and Praxinoa are depicted in intentionally humorous everyday terms (though of course the hymn is on a higher stylistic level than the mime-frame). Once again, it is surely not fanciful to see Theocritus conforming with Ptolemaic taste and cultural programme. Nor is Theocritus the only Alexandrian poet to deal with the new cults in this way. In the *Coma Berenices* (*Fr.* 110) Callimachus uses aetiology in a manner at least formally analogous to that of the hymn of *Idyll* 15, though the motivation of the *Coma* is more complex, especially in view of what may be called its baroque tone. The *Apotheosis of Arsinoe* (*Fr.* 228) also attempts to put the lives and deaths of the royal family within the Olympian framework, but in this case the use of everyday detail is evocative of impressive pathos.[101] Apollonius, too, can be fitted into the picture, for his *Foundation of Alexandria* (*Fr.* 4 Pow.) apparently treated the foundation of the capital in the traditional manner of ktistic literature, possibly tracing its origins back into the mythical past.

Thus the encomiastic poetry of early Alexandria which deals with the new city, the new cults and the new aitia demonstrates that the Ptolemies valued the authenticity that their poets could confer on their institutions by bringing them into the context of traditional Greek culture and religion.[102] The encomiastic poetry also shows that the poets themselves were willing to fit in with Ptolemaic religious and cultural programme. Moreover, the Ptolemies presumably welcomed their court-poets' use of pictorialism and everyday matter as a means of achieving their end. That they tolerated being praised in humorously low contexts is proved by Theocritus' *Idylls* 14 and 15, and Herodas' *Mimiamb* 1; and now we have the *Victoria Berenices* of Callimachus, which appears to have celebrated Berenice II's victory in the chariot-race at Nemea alongside the story of Heracles and the humble Molorchus and the discovery of the mousetrap. All this is in the starkest possible contrast with what we know of royal taste in such matters in the other Hellenistic kingdoms, for instance in that of the Attalids, whose predilections are clearly illustrated by the monumental Altar of Zeus at Pergamum. It is, therefore, evident

26 *Definitions and a Sample*

that the Ptolemies approved of the various forms of realism employed in the court-poets' encomia to them. Moreover, to judge from these poets' persistence in their use of realism in the encomia and from the way in which it fitted in with the Ptolemies' programmes, it is likely that they actually encouraged it, while perceiving very clearly that what the ordinary Greek citizenry required was a monumental entertainment like the Pompe staged by Philadelphus or the isolympic games.[103]

It is also likely, I would suggest, that the first three Ptolemies welcomed and possibly even encouraged their poets' use of realism in forms of poetry other than encomia, for it was to their taste and its use in other genres could also be made to further their cultural programme. This will have been the case particularly with epic, for that genre was especially suitable for bringing Alexandria into contact with mainstream Greek culture and hence for giving the city a cultural identity. In fact, as we shall see, the writers in the genre of epic, though we need by no means exclude lyric and iambic poetry in this connection, did realise its social potential, for they did attempt in it to bring the world of traditional Greek culture, especially myth, within the realm of the Alexandrian audience's experience and thereby assist them to come to terms with their heritage away from Greece, whether through reassurance or irony. They will thus have conformed with the cultural policy which the Ptolemies had adopted and which is illustrated by their patronage of the Museum and the Libraries. Here a comparison with Euphorion is instructive. We shall find very little pictorial, scientific or everyday realism in his extant *oeuvre*. If this is not merely the product of chance survival, then apparently these features were not in vogue at the Seleucid court at Antioch. The same is probably true of the rest of the Hellenistic cultural centres at this period, if we may judge by what little we know of the poetry written in them.

In the light of these considerations, I conclude that Alexandrian realism was primarily a response to the cultural identity crisis felt by the new city's Greek population, especially its educated members, for whom the poets were writing, but that the impact which its various forms had on such a culturally refined audience was intentionally complex. I also conclude that the growth of the phenomenon was actually fostered by the Ptolemies. The likelihood of Ptolemaic encouragement helps to explain why it was the Alexandrians of this period who developed a type of realism unique in Greek poetry. The poets of the later Alexandrian movement may not have experienced their precursors' crisis of cultural identity in quite the same way and to the same extent, but they inherited the literary canons and tastes formulated in the cultural milieu of early Alexandria, and these persisted through the following two centuries right into the very different cultural climate of late Republican and early Imperial Rome.

But now that we have surveyed the forms, function and effects of Alexandrian realism, what are its limitations? As has been remarked already, we must shed some of our experience of modern Realism when we discuss universal realism and its various historical manifestations, and it is worth studying just what this divestment means. If we want a working definition of the nineteenth-century movement, Wellek's 'objective representation of contemporary social reality' will pinpoint the main issues adequately enough. As Wellek says, his definition implies didacticism, and he goes on to talk about the basic tension in the movement between the depiction of what social reality is and what it should be.[104] This kind of didacticism is, as I have already observed, wholly absent from Alexandrian poetry.[105] So is the rather paradoxically concomitant demand for objectivity which is rightly referred to by Wellek. The Realist painters, for example, insisted that sincerity was possible only after they had rid themselves of inherited artistic conventions, Pissarro going so far as to suggest that they burn down the Louvre.[106] This would have been anathema to the Alexandrians even when they wanted to achieve their most serious realism. The traditional forms, however much they were subject to 'mixing' and other types of modification, remained the means of poetic expression, since the Alexandrians, in common with most schools of art other than the Realists, would have seen no conflict between the sophisticated, artificial and even archaistic use of the conventional media on the one hand and sincerity (inasmuch as that was an aim) on the other. Consequently, we should not look in their work for the Realists' stylistic 'flatness' or 'objectivity'. Contemporaneity is a more complicated and interesting matter.[107] In *Idyll* 15 contemporary scenes and characters are indeed presented, but they are made the objects of humour by the manner in which they are treated. The realism of this contemporaneity is thus limited to its subject-matter, a conclusion that we shall find true of Theocritus' bucolic poems and of Herodas' *Mimiambi* as well. Paradoxically for us, perhaps, the Alexandrians are more concerned with the problems of the present in their evocations of myth: these often seem to reflect the contemporary Hellenistic world's concerns with cultural identity, an approach again illustrated by *Idyll* 15. The treatment of contemporary concerns in the Alexandrians' accounts of the mythical past may be indirect, but its frequently serious tone cannot reasonably be doubted.

Three matters must be emphasised in conclusion. First of all, in examining its realism, we are only dealing with one aspect of Alexandrian poetry. The movement is characterised by other elements which cannot easily be called realistic at all. There is, for example, the intense philological interest, on the whole (but not entirely) devoid of any desire for realistic effects, which it demonstrates in the experimentation with dialects and the scholarly explanation of peculiar words and expressions found in the different parts of Greece and in danger of extinction; in etymology; in the allusive linguistic imitation and variation of earlier poetry, particularly of Homer; and in the textual criticism and lexical interpretation of 'classical' literature, again especially of Homer, whereby, for instance, a Homeric word of dubious meaning is placed in an explanatory context.[108] In fact, this kind of activity is probably often prompted by the desire to confront the past and interpret it for the present, the same impulse that I have suggested lies behind Alexandrian realism, but its methods are generally not realistic in the sense of relating to the past in some more or less tangible way. The movement's realism is perhaps a compensation for those rather cerebral pursuits. Another non-realistic preoccupation of Alexandrian poetry is the more fantastic side of mythology. Here realism may act as a counterfoil. In the *Europa* of Moschus, for example, the poet tells the miraculous story of Europa with a fully imagined pictorial precision and everyday touches of scene-setting and characterisation: as a whole, the *Europa* remains fantastic, but the interplay between the miraculous and the realistic, between distance and immediacy, creates an attractively teasing and artificial effect. Again, though an Apollonius may use love for realistic purposes, other members of the Alexandrian movement have no such motive. Lovers are characteristically placed in the most unreal situations and the fulfilment of their passion is confronted with fantastic barriers. Their emotion commonly exhibits pathological, grotesque or unnatural traits or a contrived ingenuousness. Their love-affair generally ends in spectacularly dramatic death. Side by side with this fascination with the bizarre came the desire to narrate the story in a highly wrought and artificial manner, incorporating the most sophisticated techniques of mythological allusion. This kind of approach is illustrated by the fragments of Euphorion, Parthenius' *Love Romances* and the story of Pasiphaë in Virgil's sixth *Eclogue*.

I must emphasise, secondly, that we cannot expect Alexandrian realism to be displayed with equal prominence throughout the movement: Callimachus, Apollonius and Theocritus, for example, will supply us with many examples of the three main types of Alexandrian poetry, but Euphorion will yield scarcely anything at all. Yet the facet of Alexandrian poetry that we are examining has never been systematically analysed in modern criticism, and, if it is the important and interesting phenomenon that I think it to be, then it is high time to try to repair the omission. And we may hope that an analysis of it will help put the movement's other elements into a new relation and perspective and demonstrate that Alexandrian poetry is even more varied and complex than has been thought so far.

Finally, I must make it clear that this book pursues a double theme. It is an attempt to describe and illustrate the literary forms of Alexandrian realism. But it is also concerned to explain why the new trend in poetry developed. This means that we must consider the original functions that realism is likely to have had, which in turn entails the examination of the literary phenomenon from a sociological point of view, in short an inquiry into the Alexandrian audience. This procedure is of course inevitable in the study of realism in a way that is perhaps not so urgently necessary in the study of other literary modes, but what I hope will emerge from my twofold approach is a comprehensive view of Alexandrian realism, in both its forms and its functions.

Notes

1. So Ph.-E. Legrand, *La Poésie alexandrine* (Paris, 1924), pp. 9ff.; cf. the more precise demarcations of the period indicated in the titles of A. Couat, *La Poésie alexandrine sous les trois premiers Ptolémées (324–222 av. J.-C.)* (Paris, 1882); U. von Wilamowitz-Moellendorff, *Hellenistische Dichtung in der Zeit des Kallimachos* (Berlin, 1924); J. U. Powell, *Collectanea Alexandrina: Reliquiae minores Poetarum Graecorum Aetatis Ptolemaicae 323–146 A. C. Epicorum, Elegiacorum, Lyricorum, Ethicorum* (Oxford, 1925).

2. Ziegler, second edition (Leipzig, 1966). See also L. Gil Fernández, 'La

30 Definitions and a Sample

epica helenística' in *Estudios sobre el mundo helenístico* (Seville, 1971), 91–120; J. Onians, *Art and Thought in the Hellenistic Age: the Greek World View 350–50 B.C.* (London, 1979), esp. pp. 133–42; and H. Lloyd-Jones, 'A Hellenistic Miscellany', *S.I.F.C.* 3rd Ser. 2 (1984), 58ff.

  3. The *Argonautica* of Apollonius, whom I include (against Ziegler, *Das hellenistische Epos*, p. 20) among the Alexandrians (see below), can be sharply differentiated from the mythological epics written by non-Alexandrians: see P. M. Fraser, *Ptolemaic Alexandria* (Oxford, 1972), p. 625 and Lloyd-Jones loc. cit.

  4. Ziegler, *Das hellenistische Epos*, pp. 15–23.

  5. Ibid. p. 12.

  6. Though Ziegler has been accused of exaggeration by Fraser, *Ptolemaic Alexandria*, vol. ii, p. 883 n. 58.

  7. Thus e.g. T. B. L. Webster, *Hellenistic Poetry and Art* (London, 1964) gives an unbalanced account of Hellenistic poetry by ignoring Ziegler's work.

  8. The 'geographical' definition is proposed by A. Körte, *Die hellenistische Dichtung*, (revised by P. Händel) (Stuttgart, 1960), pp. 337–40. It is also used by Fraser, *Ptolemaic Alexandria*, pp. 309, 554, 623. Such a definition is appropriate in a work like Fraser's, where the author is trying to assess the influence of the city as an intellectual capital, but it is of limited value for a literary study, like the present, which examines a poetic movement for which geographical considerations are not so relevant.

  9. For Callimachus' attitude to Aratus see *Ep.* 56 *H.E.* (with H. Reinsch-Werner, *Callimachus Hesiodicus: die Rezeption der hesiodeischen Dichtung durch Kallimachos von Kyrene* (Berlin, 1976), pp. 9–13) and to Philetas the Florentine scholia on *Pr. Aet. Fr.* 1.1–12 (R. Pfeiffer, *Callimachus*, vol. i, (Oxford, 1949), p. 3); the scholia have been variously interpreted as saying either that Callimachus is setting the short poems of Mimnermus and Philetas against long poems by different authors (reading αὐτ (ά) at line 15;, so e.g. Fraser, ibid., vol. i, p. 749 and vol. ii, p. 1053 n. 253 and p. 1058 n. 287 (with lit.)) or that the short poems of Mimnermus and Philetas are better than their long ones (reading αὐτ (ῶν) at line 15; so e.g. Pfeiffer on *Pr. Aet.* 9–12); the latter view has been convincingly defended by A. S. Hollis, 'Callimachus, Aetia Fr. 1.9–12', *C.Q.* N.S. 28 (1978), 402–6, on which interpretation Callimachus' admiration of Philetas will not have been unqualified.

  10. The Florentine scholiast to Call. *Pr. Aet. Fr.* 1.1–12, line 5 numbers Asclepiades and Posidippus among the Telchines. Asclepiades praised Antimachus' *Lyde* (32 *H.E.*) for which Callimachus expressed loathing (*Fr.* 398). For a probable parody of Call. *H.* 5.2–3 by Posidippus in an epigram which Gow and Page are probably incorrect in ascribing to Asclepiades (Asclepiades 35 *H.E.*) see Fraser, ibid., vol. ii, p. 812f. n. 144.

  11. The story of the quarrel between Callimachus and Apollonius, supposedly based on a difference of literary principles, has been discredited in recent scholarship. See T. M. Klein, 'Callimachus, Apollonius Rhodius, and the Concept of the "Big Book"', *Eranos* 73 (1975), 16–25; M. R. Lefkowitz, 'The Quarrel between Callimachus and Apollonius', *Z.P.E.* 40 (1980), 1–19 and *The Lives of the Greek Poets* (Baltimore, 1981), pp. 117–35 (q.v. for further references, though cf. below, n. 76); Lloyd-Jones, 'A Hellenistic Miscellany', 58–60

  12. For Theocritus' relations with Callimachus see A. S. F. Gow, *Theocritus*, vol. i (Cambridge, 1952), pp. xxiiff. *Id.* 7.45–8 certainly places Theocritus on Callimachus' side in the literary battle with the Telchines and Theocritus definitely resided in Alexandria for a time in the 270s (Gow, ibid., p. xvii), from which Gow concludes cautiously that they shared a professional respect and were perhaps friends. The attempt by G. Lohse, 'Die Kunstauffassung im VII. Idyll Theokrits und das Programm des Kallimachos', *H.* 94 (1966), 413–25 to minimise the extent of their agreement on literary principles has been refuted by, e.g., U. Ott, *Die Kunst des Gegensatzes in Theokrits Hirtengedichten*, *Spudasmata* 22 (Hildesheim

and New York, 1969), p. 162, n. 444. See also D. M. Halperin, *Before Pastoral: Theocritus and the Ancient Tradition of Bucolic Poetry* (New Haven and London, 1983), pp. 169–74, 202–4, 208, 212f., 218, 244–7, 252, 255–7.

13. See e.g. Fraser, *Ptolemaic Alexandria*, p. 623f.

14. See W. Bühler, *Die Europa des Moschos*, Hermes Einzelschr. 13 (Wiesbaden, 1960), pp. 74, 77, 133. For his residence at Alexandria as a pupil of Aristarchus see Fraser, ibid., p. 647.

15. See A. S. F. Gow and A. F. Scholfield, *Nicander* (Cambridge, 1953), on *Th.* 109, 457, *Al.* 62, 99, 463, 618.

16. See I. C. Cunningham, *Herodas: Mimiambi* (Oxford, 1971), pp. 16 and 194; Fraser, *Ptolemaic Alexandria*, vol. ii, p. 1050 n. 247; G. Mastromarco, *Il pubblico di Eronda*, Proagones 15 (Padua, 1979), pp. 109–42 (= Eng. trans. *The Public of Herondas*, London Studies in Classical Philology 11 (Amsterdam, 1984), pp. 65—97). On Herodas' birthplace and connection with Alexandria see Cunningham, ibid., pp. 2f. and 127f.; Fraser, ibid., vol. ii, p. 876 n. 30; S. M. Sherwin-White, *Ancient Cos: an historical study from the Dorian settlement to the Imperial Period*, Hypomnemata 51 (Göttingen, 1978), pp. 349ff. and n. 508.

17. See Fraser, ibid., pp. 650ff.

18. See below, p. 221 n. 87.

19. For Leonidas' relations with Callimachus' poetry see Fraser, *Ptolemaic Alexandria*, p. 561f.

20. Hedylus 5 *H.E.* borrows from Callimachus 56 *H.E.*; Meleager 81 *H.E.* is indebted to Callimachus 4 *H.E.*

21. Asclepiades 28 *H.E.*

22. See C. M. Bowra, 'Erinna's Lament for Baucis', in *Greek Poetry and Life: Essays presented to Gilbert Murray* (Oxford, 1936), 337ff. M. L. West, 'Erinna', *Z.P.E.* 25 (1977), 95–119 has recently rejected the authenticity of Erinna's *Distaff*; but see below, p. 102 n. 5.

23. Thus Theocritean bucolic is dismissed by Fraser, *Ptolemaic Alexandria*, p. 623; see above, n. 8.

24. See above, n. 12.

25. J. P. Stern, *On Realism* (London and Boston, 1973), pp. 168ff.

26. Ibid., p. 174; the phrases 'the Greek revolution' and 'makes and matches' allude to E. H. Gombrich's *Art and Illusion*[4] (London, 1972), pp. 99ff.

27. See R. Wellek, 'The Concept of Realism in Literary Scholarship', *Neophilologus* 45 (1961), 2–10, esp. 6 (= R. Wellek, *Concepts of Criticism* (New Haven and London, 1963), pp. 224–40, esp. p. 233).

28. See e.g. the contradictory conclusions of W. Asmus, 'Zu den historischen Grenzen des Begriffs "Realismus"', in *Probleme des Realismus in der Weltliteratur* (Berlin, 1962), 495–504 and S. Luria, 'Herondas' Kampf für die veristische Kunst', in *Miscellanea di studi alessandrini in memoria di Augusto Rostagni* (Turin, 1963), 394–415. For a forceful attack on the Marxist interpretations of Herodas see Mastromarco, *Il pubblico di Eronda*, pp. 131–40 (= Eng. trans., pp. 87–94), who also has a useful summary of the history of the view that Herodas is a realist (ibid., pp. 109–15 (= Eng. trans., pp. 65–70)).

29. For Greek art see especially G. Sörbom, *Mimesis and Art* (Bonniers, 1966).

30. See below, p. 27.

31. On which see V. G. Mylne, *The Eighteenth-Century French Novel: Techniques of Illusion* (Cambridge, 1981).

32. D. Diderot, *Oeuvres Esthétiques* (ed. P. Vernière) (Paris, 1965), pp. 34–6.

33. Ibid., p. 35.

34. See e.g. L. Nochlin, *Realism* (Harmondsworth, 1971), pp. 103–206.

35. Champfleury (J.-F.-F. Husson), *Le Réalisme* (Paris, 1857), p. 274; cf. pp. 85f., 87f., 228, 249, 258, 261f., 278, 284; and Jules Breton, *La Vie d'un Artiste* (Paris, 1890), p. 177, cited and discussed by Nochlin, ibid., p. 113.

32 Definitions and a Sample

36. See Mylne, *The Eighteenth-Century French Novel*, p. 10f. *et passim*.
37. Stern, *On Realism*, p. 179.
38. Interestingly, the Realists were vitally concerned with the preservation of vanishing popular culture and art for the depiction of peasant-life: see Champfleury, *Le Réalisme*, pp. 182–97 (his intention was 'Sauver le plus possible, pendant qu'il en est temps encore, des débris de l'art populaire', ibid., p. 196) and Nochlin, *Realism*, p. 115. John Aubrey exhibits most clearly the nostalgia involved in collecting folk-beliefs and customs even when he finds them ridiculous.
39. E. Auerbach, *Mimesis: Dargestellte Wirklichkeit in der abendländischen Literatur* (Bern, 1946) (Eng. trans. W. R. Trask, *Mimesis: the Representation of Reality in Western Literature* (Princeton, 1953)).
40. Ibid., Eng. trans. p. 22 (= p. 28 of the original).
41. Wellek, 'The Concept of Realism in Literary Scholarship', 10 (= *Concepts of Criticism*, p. 240f.). Cf. the reaction to Wellek's article by E. B. Greenwood, 'Reflections on Professor Wellek's Concept of Realism', *Neophilologus* 46 (1962), 89–97 and Wellek's response, 'A Reply to E. B. Greenwood's Reflections', ibid., 194–6.
42. So Fraser, *Ptolemaic Alexandria*, p. 663.
43. So Couat, *La Poésie alexandrine*, p. 422, Ph.-E. Legrand, *Étude sur Théocrite* (Paris, 1898), p. 133f. and Fraser, ibid., p. 672.
44. Theocritus in this *Idyll*, as elsewhere, tries to set up an ironical juxaposition of the colloquial and the heroic. Thus Gorgo's comforting words to Zopyrion, θάρσει, Ζωπυρίων, γλυκερὸν τέκος· οὐ λέγει ἀπφῦν ('Cheer up, Zopyrion, sweet child; she doesn't mean Daddy') (13), are an ironically incongruous reminiscence of Zeus urging Athene to cheer up at *Il.* 8.39 and 22.183: θάρσει, Τριτογένεια, φίλον τέκος ('Cheer up, Tritogeneia, dear child'). The subject will be discussed in detail in relation to Theocritus' other poems below, pp. 164–81. For *Idyll* 15 see F. T. Griffiths, *Theocritus at Court*, *Mnem. Suppl.* 55 (Leiden, 1979), pp. 121–3.
45. ἐς Τροίαν πειρώμενοι ἤνθον Ἀχαιοί, /κάλλιστα παίδων· πείρα θην πάντα τελεῖται (61f.). Cf. Theognis 571, Herodotus 7.9 and Pindar, *N.* 3.70 for variants of the proverb.
46. Gow on 77 reveals how little we know about this proverb and the ritual behind it, but its general drift is clear enough. Cf. K. J. Dover, *Theocritus: Select Poems* (Basingstoke and London, 1971) *ad loc*.
47. So Gow on 84f.
48. See Gow *ad loc*. for the proverb she uses.
49. For the admiration of this quality expressed elsewhere in Alexandrian poetry, see below, pp. 42–6, 94f.
50. The implications of the passage for our knowledge concerning the make-up of the population of early Alexandria are discussed by Fraser, *Ptolemaic Alexandria*, p. 65. See further below, p. 19f.
51. In the argument to the poem the scholiasts state that Theocritus modelled *Id.* 15 after Sophron's mime Ταὶ θάμεναι τὰ Ἴσθμια. See further Gow, *Theocritus*, vol. ii, p. 265f. and his n. on 2.
52. See below, pp. 144f.
53. See below, p. 145.
54. λεκτικῆς ἁρμονίας δεόμενος is the reading of E. M. Cope, *The Rhetoric of Aristotle*, vol. iii (revised by J. E. Sandys) (Cambridge, 1877), p. 86 which I accept over the *vulgata lectio* καὶ λεκτικῆς καὶ ἁρμονίας δεόμενος; Aristotle is contrasting the hexameter with the conversational iambic metre (for ἁρμονία as 'structure' see Cope-Sandys *ad loc*.). Similar comments on iambics and hexameters are made by Aristotle at *Poet.* 49^a 24–8, 59^a 10–14, 59^b 32–5, and *Rh.* 3.1.9 1404^a 31–3. His judgement is followed by Ps.-Demetrius *de Eloc*. 42f., Dion. Hal. *Comp.* 17.71 (VI.2 p. 172. 15–18 Usener-Radermacher), Ps.-Longinus *Subl.* 39.4, and by the Romans in connection with Latin speech, Cic. *Orat.* 20.67, 56.189, 57.192, *de Or.* 3.47.182 and Quint. *Inst. Or.* 9.4.76. These parallels substantiate Cope-Sandys' reading.
55. An apparent earlier exception, the *Homeric Hymn to Hermes*, perhaps

Definitions and a Sample 33

actually 'proves' the rule for the earlier period as well, for its effect depends in part on the incongruity of the everyday depiction of the baby Hermes and the grand epic medium, of which higher things seem normally to have been expected.

56. Mock-heroic poems like the *Margites* or the *Batrachomyomachia* depend for their effect on a similar incongruity, but they have a different aim, parody of the epic genre (and thus incidentally strengthen our suspicion, aroused by the *Homeric Hymn to Hermes*, that in the pre-Hellenistic period grand subjects were the normally expected material of epic and its metre); I am arguing that in *Id.* 15 humour arises first out of the tension between metre and content itself and secondly out of the lightly ironic treatment of two ordinary folk which emerges from that tension.

57. παύσασθ᾽ ὦ δύστανοι, ἀνάνυτα κωτίλλοισαι, / τρυγόνες· ἐκκναισεῦντι πλατειάσδοισαι ἅπαντα (87f.).

58. A. S. F. Gow, 'The Methods of Theocritus and some Problems in his Poems', *C.Q.* 24 (1930), 151; see also his note on 88 and G. Fabiano, 'Fluctuation in Theocritus' Style', *G.R.B.S.* 12 (1971), 521f. See further below, pp. 164f.

59. Couat, *La Poésie alexandrine*, pp. 394–402, esp. p. 399; Legrand, *Théocrite*, pp. 413ff.; L. Deubner, 'Ein Stilprinzip hellenistischer Dichtkunst', *N.Jb.* 47 (1921), 361–78, followed by W. Kroll, *Studien zum Verständnis der römischen Literatur* (Stuttgart, 1924), pp. 202ff. Auerbach in *Mimesis* talks of 'Stiltrennung' (e.g. p. 28) and 'Stilmischung' (e.g. p. 76): Trask translates these words by 'separation of styles' (e.g. p. 22) and 'principle of mixed styles' (e.g. p. 72) or 'mixture of styles' (e.g. p. 73). Cf. L. E. Rossi, 'I generi letterari e le loro leggi scritte e non scritte nelle letterature classiche', *B.I.C.S.* 18 (1971), 69–94.

60. Once again, Adonis is described as if he were a real person and not an artistic representation; cf. above, p. 10. J. Palm, 'Bemerkungen zur Ekphrase in der griechischen Literatur', *Kungl. Humanistiska Vetenskapssamfundet i Uppsala, Årsbok* 1965–1966, 146f. takes the passages as evidence of the Hellenistic age's fondness for mimetic effects.

61. Greek funerals took place before sunrise, as the rite does here (see Gow on 132 citing Dem. 43.62 and Plat. *Laws* 960a); Gow on 134 in a list of texts illustrating the expression of lamentation by baring the breast cites *Il.* 22.79, Polyb. 2.56.7, Cat. 64.64, Ov. *Met.* 3.481 and 13.688, *F.* 4.454 and Petron. 111.

62. So C. W. Vollgraff, 'χρυσῷ παίζοισ᾽ Ἀφροδίτα', *Mélanges d'archéologie et d'histoire offerts à Ch. Picard* (Paris, 1949), 1075–87, who further suggests that the enigmatic phrase may have referred to a particular cult-statue of Aphrodite–Berenice (ibid., 1087). Cf. Gow on 100f.

63. She uses the third declension form, Πατροκλῆς; the nominative of a third declension form of the name does not occur in Homer, though there are instances of its use in the oblique cases (e.g. *Il.* 16.125f., 23.65, 105, *Od.* 11.468). She (or Theocritus) may therefore be exhibiting a typically Alexandrian taste for recondite variations on Homeric diction.

64. Dover, *Theocritus: Select Poems*, p. 209f. views the hymn itself as a parody of the tastes catered for in festival-songs.

65. See below, pp. 120–4.

66. F. Cairns, *Tibullus: A Hellenistic Poet at Rome* (Cambridge, 1979), p. 13, who goes on to say stimulatingly 'the Hellenistic age seems to have felt an overwhelming sense both of the distinctness of contemporary society from the past and of its continuity with the past, and to have derived an intense and sophisticated enjoyment from its cultural heritage'.

67. The precise date of her deification (and even of her death) is uncertain. See A. Bouché-Leclerq, *Histoire des Lagides* (Paris, 1903), pp. 101, 158 n. 3, 237 n. 1, 261 and 329 n. 4; G. H. Macurdy, *Hellenistic Queens* (Baltimore, 1932), pp. 107–9; Gow, *Theocritus*, vol. ii, pp. 265 and 326; E. Bevan, *The House of Ptolemy: a History of Egypt under the Ptolemaic Dynasty* (Chicago, 1968), p. 127f.; Fraser,

34 Definitions and a Sample

Ptolemaic Alexandria, pp. 197, 224, 228, 240 and 666f.; E. E. Rice, *The Grand Procession of Ptolemy Philadelphus* (Oxford, 1983), p. 121f.

68. For an examination of Theocritus' furtherance of Ptolemaic aims in 'public relations' with the citizenry of Alexandria see especially Griffths, *Theocritus at Court*, pp. 116–28.

69. H. Diels, *Die Fragmente der Vorsokratiker*^{x}, vol. i (edited by W. Kranz) (Berlin, 1956), p. 173, *Fr.* 101a.

70. There is, moreover, a significant variation in the stylistic level of the hexameters of the mime section and of those of the hymn, the level in the hymn being more strictly in accord with the traditional. This variation concerns Theocritus' practice with the 'bucolic bridge', broken twelve times in the mime section and only once in the hymn (line 131). See below, p. 218 n. 48.

71. The following inquiry is based on remarks in my article 'The Nature and Origin of Realism in Alexandrian Poetry', *A.u.A.* 29 (1983), 135–45.

72. See below, p. 20 for the gymnasia and n. 85 below for the eponymous priesthoods.

73. See C. Vatin, *Recherches sur le mariage et la condition de la femme mariée à l'époque hellénistique*, *B.E.F.A.R.* 216 (Paris, 1970), pp. 163–80 and Fraser, *Ptolemaic Alexandria*, p. 71f. and vol. ii, p. 155 n. 239. It has been thought that Philadelphus' marriage to his sister Arsinoe was meant as an appeal to Pharaonic precedent in order to reconcile the Egyptian populace with Macedonian sovereignty: see e.g. Fraser, ibid., p. 217. That would mean a contamination of the Greek institution of marriage at the highest level of society. But there is no evidence for the notion, and there is evidence that other factors were at work, not least the powerful personality of Arsinoe: see e.g. Vatin, ibid., pp. 71–3. Indeed, there is evidence for the popularity of the marriage in the use of faience oinochoai which ordinary folk appear to have used as a means of expressing their loyalty to the queen: see D. B. Thompson, *Ptolemaic Oinochoai and Portraits in Faience: Aspects of the Ruler-Cult* (Oxford, 1973), pp. 55–7; on Arsinoe's general popularity, as demonstrated by these artefacts, see ibid., pp. 51–62, 71–5 and 120.

74. Fraser, *Ptolemaic Alexandria*, p. 78.

75. See ibid., pp. 52f., 65ff. For example, we see Zeno of Caunus, the general agent of the head of the Ptolemies' civil administration, keeping in touch with fellow Carians and aiding them in their requests for favours and advancement (ibid., p. 67f.). It would seem that in the other Hellenistic kingdoms the ties of the monarch's *philoi* to their cities of origin may have been looser than in Egypt: see C. Habicht, 'Die herrschende Gesellschaft in den hellenistischen Monarchien', *V.S.W.G.* 45 (1958), 5ff. Moreover, it is apparent that the upper-class Greeks had virtually no contact with the native Egyptians and the relationship of conquerer to conquered was maintained until the end of the third century; see Fraser, ibid., p. 70f. There is, however, not so much evidence for the middle classes on the question: see Fraser, ibid., p. 66. The problem of the ethnic 'Persian', which appears to have meant 'Hellenizing Egyptian' (see especially J. F. Oates, 'The Status Designation: ΠΕΡΣΗΣ, ΤΗΣ ΕΠΙΓΟΝΗΣ', *Y.C.S.* 18 (1963), 1–129 and Fraser, ibid., p. 58f.), is irrelevant in this connection; for a similar problem, that of the 'Macedonians', see Fraser, ibid., pp. 80 and 129.

76. *Vit.* a 5f., b 4 Wendel and *P. Oxy.* 1241/T13. Lefkowitz, 'The Quarrel between Callimachus and Apollonius', 13f. and *The Lives of the Greek Poets*, p. 130f. doubts the story of Apollonius' Alexandrian birth and argues that he was Rhodian, but her grounds are too general to carry conviction; furthermore, *Vit.* a 5f. ('he was by birth an Alexandrian of the Ptolemais tribe') is too specific to be brushed aside and Lefkowitz neglects in this connection the evidence of *P. Oxy.* 1241/T13, a list of Librarians which states that Apollonius was an Alexandrian 'called' a Rhodian.

77. For Callimachus' strong feeling for his native city we need here cite only *Ep.* 29 *H.E.*, Callimachus' epitaph for his father with its proud emphasis on the

family's achievements in the affairs of Cyrene, *Ep.* 32 *H.E.*, on the death of Melanippus and Basilo, at which 'all Cyrene bowed its head', and the *Hymn to Apollo* 65–96, where the poet stresses the association of Apollo Carneius with Cyrene; see further Fraser, *Ptolemaic Alexandria*, pp. 579, 654, 656, 662, 786 with n. 495 (vol. ii, p. 1095), 789; F. Williams, *Callimachus: Hymn to Apollo* (Oxford, 1978) on *H.* 2.68, 71, 76; and C. Meillier, *Callimaque et son temps: Recherches sur la carrière et la condition d'un écrivain à l'époque des premiers Lagides* (Lille, 1979), pp. 129–54.

78. For an analysis of the contribution made to Alexandrian life and letters by immigrants from the different Greek and non-Greek regions F. Heichelheim, *Die auswärtige Bevölkerung im Ptolemäerreich*, Klio Beiheft 18 (N.F. 5) (Leipzig, 1925), pp. 36–82 remains indispensable. A convenient list of the Alexandrian intelligentsia is provided by W. Peremans *et al.*, *Prosopographia Ptolemaica* 6, *La cour, les relations internationales et les possessions extérieures, la vie culturelle*, Studia Hellenistica 17 (Louvain, 1968), pp. 212–82. See also W. Peremans, 'Égyptiens et étrangers dans l'Égypte ptolémaïque', in *Grecs et barbares, Entretiens sur l'antiquité classique* 8 (Vandoeuvres-Geneva, 1962), 121–66, esp. 135; Fraser, ibid., p. 307f.

79. So Fraser, ibid., p. 65f. It should be noted that their failure to take on Alexandrian citizenship is apparently not to be put down to a desire to escape taxation; the Librarians and members of the Museum seem to have been exempt from taxes (see Fraser, ibid., p. 316f. with n. 84 (vol. ii, p. 470) and vol. ii, p. 870 n. 2).

80. This feeling will have been aggravated by the Greeks' numerical inferiority to the Egyptians. Diodorus 1.31.8 tells us that the total population of Egypt in antiquity was approximately 7,000,000 and that this figure had been maintained down to his day. This can be made to agree with Josephus *B.J.* 2.385 who says that the total population of Egypt, excluding Alexandria, was 7,500,000 in his time, about a century after Diodorus: see Fraser, ibid., vol. ii, p. 171f. n. 358. So the total population of Egypt under the early Ptolemies will have been about 7,000,000. Diodorus also tells us (17.52.4–6) that at the time of his visit to Alexandria (60 BC) the city had more than 300,000 'free men' resident in it and that it had grown more recently to such an extent that it was considered larger than any other city, which must mean about 1,000,000, for Rome was around 900,000 at this time: see Fraser, loc. cit. If by 'free men' Diodorus means 'all male free persons, adults and minors (citizens and resident aliens)', as Fraser argues, then the total free population will have been around 600,000. The figure will have been smaller for the early Ptolemaic period, given Diodorus' statement that the city had been in a state of continual growth, and that for the Greek population smaller still, for it will have included Egyptians, Jews and other foreigners; cf. Fraser, ibid., p. 46. As for the *chōra*, A. H. M. Jones, 'The Hellenistic Age', *Past and Present* 27 (1964), 5 allows a total figure of about 120,000 for Greek and Macedonian settlers. Thus the total Greek population in Egypt under the first three Ptolemies was perhaps only about one tenth of the total population.

81. That the Alexandrian poets studiously ignored the Egyptian population out of 'Hellenistic chauvinism' is argued by Griffiths, *Theocritus at Court*, p. 85f. C. H. Roberts, 'Literature and Society in the Papyri', *M.H.* 10 (1953), 264–79, cited by Griffiths, argues that the interest that the Greeks in the *chōra* showed in 'classical' Greek literature, as demonstrated by the papyri, was 'a natural Greek reaction to a foreign environment' and that the literary heritage of classical Greece was seen as a means of maintaining national identity. Cf. Meillier, *Callimaque et son temps*, pp. 229–32, who takes the Lille papyrus, with its commentary on Callimachus' *Victoria Berenices*, as evidence of the *chōra*'s interest in at least one contemporary Alexandrian poet, the city's most distinguished.

82. See Fraser, *Ptolemaic Alexandria*, p. 73; for the probable disadvantages

36 Definitions and a Sample

attaching to an Alexandrian's marriage to an Egyptian, if any such marriages did occur, see Fraser, ibid., p. 71f. There was of course intermarriage between Greeks and Egyptians long before the foundation of Alexandria, as witnessed for example by the Hellenomemphites, but that is a separate matter, on which see Fraser, ibid., p. 137 and A. B. Lloyd, *Herodotus Book II: Introduction*, E.P.R.O. 43 (Leiden, 1975), pp. 17–20, 118.

83. See H. I. Bell, *Egypt from Alexander the Great to the Arab Conquest* (Oxford 1948), p. 71, Fraser, ibid., p. 77 with n. 281 (vol. ii, p. 160), Peremans, 'Égyptiens et étrangers dans l'Égypte ptolémaïque', 148.

84. See Fraser, ibid., p. 28f.

85. See Fraser, ibid., p. 54. The Egyptians did, however, have protection in private law, their own courts and legal redress against the Greeks of Alexandria (see Fraser loc. cit.). For their exclusion from the influential eponymous priesthoods, see Peremans, 'Égyptiens et étrangers dans l'Égypte ptolémaïque', 134 and Fraser, ibid., p. 222.

86. Polyb. 5.65.9 and 5.107.1–3: see Fraser, ibid., pp. 60 and 75.

87. Justin 27.1.5–9 and Hieron. *In Dan.* 11.7–9; see Fraser, ibid., p. 60 with n. 179 (vol. ii, p. 143).

88. See Fraser, ibid., p. 70f. Note too the brutal murder of Agathocles and his family at the hands of the Egyptian mob (Polyb. 15.33.9); the Egyptians' reasons appear to have been simple hatred of their foreign rulers (Fraser, ibid., p. 82).

89. For further evidence on Greco–Egyptian relations in our period see in general Peremans, 'Égyptiens et étrangers dans l'Égypte ptolémaïque', 123–37.

90. Fraser, *Ptolemaic Alexandria*, p. 306; cf. pp. 116f., 251f. and 273. Even so, Soter's plan in assigning such importance to Sarapis was unsuccessful and 'the Greek population in the third century did not take him to their hearts' (ibid., p. 274): dedications to him soon became a mere stepping-stone to advancement (ibid., pp. 117, 258f., 273 and 287); significant, too, is the fact that Sarapis so rarely receives mention in the religious or encomiastic poetry of early Alexandria, in that of Callimachus or Theocritus, for example (ibid., p. 274; on Call. *Ep.* 17 *H.E.*, for a dedicatory offering to Sarapis, see ibid., p. 582.; on Call. *Ep.* 55 *H.E.* see ibid., p. 583f.; of course, there is mention of the Serapeum in *Iamb.* 1: see *Dieg.* VI 3f.), though there is the late third-century hymn from Delos by Maiistas (Pow., pp. 68ff.) commemorating the establishment of the cult on the island (Fraser, ibid., pp. 287 and 670).

91. See Fraser, ibid., p. 305f.

92. For the influence of the Lyceum on the Museum and Libraries, especially through Demetrius' mediation, see Fraser, ibid., pp. 306, 314–16, 320 and 321.

93. See Fraser, ibid., pp. 274, 287 and 295.

94. See further Fraser, ibid., pp. 289–95 and Meillier, *Callimaque et son temps*, pp. 201–7.

95. See e.g. G. M. Cohen, *The Seleucid Colonies: Studies in Founding, Administration and Organization*, Historia Einzelschr. 30 (Wiesbaden, 1978), pp. 33–7 and, for Ai Khanum, P. Bernard, 'An Ancient Greek City in Central Asia', *Scientific American* 246 (1982), 131–5.

96. See in particular F. Dunand, *Le Culte d'Isis dans le bassin oriental de la Méditerranée I: le culte d'Isis et les Ptolémées*, E.P.R.O. 26 (Leiden, 1973), especially pp. 190, 241.

97. Herodot. 2.35f.; see further Lloyd, *Herodotus Book II: Introduction*, pp. 141–7, 165f. and Lloyd, *Herodotus Book II: Commentary*, E.P.R.O. 43 (Leiden, 1976), p. 146f. *ad loc*.

98. Significantly, Theocritus purges it of its oriental aspects: see Griffiths, *Theocritus at Court*, p. 84f.

99. See R. Pfeiffer, *History of Classical Scholarship*, vol. i: *From the Beginnings to the End of the Hellenistic Age* (Oxford, 1968), pp. 128ff.

100. The most useful discussions in this connection are those of W. Meincke, *Untersuchungen zu den enkomiastischen Gedichten Theokrits* (Diss. Kiel, 1965) and Griffiths, *Theocritus at Court*.

101. Fraser, *Ptolemaic Alexandria*, p. 669 notes that the poem emphasises 'the Hellenic associations of the new gods through their links with Olympian deities'. On the role of Callimachus in advancing Ptolemaic cultural and religious policy see also Meillier, *Callimaque et son temps*, pp. 195–232, 238–47.

102. For further evidence and discussion see Griffiths, *Theocritus at Court*, especially pp. 51–106, 116–24.

103. Callixenus *ap*. Ath. 196a–203e. Indeed, the Pompe with its graphic tableaux performed a function parallel to that of the court-poets, though of course on an incomparably spectacular scale. Most importantly, it emphasised the ancestral ties of Zeus, Dionysus, Alexander and Soter, glorified the contemporary figures by their connection with the mythical and presented Alexander as a Neos Dionysos, thus legitimising the Ptolemies as Alexander's heirs in Egypt and enhancing their family's claim on divinity. See especially Rice, *The Grand Procession of Ptolemy Philadelphus*, pp. 42f., 48, 65–8, 82–6, 94f., 98f., 101f., 107f., 130f., 180f., 191f.

104. Wellek, 'The Concept of Realism in Literary Scholarship', 11–13 (= *Concepts of Criticism*, pp. 242–61); see also Nochlin, *Realism*, pp. 111–37, 179–206 and Stern, *On Realism*, pp. 142–67.

105. As it is of the poetry of the Hellenistic period in general: even Cercidas of Megalopolis, who in one passage actually recommends sharing (*Meliamb*. 2.47f. Knox), bases his social criticism on philosophical and ethical rather than specifically political considerations.

106. For the demand for sincerity see Champfleury, *Le Réalisme*, pp. 42, 81, 99, 111 ('le style plat'), 189f., 192, 263, 283, Wellek, 'The Concept of Realism in Literary Scholarship', 13–16 (= *Concepts of Criticism*, pp. 246–51) and Nochlin, *Realism*, pp. 34–40.

107. See Champfleury, ibid., p. 275, cited by Nochlin, ibid., p. 28, and Nochlin's discussion, ibid., pp. 103–78.

108. For these aspects of Alexandrianism see the general surveys of Pfeiffer, *Hist. Class. Schol.*, vol. i, pp. 87–233 and Fraser, *Ptolemaic Alexandria*, pp. 451, 452, 456, 633–7, 643, 644, 663, 735, 746f., 760f. Among the more specialised studies mention may be made here of e.g. H. Erbse, 'Homerscholien und hellenistische Glossare bei Apollonios Rhodios', *H*. 81 (1953), 163–96, G. Giangrande, '"Arte Allusiva" and Alexandrian Epic Poetry', *C.Q.* N.S. 17 (1967), 85–97 and the same scholar's 'Hellenistic Poetry and Homer', *A.C.* 39 (1970), 46–77.

2 The Hellenistic Theory of Pictorial Realism

The type of Alexandrian realism that I propose to examine first is the pictorial. It will prove instructive to describe the fourth-century and Hellenistic theory of pictorial realism and then to locate the Alexandrians' achievement in the context of contemporary literary criticism and fine art.

An inquiry into the concept of *mimēsis* in authors like Xenophon, Plato and Aristotle might appear a useful starting-place, but in fact it yields negative results. *Mimēsis* for these writers refers to the process, in both fine art and literature, of taking a general type or 'mental image' drawn from a number of instances of the type, and individualising it by imposing the particular traits of the model.[1] It is worth noting that the realism resulting from such a process would strike us as limited, but we must remember the part that convention plays in making and matching. So, for instance, the satyrs in Aeschylus' *Theoroi* or *Isthmiasthai* admire the accuracy of certain likenesses of themselves whereas these images must have been very stylised:[2] any progress towards matching image to model appears realistic, which is why Xenophon, Plato and Aristotle can all express their admiration for (or disparagement of) *trompe l'oeil* effects.[3] But the important thing here is that *mimēsis* and its congeners are never used to denote literary pictorialism.[4]

The scholars who created a terminology to cope with literary pictorialism were Hellenistic; the basic term was *enargeia*.

The significance of *enargeia* has been underrated and its history misunderstood.[5] *Enargeia* is defined by Dionysius of Halicarnassus when commenting on the style of Lysias the orator.[6] He means by *enargeia* the stylistic effect in which appeal is made to the senses of the listener and attendant circumstances are described in such a way that the listener will be turned into an eye-witness: he will inevitably see the events Lysias depicts and, as it were, feel as if he is in the presence of the characters introduced. The importance attached to sight is clear in Dionysius' definition as it is in the rhetors' when they discuss *ekphrasis* or pictorial description.[7] *Enargeia* is for the rhetors one of the 'virtues of *ekphrasis*', which Theon (first or second century AD) calls 'in particular clarity and the *enargeia* whereby you can almost see what is being related'[8] and Hermogenes (second century AD) calls 'clarity and *enargeia*, for the expression ought almost to create the picture through the sense of hearing'.[9] Among the Latin authors *enargeia* is translated variously by *demonstratio, euidentia, illustratio, repraesentatio* and *sub oculos subiectio*, and the same emphasis on sight is present in their discussions. For example, the treatise *ad Herennium* says of *demonstratio* 'demonstratio est cum ita uerbis res exprimitur ut geri negotium et res ante oculos esse uideatur' ('*demonstratio* is when an event is described in words in such a way that the business seems to be happening and the subject seems to be before our eyes').[10] Cicero, talking of *inlustris oratio*, says 'est enim haec pars orationis, quae rem constituat paene ante oculos; is enim maxime sensus attingitur, sed et ceteri tamen et maxime mens ipsa moueri potest' ('for this is the department of oratory which almost puts the fact before the eyes, for that sense in particular is appealed to, though it is, however, possible for both the other senses and especially the mind itself to be affected').[11]

These definitions come from treatises on rhetoric. But *enargeia* was considered to have been a device originating in poetry and history. We have, for instance, an explicit statement to that effect in an *Ars Rhetorica* probably to be dated to the first century AD;[12] it discusses *ekphrasis*, to which we have seen *enargeia* is integral, and says 'This fault [the so-called *ekphraseis*] has infiltrated declamations through an emulation of history and poetry' (*Ars Rhet.* 10.17;II.372.9 Usener-Radermacher). Similarly, Horace complains of poetic *descriptio* that the poets of his time too often succumb to the temptation to 'stitch in' an untimely 'purple patch' — to the ruin of the unity of their poems.[13] Pictorial vividness was considered a particular beauty of Homer, as is clear from Cicero's famous statement on the blindness traditionally ascribed to him.[14] Further evidence of the word's application to poetry is found in Philodemus' *On Poetry*, discussed below.

It is not surprising that *enargeia* is the central term for all ancient theory on literary pictorialism. We have seen its importance for *ekphrasis* and *descriptio* in poetic as well as rhetorical contexts. Two equivalents of *ekphrasis, diatyposis* and *hypotyposis*, are discussed by Quintilian in his section on *sub oculos subiectio*.[15] It is also relevant to the concept of *phantasia* or *uisio*. Quintilian tells us that this is the accurate mental visualisation of objects and that

The Hellenistic Theory of Pictorial Realism   41

enargeia will be a consequence of it, and he illustrates his point by several quotations from the *Aeneid*.[16] Ps.-Longinus also associates *enargeia* with *phantasia*, though he differs from Quintilian in limiting 'visual vividness' to rhetoric, the aim in poetry being 'astonishment' (ἔκπληξις).[17]

The dating of the coinage of the term in literary criticism is bound to be less certain than its definition, but the evidence shows that it was current by the second century BC and that in all likelihood it predated the other terms like *ekphrasis*.[18] Our main evidence is Philodemus' *On Poetry* Book 5. In one section Philodemus reports and attacks the view of an unidentified Hellenistic critic that *enargeia* was the prime object of poetry;[19] elsewhere he shows that a certain Zeno, quite probably Zeno of Sidon, Philodemus' teacher, mentioned in his writings another critic's view that if only poets write 'with *enargeia*, expressiveness and concision' it is 'impossible to go wrong'.[20] Moreover, the concept of *enargeia* is evidenced as current in second-century historiography by Polybius who alludes to it when he expresses his hope that his readers will profit by certain examples of tactical skill and courage described in his *Histories* 'by recalling some events and picturing others'.[21] The evidence, therefore, only takes us back to the second century BC, when it appears to have gained the status of an established tool of criticism. Contrary to common belief, *enargeia* denoting visual immediacy in literature is not discussed in any of the extant works of earlier critics like Plato, Aristotle or Theophrastus,[22] though, of course, the style had been affected in literature since Homer and the concept of pictorialism may have been hinted at in Simonides' saying that 'painting is silent poetry, poetry talking painting'.[23] We may conclude that *enargeia* as a literary term central to all ancient theory on literary pictorialism is of firmly Hellenistic provenance.[24]

The history of the term *enargeia* sheds useful light on our inquiry and indeed on the whole development of visual perception in the Hellenistic period. First, we can see in *enargeia* a technical term developed to refer to pictorialism in *literature*, whereas earlier criticism only had words, like *mimēsis*, to denote the pictorial representation of fine art. The Hellenistic age clearly felt an intellectual and aesthetic need for discussion of literary pictorialism. The poets of the Alexandrian period were concerned, as no other period before, to exploit pictorial effects, so that the preoccupation was common to practitioner as well as theorist. Secondly, there has been a crucial shift of ground in the debate over visual representation. We have seen that underlying the fourth-century discussions was the tendency to regard the objects of *mimēsis* as general types. Yet in the concept of *enargeia* there is an inherent assumption that the objects of literary pictorial description are individual, particular phenomena as they appear to the eye so that they will be immediate and visually vivid to the audience. This shift from the general to the particular in representation is strikingly evidenced in the writings of Plutarch. Taking up Simonides' comment that 'painting is silent poetry, poetry talking painting', he argues that the link between the arts is pictorial vividness. He regards poetry as 'an imitative art and faculty analogous to painting' because both arts in their different materials and means aim at the vivid and accurate depiction of the subject as it is in reality in order to produce the emotional effects desired (*Mor.* 17f–18a). This will often entail the use of pictorialism: at *Mor.* 347a–c Plutarch argues that Thucydides aims to 'make the reader a spectator'[25] and talks of the 'graphic *enargeia*' which characterises his descriptions; a second aim, concomitant with pictorial vividness, is the production in the reader's mind of the emotions felt by the original witnesses. Plutarch, therefore, demonstrates that the aim of *enargeia* is not mere verisimilitude but a vivid and precise copy of the subject, and he also makes explicit the analogy between fine art and literature which was implied in all earlier discussion of *enargeia*.[26] We have, then, a shift from what has been called 'archaic intellectualism'[27] to a more empiricist particularism in pictorial representation, and one quite close to that of modern Realism.[28]

Now that we have surveyed the evolution of literary-critical terms associated with literary pictorialism, we are perhaps entitled to attempt to come to some conclusions about the origins of the preoccupation with pictorialism not only in Hellenistic criticism but in the practice of Alexandrian poetry itself.

I suggest that an important clue lies in the way the Alexandrian poets talk about fine art. There is a striking number of passages in which they explicitly express admiration for *trompe l'oeil* effects. They celebrate in particular the effects achieved by artists of the second half of the fourth century, such as Apelles. Up till that time, artists and their public were content merely with the verisimilitude in art-objects that arises from the representation of general types of subject-matter. The fact that viewers before then could single out effects in works of art as lifelike should not surprise us, for, as we have seen, any art which 'matches' nature in a strikingly new way appears realistic. With the advent of artists like Apelles, however, people were concerned with the realism which springs from the depiction of particular phenomena as they exist in nature, and an astonishing new dimension was added to *trompe l'oeil* illusionism. Herodas, for instance, in his fourth *Mimiamb* describes the reactions of two women viewing sculptures on show in the temple of Asclepius on Cos. Coccale, to be sure the more naïve of the two women, exclaims:

> μᾶ, χρόνῳ κοτ' ὤνθρωποι
> κῆς τοὺς λίθους ἕξουσι τὴν ζοὴν θεῖναι —
> τὸν Βατάλης γὰρ τοῦτον, οὐχ ὁρῆς, Κυννοῖ,
> ὅκως βέβηκεν, ἀνδριάντα τῆς Μύττεω;
> εἰ μή τις αὐτὴν εἶδε Βατάλην, βλέψας
> ἐς τοῦτο τὸ εἰκόνισμα μὴ ἐτύμης δείσθω. (33–8)[29]

Heavens, one day men will be able to put life even into stone! Cynno, don't you see how this statue of Batale, Myttes' daughter, stands? Anyone who hasn't seen Batale herself could look at this likeness and not need the real Batale.

The fact that they are common folk and that Coccale is characterised for her wide-eyed naïveté should not make us think Herodas considers their judgements lightly. Indeed, there is a tradition that Apelles himself thought the common folk a more exacting critic of his work than *he* was.[30] There is, moreover, the eulogy of Apelles by Cynno, the more serious-minded of the pair:

> ἀληθιναί, φίλη, γὰρ αἱ Ἐφεσίου χεῖρες
> ἐς πάντ' Ἀπελλέω γράμματ', οὐδ' ἐρεῖς 'κεῖνος
> ὤνθρωπος ἐν μὲν εἶδεν, ἐν δ' ἀπηρνήθη,'
> ἀλλ' ὅ οἱ ἐπὶ νοῦν γένοιτο, καὶ θέων ψαύειν
> ἠπείγεθ'· ὃς δ' ἐκεῖνον ἢ ἔργα τὰ ἐκείνου
> μὴ παμφαλήσας ἐκ δίκης ὀρώρηκεν,
> ποδὸς κρέμαιτ' ἐκεῖνος ἐν γναφέως οἴκῳ. (72–8)

Yes, dear, the hands of Apelles of Ephesus are true in all his lines, and you can't say that he looked at one thing but rejected the other: whatever came to his mind he was quick and eager to

44 The Hellenistic Theory of Pictorial Realism

attempt, and if anybody gazes at him or his works and doesn't view them fairly, may he be hung up by the foot at the fuller's!

Apart from Apelles, other fourth-century artists are named: the sons of Praxiteles (23), Cephisodotus and Timarchus. These three artists were all involved in the revolution in art in which general types were discarded for the depiction of phenomena as they exist in nature.[31] Admiration is here expressed for them precisely on the grounds of their achievements in the new realism.[32]

Similar admiration is expressed by Theocritus in *Idyll* 15 which is clearly connected with Herodas' *Mimiamb*:[33]

ὡς ἔτυμ' ἑστάκαντι καὶ ὡς ἔτυμ' ἐνδινεῦντι,
ἔμψυχ', οὐκ ἐνυφαντά. (82f.)

How true they stand and how true they move about; they're alive, not woven.

And in *Epigram* 15 H.E. he bids the passer-by examine the statue of Anacreon in Teos: if the stranger describes the statue to his friends at home and adds that Anacreon was fond of young men, he'll be describing the whole man accurately.[34]

Apollonius shares the predilection, as we can see from his description of Jason's cloak:

ἐν καὶ Φρίξος ἔην Μινυήιος, ὡς ἐτεόν περ
εἰσαΐων κριοῦ, ὁ δ' ἄρ' ἐξενέποντι ἐοικώς.
κείνους κ' εἰσορόων ἀκέοις ψεύδοιό τε θυμόν,
ἐλπόμενος πυκινήν τιν' ἀπὸ σφείων ἐσακοῦσαι
βάξιν, ὅτευ καὶ δηρὸν ἐπ' ἐλπίδι θηήσαιο. (1.763–7)[35]

On it was Phrixus the Minyan as though really listening to the ram, which looked as if it were speaking. Looking at them you would fall silent and delude your mind with the hope of hearing some wise speech from them, in expectation of which you would gaze long at them.

There is, moreover, a plethora of comments illustrating the notion in epigrams from Hellenistic times: for example, a group centres around Apelles' *Aphrodite Anadyomene* and Myron's *Cow*, once again fourth-century works.[36] Leonidas of Tarentum seems to have started the series of epigrams on the former[37] with the following:

Τὰν ἐκφυγοῦσαν ματρὸς ἐκ κόλπων, ἔτι
ἀφρῷ τε μορμύρουσαν εὐλεχῆ Κύπριν
ἴδ' ὡς Ἀπελλῆς κάλλος ἱμερώτατον
οὐ γραπτὸν ἀλλ' ἔμψυχον ἐξεμάξατο.
εὖ μὲν γὰρ ἄκραις χερσὶν ἐκθλίβει κόμαν,
εὖ δ' ὀμμάτων γαληνὸς ἐκλάμπει πόθος,
καὶ μαζός, ἀκμῆς ἄγγελος, κυδωνιᾷ.
αὐτὰ δ' Ἀθάνα καὶ Διὸς συνευνέτις
φάσουσιν, 'ὦ Ζεῦ, λειπόμεσθα τῇ κρίσει.' (23 H.E.)

Behold Cypris, the bringer of happy unions, just escaped from her mother's bosom, still streaming with foam, and behold how Apelles has captured her most lovely beauty, which is not painted but alive. Beautifully she wrings her hair with her fingertips, beautifully does tranquil desire radiate from her eyes, and her breasts, the harbingers of maturity, swell like quinces. Athene herself and the consort of Zeus will say 'O Zeus, we were the inferiors at the judgement'.

Likewise, Leonidas' epigram on Myron's *Cow* found an imitation in, among others, Antipater of Sidon and the series in the *Palatine Anthology* Book 9 which is, as Gow and Page put it,[38] a 'somewhat tedious competition in thinking of a new way to say that it was a very lifelike representation of a cow':

Οὐκ ἔπλασέν με Μύρων· ἐψεύσατο, βοσκομέναν δὲ
ἐξ ἀγέλας ἐλάσας δῆσε βάσει λιθίνῳ. (88 H.E.)

Myron did not mould me. He lied: driving me from my herd as I grazed, he tethered me with a stone base.

Now we have seen that lifelikeness in art had been a matter for admiration among the Greek poets from Homer onwards. But praise for it never reached the pitch it did among the Alexandrian poets. The mere volume of passages like those just quoted is an index of the Alexandrian poets' interest in pictorial realism and its effects. It is hardly surprising, therefore, that their pictorialist powers were lavished on descriptions of works of art, some of which will be discussed in the next chapter. However, adequate evidence has been adduced to show how alert the eye of the poets had become; moreover, for them, as for Apelles, mere verisimilitude was no longer sufficient, and the visual matching of art to reality had become the aim, a fact demonstrated by Coccale's admiration for the portrait of Batale. It looks, furthermore, as if the eye of the poets had actually been trained by the artists of the fourth-century revolution, if only to judge by the frequency with which the latter are named.

After all, the idea that poetry and fine art are in some sense parallel arts was of hallowed antiquity, even though the question of pictorialism was, interestingly, seldom raised before the Hellenistic period. The first instance is the comment of Simonides about poetry and painting recorded by Plutarch. Even here it is uncertain to what extent pictorialism pure and simple is the link between the arts.[39] What Simonides may have had in mind, for instance, was that poetry has all the potential for the *apatē* of painting but adds the element of language, so that it may convincingly tell a story. But the fact remains that with Simonides the parallel was explicitly drawn. The next occurrence of the idea is found in the sophistic *Dissoi Logoi* (3.10), dated *c.* 400 BC,[40] which compares tragedy and painting. But the author does not claim for tragedy any pictorial realism. He is, as perhaps Simonides before him, thinking of the principle of *apatē*, of 'deceiving' the hearer or viewer by producing things like the truth. Plato and Aristotle regard the fine arts as the clearest example of the mimetic principle shared by all the arts, particularly literature, though they make no inference about pictorialism in the last. Aristotle, however, goes further than that and illustrates certain facts about tragedy by drawing on parallels from fine art. For example, after dividing the subjects of artistic *mimēsis* into three categories, people who are 'our betters', 'lower' and 'like you and me',[41] he uses painters as examples justifying the division, Polygnotus, Pauson and Dionysius representing the different groups respectively (*Poet.* 48^a 5f.).[42] Nowhere, however, does he suggest pictorialism as the link between the two branches of art. Indeed, at the very beginning of the *Poetics* he differentiates between them on the basis of the different media they employ in representation; painting uses colour and form, poetry rhythm, speech and melody.[43]

In the Hellenistic period, on the other hand, the parallelism is extended to pictorialism itself. In the history of the word *enargeia*, current in second-century literary criticism, we can see the invention of a technical term conveying for literature what *mimēsis* had, from the fourth century onwards, come to convey for fine art: at first, visual accuracy of representation and, after the Greek revolution in art, realistic, *trompe l'oeil* representation of objects as they appear in nature. Pictorialism had at last received explicit recognition as an aim of poetry itself.[44]

In the light of such evidence, I wish to propose that the Alexandrian poets had been alerted to the possibilities of pictorialism by the example of the realistic visual effects achieved by the artists of the latter half of the fourth century, in short that they were inspired to capture these effects in the medium of poetry. In support of this hypothesis there is, above all, the interest shown by the Alexandrians in pictorially vivid description. It will be the province of the following chapter to explore that subject in detail, but it may be noted here that the poets demonstrate an interest in pictorial effects unprecedented in Greek poetry, as far as we can tell. For the present purposes it will be sufficient to cite three examples. The first is to be found in Apollonius Rhodius' description of Jason's cloak and is the *genre*-picture of Aphrodite holding the shield of Ares:

ἑξείης δ' ἤσκητο βαθυπλόκαμος Κυθέρεια
Ἄρεος ὀχμάζουσα θοὸν σάκος, ἐκ δέ οἱ ὤμου
πῆχυν ἔπι σκαιὸν ξυνοχὴ κεχάλαστο χιτῶνος
νέρθε παρὲκ μαζοῖο· τὸ δ' ἀντίον ἀτρεκὲς αὕτως
χαλκείῃ δείκηλον ἐν ἀσπίδι φαίνετ' ἰδέσθαι. (1.742–6)

Next Cytherea with the low tresses was represented holding the swift shield of Ares; the joining of her tunic had fallen from her shoulder on to her left arm beneath her breast; in front of her, exactly reproduced, her image appeared visible on the bronze shield.

The lifelike detail of Aphrodite's concern with her image, the precise description of the drapery of her tunic and the observation that her frontal image was clearly reflected on the shield all demonstrate how sophisticated pictorialism has become;[45] though we do not know of any precisely parallel model for the scene,[46] it is obvious that the poet's eye has been trained by fine art. My second example is also drawn from Apollonius. It shows his interest in the sensuousness of light-effects and the use of pictorialism for character-motivation, and demonstrates his skilful deployment of pictorialism in narrative. It is the scene where Hylas is espied by the nymph at the spring called Pegae as he gathers water for his lord, Heracles:

> τὸν δὲ σχεδὸν εἰσενόησεν
> κάλλεϊ καὶ γλυκερῇσιν ἐρευθόμενον χαρίτεσσιν,
> πρὸς γάρ οἱ διχόμηνις ἀπ' αἰθέρος αὐγάζουσα
> βάλλε σεληναίη· τῆς δὲ φρένας ἐπτοίησεν
> Κύπρις, ἀμηχανίῃ δὲ μόλις συναγείρατο θυμόν. (1.1229–33)

She noticed him nearby in the rosy flush of his beauty and sweet charm, for the light of the full moon beamed on him from the sky. Cypris made her heart flutter and in her confusion she could scarcely collect her wits.

The emphasis on the erotically pictorial sensuousness of the scene is apparent; we can picture vividly the colour of Hylas' countenance, gracefully blushing, and the enhancement of his beauty in the subdued light of the half moon. Moreover, the pictorial element explains why the nymph falls in love so precipitately, thus explaining the psychological motivation of the scene. A further telling visual detail is the way Hylas dips the pitcher in the stream, leaning to one side. In this position, which renders his footing unsure, he is seized by the nymph: she places her left hand behind his neck to kiss his mouth, grasps his elbow with her right hand and pulls him down to the spring (1234–9). The whole episode is pictorially realistic and the sequence of events is explained in pictures.[47] My final example is the cup of Theocritus in *Idyll* 1 (27–56). I wish here only to draw attention to the arrangement of the figures within each of the three scenes depicted on the cup, whatever the overall arrangement of the scenes on it.[48] Theocritus bases the composition of the outer scenes on an ABA pattern:[49] in the first, two young men stand on either side of the girl whom they are wooing; in the third, the boy watching the vineyard is flanked by two foxes, who, unobserved by the boy, are engaged in stealing from him; the second scene is that of the solitary old fisherman; another ABA pattern is thus established by the framing effect of the triadic scenes around the one-figure scene.

Quite apart from the thematic coherence of the vignettes — adolescence and romantic involvement, old age and absorption in work, childhood and innocence — Theocritus is plainly concerned with the formal aspects of pictorial composition, and the impulse seems very probably to have been his viewing of fine art, though once again there is no need to think he is describing an actual cup. I trust that these examples will suffice for the moment to put us on the alert for further evidence of the Alexandrian poets' powers of observation and to lend weight to my suggestion that the educative factor was recent and contemporary fine art.

The second reason for proposing my hypothesis is the coherence of the chronological sequence. The fine artists of the later fourth century were characterised by their exploitation of unprecedentedly realistic visual effects. The poets of the Alexandrian period demonstrate a parallel preoccuption in their descriptive passages, which, as we shall see, are numerous, and in the second century (or perhaps earlier) we have attestation for the explicit approval of *enargeia* in literature. To allay the suspicion that I am merely arguing *post hoc ergo propter hoc*, we have the Alexandrian poets' expression of admiration for the effects achieved by fine artists from the latter half of the fourth century onwards, whom they actually name.

There is a rider to all this. To say that Alexandrian poets were inspired by fine artists to strive for remarkable visual effects is not the same as postulating direct influence of specific works of art on any particular descriptive passage of poetry. A modern scholar has remarked that pictorialism 'can thrive quite independently of the visual arts'; that general statement has a particular relevance to Alexandrian poetry.[50] Yet precisely because of the 'plastic' nature of pictorial descriptions in Alexandrian poetry many modern critics feel the temptation to posit actual works of art behind passages of strikingly vivid visual appeal.[51] In this they are presumably also encouraged by the fact that the art of the time was concerned with certain realistic effects. Perhaps a further stimulus is what I consider a mistaken view of the frequency with which the poets themselves praise these effects. Such speculations are generally incapable of proof[52] except in more obvious cases[53] and where the poet actually names the work he is describing.[54] I suggest that apart from such clear cases it is more satisfactory to explain the 'plastic' nature of many descriptions of this kind as the product of the Alexandrian taste for *enargeia*, which we have seen was conceived as an aim of literature in itself, rather than to feel obliged to postulate any direct influence from particular works of fine art. Even in the descriptions of works of art, like the cup in Theocritus' first *Idyll*, Jason's cloak in Apollonius and the basket in Moschus' *Europa* (37–62), the same conclusion is preferable. The poet in each of these descriptions is concerned with detailed verbal scenes and has not bothered to make the distribution of scenes clear;[55] both facts are best accounted for if we suppose that each poet is acting in a manner analogous to the artists of the time, because of the similar effects of literary *enargeia* and artistic realism, and is using the opportunity which his subject offers to draw separate, individual scenes rather than describing a work of art.[56] Which brings us back to the point that realism may only pretend to present what is real.

Notes

1. See especially G. Sörbom, *Mimesis and Art* (Bonniers, 1966); D. W. Lucas, *Aristotle: Poetics* (Oxford, 1968), pp. 258–72.
2. *P. Oxy.* 2162, discussed by Sörbom, ibid., pp. 41–53.
3. See e.g. Xen. *Mem.* 3.10.6–8; Pl. *Rep.* 472d. 595a–602b, *Soph.* 234b; Arist. *Poet.* 48^b 10ff.
4. Duris of Samos *ap.* Phot. *Bibl.* 176 p. 121a 41 (= *F.G.H.* 76 F1) criticised Ephorus and Theopompus for lacking *mimēsis*, which Jacoby (in *F.G.H.* ad loc.) takes to refer to pictorialism. But this is unnecessary: cf. R. B. Kebric, *In the Shadow of Macedon: Duris of Samos, Historia Einzelschr.* 29 (Wiesbaden, 1977), pp. 15–18, 39–41 and 77, who argues that what Duris missed in the histories of Ephorus and Theopompus was the recording of events as they 'actually happened'. See J. H. Hagstrum, *The Sister Arts: the Tradition of Pictorialism and English Poetry from Dryden to Gray* (Chicago, 1958), pp. 3ff. on the way later pictorialist theory benefited from the association of fine art and literature in Plato and Aristotle.
5. See my 'Enargeia in the Ancient Criticism of Poetry', *Rh.M.* N.F. 124 (1981), 297–311. Cf. C. Imbert, 'Stoic Logic and Alexandrian Poetics', in M. Schofield *et al.* (eds.), *Doubt and Dogmatism: Studies in Hellenistic Epistemology* (Oxford, 1980), 182–216; R. L. Hunter, *A Study of Daphnis and Chloe* (Cambridge, 1983), pp. 43–6.
6. *Lys.* 7; I.14.17 Usener-Radermacher.
7. E.g. Theon: 'an *ekphrasis* is a descriptive speech which brings the subject before our eyes with *enargeia*' (*Prog.* 11; II.118.6 Spengel). The use of the term to denote exclusively the description of works of plastic art is modern: cf. e.g. G. Kurman, 'Ecphrasis in Epic Poetry', *C.L.* 26 (1974), 1.
8. *Prog.* 11; II.119.27 Spengel.
9. *Prog.* 10; II.16.32 Spengel.
10. *Ad Herenn.* 4.55.68.
11. *Part. Or.* 6.20; for further references, including the relevant passages in Quintilian, see Zanker, 'Enargeia', 298f.
12. It is falsely ascribed to Dionysius of Halicarnassus.

The Hellenistic Theory of Pictorial Realism   51

13. *A.P.* 14–23.
14. *Tusc.* 5.39.114. For additional references, see Zanker, 'Enargeia', 300–4.
15. *Inst. Or.* 9.2.40ff.: see further Zanker, ibid., 302f.
16. *Inst. Or.* 6.2.29ff.
17. *Subl.* 15.1f.; however, he does not follow this up in practice, for he quotes as examples passages from Euripides for which he claims brilliant visual appeal (15.2): see further Zanker, 'Enargeia', 303f. and n. 28.
18. Zanker, ibid., 304ff. The Homeric scholia do not help us in dating the terms: ibid., n. 17. It may be asked whether the scholia influenced the Alexandrian poets in the matter of poetic *enargeia*, but for Callimachus, Apollonius, Theocritus and other members of the early movement it is really only Zenodotus who comes into question, and there are no usages in the scholia of words like *enargeia* which are attributable to him (see K. Nickau, *Untersuchungen zur textkritischen Methode des Zenodotos von Ephesos, Unters. zur ant. Lit. u. Gesch.* 16 (Berlin and New York, 1977). R. R. Schlunk, *The Homeric Scholia and the Aeneid: A Study of the Influence of Ancient Homeric Literary Criticism on Vergil* (Ann Arbor, 1974) is on safer ground in the case of Virgil.
19. *On Poetry* Book 5, col. 3.12–31, discussed in Zanker, 'Enargeia', 305f.
20. *On Poetry* Book 5, col. 27.17–25, discussed in Zanker, 'Enargeia', 306f.
21. 9.9.10 See Zanker, ibid., n. 12 for further references.
22. See Zanker, ibid., 307ff. and nn. 40 and 41 where the arguments in favour of this conclusion for fourth-century criticism as a whole are documented in detail. Suffice it here to correct a common misconception about *energeia* in Aristotle *Rh.* 3.11.1ff. 1411^b 22ff. The word refers to the representation of things in a state of actuality, which includes personification and describing events as happening; it is thus quite distinct from *enargeia*, though the distinction is not always clearly perceived.
23. Plu. *Mor.* 346f; cf. 17f, 58b, 748a, *Vit. Hom.* 216.
24. On the invention of the term, I have tentatively suggested ('Enargeia', 308ff.) that it was borrowed from Epicurean philosophy, just as *phantasia* was from Stoicism; it is possible, however, that, since the Stoics appropriated the term *energeia* from the Epicureans (see F. H. Sandbach, 'Ennoia and Prolepsis in the Stoic Theory of Knowledge', in A. A. Long (ed.), *Problems in Stoicism* (London, 1971), 32), the word was actually introduced into literary criticism by Stoic scholars, who are the likely originators of the related term *phantasia* (see 'Enargeia', 303f.).
25. Cf. e.g. Theon and Hermogenes on the purpose of *enargeia* in *ekphrasis*, quoted above, pp. 39f.
26. He did, however, notice the important difference that painting represents 'events as if happening' and literature 'events as if having happened' (*Mor.* 346f.), though we can hardly assume that Simonides was conscious of the distinction. For the later history of the connection see Hagstrum, *The Sister Arts*, pp. 10ff. *et passim* and J. Palm, 'Bemerkungen zur Ekphrase in der griechischen Literatur', *Kungl. Humanistiska Vetenskapssamfundet i Uppsala, Årsbok* 1965–66, 158ff. Hagstrum, ibid., p. 9f. illustrates the shift in viewing by recourse to Horace *A.P.* 1–9, but the example is unsatisfactory, for all Horace has in mind there is verisimilitude (so C. O. Brink, *Horace on Poetry: the 'Ars Poetica'* (Cambridge, 1971), p. 85) and the passage, therefore, does not imply 'the imitation of the object as it exists in nature'.
27. So e.g. Sörbom, *Mimesis and Art*, p. 88 *et passim*.
28. Cf. e.g. the remarks on the pictorial realism of Zola's *Germinal* in E. Auerbach, *Mimesis: Dargestellte Wirklichkeit in der abendländischen Literatur* (Bern, 1946), pp. 451ff. (= Eng. trans. W. R. Trask, *Mimesis: the Representation of Reality in Western Literature* (Princeton, 1953), pp. 506ff.), and L. Nochlin, *Realism* (Harmondsworth, 1971), p. 44f. for the enthusiastic use of photography by Courbet, Degas and others 'as an aid to capture the appearance of reality' in their paintings.
29. Other objects exciting the girls' admiration are a relief (most probably) of a girl looking longingly at an apple (27–9), a statue of an old man (30), one of a boy

52 The Hellenistic Theory of Pictorial Realism

strangling a goose (30–3), a panel-painting depicting a sacrificial offering (so W. Headlam, *Herodas: the Mimes and Fragments* (edited by A.D. Knox) (Cambridge, 1922) *ad loc.*) with a naked boy, whose flesh seems to pulse (59–62), a silver toasting-iron, a frightening ox, its leader, a girl in attendance, a hook-nosed man and a snub-nosed man (62–71: n.b. 68).

30. Pliny *N.H.* 35.84f. (Apelles and the shoemaker). For traditional stories celebrating fourth-century illusionism, especially that of Apelles, see Pliny *N.H.* 35.88 (Apelles and the physiognomists), 35.89 (Apelles and Ptolemy's jester), 35.95 (Apelles and the horse), 35.65f. (Zeuxis' grapes), 36.21f. (Praxiteles' *Cnidian Aphrodite* and *Eros at Thespiae*).

31. For the illusionism of Cephisodotus, see Pliny, *N.H.* 36.24. On the revolution in art see e.g. E. H. Gombrich, *Art and Illusion*[4] (London, 1972), pp. 99–125 and Sörbom, *Mimesis and Art*, pp. 44–53.

32. For extant examples of this realism one need only think of figures like the *Drunken Old Woman* in the Glyptothek in Munich or the *Boxer* in the Terme Museum: see G. M. A. Richter, *The Sculpture and Sculptors of the Greeks*[4] (New Haven, 1970), figs. 79 and 847.

33. See Gow on *Id.* 15.79–83 and Headlam-Knox on *Mim.* 4.56ff. *et passim*; cf. G. Mastromarco, *Il pubblico di Eronda*, Proagones 15 (Padua, 1979), pp. 104f. (= Eng. trans. *The Public of Herodas*, London Studies in Classical Philology II (Amsterdam, 1984), pp. 62f.). It has even been argued that Apelles was at the basis of a political and aesthetic feud between Theocritus and Herodas: so S. Luria, 'Herondas' Kampf für die veristische Kunst', in *Misc. Rostagni* (Turin, 1963), 394–415, refuted by Mastromarco, ibid., p. 134f. (= Eng. trans., p. 89f.).

34. Cf. Leonidas of Tarentum 31 *H.E.* For illusionism in art as a theme of Hellenistic epigrams, see Palm, 'Bemerkungen zur Ekphrase in der griechischen Literatur', 150ff. See O. Benndorf, *De Anthologiae Graecae Epigrammatis quae ad Artes spectant* (Diss. Bonn, 1862) for a general history of epideictic epigrams on works of art and an evaluation of their use to historians of art (esp. pp. 71–3 for illusionism as a commonplace in these epigrams).

35. Palm, ibid., 138 draws attention to the fact that the 'Illusionswirkung' is emphasised by the placing of these lines at the end of the cloak *ekphrasis*. As he notes, too, the effect of this is to make all the preceding pictures all the more 'vollkommen lebendig ausgeführt'. It shows what store Apollonius set by this kind of realism.

36. Praxiteles' *Cnidian Aphrodite* also is celebrated in *A. Plan.* 159–70, which includes Antipater of Sidon 44 *H.E.* and Hermodorus 1 *H.E.*, although the latter compares it unfavourably with a statue of Athene at Athens, most probably the *Parthenos* of Pheidias (Gow-Page *ad loc.*). Praxiteles' *Eros at Thespiae* is also a favourite subject (Ant. Sid. 44, Leonidas 89, Meleager 110 and 111 *H.E.*). See further above, n. 30.

37. Leonidas is copied e.g. by Ant. Sid. 45 *H.E.*, on which see Gow-Page for further imitations, adding *Fr.* 974.9–12 *S.H.* (cf. *Fr.* 981 *S.H.*).

38. *H.E.* vol. ii, p. 64 on Ant. Sid. 36; on p. 63 Gow and Page list the imitations of Leonidas' epigram.

39. R. Harriott, *Poetry and Criticism before Plato* (London, 1969), p. 143f. inclines to the view that Simonides is talking about pictorialism, adducing the Danae poem (*P.M.G.* 543) as an instance of pictorial narrative in Simonides, though she herself notes that the poet's death in 468 BC antedates the introduction of the illusionistic style in painting.

40. H. Diels, *Die Fragmente der Vorsokratiker*[x], vol. ii (edited by W. Kranz) (Berlin, 1956), p. 405.

41. The categories are discussed below, pp. 139–42.

42. See also *Poet.* 50^a 23–9, 50^a 39–50^b 2, 54^b 8–11 and 60^b 8–11.

43. *Poet.* 47^a 18–47^b 29; for ἁρμονία translated as 'melody' see Lucas on 47^a 22.

44. Of history, too: see above, p. 41.
45. Cf. the discussion of Palm, 'Bemerkungen zur Ekphrase in der griechischen Literatur', 140.
46. Cf. the fallen Persian's face mirrored in his shield on the *Battle of Alexander and Darius* mosaic (see G. Becatti, *The Art of Ancient Greece and Rome* (London, 1968), pl. 207). The motif has been exploited in more recent times, of course; for example, Aphrodite's face is seen only in the mirror into which she is looking in Velasquez' *Rokeby Venus* in the London National Gallery.
47. For discussions of this episode see especially A. Köhnken, *Apollonios Rhodios and Theokrit: die Hylas- und die Amykosgeschichten beider Dichter und die Frage der Priorität, Hypomnemata* 12 (Göttingen, 1965), pp. 58–67 and P. Händel, *Beobachtungen zur epischen Technik des Apollonios Rhodios, Zetemata* 8 (Munich, 1954), pp. 27–33. An incidental touch of realism is found, as Köhnken, ibid., p. 64 notes, in the description of the sound of the water entering the bronze pitcher and the way it resounds as it is filled (1235f.).
48. See further below, n. 55, p. 80 and p. 107 n. 89.
49. Well discussed by G. Lawall, *Theocritus' Coan Pastorals: a Poetry Book* (Cambridge, Mass., 1967), p. 28f.
50. Hagstrum, *The Sister Arts*, p. xvi: cf. Palm, 'Bemerkungen zur Ekphrase in der griechischen Literatur', 142. There are striking instances of this independence in modern times: for example, after visiting an exhibition of Cézanne, Rilke recognised in that painter an artist working analogously to himself in poetry (see his letters to his wife, Clara, of October 1907, especially that of the 18th).
51. A few examples: H. Brunn, 'Die griechischen Bukoliker und die bildende Kunst', *S.B.A.W.* 1879 (2), 1ff. (= *Kl. Schr.*, vol. iii, Leipzig, 1906, 217–28); H. Herter, 'Bericht über die Literatur zur hellenistischen Dichtung seit dem Jahre 1921, II: Apollonios von Rhodos', *Bursians Jahresbericht* 285 (1944–1955), 370; T. B. L. Webster, *Hellenistic Poetry and Art* (London, 1964), pp. 88, 174; K. Ziegler, *Das hellenistische Epos: ein vergessenes Kapitel griechischer Dichtung*^{2} (Leipzig, 1966), p. 42f.; Lawall, *Theocritus' Coan Pastorals*, pp. 80–2.
52. See e.g. Ph.-E. Legrand, *Étude sur Théocrite* (Paris, 1898), pp. 214ff.; Wilamowitz, *H.D.* vol. i, pp. 89, 141; Palm, 'Bemerkungen zur Ekphrase in der griechischen Literatur', 139 n. 1.
53. Even Legrand, ibid., p. 224 admits Theoc. *Id.* 4.50–7 to have been suggested by the *Thorn Puller* group (M. Bieber, *The Sculpture of the Hellenistic Age* (rev. edn) (New York, 1961), figs. 633–5).
54. E.g. Callimachus and Pheidias' Zeus at Elis (*Fr.* 196).
55. On Theocritus' cup see Gow on 1.27,30f., U. Ott, *Die Kunst des Gegensatzes in Theokrits Hirtengedichten, Spudasmata* 22 (Hildesheim and New York, 1969), pp. 93ff. and n. 264 and Legrand, *Théocrite*, pp. 222ff., who shows most clearly the difficulties involved in thinking that Theocritus had a real cup in mind. See D. M. Halperin, *Before Pastoral: Theocritus and the Ancient Tradition of Bucolic Poetry* (New Haven and London, 1983), p. 161 n. 50 for literature. In the case of Apollonius' description of Jason's cloak P. Friedländer, *Johannes von Gaza und Paulus Silentiarius* (Leipzig, 1912), p. 12 notes that the poet is evidently concerned with a series of individual scenes, for he writes 'on each margin many devices had been skilfully woven *separately*' (1.728f.). For Moschus' basket see Friedländer, ibid., p. 15 and Palm, 'Bemerkungen zur Ekphrase in der griechischen Literatur', 147f.: Friedländer points out that the scenes are described in straightforward juxtaposition after the manner of the Ps.-Hesiodic *Shield of Heracles*.
56. Free poetic invention drawing on features of real art may well have been traditional in Greek poetry. See for example J. T. Kakridis, 'Erdichtete Ekphrasen: ein Beitrag zur homerischen Schildbeschreibung', *W.S.* 76 (1963), 7–26; K. Fittschen, 'Der Schild des Achilleus', in F. Matz and H.-G. Buchholz (eds.), *Archaeologia Homerica: Die Denkmäler und das frühgriechische Epos*, vol. ii

(Göttingen, 1973), Ch. N. Pt. 1, 17 *et passim*; H. A. Gärtner, 'Beobachtungen zum Schild des Achilleus', in H. Görgemanns and E. A. Schmidt (eds.), *Studien zum antiken Epos*, *Beiträge zur klassischen Philologie* 72 (Meisenheim am Glan, 1976), 46–65.

3 The Practice of Pictorial Realism

Now that an attempt has been made to analyse the Hellenistic theory of pictorialism, we may try to ascertain how far practice agreed with theory and determine the nature and extent of pictorialism in Alexandrian poetry itself. Of course, this naturally entails an element of subjectivity and our conclusions will be the more persuasive where we have the literary models on which visually detailed passages in Alexandrian poetry are based, or at least parallels from earlier literature, for then we may compare the respective attitudes to pictorialism. I propose first to discuss Philetas, Erinna, Callimachus, Apollonius, Theocritus, Herodas, Euphorion, Moschus and Bion. For reasons inherent in the genre, we shall here be mainly concerned with epic, though of course elegy, iamb and mime will also come under our scrutiny. We shall deal secondly with the epigrammatists. Epigram may most conveniently be treated as a separate genre. The compass of the epigrams is so small that to some extent they must be treated collectively, but where possible the poets will be treated as separate personalities and we may still hope to see if there is any general development in pictorial approach. The didactic poets, Aratus, Eratosthenes and Nicander, will be considered last, for their pictorialism may have motivations other than the purely poetic, though the latter will be found to play an important role.

We begin, then, with the figure commonly described as the father of the Alexandrian movement, Philetas of Cos.[1] Unfortunately, the remains of his poems are so meagre — no fragment exceeds four lines — that it is impossible to come to any firm conclusion about his pictorialism. We can say that his epyllion, the *Hermes* (*Frr.* 5–9 Pow.), in which Odysseus tells Aeolus of his wanderings including his descent to Hades (*Fr.* 6), would have afforded an obvious opportunity for extended, vivid narration, especially since Parthenius[2] tells us that in it Aeolus offered Odysseus hospitality for a long time in order to question him in detail 'about the sack of Troy and how the Achaean ships were scattered on the way home'; and Philetas has altered the Homeric sequence of Odysseus' adventures, making the journey to Hades, for example, precede his meeting with Aeolus so that it too can be described.

Fr. 17 is interesting because it describes an unidentified character in sorry plight. The two lines, with their reference to the character's dirty tunic and the covering of plaited rushes wrapped around his waist, which is 'thin', one imagines, through starvation, create quite a vivid picture; pictorial realism thus accompanies the depiction of low life.

Finally, we should consider *Fr.* 24; νάσσατο δ' ἐν προχοῇσι μελαμπέτροιο Βυρίνης ('He[?] dwelt at the mouth of black-rocked Bourina'). Theocritus describes Bourina, the spring on Cos, at *Idyll* 7.6–9, where the scholiasts quote the line of Philetas; it is just possible that Theocritus has Philetas in mind, especially given his praise of the older poet at lines 39–41, and perhaps Philetas described the spring too.[3]

Now though all this can give nothing like solid evidence for the extent of pictorialism in Philetas, we may perhaps conclude that descriptive writing figured in his verse at least to some degree. Moreover, if he did avail himself of the opportunity for pictorially vivid narration offered by his *Hermes*, he will have done so in a poem which seems to have experimented with the inclusion of new subject-matter in epic poetry, love; pictorialism and the depiction of the common human passion may, therefore, have been central features of the epyllion, in a combination we shall find to be typical of the Alexandrian movement.

We may at this juncture examine the *Distaff* of Erinna (*Fr.* 401 *S.H.*), but I include her here with some hesitation, for her date is disputed. Eusebius puts her *floruit* at 353–2 BC and the date is commonly accepted.[4] But Bowra has proposed that it be brought down nearer to the time of Theocritus on the grounds that in her choice of metre, her vocabulary, dialect and tone she has striking points of contact with him.[5] Membership of the generation of Asclepiades and Theocritus would certainly entitle her to a place in our study,[6] but, even if she can only be said to have written in the later fourth century,[7] she may still with justification be called a forerunner of the Alexandrian age, given her style, her choice of the hexameter for a dirge, and her subject-matter.[8]

In the *Distaff* Erinna describes the games and everyday tasks she and Baucis shared as girls. The fragmentary text which has come down to us allows us only to speculate over the details of the Tortoise game they played (1–17), but it is clear that she dwelt upon the picture. The game, which resembles our modern 'Catch', followed a question and answer pattern, concluding with the question 'How did your son die?' and the answer 'From his white horses into the sea he *leapt*',[9] at which the Tortoise, surrounded by her playmates, suddenly jumped and tried to catch another child, who became the Tortoise in turn.[10] Erinna appears to have pictured how Baucis caught her[11] and how she chased Baucis over the farmyard (16–17).[12] It seems most likely that they are described as playing the game till the moon rose.[13] The second description is of the bogy, Mormo, invoked by Erinna's mother either to wake them in the morning or to hurry them on to their place at the loom with the wool-workers:[14] she has great ears on her head, walks on four feet and changes from one appearance to another (26–7).[15] In picturing Mormo with such naïve clarity Erinna charmingly reconstructs a child's imagination at work. The pictorial realism of both descriptions is employed in close association with everyday realistic details[16] and lends a rare pathos to Erinna's expression of grief.

In the case of Callimachus of Cyrene, however, we have indisputable evidence of a keen yet judicious interest in pictorial realism, even though two works of great importance to this book, the *Aetia* and the *Hecale*, are in a fragmentary state.

To consider the *Aetia* first, it must first be noted that cult-origins will not have been a theme naturally conducive to pictorial description. Callimachus is in general more interested in the brief delineation of the history which led to the founding of cults. Even so, *Fr.* 114.1–17 takes the form of a dialogue between Callimachus and a statue of Apollo, and in the course of the conversation an explanation is given of why Apollo is carrying a bow in his left hand and the Graces in his right; a definite picture of the statue emerges, though it appears to have been meant only as the occasion for Callimachus' explanation of its peculiarities.[17]

The *Hymns* yield much interesting evidence for Callimachus' approach to pictorialism and the contexts to which he thought it appropriate. The third, that to Artemis, claims our particular attention. The poem opens with a family tête-à-tête, where little Artemis, still a child, is seated on her father Zeus' knee and in a forthright, ironically naïve manner asks for her divine attributes as maiden goddess of the hunt and of childbirth and for polyonymy:

["Ἄρτεμιν . . . ὑμνέομεν]
ἀρχμενοι ὡς ὅτε πατρὸς ἐφεζομένη γονάτεσσι
παῖς ἔτι κουρίζουσα τάδε προσέειπε γονῆα·
'δός μοι παρθενίην αἰώνιον, ἄππα, φυλάσσειν,
καὶ πολυωνυμίην, ἵνα μή μοι Φοῖβος ἐρίζῃ,
δὸς δ' ἰοὺς καὶ τόξα . . .' (4–8)

ὡς ἡ παῖς εἰποῦσα γενειάδος ἤθελε πατρός
ἅψασθαι, πολλὰς δὲ μάτην ἐτανύσσατο χεῖρας
μέχρις ἵνα ψαύσειε. πατὴρ δ' ἐπένευσε γελάσσας,
φῆ δὲ καταρρέζων· 'ὅτε μοι τοιαῦτα θέαιναι
τίκτοιεν, τυτθόν κεν ἐγὼ ζηλήμονος Ἥρης
χωομένης ἀλέγοιμι.' (26–31)

Of Artemis we sing, . . . beginning at the time when, still a little child, she was sitting on her father's knees and addressed her parent with these words: 'Daddy, grant that I may keep my virginity forever, and grant me many names, so that Phoebus won't vie with me, and grant me arrows and a bow . . .' With these words the child wanted to touch her father's beard, and she kept stretching her hands in vain so that she might touch it. With a laugh her father nodded assent and said, caressing her, 'When goddesses bear me children like this, little need I bother about Hera's jealous anger.'

The homely visual details of the little goddess, repeatedly straining to touch her father's beard and being unable to reach, Zeus' delighted laugh and his spite for his wife, Hera, are carefully emphasised. Now one of Callimachus' models is a scene in the *Iliad* and a brief comparison will prove instructive. In Homer, Artemis, who is unlike her counterpart in Callimachus in that she is adult, has been put in her place by her step-mother, Hera, for meddling in the affairs of gods greater than herself in the divine struggle over Troy. She flies home to her father and sits weeping on his knee, her robe trembling with her sobs; Zeus makes her look at him and with a smile asks her who is troubling her and she tells him it is Hera and blames her for the gods' dissension (*Il.* 21.505–13). The pose of the daughter on her father's knee, Zeus' laughter and the family frictions are already present in Homer, but Callimachus' version is even more intent upon highlighting amusing domesticities, again of a predominantly visual nature, and upon giving the scene individuality and vividness by so doing; its aim is to dwell on the particular, individualising detail, whereas the Homeric passage gives the impression of stylisation, not only because of its formulaic phraseology, but also because a sense of decorum is preserved to a greater degree; Callimachus dwells upon characterising, homely strokes and invests the portrayal of the behind-the-scenes dealings of the gods with a feeling of *tout comme chez nous*. Another main model seems to be a hymn to Artemis by Alcaeus (304 Lobel-Page (= Sappho 44A Voigt)) in which Artemis makes her vow of chastity with a solemnity which contrasts pointedly with the tone of the Callimachean Artemis' request, and in which the pictorial is scarcely discernible at all. The comparison with these two models thus reveals Callimachus' heightened concern with visual detail; it also illustrates the close connection between pictorialism and the depiction of the everyday which of course lends the scene its humour.[18] The fusion of vividly pictorial representation of realistic matter and momentous grandeur of setting is curiously paralleled in baroque art.[19]

The second chief section of the hymn maintains a pronounced emphasis on the pictorial. At lines 46ff. Artemis goes to Hephaestus' workshop to ask the Cyclopes for a bow, arrows and a quiver. The giants are at work around a red-hot mass of iron and an anvil (48f.). The attendant nymphs are terrified at the sight of them, and Callimachus does not miss the opportunity to give a vivid picture of the Cyclopes' appearance: they are 'dread monsters that look like the crags of Mount Ossa and beneath their brow their single eyes, like a shield with four folds of hide,[20] glare fearfully' (51–4). The nymphs are frightened, too, by the noise the smiths make and, once again, we are given a picture of the Cyclopes as they swing their hammers above their shoulders and strike the iron or bronze hissing from the furnace, their hammer-blows falling in alternate succession (59–61).[21] But no shame to the nymphs, Callimachus remarks, for not even the goddesses who are already past their childhood look upon the Cyclopes without a shudder (64–5). Moreover, he says, divine mothers bring their disobedient daughters to heel by calling the Cyclopes to frighten them; or Hermes comes out from inside the house, all stained with ashes, and plays bogy with the child, who covers her eyes with her hands and runs to her mother's lap (66–71).[22] But Artemis is different from the nymphs. On an earlier occasion, when she was only three years old (72) and needed her mother, Leto, to carry her (73), she had visited Hephaestus who had promised her the presents customarily given to a new-born child when an adult sees him for the first time (ὀπτήρια:74; again an everyday detail); the little goddess sat on Brontes' knees and tore a handful of hair from his chest (76f.);[23] 'even to this day', we are told, there remains a bald patch on Brontes' chest,[24] just as when a man gets mange and loses his hair (78–9). So now Artemis finds no difficulty in framing her request boldly (80). Homely realistic detail and thoroughgoing pictorial portrayal of it form the appeal of the passage and humorously contrast with the grandeur of the metre and the dignity of treatment normally expected in a hymn.[25]

Though Callimachus' pictorialism is evidenced most clearly in the *Hymn to Artemis*, it is by no means exclusively confined to that poem. Consider Callimachus' account in the *Hymn to Delos* of the crucial moment when Leto finally gives birth to Apollo: she comes to rest and sits by the River Inopus, undoes her girdle and, wearied by her pain, leans backwards with her shoulders supported by the trunk of a palm-tree;[26] her whole body is covered in sweat; she addresses her unborn child and begs him to come forth (205–12). The visual elements here employed to heighten the pathos of the scene may certainly be called realistic. Callimachus' model is the *Homeric Hymn to Apollo* and a comparison will illustrate the Alexandrian poet's realism. In the Homeric hymn, the birth of the god is mentioned briefly at lines 25–7, but is treated at greater length ninety lines later (115–19). Eileithyia visits Delos and Leto longs to give birth; she throws her arms around the palm-tree, kneeling on the soft meadow, and the earth smiles beneath; Apollo springs forth into the light of day and all the goddesses shout for joy. The scene is pictorial enough, though perhaps less precisely observed, but the birth is an easy one and Eileithyia is allowed to help Leto, whereas Callimachus makes no mention of her presence at the birth.[27] Callimachus has invested the scene with a dramatic force and pathos absent from his model; his choice of pictorial detail from actual childbirth with its emphasis on pain and particularly his alteration of Leto's pose to one realistically evocative of utter exhaustion[28] are the main means of achieving his effect. And once again we have evidence of just how closely the aims of *enargeia* and *mimēsis biou* are connected.[29]

Now this passage is set in an account of Leto's flight in which

The Practice of Pictorial Realism 61

Callimachus has gone far out of his way to introduce incidents which are realistically quite fantastic and incredible. We can hope to understand the motivation behind his procedure only once we have analysed, in their proper place, the other aspects of the scene's realism.

Also in the *Hymn to Delos* is the description of Iris, where the messenger-goddess sits down after informing Hera that Leto has given birth to Apollo:

ἣ καὶ ὑπὸ χρύσειον ἐδέθλιον ἷζε κύων ὥς,
Ἀρτέμιδος ἥτις τε, θοῆς ὅτε παύσεται ἄγρης,
ἷζει θηρήτειρα παρ' ἴχνεσιν, οὔατα δ' αὐτῆς
ὀρθὰ μάλ', αἰὲν ἑτοῖμα θεῆς ὑποδέχθαι ὁμοκλήν·
τῇ ἰκέλη Θαύμαντος ὑπὸ θρόνον ἷζετο κούρη.
κείνη δ' οὐδέ ποτε σφετέρης ἐπιλήθεται ἕδρης,
οὐδ' ὅτε οἱ ληθαῖον ἐπὶ πτερὸν ὕπνος ἐρείσει,
ἀλλ' αὐτοῦ μεγάλοιο ποτὶ γλωχῖνα θρόνοιο
τυτθὸν ἀποκλίνασα καρήατα λέχριος εὕδει.
οὐδέ ποτε ζώνην ἀναλύεται οὐδὲ ταχείας
ἐνδρομίδας, μή οἵ τι καὶ αἰφνίδιον ἔπος εἴπῃ
δεσπότις. (228–39)

So she spoke and sat at the foot of the golden throne like a hunting hound of Artemis which, after the swift chase, sits at her feet, its ears pricked up, always ready to receive the goddess's call; like that, Thaumas' daughter sat at the foot of the throne. She never neglects her post, not even when sleep brushes its wing of forgetfulness against her, but there by the corner of the great throne she sleeps tilting her head aslant a little. She never undoes her girdle or her swift hunting-boots in case her mistress gives her even a sudden command.

Pindar's passage on Zeus' eagle being lulled to sleep by the phorminx (*P*. 1.6–10) is in some ways interestingly comparable. The eagle's external appearance is clear enough: the bird is perched on Zeus' sceptre, its wings relax, its head droops, its eyes are closed, and its supple back rises and falls as it breathes. But Pindar moves easily from this external picture to the less pictorial imagery of the dark cloud which the phorminx spreads over the eagle's head, 'a sweet seal for his eyelids', and of the dream and enchantment that the phorminx induces. Callimachus is far more pictorial and, moreover, limits his less visual sleep-imagery to the motif of the brushing of sleep's wing. The lines present an image of Iris so graphic and precise in its detail that scholars have claimed that they are inspired by particular works of plastic art, though unanimity has never been reached over which.[30] The picture may well have been influenced in its general conception and composition by works of art and the poet's eye may have been opened to the possibilities of pictorialism by his contemplation of art, a point I have already argued, but there is no need to postulate the influence of any particular statue or the like, given the fact that for Callimachus and his movement pictorialism, which we have found denoted in second-century criticism by the word *enargeia*, was in itself a well-attested aim in literature. Still, in the case of the description of Iris one may agree with a modern scholar that 'in general Callimachus' imagery is less static than this'.[31] As we shall see, however, other Alexandrian poets, notably Apollonius and Theocritus, offer us even more detailed and extended descriptive passages.

One further aspect of the *Hymns* deserves mention here. It is the 'mimetic' approach of the *Hymn to Apollo*, *The Bath of Pallas* and the *Hymn to Demeter*. The most recent editors of these poems agree that they are literary pieces and are meant only to create the illusion that they accompany actual rituals: the audience, consequently, was not present at them.[32] The narrators, who are identifiable with the masters of ceremonies at the different festivals, realistically evoke for Callimachus' audiences an atmosphere of religious excitement by reporting the different stages of the rites, by urgent commands to the participants, by addresses to the deity and by expressions of awe at his or her epiphany. This realism is not pictorial, but it is analogous to pictorial realism as a style lending immediacy to its subject.

It is now time to examine a poem by Callimachus which exhibits, despite its fragmentary state, all the major aspects of Alexandrian realism and may be called the centre-piece of this book. It is the *Hecale*.[33] The fragments provide ample evidence that Callimachus throughout the epyllion aimed at pictorially realistic description.

We possess a fragment which appears to have described the weather on the day Theseus left (*Fr.* 238.15–30). It describes first, I take it, the weather as it was at noon:

⌊ὄφρα μὲν οὖν ἔνδιος ἔην ἔτι, θέρμετο δὲ χθών,
τόφρα δ' ἔην ὑάλοιο φαάντερος οὐρανὸς ἠνοψ⌋
οὐδέ⌋ ποθ⌊ι⌋ κν⌊ηκὶς ὑπεφαίνετο, πέπτατο δ' αἰθήρ
ἀγ[ν]έφελος. (*Fr.* 238.15–18)

So while it was still noon and the earth was warm, the bright sky was clearer than glass and not a wisp of cloud appeared anywhere, and the heavens stretched cloudless.

Evening is described as 'the time when girls take the wool they have spun to their mother, ask for their evening meal and take their hands from their work' (19–20),[34] in itself a picturesque scene. It is then that the storm suddenly breaks over Attica; the clouds, the wind and the lightning are described; and the mountains of Attica over which the storm passes, Parnes, Aegaleos and Hymettus, are detailed (21–30). This will be the storm which forced Theseus to lodge with Hecale, and it is evident that Callimachus has taken much care over presenting a vivid picture of it and the time it occurred. Moreover, the storm he describes motivates Theseus' taking refuge in Hecale's hut.

Callimachus' portrayal of Hecale herself is of key importance to this book. Her person, life and milieu are described with a remarkable visual realism, and her poverty is emphasised largely by means of it; *enargeia* and *mimēsis biou* are therefore once again inseparable. Callimachus' presentation of her as a figure of low realism in fact depends for its impact on his vivid description of her, so that the real point of his pictorialism is only intelligible once the background to low realism has been explored. Discussion of the description of Hecale must therefore wait till that has been done. It is sufficient here to note that the 'heroine' of the epyllion — who, after all, gives it its name — is described extensively and in arresting detail, and that the poem's real point (aside from its formal, aetiological one), namely that appearances may be deceptive and that moral nobility can be found in people of lowly circumstances, actually depends upon pictorialism.

It looks as if Theseus' victory over the bull of Marathon was also described. One fragment tells how Theseus 'forced the terrible horn of the beast down to the ground' (*Fr.* 258). We learn from *Fr.* 288.1 *S.H.* (= *Fr.* 260.1 Pf.) that Theseus probably broke off one of its horns with his club.[35] Another fragment describes how after the struggle Theseus 'dragged [the bull] and it followed, a reluctant travelling-companion' (*Fr.* 259).³⁶ A more substantial fragment (*Fr.* 288.1–15 *S.H.* = *Fr.* 260.1–15 Pf.) depicts Theseus' triumphal procession, dragging the bull by its remaining horn, and relates how the country-folk grew frightened at the sight of the hero and the animal and showered him with leaves in a ritual φυλλοβολία; the simile describing the number of the leaves, and hence the people's relief, is also graphic:

οὐχὶ νότος τόσσην γε χύσιν κατεχεύατο φύλλων,
οὐ βορέης οὐδ' αὐτὸς ὅτ' ἔπλετο φυλλοχόος μ<ε>ίς,
ὅσσα τότ' ἀγρῶσται περί τ' ἀμφί τε Θησέϊ βάλλον,
. . . .] . . . περίστατον, αἱ δὲ γυναῖκες
[στόρνῃσιν ἀνέστεφον] (*Fr.* 288.11–15 *S.H.*)

The south wind does not spread so great a fall of leaves, nor even the north wind itself when it is the month of falling leaves, as the country folk then showered Theseus with, around and on both sides of him, . . . surrounded by the crowd[?], and the women . . . crowned him with girdles . . .

The fragments permit us, surely, to conclude that Callimachus' narration of the victory was pictorially vivid.

The description of the dawn at which Theseus returns to Hecale is a charming mixture of everyday and pictorial detail. Dawn is called the time when burglars have given up searching for loot; the early morning lanterns are beginning to appear and many a water-bearer is singing the Song of the Well; people whose house is on the road-side are woken by the axles squeaking under wagons; and blacksmiths are either being troubled for a light or are troubling others for it (*Fr.* 288.65–9 *S.H.* = *Fr.* 260.65–9 Pf.).³⁷

There is only one more poem of Callimachus that need be discussed here to demonstrate that pictorialism was by no means limited to the poet's epos. In *Iambus* 6 (*Fr.* 196) Callimachus goes to inordinately painstaking lengths to describe the statue of Zeus at Elis to a friend sailing off to see it. The Diegete tells us that he describes the length, height and width of the base, the throne, the footstool and the god himself, and how much the whole group cost. The fragments mention the winged Victory in Zeus' hand (39), the Horae (42) and, conjecturally, the Graces (44f.), attested elsewhere as adornments of the statue.³⁸ The poem, as we know it, looks like a monstrous display of erudition, and its joking point may have been to render Callimachus' friend's visit to Elea unnecessary.[39]

We have now surveyed sufficient evidence to allow us to conclude that pictorial realism is used extensively by Callimachus. Whenever we have been able to compare Callimachus' treatment of earlier, especially Homeric models, we have seen that he extends the everyday, low and pictorialist elements in his version. Sometimes pictorialism is used to give high-flown material an impression of immediacy or ironic *tout comme chez nous*, as in the *Hymns*, sometimes it is integral to his thematic point, as in the case of the *Hecale*, but it is always an important aspect of his poetry.

Now it has been claimed that '[Callimachus'] pictures are less clearly outlined than those of Apollonius, and do not create the same impression of a pictorial art.'[40] A claim like this, together with our findings on Callimachus' pictorialism, leads us to expect a very highly developed type of pictorial realism in Apollonius, to whom we may now turn.

A factor crucial to our examination is the literary genre to which the *Argonautica* belongs. It had always been the peculiar task of the epic poet to render his material immediate to his audience. Because of social change, when for example, national pride had been hurt by defeat or emigration, the exploits of a nation's ancestors became endowed with a grandeur that we sometimes rather uncharitably label 'epic exaggeration'. This is generally held to be the case with Homer.[41] The problem for the poet and his audience then becomes the ability to assimilate the epic's heroes and narrative. Now the reasons for 'epic exaggeration' in Apollonius' epic are not the same as in the *Iliad* or the *Odyssey*; it may be put down in his case to the yearning for unity with mainstream Greek culture and the sense of identity which the Greeks in Alexandria seem to have derived from Greek mythology. But the problem for Apollonius, that of relating his epic to his audience's experience, was the same as that for Homer; it was, perhaps, even more acute. To demonstrate this, we may compare an authorial comment in Apollonius with one in the *Iliad* upon which it is modelled. At *Iliad* 12.447-9 Hector, in order to break down the gate of the Achaean encampment, picks up a stone: 'not even the two best men of the community', Homer remarks, 'such as men are now, could easily have heaved it up from the ground on to a wagon.' Apollonius borrows the motif when describing the stone

Jason picks up to throw at Aeetes' Earthborn Men: 'four stout men could not have lifted it a little from the earth' (3.1366f.). The escalation in number is symptomatic of how remote from modern life Apollonius felt his material to be; he may even be teasingly exploiting the 'incredibility' of Homeric epic.

Pictorial realism was one of Apollonius' main methods for bringing the grand, mythical saga of the Argonauts within his audience's experience, thus allowing them the more easily to enter into the fiction of his epic.[42] And this realism is one of his chief glories. An extraordinary example of it occurs early in the poem, in the scene where the Argo is launched (1.363–93). How was Apollonius to get his audience to feel involved with the fabulous Argo? Athene, tradition related, had even fitted her out with a divine oak from Dodona, which ran along the middle of her cutwater, so that she was endowed with the powers of speech.[43] Apollonius' technique is to describe her launching with a visual precision which takes nothing for granted and which probably draws upon details of any real launching such as he might himself have watched. In this extended description, lasting over 30 lines, he even tells us where the Argonauts put their clothes when they had stripped off for the work, indeed an important matter, as every yachtsman knows, but the poet is careful to tell us that it was outside the reach of the waves, adding that the sea had cleaned the beach in a storm long ago! He thus allows a motif drawn from ordinary life to intrude upon the grand moment. The Argo is girded with ropes 'well twisted within' so that the rivets might grip the timbers better.[44] A trench the width of the Argo's hull is dug right down to and into the sea, just as far as she would run with the Argonauts pushing her; the trench is dug on a slant to make her roll easily, and smoothly turned rollers are put into place in it. The oars are placed and tied in their thole-pins, blades inboard, so that their handles, projecting a convenient cubit, can be used by the heroes for pushing the ship, a procedure surely adopted on slipways in actual launchings.[45] The coxswain, Tiphys, leaps on board to give the timing, the Argonauts strain on both sides of the Argo, leaning into the oars with their chests and arms, with one push the ship moves, the rollers groan under the weight of her keel and give off dark smoke from the friction, she gathers way and the heroes check her so that she doesn't career. Once she is launched, the oars are put in their rowing position in the thole-pins, and the mast, the sails and the provisions are stowed on board.

The Practice of Pictorial Realism 67

All in all, this is an admirably engaging description, and it is clear that Apollonius has thought through the scene in a most detailed manner, doing everything in his power to 'bring the scene before the eyes of his audience'; the result is that the great moment, the launching of the mythical Argo, known to everybody from *Odyssey* 12.70 as 'the Argo, in everyone's thoughts', can be clearly visualised and appears quite within the bounds of possible experience.

This is often the basic rationale behind Apollonius' descriptive passages. It is revealed more clearly when he has a Homeric model in mind. An example is the treatment of the motif of setting sail. In *Odyssey* 2.414–34, the most extended passage of this kind,[46] Telemachus takes his men with their equipment down to the ship; at Athene's direction — she is disguised as Mentor — he embarks and sits in the prow; the others follow and sit on their benches; Athene sends a following wind; Telemachus orders his men to pick up the tackle and they raise the mast and step it in its slotted thwart, securing it with the forestays, and hoist the white sails with well-twisted ox-hide ropes. The wind blows into the middle of the sail and the waves plash about the cutwater as the ship gets under way. The men secure the ropes and pour a wine-libation to Athene. It is plain that Homer in this version of the motif is interested in the visual effect.

But Apollonius again and again shows an unwillingness merely to reproduce formulaic passages of Homer, and in his re-working of the Homeric model he is intent upon making the scene even more visually appealing. The motif is in fact spread over more than sixty lines (1.519–79) with the addition of much extraneous material. There is pictorialism in the descriptions of dawn (519–220), and of the motifs of the heroes taking up their benches, Heracles putting his club beside him and making the Argo's keel sink beneath his tread (528–33), the slipping of the hawsers and the libation (533f.), the water eddying over the oars (540–3), the Argonauts' gleaming armour (544f.), the Argo's wake (545f.), the stepping of the mast and the hoisting of the sail (599–63). There is also the graphic simile comparing the rowers with youths dancing to Apollo, which evokes a clear image of the ease and grace of their blade-work (536–9). Human touches are present in Jason's sadness at leaving his homeland (535) and Cheiron's appearance at the water's edge with his wife, who holds up the baby Achilles for his father Peleus to see, a gesture of some pathos, in view of the separation of

Peleus and Thetis (553–8).⁴⁷ Workaday matter, too, can be found in the simile comparing the fish that follow the Argo and Orpheus' singing with sheep which follow their shepherd as he plays on his pipes (569–79). The simile is important for it points up an interesting facet of Apollonius' realism. That fish might follow Orpheus' harp is well within the realism of the magical. But fish do follow ships, and Apollonius has chosen to illustrate their action by a simile drawn from low life. He seems intent upon juxtaposing in a piquant manner the incredible elements of his narrative and the observable and everyday. Likewise the miraculous is highlighted when the Argo herself, speaking with the Dodonian oak fitted by Athene, urges the heroes to embark (524–7). The effect of this is perhaps to 'define' the incredible, which is another way of helping the audience to relate to such things, even if irony is intended — a point I raised in Chapter 1.⁴⁸

Apollonius' pictorial realism can also be observed in his account of the boxing-match between Polydeuces and Amycus (2.67–97). He has two Homeric models in mind, *Iliad* 23.685–99 and *Odyssey* 18.89–99. The description of Epeius and Euryalus' match in the *Iliad* is quite brief; mention is made of details like sweat and teeth-clattering, Epeius lunging and successfully landing his punch, and Euryalus spitting blood and being dragged off by his friends. The contest between Odysseus and Irus has about the same amount of detail. But in Apollonius we have a veritable boxing-commentary: Amycus tries to tire Polydeuces, who, however, succeeds in staying out of trouble, both get exhausted, Amycus re-opens the fray by trying to smash his fist down on Polydeuces' head, Polydeuces weaves, taking the blow on his shoulder, penetrates the king's guard and lands a fatal punch above his ear. The scene is eminently picturable and every movement clearly described.⁴⁹ As we shall see, however, this pictorialism is taken to its extreme in Theocritus' account of the fight.

Interesting background to this taste for pictorial realism is provided by Apollonius' description of Jason's cloak (1.721–67). This is important as evidence not only for assessing Apollonius' approach in describing works of art in comparison with, say, Homer's or that of the composer of the Ps.-Hesiodic *Shield of Heracles*, but also, as has already been pointed out, for how the poet actually *saw*, and for how he realised that visual effects could be exploited in art and poetry.

First, he tells us all we need to know about the disposition of the figures: they are woven separate from each other on each border of the cloak (728f.). This is a refinement on the procedure of Homer in his description of Achilles' shield (*Il.* 18.478–608), where the arrangement of the scenes still defies convincing reconstruction.[50] Having clearly stated where the scenes are on the cloak, however, Apollonius can proceed with traditional tags like 'on it there were . . .' (ἐν μὲν ἔσαν),[51] but the important fact has already emerged that Apollonius views the cloak as a work of art, more self-consciously than Homer does with Achilles' shield, where the scenes are treated as actions, not merely as depictions. In line with Apollonius' different procedure is the fact that he captures each of the seven scenes at one moment in time,[52] thus showing he knows the limitations of the art he is describing: so, for example, the Cyclopes are just completing a thunderbolt for Zeus and it just lacks one more ray, which they are forging (730–4); Zethus and Amphion are laying the foundations of Thebes, which is still without towers (735–41); the Teleboae and sons of Electryon are represented at one specific moment in the defence of their oxen against the Taphian pirates (747–51); Pelops and Hippodameia are escaping in a chariot at just the moment when Oenomaus' axle breaks (752–8); Phoebus is shooting at the monster Tityus who is raping his mother (759–62). Here Apollonius gives us Tityus' lineage which a weaving could not reveal. This procedure is in striking contrast with that of Homer, who includes quite extensive narrative elements which would be impossible in an artefact.[53] Clearly, Apollonius is conscious of the boundaries of plastic art, and his description of Jason's cloak, for all that each scene is drawn from mythology, is realistic in this respect as in its pictorial detail.

Secondly, there is the fine description of an optical effect, discussed in the preceding chapter, of the passage in which Aphrodite is depicted looking at her image in Ares' shield (742–6), which shows how sophisticated Apollonius' eye is; we have a poetic description of a reflected image in a woven picture. We have also remarked the everyday element in the scene of Aphrodite at toilet. The final scene of the group, the flight of Phrixus on the ram (763–7), has also been discussed; it emphasises the artistic illusion that the ram is actually speaking to Phrixus. Coming last in the description, the scene suggests that the preceding ones were executed in a similar vein of *trompe l'oeil*.[54] The description of

Jason's cloak, therefore, gives precious insight into the extent to which Apollonius valued illusionism in art, how far his eye appears to have been trained by that art and how he tried to realise its potential in poetry. Its relation to the surrounding narrative will be discussed presently.

We have, I trust, seen sufficient evidence of how Apollonius tries by means of pictorial realism to help his audiences assimilate moments and scenes in his epic. But we find that he often combines with pictorialism two other methods of achieving his aim: employing everyday material and enlisting the aid of science. The description of the scene of Aphrodite gazing at her mirror-reflection on Jason's cloak is one obvious example of how the poet combines the pictorially vivid with the everyday detail of a beautiful woman admiring herself. The motif of Aphrodite at toilet recurs in Book 3 when Hera and Athene come to ask the queen of love to help Jason (43–51). The everyday, domestic element in the passage is quite pervasive; Aphrodite appears just like any beautiful woman disturbed while preening herself,[55] though she regains composure enough to tease her visitors. The intention of Apollonius' pictorial detail and his use of the everyday is plain; it is humour and to make the grand ladies of Olympus look 'just like us', and so fix them on a scale of reality which helps us to relate to them. We have seen this procedure in Callimachus.

The same combination can be observed a little later, when Aphrodite has agreed to try to induce Eros to make Medea fall in love with Jason. She goes looking for Eros and finds him in Zeus' orchard playing dice with Ganymede, whom Zeus, we are told, has settled on Olympus out of desire for his beauty. The sublime tone is soon lowered, however, for the boys are introduced playing knucklebones, 'as any boys of similar temperament do'; Eros stands, holding his left hand, full of pieces, beneath his breast and there is a ruddy bloom to his cheeks; Ganymede crouches, silently sulking; he has two pieces left which he throws in one after the other to no avail, angered by Eros' laughter; having lost his pieces he leaves empty-handed and doesn't notice Cypris' approach; she grasps her son by the chin and accuses him of cheating his playmate (114–30). Here again we are given a gorgeously detailed picture — the poses of Eros and Ganymede are quite statuesque, and again show how Apollonius' eye had become attuned to the effects possible in fine art;[56] this time the picture is of the problem-child of Olympus. The literary implications of this treatment of

Eros are crucial here. For instance, the irresponsible, carefree playfulness of the god contrasts with the pain that he is soon to inflict on Medea, a point that we shall return to. Pictorialism plays its part in that thematic development, but it also performs the role of helping us to relate to Apollonius' material. The depiction of divine children in emphatically human terms is already familiar to us from Callimachus' *Hymn to Artemis*. It is a typically Alexandrian trait and goes far beyond counterparts in earlier literature, like the *Homeric Hymn to Hermes*, in its frequency, its use of the everyday and its pictorial detail.[57]

We have seen enough evidence of Apollonius' fondness for describing the ordinary lives of children and adults, but he by no means discounts old age as a proper subject for representation. We have, for example, the touching moment when Iphias, the old priestess of Artemis, kisses Jason's hand as he proceeds from Iolcus to the Argo, but is left behind in the crush of the crowd (1.311–16). Another old woman is similarly described at 1.668–74: she is Polyxo, Hypsipyle's nurse, a description of whose appearance is particularly relevant for, in advising that the Lemnian women give a friendly reception to the Argonauts, she stresses that, whereas she herself will have people to bury her, the present generation will have no one if they leave no offspring (1.681–96).

Another aspect of Apollonius' descriptive power is the remarkably scientific nature of some of his descriptions. A good example is his passage depicting the Acherousian headland, which according to tradition had been passed by the Argonauts on the Black Sea (2.727–49). The description is observed with a scientific accuracy. There is, for example, the detail of the rime at the mouth of the cave of Hades. Frost formed during the night remains on the entrance of a cave if the latter is covered with rock or heavy vegetation and if it is not exposed to the sun. Apollonius describes these conditions explicitly and mentions the midday sun which melts the rime. His only 'mistake' is that the rime could not have been deposited by the subterranean draughts he mentions. These are caused by factors like rivers or a nearby sea, which the description includes, though that may not have been known in Apollonius' time.[58] Now the scholiast on the passage tells us that the historian Nymphis had described the headland and that Apollonius is probably borrowing from him.[59] If that is correct, Apollonius' pictorial and scientific realism may derive from

72 The Practice of Pictorial Realism

Nymphis' researches. It is, however, typical of the poet that he should have selected telling visual details for his account. It is also typical of him that he has appealed to contemporary geographical scholarship in order to give his material scientific credibility, for that accords with his general practice in his use of science, as we shall see in the next chapter. The fact that the promontory has actually been identified[60] is therefore irrelevant, because Apollonius obviously did not see the cave for himself and probably felt that he had been as realistic as could reasonably be expected by his following a scientific source. As for his reference to the Megarians, that is perhaps motivated by an urge to fix the Argonauts' passage past the headland on a 'verifiable' time-scale. The history of their journey is catalogued in ancient geographical works[61] and Apollonius seems to be drawing on a historical tradition for the details. He is thus evidently trying to connect his own age with the mythical past to lend credibility to the mythical events he is describing. The passage on the Acherousian headland is therefore realistic in three main senses: it aims at pictorially precise and vivid description; it strives for scientific accuracy of observation and appeals to actual geographical research; and it gives the audience a chronological perspective which will help them relate to the mythical material.

Sometimes, however, Apollonius' descriptions are deeply indebted to actual scientific research carried out in Alexandria. Medicine in particular provides him with material to make his descriptions more convincing and immediate. An example is the first sight the Argonauts get of Phineus. After a lengthy description of his wretched state, we are told how his knees give way, he sits on the threshold of the yard, a dark swoon (κάρος πορφύρεος) enshrouds him, he thinks the earth is whirling around beneath him, and he lies speechless and fainting with weakness (ἀβληχρῷ δ᾽ ἐπὶ κώματι) (2.197–205). The emphasis is once again on visual elements which both demonstrate the misery of Phineus' existence and motivate the heroes' pity and horror. Apollonius' description is detailed and even scientifically accurate. Two usages of medical terms have been detected in the passage:[62] the expression ἀβληχρὸν κῶμα, modelled after the phrase θάνατος ἀβληχρός ('a feeble death') of *Odyssey* 11.134f., only gains full significance when it is realised that the condition underlying the words is καταφορά, the dizziness between sleeping and waking;[63] secondly, the term κάρος πορφύρεος belongs to the same area of medicine.[64] This remarkable enthusiasm for precision in an account of a pathological state is plainly the consequence of a desire for realism.

There are also passages of narrative in the *Argonautica* which actually depend on visual cues, just as good modern films will fully exploit the particular advantage of their medium, its capacity for visual motivation. And certain descriptions in the epic have quite a subtle relationship with its main theme and narrative. In both these respects Apollonius is something of a pioneer and we must here discuss his achievement.

The rape of Hylas is an instance where he has tried to render plausible the motivation of each link in the chain of events he is narrating (1.1153–279).[65] The first link is the moment when Heracles breaks his oar as he pulls the Argo along single-handed, having worn out the rest of the crew; in such circumstances, it is not surprising that he breaks the oar in half. We may sense some irony in the portrayal of the way the superman Heracles does something as 'ordinary' as breaking an oar (a feeling underlined by the picture painted of him looking slightly ridiculous as he falls from his seat, sits up and glares around him, unaccustomed to his enforced idleness: 1153–71), but the event does help define our relation with the mythical strong-man. More importantly in this context, the event, despite Heracles' superhuman qualities, motivates the narrative, for now the Argonauts must land so that Heracles can make a new oar. The felling of the pine which Heracles selects for the purpose is graphically detailed. He first puts down his quiver and lion's skin (an everyday touch which reminds us of how the poet had made the Argonauts strip off before launching the Argo). He loosens the tree's grip on the ground by knocking it with his club and then grasps it near the bottom, pressing his shoulder against it with his legs wide apart, the perfect stance for a man of Heracles' strength to drag a tree up by the roots. With tremendous effort, he raises the tree, earth still clinging to its roots. He then also picks up his bow and arrows, lion skin and club, and heads home (1172–206).

Hylas' water-search is likewise in part motivated by pictorial details,[66] the realism being, as so often, deployed on a quite fantastic event, in the piquant manner that is becoming quite familiar to us. We have already examined the passage in which the nymph falls in love with his beauty, enhanced in the moonlight (1207–39).[67] The point to note here is that the pictorial element explains the motivation of the nymph's falling in love. The same is true of her ability to drag him into the spring: his position, as he leans into the spring to scoop water in his pitcher, is clearly precarious, and the nymph's success is made credible by the pictorial realism of the depiction of it.[68]

Then there is the final 'shot' in the sequence. Polyphemus is waiting for Heracles' return and heads out to meet him; he is thus alert to the sounds of a man's approach. This 'detail from the heroes' everyday life' realistically explains why he alone of the Argonauts hears Hylas' shout.[69] Polyphemus shouts and roams about in desperation. He draws his sword, his immediate thoughts being of wild beasts or ambushers in the strange place. He meets Heracles to whom he tells what he has heard — breathlessly, for he has been running. Heracles' physical reaction is expressed in the most visual terms: as he listens, sweat pours from his temples and the blood seethes hot deep within his heart (1261f.); he throws down his pine and runs, alternately rushing on and stopping to shout. Meanwhile, the morning star has risen and the Argonauts set forth with the dawn, leaving Heracles, Hylas and Polyphemus behind.[70]

This is a fine example of what the Greek rhetors were to call ecphrastic narration.[71] The passage takes time to draw a series of graphic pictures; sequence and causation are explained with particular reference to the visual, one effect of which is to define the myth's relation with reality as it is perceived, right from the moment when Heracles breaks his oar, which renders natural his separation from Hylas, as he goes in search of a tree for a new one, till the appearance of the morning star which motivates the Argonauts' departure. The emphasis on the visual for motivating narrative is not evidenced to such a degree in earlier Greek epic as we know it: the narration of Odysseus' adventure with the Cyclops at *Odyssey* 9.166–566, for example, is both extended and brilliantly detailed, and offers an admirably clear exposition of the circumstantial details necessary to the development of the tale, but perusal of it will reveal that the actual pictorial content is small in comparison with Apollonius' narrative of the Hylas episode. Perhaps a closer approximation to Apollonius' intensity of detail can be found in the messenger-speeches in tragedy.

We may now examine instances of descriptions for their close relation, aesthetic or thematic, to the main narrative. An example of a description whose relation to the narrative is aesthetic is the famous passage describing nightfall in Book 3 (744–50): night brings darkness over the earth; sailors look from their ships at the constellations; many a traveller and porter longs for sleep and deep sleep falls even upon a mother whose children have died; throughout the city barking is no longer to be heard, nor rowdy talk; silence reigns in the deepening gloom. The picture drawn here contains several visual motifs, though, to be sure, it appeals to hearing also and evokes an intense atmosphere of silence;[72] moreover, it includes a deal of matter from ordinary human life. But the point of the passage is of course that its mood contrasts markedly with the turmoil of Medea's heart as she ponders whether to help Jason (751ff.).

The dream of Medea, described at lines 617–32, also stands in a close thematic relationship with its frame. Medea dreams that Jason has accepted Aeetes' challenge to plough the field of Ares and conquer the Earthborn Men, not in order to win the fleece but to take her home to Hellas and marry her; she dreams that she herself faces the task and succeeds, but that her parents go back on their promise because they had challenged Jason, not her; an argument ensues between Jason and her parents who leave the decision to her; she chooses Jason, her parents shriek in indignation and she wakes. Now of course dreams had traditionally performed the function of prefiguring future events; one need only think of Penelope's dream of the eagle and geese at *Odyssey* 19.535ff. to demonstrate that. But Apollonius' description contains all the inconsequence of a real dream. Indeed, he may have been influenced by medical treatises and perhaps even current research on wish-fulment in dreams;[73] certainly, it is a psychologically as well as visually realistic account. But it also serves to illuminate Medea's actual feelings towards Jason, and is thus integral to Apollonius' characterisation of her, and to give an accurate prediction of the course of events.

My final example has been the subject of hot dispute. It is the description of Jason's cloak, discussed earlier. What purpose *does* it serve, if any? It is generally recognised that the description is meant as a counterpart to Homer's description of Achilles' shield in *Iliad* 18.[74] There the description is perhaps best seen as an expansion of a component of the traditional bardic motif of the hero arming, like that of Agamemnon at *Iliad* 11.15–46, and as a prelude to the grand but terrible moment of the combat of Hector and Achilles; arguably, too, it bears a direct relation to the poem's main narrative in that it offers a panorama of ordinary human life, both in war and peace, in country and city and so on, which is meant to contrast with the picture of heroic life evident throughout the rest of the epic.[75] On the

76 The Practice of Pictorial Realism

question of how Apollonius' description is related to its frame a consensus seems to be emerging. It seems intended as a *contrast* with the Homeric passage:[76] Achilles' shield is a prelude to heroic combat, Jason's cloak to love-making; the cloak emphasises the theme of love in its central scenes of Aphrodite and the elopement of Pelops and Hippodameia to a degree to which the shield does not;[77] the description of the cloak thus helps motivate the Lemnian women's desire for Jason (774–84), though surely their desire in the circumstances was already understandable enough; it heralds a love-encounter and, by contrast with Achilles' shield, tells us something of Jason's status as a hero, namely that he is a 'love-hero'.[78] If this reconstruction of Apollonius' intentions is true — it is an interpretation to which most commentators at least incline — then the description has a quite complex relationship with the narrative into which it is inserted.

There is one final aspect of Apollonius' pictorialism that must receive brief attention. It is his use of the simile, which is integral to the task of relating the grand material of epic to his audience's experience. An exhaustive study of this topic is unnecessary here for it has in any case been well worked over.[79] The links of the simile with visual description are obvious: simple removal of the 'even as' or 'just as when' component will very often leave us with a passage vividly pictorial in its own right.[80] Two similes of the *Argonautica* will have to stand for many and the first will involve a comparison with a Homeric model. It concerns the motif of the woman who spins wool for daily hire. The Homeric version occurs at *Iliad* 12.433–5. The context is the equally balanced battle line of the Achaeans and Trojans at the breach in the Achaeans' wall:

ἀλλ' ἔχον ὥς τε τάλαντα γυνὴ χερνῆτις ἀληθής,
ἥ τε σταθμὸν ἔχουσα καὶ εἴριον ἀμφὶς ἀνέλκει
ἰσάζουσ', ἵνα παισὶν ἀεικέα μισθὸν ἄρηται.

But [the Achaeans] held their ground, as a careful woman who spins for daily hire holds the balance and, raising the weight and the wool in each scale, lifts them to make them equal, so that she may win a meagre wage for her children.

The motif is employed in the *Argonautica* when Medea has fallen in love with Jason, and love in its destructive aspect envelops her heart and sets it aflame:

ὡς δὲ γυνὴ μαλερῷ περὶ κάρφεα χεύατο δαλῷ
χερνῆτις, τῇπερ ταλασήια ἔργα μέμηλεν,
ὥς κεν ὑπωρόφιον νύκτωρ σέλας ἐντύναιτο,
ἄγχι μάλ' ἑζομένη· τὸ δ' ἀθέσφατον ἐξ ὀλίγοιο
δαλοῦ ἀνεγρόμενον σὺν κάρφεα πάντ' ἀμαθύνει. (3.291–5)

As a spinning woman who lives from wool-working heaps dry twigs around a raging brand so that she may prepare a fire beneath her roof at night, sitting very close to it, and the blaze rises prodigiously from the tiny brand and consumes all the twigs together . . .

The altered milieu of the motif is, first, typically Apollonian. In Homer the lowly struggle for survival of the poor woman and her careful weighing of her wool is juxtaposed and, at first sight, contrasted with the heroic world of men and war. (In a deeper and more poignant sense, of course, the plight of both the warriors and the spinster is one and the same.) But Apollonius sets his simile in the context of the passionate love of a woman. Secondly, and more importantly in this connection, Apollonius shows a predilection for drawing a graphic picture: the poor woman is busied with lighting a fire from a brand to warm herself, and she sits close to it;[81] the flame grows larger from the tiny brand as the twigs catch. Homer's picture is of a woman weighing her wool carefully; we are told that her care is to get the most she can as a 'meagre wage' to feed her children, but the explanation does not add to the picture in itself, although it charges it with deep pathos. Apollonius' simile is decidedly more visual and detailed, suppressing the explanation Homer gives for the woman's hard work, which is not appropriate to the new context.[82]

Similes seem traditionally to have taken everyday and low life as their subject-matter. For Homer, the simile seems to have been one of the means of including such material in his heroic narrative, presumably being intended to appeal to the experience of at least a section of his audience. Apollonius in general adheres to the tradition, though, as we have by now become accustomed to expect, he expands the pictorial element and seems to dwell longer on details from low life. Consider the following time-designation, analogous to a simile;

78 The Practice of Pictorial Realism

ἦμος δ' ἀγρόθεν εἶσι φυτοσκάφος ἤ τις ἀροτρεύς
ἀσπασίως εἰς αὖλιν ἐήν, δόρποιο χατίζων,
αὐτοῦ δ' ἐν προμολῇ τετρυμένα γούνατ' ἔκαμψεν
αὐσταλέος κονίῃσι, περιτριβέας δέ τε χεῖρας
εἰσορόων κακὰ πολλὰ ἑῇ ἠρήσατο γαστρί —
τῆμος ἄρ' οἵγ' ἀφίκοντο Κιανίδος ἤθεα γαίης
ἀμφ' Ἀργανθώνειον ὄρος προχοάς τε Κίοιο. (1.1172–8)

At the time when a gardener or ploughman goes gladly from the field to his hut, longing for dinner, and there, parched with dust, he bends his stiff knees on the threshold and, looking at his hands worn with work, he pours many a vile curse on his belly, at that time [the Argonauts] reached the locality of the Cianian land near the Arganthonian mountain and the mouth of Cius.

Now Apollonius could not have lavished so much detail on the direct depiction of the Argonauts' weariness without very much reducing their stature, so he indirectly alludes to it in the time-designation,[83] while drawing at the same time a graphic, independent picture. In sum, the simile and related devices had always been realistic in their pictorialism, in the incorporation of material from everyday life and in the intention to link the grand moments of the main narrative to the experience of more humble realities, but Apollonius seems to extend the simile's realism to extraordinary lengths.[84]

We may conclude this section on Apollonius' pictorial realism with a summary of our findings. Comparison with Homeric models has again and again revealed the later poet's preoccupation with pictorialism, and he shows an at times astonishing alertness of eye for remarkable visual effects. Like that of his teacher, Callimachus, his pictorialism is very often combined with material and motifs drawn from everyday and low life. Like Callimachus, too, he incorporates into his descriptive passages scientific observation, especially in medicine, to lend the weight of science to them, an aspect of his poetry we shall return to in the next chapter. Moreover, Apollonius calls upon the evidence of the graphic visual images he draws to motivate sections of his narrative; indeed, pictorialism is part of his narrative art. Finally, he often dwells upon a realistic picture in order to give greater point to his narrative, at times as if in correction of, say, a Homer. In all this we can see a realist at work. He tries to help his Alexandrian audiences relate to his narration of events, events from which they apparently felt some degree of remoteness. Even if this relation is ironical, the poet's realism is not necessarily the lesser. Pictorialism is thus essential to Apollonius as an epic poet.

Our next task is to survey the pictorial realism of Theocritus, the third major poet active in Alexandria (at least for some part of his life)[85] during the first three decades of the third century BC. He puts pictorial realism to different uses appropriate to the different types of his *oeuvre*. For a clear understanding of his approach we must therefore examine a selection of visually descriptive passages which will illustrate it in each branch of his poetry; I propose to take pastoral idyll first, then briefly refer to urban mime and encomium, and finally deal with epyllion.

There are several extended pictorial descriptions in Theocritus' pastoral *Idylls* and they have been castigated for their length, but none is in fact otiose; rather, they each perform a specific function, some for a purely aesthetic effect, some to illustrate country life to what one presumes was a predominantly city audience, some to underline a thematic point, and some combining any or all of these.

The validity of this assessment can be tested by considering what is perhaps Theocritus' most famous description, that of the Goatherd's cup in *Idyll* 1 (27–56), which is composed, like the passage on Jason's cloak in the *Argonautica*, in the tradition of Homer's shield of Achilles and the Ps.-Hesiodic *Shield of Heracles*.[86] We have already noticed the ABA arrangement of the figures on it to demonstrate Theocritus' interest in the formal aesthetic effects of pictorial representation; we concluded that his interest may owe something to his viewing of contemporary objets d'art, though it is unlikely that he is describing a real cup.[87] It is an extensive example of pictorialist writing. Indeed, when Virgil imitated the passage in *Eclogue* 3 and took twelve lines, which in fact describe two cups (36–43 and 44–7), instead of thirty lines, he may have been tacitly criticising his model. Pope's condemnation of its prolixity is quite explicit: 'He [Theocritus] is apt to be too long in his descriptions, of which that of the Cup in the first pastoral is a remarkable instance.'[88] But let us examine the passage afresh. Apart from outlining the overall shape, materials and ornamentation of the cup (27–31), Theocritus represents three pictures, all precisely delineated. The first is of a woman: her dress is described and on either side of her stand two men, hollow-eyed with love for her; her affections tend now this way, now that, she smiles at one and then looks with favour on the other (32–8).[89] Next (39–44) comes the picture of an old fisherman which we shall presently examine in detail. Finally, we have the scene in which a young boy guards a vineyard, the grapes of which are ripe (45–54): he is sitting on the dry-stone wall of the vineyard; there are two foxes at each side of him, one stealing the grapes and the other, a vixen, trying to rob the boy's wallet, but his attention is absorbed in plaiting a cricket-cage out of asphodel and rush. The two framing pictures thus have a formal symmetry of a central figure surrounded by two others, as we have already observed. But what about the carving of the old fisherman?

> τοῖς δὲ μετὰ γριπεύς τε γέρων πέτρα τε τέτυκται
> λεπράς, ἐφ' ᾇ σπεύδων μέγα δίκτυον ἐς βόλον ἕλκει
> ὁ πρέσβυς, κάμνοντι τὸ καρτερὸν ἀνδρὶ ἐοικώς.
> φαίης κεν γυίων νιν ὅσον σθένος ἐλλοπιεύειν,
> ὧδέ οἱ ᾠδήκαντι κατ' αὐχένα πάντοθεν ἶνες
> καὶ πολιῷ περ ἐόντι· τὸ δὲ σθένος ἄξιον ἅβας.
> τυτθὸν δ' ὅσσον ἄπωθεν ἀλιτρύτοιο γέροντος . . . (39–45)

Next to them are wrought an old fisherman and a rough rock, on which the old man energetically drags in a huge net for a cast, looking like a man working hard. You'd say he was fishing with all the strength of his limbs, so swollen are the muscles all around his neck, even though he is grey; his strength is worthy of youth. Just apart from the sea-beaten old man . . .

This is a striking example of pictorial realism. Theocritus exhibits an acute power of observation when he describes the physical effect of the man's effort, the sinews standing out from his neck (43).[90] The immediate ancestor of this motif is Ps.-Hesiod's *Shield of Heracles* (213–15):

> αὐτὰρ ἐπ' ἀκτῆς
> ἧστο ἀνὴρ ἁλιεὺς δεδοκημένος, εἶχε δὲ χερσὶν
> ἰχθύσιν ἀμφίβληστρον ἀπορρίψοντι ἐοικώς.[91]

But on the shore sat a fisherman waiting, and he had in his hands a net for fish, and seemed like a man about to make a cast.

How much more pictorial detail Theocritus has incorporated in the motif! In the *Idyll* the fisherman has become a weather-beaten, old, grey-haired man, as strong and energetic as a youth; moreover, his activity has become more specific, for he is gathering in the net and not just holding it; finally, the picture as a whole is much more immediate, not least because of the address to the reader (42).[92]

The cup description clearly demonstrates that Theocritus, too, is an Alexandrian fascinated with pictorial realism, though we have already seen evidence of that in connection with *Idyll* 15. But the passage does more than dwell on the visual content of the cup for its own sake. First, as has long been realised, the description is an artful substitute for a song to balance that of Thyrsis, thus at once conforming to and breaking with the amoebean form of pastoral.[93] Secondly, there have been several theories put forward regarding its thematic relationship to the frame,[94] but perhaps its real thematic point is to illustrate country life on a more quotidian plane than the emotionally tense struggle of the neatherd Daphnis against Aphrodite described in Thyrsis' bucolic song. Indeed, human life in the country is illustrated at all its stages: childhood, caught up with its play; youth and its concern with love; and old age faced with the realities of work and making a living. Thus everyday and low life, this time that of the country, is once again depicted in the most visually realistic terms, but, more than that, a contrast is effected between the cup description, with its low tone and humble pictorial detail, and the elevated tone of the song of Thyrsis.[95] If that is so, then the pictorial realism of the description has a sophisticated aesthetic and thematic relation to the latter half of *Idyll* 1.

Idyll 7 has two extended descriptive passages, one describing Lycidas the goatherd *par excellence* (11–20), the other the pleasance at the harvest festival (132–57). The description of Lycidas, with its emphasis on lowly rustic detail like the tawny rustic goatskin smelling of rennet, might at first appear to have been just the sort of passage Pope had in mind in his criticism.[96] Yet in fact it is the only description the poet gives of his herdsmen, and Lycidas might be meant to act as a representative example. If so, the description could hardly be called prolix. Yet there is perhaps another level to it. In the notorious inquiry as to whether Lycidas represents a real person, and, if he does, whom,[97] it has been proposed that he is no less than Apollo; the arguments for the identification are impressive.[98] If the identification is correct, then the humble appearance of the god would assuredly have been appreciated by an Alexandrian audience and the point of the description would be ironic contrast. The description of the pastoral pleasance, on the other hand, probably has purely aesthetic aims. Though the picture of the Coan spring Bourina at the beginning of the poem (7–9) is not to be identified with the later scene, as has been suggested,[99] the two *loci amoeni* do act as a frame to the heat and bustle of Simichidas' midday walk to the harvest festival (21–6); the effect is a pleasantly circular sequence of shade, heat and cool repose.[100] Moreover, it should be noted that the closing scene appeals to all the senses: touch in the couches of rush and vineleaves, hearing in the water plashing from the cave and in the cries of the cicadas and birds and in the humming of the bees, smell in the autumn richness, taste in the wine, the pears and apples rolling on the ground in plenty and branches bending with the weight of sloes, a detail which also contributes to the overall appeal to sight in the shade, the couches, the grotto and the vegetation.[101] Obviously, it is a sensuous picture, and, once again, it is unique in Theocritus' pastorals, for not even the descriptions which the singers give of the sites they propose for their singing matches contain such richness of detail, as we shall see. Here too, perhaps, Theocritus' intention was to make immediate to the city audience the pleasures of the countryside and make the attempt once only. (To be sure, he paints effective country-scenes in the non-pastoral poems, *Id.* 16.90–7 and *Id.* 22.36–43, but in both cases, we shall find, his aim seems to be different.) There are other vignettes in *Idyll* 7 like the scene Lycidas paints in his song of the melancholy feast at his Ageanax' departure (63–72) and the humorous picture Simichidas draws of his dawn vigils with Aratus at the door of the latter's beloved, Philinus (122–5); but the two main descriptions are crucial to Theocritus' pastorals, for they supply unique visual information about the countryside.

The other pastoral *Idylls* have several instances of pictorialism too. The descriptions of the sites of the singing matches, for example, contain just enough visual material to set the tone for the match.[102] In *Idyll* 1 the sweetness and pleasantness of the sites is emphasised (1–23) and the tone of peace and harmony is set for the ensuing exchange.[103] In *Idyll* 5, however, Comatas and Lacon pour sarcasm over one another's choice of ground and eventually sing from separate sites (45–61); the descriptions here illustrate the bitterness of the two men's relationship. These passages thus serve to set the mood of the amoebean contests and to tell us something of the personal relations of the singers.[104]

The conversational fourth *Idyll* presents us with the scene of Battus and Corydon pulling a thorn out of the former's foot (50–7). This is the one passage in Theocritus that might have been directly influenced by plastic art. We have already considered the likelihood that Theocritus has in mind the motif of the Thorn Puller common in Hellenistic art; furthermore, the passage has no literary forbear, as far as we know.[105] But, for all the passage's pictorial realism, it is not necessary to assume that Theocritus has a specific statue in mind; art will have supplied him with the general motif, perhaps, but his well-attested fondness for *enargeia* will have provided the stimulus for integrating it into his poem.

We may close this section on Theocritus' pastoral poems by observing the close relationship between pictorial description and an important theme of the poems, that of self-delusion. The relationship can be most clearly observed in the poems on Polyphemus and Galatea, for example in the two companion-pieces on the theme sung by Daphnis and Damoetas in *Idyll* 6. Damoetas' song has Polyphemus claiming that he recently looked on the sea when it was calm and reflected his image; he fancied his beard and his single eye were handsome and his teeth gleamed whiter than Parian marble, so much so that he spat into his breast to avert the evil eye (35–40). The dramatic irony is patent. Daphnis has earlier teased Polyphemus by saying Galatea was merely playing hard-to-get, 'for often the unlovely has appeared lovely in the eyes of love' (18f.). That Polyphemus is unlovely is all too true (to all but a Cyclops),[106] but it is equally obvious that it is he and not Galatea who is in love, and that it is thus he who is love's dupe. True, the pictorialism of *Idyll* 6 is limited (though the picture of the dog barking on the shore at Galatea and mirrored in the water is both graphic and evocative: 9–15), but there is sufficient to point the contrast between Polyphemus' appearance and his false apprehension of it. *Idyll* 11, on the other hand, makes more extensive use of pictorialism in underlining the theme. There Polyphemus shows a pathetic concern with his looks by admitting the ugliness of his single eye and eyebrow (30–3), but fondly deludes himself about his desirability by describing at length to Galatea — and to himself — his wealth on land (34–66),[107] adding what he construes to be the favour he finds among the local girls, who are probably in fact coquettishly teasing him for his ugliness (75–9). Pictorial realism is thus integral to one of the major themes of Theocritus' pastoral poetry.[108]

Among Theocritus' urban mimes we have already found that one of them, *Idyll* 15, has an extensive pictorial element, that contained in the hymn to Adonis and Aphrodite (100–44); this pictorialism, as we saw in Chapter 1, is in close proximity to the everyday depiction of the Syracusan women. But in *Idyll* 2, *The Sorceress*, and *Idyll* 14, *Aeschinas and Thyonicus*, the pictorial realism is quite limited.

The encomia of Theocritus are not strikingly pictorial either. There is the charming picture in Theocritus' address to Hiero II of Syracuse (*Id.* 16) of the poet's 'Graces' who are sent back to him after a long and fruitless journey to some patron and of how they grumble to the poet about their task as if they were the divine Graces themselves and rest exhausted, their heads slumping over their numbed knees in the bottom of the box where the poet usually stores his poems (6–12). The passage is full of vivid everyday touches besides its appealing pictorialism, and it is through the two elements, seen once again in close association, that the Graces are personified. In fact it is only when the poet talks of his bookbox that the reader is absolutely sure that personification is involved at all, and the knowledge comes as a pleasant surprise. In the same *Idyll* there is a highly effective passage of some pictorial power on the peace that will ensue in the Sicilian countryside after Hiero's defeat of the Carthaginians who have been occupying part of the island (90–7).[109] Apart from these, there is really only the passage in *Idyll* 17, addressed to Philadelphus, which pictures Soter and Alexander in heaven in the company of their ancestor, Heracles, whom they escort home after feasting, Soter entrusted with his bow and quiver, Alexander with his club (13–33); the detail of Heracles' hunger is clearly alluded to, and there seems to be a light comic element in Theocritus' picture, the motivation for which we considered briefly in Chapter 1. Finally, mention should be made of the catalogue of Philadelphus' kingdom (77–94),[110] but it is not especially pictorial.[111] In the encomia, then, Theocritus' pictorial realism is not at its most extensive, though the lines on the Graces, on the peace that Hiero will bring to the Sicilian countryside, and on Soter, Alexander and Heracles on Olympus are quite graphically imagined.

It is, however, at its most developed and arresting in his epyllia,[112] which we shall now consider.

Idyll 13, the story of Hylas, invites comparison with the same episode as treated by Apollonius.[113] As we have seen, Apollonius deals with it in such a manner that the visual elements actually motivate the narrative. That is not the case in Theocritus' account. Certainly, there are descriptive passages, notably that of the spring at lines 39–42, and there are a number of graphic similes: evening is denoted as the time when chickens begin to roost — a *genre-*picture (10–13); Hylas' plunge is likened to that of a shooting star, at which sailors prepare for a rising wind[114] — another simile from ordinary life, though it is Homeric in origin (50–2);[115] and Heracles' frenzied pursuit of Hylas is compared with a hungry lion's hunt for a fawn whose cry it has heard (61–3).[116] Moreover, Theocritus achieves a curious effect at lines 58–60: when Heracles calls 'Hylas!' three times, the boy replies at each call, but, since he is under water, his shout appears to come from a distance while in fact he is nearby. Of course, you cannot shout under water, nor would you be heard on the surface if you could. But if we accept Theocritus' revisions of natural acoustics here, his novel law, by which sound appears to come from a distance if rising from under water, seems in its own way credible, and produces a strangely moving effect,[117] a variation on the theme of lovers who are near yet far. The actual rape is carried out here by three nymphs, which gives the scene a more impersonal and formal impression than its counterpart in Apollonius, where only one nymph is involved,[118] despite the fact that Theocritus spends more time drawing a tender picture of the nymphs comforting the tearful boy (53–4). There is, moreover, none of the visual motivation for their love that is found in Apollonius, nor is Hylas' position detailed as precisely: Hylas merely reaches down to dip his pitcher in the spring (46f.). Finally, it should be noted that Theocritus does not motivate the departure of the Argonauts in the detailed manner of Apollonius;[119] in the *Idyll*, the heroes merely wait for Heracles' return, but head off, rather arbitrarily one feels, at midnight and mock him as a deserter. The reason for the comparative lack of pictorial detail in *Idyll* 13 is, I suggest, that Theocritus was more concerned in a poem of small compass to contrast the themes and paraphernalia of epic with emotions felt in everyday life: hence, for example, the contrast of a homely simile (that of the chickens) with the epic notion of the education of a squire and the reverse procedure, whereby the two similes from Homeric epic, those of the shooting star and of the lion, illustrate moments of erotic tension. Now Apollonius is aiming at a similar juxtaposition, a point which will be argued at a more appropriate juncture,[120] but he has a broader canvas in which to do so — he takes over thirty lines to describe the episode at the spring alone — and can devote more space to evoking the sensuousness of the scene; as we have noticed, pictorialism is his chief means.

We come now to *Idyll* 22, the *Dioscuri*. If Theocritus' poem on Hylas has less pictorial realism than Apollonius' account, the situation is reversed in the two poets' versions of the fight between Amycus and Polydeuces.[121] But pictorial realism is given a prominent role right from the start of the *Idyll*, when Theocritus describes a storm from which the Dioscuri save sailors. We have details of how before the arrival of the gods the waves fill the hold and break the bulwarks, and the tackle and sails are in disarray, but once the gods arrive, the winds die, an oily calm returns to the sea, and the clouds disperse to reveal the constellations signifying fair sailing weather (10–22). Vivid description is thus an integral method for celebrating the gods, though of course appeal is also made to hearing in the detail of the roar of the sea as it is lashed by gusts and hail.[122]

The whole of the Amycus episode is related in a manner that could almost be called cinematographic. First we are presented with a 'still' while Theocritus describes in detail the landscape forming the background to the main action, the spring in which pebbles can be seen shining and around which tall trees and fragrant flowers grow (37–43). Next comes a passage exhibiting equal attention to visual detail, the description of Amycus himself: he is sitting in the sun; his ears are crushed from boxing; iron skin and muscles cover his chest and back; the muscles in his mighty arms stand out like boulders rolled and rounded by a swollen river in winter; a lion-skin hangs on his back and neck, its paws fastened together (44–52). The precision and realism of this monstrous figure, down to the detail of his 'cauliflower ears', has even prompted critics to regard the bronze statue of the seated Terme boxer, gnarled, colossal and cauliflower-eared as he is, as a representation of Amycus and Theocritus' picture of him, such is the emphatically 'plastic' nature of the description.[123] Moreover, the point of juxtaposing the two passages seems to be to contrast the idyllic scene with the hideousness of Amycus, and we have in them evidence for Theocritus' receptiveness to the aesthetic possibilities of detailed, vivid description. There follows a twenty-line passage of stichomythia between Amycus and Polydeuces, the point of which seems to be to underline the politeness of the son of Zeus.[124]

It is, of course, the boxing-match in which Theocritus invests his most extraordinary powers of observation, and this is made all the more obvious, if that were needed, by comparison with Apollonius' version; the boxing-fights in Homer appear very remote ancestors indeed. We gain the impression that the poet has set himself the question: 'Precisely how would a hero out-box a giant of a man like Amycus?' In answering it, he shows a shrewd knowledge of the noble art, as critics have noted.[125] Throughout, Polydeuces' 'finesse' is emphasised as against the brute force of Amycus. Though there is a wealth of pictorial detail in the earlier stages of the fight (75–114),[126] it is remarkably precise in the final exchange. Amycus chooses a punch known nowadays as a right uppercut. His delivery is almost 'classical'; he takes Polydeuces' left hand in his own left (of course not allowed in modern boxing), leans forward bringing his body at an angle to his earlier stance (right shoulder now forward, we infer), using his left foot behind him as a spring to bring his whole weight to bear on his delivery, which he makes with his right hand coming up from his flank, indeed a dangerous punch as Theocritus remarks; but Polydeuces weaves to one side and strikes Amycus on the left temple (118–25). Theocritus has thought the body-positions out perfectly: Amycus is holding Polydeuces' left hand with his own and has exposed the left side of his head by doing so; Polydeuces' right fist is free and can be used on Amycus' unguarded left temple efficiently and from close range. He follows up his punch with a left to Amycus' mouth so that his teeth rattle, and after some quick fist-work the fight is ended (126–30). The effect of the passage is 'filmic', to use a vogue term.

Now the pictorial realism in the first part of *Idyll* 22 may be intended to serve thematic ends. The second half of the poem tells of how Polydeuces and Castor carried off the daughters of Leucippus from Lynceus and Idas, to whom they were about to be wed. The episode is understandably not as pictorially detailed as the preceding, though the fight between Castor and Lynceus is both graphically and realistically narrated (181–204);[127] but it amply illustrates the disquieting moral with which Theocritus concludes the poem, that it is not a light matter to war with the Dioscuri, whom Theocritus in his poem has called 'saviours of mankind' (6).[128]

The twenty-fourth *Idyll*, the *Heracliscus*, further attests to Theocritus' fascination with realistic pictorial effects. The comparison between the poem and Pindar's first *Nemean*, which narrates the same episode and seems to be Theocritus' model, is illuminating. It has been made by several critics,[129] but we shall concentrate here on what it demonstrates about Theocritus' pictorial realism, though it will become apparent just how artificial it is to dissociate that from the everyday material in the poem. In fact, Theocritus probably also had before him Pindar *Paean* 20 Snell, in which the older poet again deals with the story, but our fragment of it tells us more about the use of the everyday in the *Idyll* than about its pictorialism, and so will be reserved for consideration in Chapter 6.

The opening scene depicts Alcmena tucking in the ten-month-old Heracles and his brother Iphicles.[130] The picture is lacking in Pindar, who in any case represents the episode as occuring during the daytime. Theocritus' choice of night as the time of the episode allows him, among other things, greater latitude for visual effects and scenes, of which the opening domestic picture is only the first example. The snakes are described in an emphatically pictorial manner (14–20). Though the description of them might not be scientifically realistic,[131] it is precise, if imaginative, and completely suceeds in explaining Iphicles' fear and highlighting Heracles' bravery as a little boy. Zeus' miraculous light sets in motion three events. First, Iphicles sees the snakes, which he could not have done in the dark, and his reaction is detailed graphically (23–6). Secondly, Heracles faces them and throttles them (27–33). Thirdly, Alcmena hears Iphicles' shout, senses danger from it and the strange light, and rouses Amphitryon from bed to see what is wrong, without letting him put on his sandals (34–40). When he takes down his sword from its peg, the light disappears and he calls the sleeping servants to bring lamps (41–53). The household is greeted with the sight of Heracles proudly holding out the dead snakes for his father to see and lightheartedly laying them at his feet (54–9); again the visual effect, lamp-light and all, is paramount. It is clear that the pictorial element in *Idyll* 24 motivates the sequence of events; moreover, Theocritus' night-setting of the episode gives him freer play with realistic visual effects than is found in Pindar,[132] besides allowing him to describe the heroic event as a realistically everyday picture of a happy family disturbed at night. Theocritus' emphasis on the visual makes the episode appear well within the range of the conceivable, and again we are invited to juxtapose the heroic and the everyday. Irony is of course a major effect, but so too, by the process that I have described, is realistic 'relating'.[133]

It will be convenient here to discuss *Idyll* 25, the *Heracles Leontophonos*. This splendid piece cannot definitely be ascribed to Theocritus, but it seems safe to conclude with Gow that its date is the third century and that it 'belongs to the school of Theocritus and Callimachus'.[134] It is almost entirely pictorial. The garrulous rustic describes the flocks of Augeas at considerable length (7–33). The sight of Heracles' lion-skin and club prompts the old man's desire to ask who he is but he refrains out of politeness (62–7). There is a brilliant vignette of the rustic's dogs barking at Heracles and fawning on the old man (68–83). A description of the stalls begins at line 95 and leads naturally to Heracles' encounter with the head of the herd, the bull Phaethon. Phaethon is the best of Augeas' twelve most noble bulls who attack wild animals preying on the herd. It is therefore quite plausible that when he sees Heracles' lion-skin he charges. As he does so, Heracles grasps his left horn and wrenches his neck to the ground, using all the strength of his shoulder; the muscles of his upper arm flex and stand out;[135] Augeas, Phyleus and the herdsmen standing nearby marvel at the sight (138–52). It is already plain that the poet motivates the action he describes by means of visual cues. Later Phyleus guesses from the remarkable lion-skin, to which attention has been drawn in the incident with Phaethon, that it came from the Nemean lion and that his companion is its slayer, and he asks him to tell how he conquered it (153–88).[136] Heracles obliges with an accurately drawn and easily visualised picture; his pose astride the lion throttling it from behind is almost plastic in the visual impression it creates.[137] The action is narrated with step-by-step, pictorially vivid motivation, and the poet thereby brings the exploit, remote from human experience as it is, into the ironic-realistic relation to the everyday that we are now familiar with.[138] It should be noted, too, that the poem as a whole consists of three vignettes in which Heracles faces animals: first the dogs, which the rustic easily quietens; secondly Phaethon, which Heracles demonstrates his strength in mastering; and thirdly the Nemean lion.

Moreover, these pictures are arranged in ascending order of gravity and excitement and, closing each section of the poem as they do, provide a thematic framework for the whole. Pictorial realism is thus integral to the structure of the poem and is indeed its most arresting feature, if not its actual point.[139] Finally, the poem is very similar to the *Hecale* in its admission of humble detail into epic, and here too pictorial realism is seen in close association with realism of the everyday and low; the rustic may, it is true, remind us of Eumaeus,[140] but the space devoted to the representation of the rustic is proportionately far greater than Homer allowed for the depiction of Odysseus' servant.[141]

We may now take stock of our findings on Theocritus. He evinces an extraordinary talent for evoking precise mental images and makes extensive use of it in the genres of pastoral and epyllion (though his use of it in the urban mimes and encomia is more sparse). Moreover, each of his descriptive passages has some specific function to fulfil. First, pictorial passages may serve a structural role, as in the cup of *Idyll* 1 or in the *Heracles Leontophonos* (if it is by Theocritus). Secondly, they may be employed to give a picture of people and objects outside the audience's experience and thereby to confer immediacy on the poet's material. Thirdly, Theocritus makes effective use of detailed pictorial realism in narrative, so that each stage of the action he describes is eminently picturable and can hence be more easily related to our experience, as in the first part of the *Hymn to the Dioscuri*. The problem of credibility is one that evidently exercised Apollonius, but Theocritus differs from his rival in that his pictorial realism often seems designed to lend even more obviously ironical humour to his new subject-matter, as in the *Heracliscus*. The fourth function of his descriptions is thematic. In the pastoral poems pictorial realism is integral to the important theme of self-delusion. Finally, we have observed in Theocritus' poems the close relationship between *enargeia* and *mimēsis biou* which has already been amply attested in Callimachus and Apollonius, so that we may now consider it a fundamental aspect of the poetry of the Alexandrian movement's most prominent members.

Herodas may be mentioned only briefly in this chapter, for his *Mimiambi* do not, except for the eighth, contain any extended pictorial descriptions. We would not normally expect that in a dramatic art-form like the mime.[142] Even *Mimiamb* 4, mentioned in the last chapter, is interesting not so much for any picture it gives of the works of art seen by Cynno and Coccale — indeed, the subjects of the objets d'art are only hinted at, as we found — but for the impression we gain of the characters commenting on the artefacts and their reactions to them;[143] in this it differs from its counterpiece, Theocritus' *Idyll* 15, for the hymn there contains the description of the Adonis-tableau. On the other hand, *Mimiamb* 8, which is the poet's manifesto (and therefore possibly non-dramatic), describes a dream retold by Herodas to a trustworthy slave. The poem is in an extremely fragmentary state, but we are in a position to make a rough assessment of its pictorialism. At lines 36ff. of the narrative, for instance, a contest is described: it is the Dionysiac ἀσκωλιασμός, in which competitors try to stand upright on an inflated wineskin; some, plunging into the dust head first like divers, strike the ground violently, others are thrown on to their backs; the whole scene is 'a mixture of laughter and pain' (43f.). Herodas is apparently successful in his attempt and is applauded (45–7). The description of the contest is lively and picturesque and acts as an effective 'build-up' to the literary point, whatever it is, that Herodas makes in his interpretation of the dream (66–79).[144]

We may now turn to members of the Alexandrian movement writing after its acme in the first half of the third century. Euphorion of Chalcis first claims our attention.[145] To judge from the surviving evidence, pictorial realism does not seem to have been a major factor in his poetry. This is demonstrated by our longest connected piece, from the *Thrax* (*Frr.* 24–9 v. Gr.): it contains a lament for a dead person preceded by a curse directed at a third person, probably the murderer[146] (*Fr.* 24c. 67–70 = *Fr.* 415 col. ii 23–6 *S.H.*); the poet expresses his hope for vengeance on the murderer, apparently citing as *exempla* the grim fates of the evil-doers Clymenus (*Fr.* 24a = *Fr.* 413 *S.H.*) and Trambelus (*Fr.* 24c 12–19 = *Fr.* 45 col. i 12–19 *S.H.*) and wishes for the return of Themis and Dikē (*Fr.* 24c 45–66 = *Fr.* 415 col. ii 1–22 *S.H.*). This kind of material does not exactly lend itself to pictorialism, especially given the allusive treatment of the myths.[147] However, we do possess a descriptive passage written by Euphorion which comes from a poem of unknown title. It is the description of Cerberus being dragged up from Hades by Heracles (*Fr.* 57):[148] either Cerberus is called 'tawny' or Heracles 'fair' (2); Cerberus is in a state of fear and his thick hair is matted with froth (3–4); his tail consists of snakes which cower beneath his shaggy belly, their tongues flickering around his ribs (5–6); the eyes beneath his eyelids beam darkly (7); thus do the flashes in the forges or on Meligunis[149] leap into the air when iron is beaten with hammers and the anvil roars under the mighty blows — or on smoky Aetna, the abode of Asteropus (8–11); when Heracles returns alive to Tiryns, women with their children tremble at the sight of him at the crossways of Mideia, rich in barley (12–15). This is the sole instance in the fragments of an interest in pictorial vividness; indeed, the description of Cerberus has been called 'overwritten'.[150] With this exception, therefore, the fragments do not permit us to come to any firm conclusion whether Euphorion went in for pictorialism to the extent that the other Alexandrians did.[151]

We come now to the last narrative epic poem we possess from the Greek Alexandrian movement. It is the *Europa* of Moschus.[152] The *Europa*, like the other Alexandrian epyllia, exhibits an overriding concern with pictorial effect. It is, however, especially interesting, for, dependent as it is on earlier poetry for many of its motifs, it is none the less entirely original in its deployment of pictorialism and represents a remarkable achievement in this respect.

The poem opens with the description of the dream sent to Europa by Aphrodite in which Europa imagines she sees two continents, in the form of ordinary women, fighting over her, Asia and 'the one opposite' (Europa must not know that it is she who will give it a name!) (1–15). Now, though it has literary precedents including, for example, Nausicaa's dream at *Odyssey* 6.15ff. and, indeed, Medea's dream in the *Argonautica* (3.617–31),[153] Europa's dream has the function not of directing the heroine to a course of action, as in the case of Nausicaa, nor of helping her towards a decision; indeed, the very point — and charm — of the description of the dream is that Europa has no inkling of what it means. Rather, it gives the *audience* a premonition of what is to happen and supplies information about what happens outside the poem, in particular about the naming of Europe, after Europa and Zeus reach Crete (162–6).[154]

When Europa awakes and joins her friends and goes with them to the meadows by the sea (28–36), she carries a basket which is described at length (37–62).[155] On it are three scenes from the myth of Io, Io in the form of a heifer in the sea, Zeus at the mouth of the Nile returning her to her normal form, and Hera's watchdog, Argus, whom Hermes has killed. The basket is described quite extensively: a pleasant detail is the way the peacock's tail surrounds the lip of the basket (58–62) for there the representation becomes part of the ornament;[156] some motifs, moreover, seem meant to suggest an artist's 'filling in', like the men watching Io from the cliffs. Yet the emphasis on visual illusionism is not as great as in, say, Theocritus or Apollonius. The point in this case lies elsewhere. First of all, the basket description, unlike its predecessors, deals with scenes which are connected in that they represent three moments of the same myth. The description thus has a unity that is not evidenced in its earlier counterparts.[157] This unity extends to an internal connection between the inset and its frame. The description forms a narrative illustrating Zeus' desires, Hera's thwarted attempts at hindering their fulfilment and his leniency once he has accomplished his aim. There is, therefore, an unmistakable parallelism between the scenes on the basket and the framing story of the rape of Europa, the owner of the basket.[158] And, as in the case of the dream, Europa is unconscious of how closely the decoration on her basket foretells her own fate; that is again something for the audience to appreciate, and adds considerably to the effect of the description.[159] The description of a work of art has become a method for prefiguring the outcome of the poem's main action,[160] and is the direct ancestor of the description of the bedspread in Catullus 64,[161] or Aeneas' shield in *Aeneid* 8.626–731, where actual events in Roman history are 'prophesied'.[162] The basket description thus constitutes perhaps the most sophisticated artistic use of a description of a work of art in Alexandrian poetry and shows how brilliantly the movement can exploit pictorialism.

The abduction-scene also pursues the aim of *enargeia*. It is the *sight* of Europa picking flowers in the meadow that moves Zeus to action (74f.), and it is the sight of the handsome bull that motivates Europa's interest in him and emboldens her to mount him. There is also the famous picture of the procession in which Europa and the bull voyage over the sea (115–36). A noteworthy motif is the way Europa grasps one of the bull's horns in one hand and with the other draws up the folds of her robe so that it does not trail in the salt water; it billows about her shoulders like a ship's sail and lifts her as it is caught in the wind. Now critics are keen to point to representations of the scene in fine art,[163] but the main inspiration is literary; *Iliad* 13.27ff. describes Poseidon travelling over the Aegean and is clearly Moschus' model,[164] though he has predictably expanded the pictorial element and added everyday elements, like Europa's concern for her dress. There is thus no need to explain the existence of pictorialism in the passage by recourse to fine art, though that too will have aided Moschus' imagination in a general way and will have been a simultaneous but secondary influence.[165]

The *Europa* thus forms a fitting conclusion to this section of our discussion. Its three main scenes are all eminently picturable and demonstrate several aspects of Alexandrian pictorialism, including its pervasiveness, its delight in detail, its association with *mimēsis biou*, and its use in motivating narrative. The basket description, moreover, represents a striking poetic achievement in its prefiguration of Europa's fate. Yet here the interplay of the miraculous and the realistic results in a degree of pleasantly humorous irony surpassed perhaps only by Theocritus. There is no aim to convince us of the authenticity of Moschus' account of the myth, no desire to help us relate to the narrative. It has been rightly observed that Moschus has captured an atmosphere of 'soft romantic charm',[166] and that is due principally to the sensuous richness of his epyllion's pictorialism.[167]

We may now turn to a brief examination of pictorial realism in epigram. It is commonly said that the form of the epigram does not lend itself to extensive pictorialism.[168] The point may be illustrated by the example of the epigram type which might be expected to exhibit descriptive writing. We have already seen how epigrams begin in the Alexandrian movement to celebrate the illusionism of fourth- and third-century art. So Asclepiades praises Lysippus' *Alexander* for its depiction of the king's daring (43 *H.E.*); Posidippus tries to cap Asclepiades' poem (18 *H.E.*) and in another epigram interprets, by means of a dialogue held between an onlooker and the statue, the allegorical depiction of Kairos by Lysippus (19 *H.E.*); Erinna expresses her admiration of a likeness of Agatharcis (3 *H.E.*) and Nossis has similar pieces on portraits of women (6–9 *H.E.*); Leonidas, as we saw, says Apelles' *Aphrodite Anadyomene* depicts the goddess 'not painted but alive' (23 *H.E.*), comments in similar terms on Praxiteles' *Eros* (89 *H.E.*), and makes his famous remark on the lifelikeness of Myron's *Cow* (88 *H.E.*); the last is imitated by, for example, Antipater of Sidon (36 *H.E.*; cf. 37–9), who also admires the lifelike quality of Praxiteles' *Eros* (44 *H.E.*), as does Meleager (110 and 111 *H.E.*); and so on. What is important to note here, however, is that, though these poems are invaluable indexes of the Alexandrian admiration of *trompe l'oeil*, they in general only actually describe the works of art in sufficient detail to identify them for the reader.[169]

Yet we do have several instances where the Alexandrians employed it, like all the other genres, for the purpose of pictorial realism. Leonidas, for example, has an epigram of the most traditional kind, the funerary, which draws a quite detailed picture (72 *H.E.*): an old woman, Platthis, has died at eighty; she was a spinner and weaver, and is pictured in her old age singing at her distaff and loom, smoothing and rounding the yarn by rubbing it on her wrinkled knee, working long hours. Thus the Alexandrians introduced pictorial realism (and in Leonidas' case low realism is often included, as in the poem on Platthis) into epigrams of a traditional type which did not normally depend on it for pathos.[170] On the other hand, they made extensive use of it in a type they themselves initiated, the erotic epigram. For example, there is Asclepiades' piece on Nicagoras, who denied that he was in love, but was given away at a party by his frequent love-toasts, his tears, nods, downcast look, and by his garland which would not stay in its place (18 *H.E.*).[171]

Again, epigrams now begin to describe places. Anyte has a poem on a precinct and statue of Aphrodite overlooking the sea which the goddess likes to see sunlit and calm for sailors (15 *H.E.*). Theocritus describes a precinct of Priapus with its statue, its stream surrounded by trees, its vines and birds (20 *H.E.*). Posidippus describes the Pharos lighthouse (11 *H.E.*) and a shrine of Arsinoe-Aphrodite on Zephyrium (12 and 13 *H.E.*). These last may be compared with a remarkable anonymous epigram dated to the late third century BC,[172] though they are far less pictorially detailed than it. It describes at extraordinary length and in technical architectural terms a Nymphaeum or a fountain. In its purely descriptive pictorial realism it resembles Callimachus' sixth *Iambus* (*Fr.* 196) on Phidias' Zeus at Elis; the approach obviously had enjoyed quite a vogue among the Alexandrians.

A very common type is the epigram intended for inscription on a work of art; it is to be differentiated from that solely concerned with illusionism in that it actually describes the subject of the work of art. So, for example, Anyte describes what is apparently a picture or relief of a goat near a temple: children have put reins and a noseband around the animal's shaggy mouth and are playing horses on it so that the god may look upon their play (13 *H.E.*);

this is, again, pictorialism and *mimēsis biou*.[173] Leonidas describes a statue, most probably, of Anacreon drunk and singing to his lyre (31 *H.E.*): the old man in his cups gives languishing glances with his lecherous eyes; his cloak trails in disarray; he has lost one of his slippers though the other is still on his wrinkled foot; he sings of his boy-loves to his melancholy lyre; the poet asks Dionysus to protect his attendant and not let him fall in his drunken state.[174] This description of a work of art has been considered exceptionally extensive,[175] but we have already seen a number of poems which are almost equally so. Yet even Leonidas' pictorialism is outdone by Meleager's poem on a painting of Niobe (128 *H.E.*). The poem is strikingly original in the introduction of a messenger who describes the slaughter of Niobe's children as a messenger would in a tragedy and the picture he gives is as vivid as any tragic messenger's speech:[176] he tells Niobe of the death of her sons, but then describes the death of her daughters as they are killed in front of him, as if on a stage; 'But what is happening now? What do I see?', he cries and describes what he sees in front of him: one daughter dies at Niobe's knees, another in her arms, another on the ground, another at her breast, another looks in horror at a shaft pointed at her, another cowers from the arrows, and another is still alive; but Niobe is struck dumb with horror, 'like a stone'. This is a remarkable experiment in pictorial description and creates in our mind an image the more full of pathos through its precision. These inscriptional epigrams yield further evidence for the Alexandrian poets' admiration for realistic effects in fine art and for the way they tried to emulate it in their own medium.

Clearly, then, the literary genre of epigram became in the hands of the Alexandrians another vehicle for pictorial realism, however refractory the form of the epigram may have seemed for the purpose. Moreover, the feature is present in all the Alexandrian epigrammatists, though, notably, it is not on the whole favoured by Callimachus, who chooses other forms of imagery for his effects.

We come, finally, to didactic poetry. Eratosthenes' comment that poetry aims at entertainment and not education has been taken to mean that the scientist found the genre foreign to his taste, and Callimachus himself has been credited with the view.[177] But it is hardly certain that Alexandrian didactic poetry was seriously educational. We shall, for example, see Eratosthenes incorporating scientific material in his poetry, and Callimachus expresses praise on a purely literary level for Hesiod's poetry and for Aratus' 'subtle discourses' (*Fr.* 2 and *Ep.* 56 *H.E.*).[178]

Callimachus' epigram coupling Aratus with Hesiod invites a comparison between the two poets. Realistic description was of course a primary concern to Hesiod in the *Works and Days* and it is one of the poem's chief delights; one need only think of the descriptions of winter and summer at lines 504–60 and 582–96 and of ploughing at 465–72 to be convinced of the truth of Fränkel's observation that 'more than any other early Greek work, this poem invites illustration by small pictures in the margin'.[179] And yet in Aratus' *Phaenomena* the expressed intention of describing the heavens and weather-signs for sailors and farmers is really only an occasion for the poet to describe to his educated readership his concept of Stoic benevolence.[180] In fact, strict pictorialism is quite rare. On the whole, the poet simply gives us enough detail to identify the constellation or weather-sign to which he is referring. A representative example is his description of the Dragon (45–62). The different portions of the constellation are located clearly enough, but the description is rather jejune, and that is true of Aratus' treatment of most of the other constellations too.

Apart from the merely identificatory passages like that on the Dragon, there none the less exist set descriptions which seem to be intended for variety. At lines 342–8 the constellation of Argo is compared with a real ship in a simile: the Argo moves backwards in the heavens just as when a real ship makes her final approach to her berth the sailors turn her stern towards the shore and backwater with their oars. This graphic comparison is obviously based on the poet's own observation. The two storm descriptions (287–99 and 422–9) are more literary in inspiration, and belong to the long tradition of such passages starting with the *Odyssey*, which Aratus emulates.[181] In the first, Aratus advises against sailing in December, the month of the winter solstice; daylight is short and so long journeys cannot be made; and if you sail at night, dawn will be slow to rise, however much you may be afraid in the darkness and shout for fear; the south winds buffet and frost numbs the sailor; even so, sailors throughout the year have to put up with the thought of deep water beneath them, and we sit gazing at the sea, our heads turned towards the shores which, further and further from us, are beaten by the surf; and thin timbers save us from death. In the second description, Aratus gives the advice that if clouds bank up above the Altar a storm is brewing; if a gust unexpectedly strikes the ship, it throws the sails into disarray, and sailors sometimes find their decks awash and sometimes, if they gain Zeus' aid by their prayers and the north wind brings lightning, they can look at one another again on board after their struggle. Now Ps.-Longinus[182] compares the first passage with an Iliadic simile of a wave striking a ship and covering her while the wind blusters about the mast and the sailors are terrified by their narrow escape from death (*Il.* 15.624–8); he feels that Aratus' phrase 'thin timbers save us from death' defines the action too closely; Homer's description, on the other hand, depicts men continually at the point of death, which adds to the sense of the sailors' terror. That may be true, but it can be said that Aratus' descriptions are more *realistic* than the rather hyperbolic passages in Homer, and it is significant that Ps.-Longinus quotes the first description in a section on the vividness of the imaginary second person[183] and praises Aratus for his *enargeia*.

Moreover, as befits a poem like the *Phaenomena* with its Stoic insistence on the ultimate providence of Zeus in aiding mankind with signs, Aratus occasionally expresses awe at the sight of the heavens, examples being his passages on Orion and the Milky Way seen on a clear night (322–5 and 469–79) where a sense of visual grandeur is conveyed deftly and concisely.

The section on weather-signs gives Aratus even more scope for imaginative visual writing. At the end of a storm, 'one would think the ravens are glad' from the way they shriek at evening, flitting now around the foliage of a tree, now on it to roost, now, although they have just landed, flapping their wings for sheer joy (1005–9).[184] Shepherds will be warned of a coming storm by flocks of sheep when they rush with more than usual eagerness to pasture, rams and lambs playfully butting with their horns, the younger, skittish sheep leaping up, all four feet off the ground, and the older sheep with horns rearing with two feet in the air, or when they are loathe to leave the pasture though it is evening, and they keep stopping to chew grass even though they are urged to move on by many a stone (1104–12). Here for once Aratus has allowed comparatively wide play to his descriptive powers and a graphic country scene emerges.[185] There is even gentle irony when he tells how ancient man noted that mice and dogs herald the onset of bad weather by their antics: 'then even the mice act as storm-prophets' (1132–7).[186]

Besides his informative descriptions, then, Aratus illustrates an economical but effective employment of verbal picture-painting, the function of which is to introduce variety where it does not express the poet's awe at his subject-matter. The extent of pictorial realism is, however, noticeably less than that of Hesiod or, for that matter, of Virgil's *Georgics*.[187]

An Alexandrian poem whose pictorialism Virgil paid the compliment of imitation at *Georgics* 1.233ff. is the *Hermes* of Eratosthenes. Its fragmentary state does not permit us to say for certain that it was a didactic poem. It seems to have combined mythology and astronomy, telling some amusing anecdotes about the god's childhood and how he ascended to heaven, and describing the universe as the god saw it from there. An extant fragment (*Fr.* 16 Pow.), containing the passage imitated by Virgil, depicts the five zones of the terrestrial globe in eighteen verses of great visual appeal, though the sequence of the description is a little unclear: the two polar zones are darker than dark-blue enamel (4); the torrid zone is dry and red as fire and is ablaze when it inclines beneath the Dog-Star (5–8); the two polar zones are always icy cold and dripping with water, ice covering the land, which men cannot penetrate (9–13); the conditions at the temperate zones are between summer heat and icy cold, and there the rich bounty of Demeter flourishes, and antipodean men dwell in the one of them (14–18). The lines convey an undeniable sense of grandeur through their pictorialism, and show Eratosthenes' willingness to include scientific material in poetry.[188]

We may conveniently include Nicander for discussion here, for, though his date is disputed, his most recent editors have tentatively favoured placing it at around the middle of the second century BC,[189] in which case he is later than Eratosthenes. His extant works, the *Theriaca* and *Alexipharmaca*, as well as fragments of his *Georgica*, reveal him to be a minor talent, but his approach to pictorialism warrants consideration.

The expressed aim of the two complete extant treatises is to enable the reader to identify snakes, spiders, poisonous plants, their effects on humans and the appropriate antidotes. The theme itself thus leads us to expect precise descriptions in which the visual element will predominate. Accordingly, for example, we have the admirably vivid description of the asp and its bite (*Th.* 157–89). The description of the death inflicted by the asp is interesting because it tallies with those of the medical writers,[190] but is more particulary so for its agreement with the account by Apollonius

Rhodius of the death of Mopsus, who is bitten by an asp, in *Argonautica* 4.1522–5, a passage which we shall examine in the next chapter. There are of course other examples of similar precision and pictorial vividness,[191] but scholars have found that many of his snakes and plants cannot now be identified from the description Nicander gives of them and that his descriptions can be quite unreliable.[192] It is evident that he is not describing 'from the life' but is dependent on his source, a certain Apollodorus.[193]

Nicander's pictorialism is not confined to graphic, if inaccurate, descriptions of venomous creatures and plants. In the prologue to the *Theriaca*, he states that the people he hopes will benefit from his writings are lowly folk, ploughmen, herdsmen and woodcutters, who are most likely to be afflicted by snake-bite at their several tasks, in the woods or at the plough (4–7). We therefore find in his poems many pictorial passages describing scenes from the lives of ordinary and low people. For example, he describes at some length the common habit of sleeping out of doors on straw beds in summer when it is too hot to stay indoors; he depicts the places one would choose, like fields, hills, glens, the threshing-floor, the water-meadows covered in rich grass, and woods; the picture leads straight in to his advice about fumigation, as a result of which, he says, one may sleep safe from snakes (21–56).[194] Another striking picture is that of the child who has just come out of swaddling-clothes, has stopped crawling and can walk 'without a cautious nurse'; his front teeth are just appearing in his gums and, to relieve the attendant itching, he might chew noxious plants, like hen-bane (*Al.* 417–22). There are several similar scenes from ordinary life elsewhere in his poems.[195] They are all plainly ornamental and call forth some of the poet's most attractive pictorial realism.

But what was Nicander's real aim in his two treatises? It has been argued that his style reveals his expressed intentions and intended audiences to be a fiction and that his actual purpose is the display of a philological erudition which will contrast with his unpoetic material.[196] Cicero was surely right in saying 'scholars agree that Nicander, though a man out of contact with country life, wrote excellently, but with a flair for poetry rather than for the countryside' (*de Or.* 1.16.69). Perhaps, then, it is true to say that his deployment of *enargeia* (often associated with *mimēsis biou*) is motivated by these purely poetic impulses. That would explain both his vivid pictorialism and his insouciance over accuracy.

Finally, we possess a fragment of an anonymous *Georgic*, which, whatever its actual date and provenance, probably came from Alexandria, to judge from its repeated reference to the Nile.[197] Two plants are described, the cyclamen and the persea. The cyclamen has deep roots so that, if the Nile were ever not to flood, it would still bring forth fruit for people to pick, not that that would ever happen, for the Nile brings such smiling abundance to the corn that it can be exported; the persea should produce beautiful fruit beneath its verdant leaves and will not ripen until its twigs flower around its first crop; its hardiness endures the Nile flood[198] and the lack of dew. In its detail the fragment reminds us of Virgil's pictorialist approach in the *Georgics*.

In sum, then, Alexandrian didactic poetry possesses, alongside the at least formally functional descriptions demanded by the genre, instances of a pictorialism which goes far beyond the mere exigencies of identification and even includes the representation of everyday and low life; it seems intended primarily as a poetic, ornamental device.

We may conclude this chapter with a summary of our findings. Pictorial realism is a pervasive characteristic of Alexandrian poetry. Traces of it are found in the fragments of poets as early in the movement as Erinna and Philetas; it is employed economically but with splendid effect by Callimachus especially in his *Hymns* and in the *Hecale*; it is pre-eminently observable in Apollonius' *Argonautica*, where problems posed by the genre of epic, like exaggeration, are confronted especially by means of the poet's insistence on visual realism to an extent far beyond that found in Homer; Theocritus' *Idylls*, especially the epyllia, seem meant as picture-poems, embracing description both of the static and the active. Moschus' *Europa* is an even more striking example of a series of pictures, though we surmised that even there the inspiration is primarily from literature rather than fine art. Euphorion's interest in pictorialism is harder to gauge, given the paucity of the fragments that have come down to us. The epigrammatists of the movement created graphic scenes and images, at times all the more effective precisely because of the form's brevity. The didactic poets, too, on occasion dwell on a picture for the aesthetic pleasure involved and to enliven what could be arid writing. A major impulse behind this pictorial realism seems to be a desire to bring the Alexandrians' sophisticated audiences into a well-defined relation with their poetic subjects, from which, as I

102 The Practice of Pictorial Realism

have argued, they had reason to feel cut off in time, place and spirit. It is obvious that the precise visual description of, for example, the grand world of myth is often playful or even ironical, but, as I have tried to suggest, the realism of 'building bridges' need in no way necessarily be precluded by that: irony, indeed, may even aid such realism, as can be seen when a Theocritus employs it in the very process of authenticating the Ptolemies' claim to links with the Hellenic past.

Notes

1. For literature see P. M. Fraser, *Ptolemaic Alexandria* (Oxford, 1972), p. 556 with nn. 21-33 (vol. ii, p. 792ff.).

2. *Love Romances* 2. The caveat should be entered here that the attributions in the *Love Romances* seem not to be by Parthenius himself: see M. Papathomopoulos, *Antoninus Liberalis: Les Métamorphoses* (Paris, 1968), pp. XI-XX.

3. See further *Fr.* 13 which possibly stands in the tradition of sea-storm descriptions.

4. So e.g. Wilamowitz, *H.D.* vol. i., p. 108 and K. Latte, 'Erinna', *Gött. Nachr.* 1953, 90f. (= *Kl. Schr.* (Munich, 1968), 521f.).

5. C. M. Bowra, in *New Chapters in the History of Greek Literature*, 3rd series (ed. J. U. Powell) (Oxford, 1933), 183f. and *Greek Poetry and Life: Essays presented to Gilbert Murray* (Oxford, 1936), 337ff. (= *Problems in Greek Poetry* (Oxford, 1953), pp. 151-68). M. L. West, 'Erinna', *Z.P.E.* 25 (1977), 117ff., arguing that no nineteen-year-old girl could have written a poem as sophisticated as the *Distaff*, concludes that it is a forgery by 'one of the poets of Cos or Rhodes who flourished toward the end of the fourth century or very early in the third'; it is, however, stretching credibility to imagine that a forger should be so close in time and place to Asclepiades (who praises the poem (28 *H.E.*)) and to Theocritus (who is influenced by it) without the fraud being detected by them. See further S. B. Pomeroy, 'Supplementary Notes on Erinna', *Z.P.E.* 32 (1978), 17-22.

6. Gow-Page, *H.E.* vol. ii, p. 282 includes her on the same grounds.

7. So Fraser, *Ptolemaic Alexandria*, p. 555; cf. D. N. Levin, 'Quaestiones Erinneanae', *H.S.C.P.* 66 (1962), 104; *H.E.* vol. ii, p. 281.

8. So Bowra in *Gk. P. and L.*, 341f.; cf. Levin 'Quaestiones Erinneanae'. Her 'crossing of genres' in composing a dirge in hexameters is scarcely conceivable before the fourth century: the dirge was traditionally composed in choral metres (Bowra, ibid., 337). See further below, p. 193.

9. Pollux 9.125. Cf. M. Michelazzo Magrini, 'Una nuova linea interpretativa della Conocchia di Erinna', *Prometheus* 1 (1975), 225-36; West, 'Erinna', 102f.

10. So Bowra, in *Gk. P. and L.*, 328; F. Scheidweiler, 'Erinnas Klage um Baukis', *Philol.* 100 (1956), 41f. and West, ibid., 101ff.; cf. Latte, 'Erinna', 83 (= *Kl. Schr.*, 512).

11. So West, ibid., 104; cf. Bowra, ibid., 328 and Scheidweiler, ibid., 42.

12. So West, ibid., 104; cf. Bowra, ibid., 328 and Latte, 'Erinna', 83 (= *Kl. Schr.*, 512); Scheidweiler, ibid., 41f.

13. So Scheidweiler, ibid., 42f.; cf. Bowra, ibid., 382f.; West, ibid., 103.

14. Scheidweiler, ibid., 47 proposes the former alternative; West, ibid., 107 suggests the latter.

15. See Scheidweiler, ibid., 46f. and West, ibid., 106f.
16. Relevant also is the reference to the girls' dolls at 21: Scheidweiler, ibid., 47; West, ibid., 105.
17. The fragment is discussed in detail by Fraser, *Ptolemaic Alexandria*, p. 731. C. Meillier, *Callimaque et sons temps: Recherches sur la carrière et la condition d'un écrivain à l'époque des premiers Lagides* (Lille, 1979), pp. 174–91 argues for the likelihood that Callimachus' descriptions of works of art — and of places like Attica and Delos — are in general inspired by the literary tradition of *ekphrasis* rather than based on autopsy.
18. See further especially H. Herter, 'Kallimachos und Homer: Ein Beitrag zur Interpretation des Hymnos auf Artemis', *Xenia Bonnensia* (Bonn, 1929), 50–105, reprinted in part in *W.d.F.* 296, 354–75. Cf. G. Th. Huber, *Lebensschilderung und Kleinmalerei im hellenistischen Epos: Darstellung des menschlichen Lebens und der Affekte* (Diss. Solothurn, 1926), p. 34f. The *genre* in the passage is further discussed below, pp. 182–7, where Callimachus' third major model, Zeus comforting Thetis at *Il.* 1.495–532, is also discussed.
19. See Wilamowitz, *H.D.* vol. i, pp. 90, 143 and 199; and L. P. Wilkinson, 'The Baroque Spirit in Ancient Art and Literature', *T.R.S.L.* 25 (1950), 2–11.
20. See below, pp. 124f.
21. The motif of the Cyclopes at work seems to have captured Callimachus' imagination: see *H.Del.* 141–7.
22. This is again a striking *genre*-picture; we are reminded of Erinna's *Distaff* 22–7.
23. The motif is also found in the story of Theiodamas in the *Aetia*, *Fr.* 24.1–3.
24. There seems to be some aetiological allusion behind these lines: A. H. Griffiths, 'Six Passages in Callimachus and the Anthology', *B.I.C.S.* 17 (1970), 33–5 argues that Callimachus is referring to the Cyclopes' mountain Aetna, with its bald peak as described by Strabo 273.
25. See below, pp. 186f. for the picture of Heracles at 142ff.
26. The palm-tree was most commonly considered the tree against which Leto rested, though other trees competed for the honour: see the *Homeric Hymn to Apollo* 117 with the note of T. W. Allen *et al. The Homeric Hymns*² (Oxford, 1936) *ad loc.*; cf. *Od.* 6.162f., Theogn. 5f. and Call. *H. Apol.* 4f.
27. At line 132 the river-god Peneius enjoins Leto to call on Eileithyia and, when Apollo has been born, the Delian nymphs sing the holy chant of Eileithyia, for, Callimachus tells us, Zeus has made Hera's anger abate (255–9). To that extent alone is Callimachus prepared to include the traditional motif; at the actual birth Leto is on her own.
28. Leto's pose in the Homeric hymn was the traditional one: see Theogn. 5f. and cf. Herodot. 5.86 and Paus. 8.48.7; delivery in the kneeling position was the general practice: see F. G. Welcker, 'Entbindung', *Kl. Schr.*, vol. iii (Bonn, 1850), 185–208 and Allen *et al., The Homeric Hymns* on *H. H. Apol.* 117. Thus Callimachus' alteration of Leto's position would have been all the more striking. Indeed, if Callimachus is following the physician Herophilus' recommendations on the posture appropriate to childbirth (see below, p. 125) his account may be scientifically realistic as well as dramatic.
29. See below, p. 189.
30. Without actually claiming direct influence, Wilamowitz, *H.D.* vol. ii, p. 73 compares Iris with the dog who waits on Meleager in the statue from the school of Scopas and also with the Attic gravestones on which slaves attend their masters; T. B. L. Webster, *Hellenistic Poetry and Art* (London, 1964), p. 174 considers that the statue of Cerberus at Sarapis' throne may have inspired the passage.
31. Fraser, *Ptolemaic Alexandria*, vol. ii, p. 931, n. 373.
32. F. Williams, *Callimachus: Hymn to Apollo* (Oxford, 1978), pp. 2–4; N. Hopkinson, *Callimachus: Hymn to Demeter*, Cambridge Classical Texts and Com-

104 The Practice of Pictorial Realism

mentaries 27 (Cambridge, 1984), pp. 3f., 35–9; A. W. Bulloch, *Callimachus: The Fifth Hymn*, Cambridge Classical Texts and Commentaries 26 (Cambridge, 1985), pp. 3–8.

33. I have made a preliminary study of the poem's realism, 'Callimachus' Hecale: A New Kind of Epic Hero?', *Antichthon* 11 (1977), 68–77.

34. After Pfeiffer *ad loc*.

35. See H. Lloyd-Jones and J. Rea, 'Callimachus, Fragments 260–261', *H.S.C.P.* 72 (1968), 133–5.

36. A. Couat, *La Póesie alexandrine sous les trois premiers Ptolémées (324–222 av. J.–C.)* (Paris, 1882), p. 386 observes that Callimachus' narration of the encounter, like Ps.-Theocritus' account of Heracles' mastery over the bull Phaethon (*Id.* 25.138–49) and Apollonius' description of Jason yoking the brazen steers (3.1306–10), aims at reproducing the impression created by a work of art.

37. See Lloyd-Jones and Rea, 'Callimachus, Fragments 260–261', 145. For further examples of pictorial realism in the poem see *Fr.* 288.51-2 *S.H.* (= *Fr.* 260.51-2 Pf.), where one of the crows swears by her 'wrinkled skin' (the lines are given to the crow by Lloyd-Jones and Rea, ibid., 142ff., against e.g. C. A. Trypanis, *Callimachus: Aetia, Iambi, Lyric Poems, Hecale, Minor Epic and Elegiac Poems, Fragments of Epigrams, Fragments of Uncertain Location* (Cambridge, Mass. and London, 1958) *ad loc.*, who attributes them to Hecale), and *Fr.* 304, which describes a Thessalian hat. See below, pp. 209f. for the description of Hecale herself.

38. Paus. 5.11.7; Strabo 353.

39. On the question of whether *Iambus* 6 is a joke see C. M. Dawson, 'The Iambi of Callimachus. A Hellenistic Poet's Experimental Laboratory', *Y.C.S.* 11 (1950), 72; H. Reinsch-Werner, *Callimachus Hesiodicus: die Rezeption der hesiodeischen Dichtung durch Kallimachos von Kyrene* (Berlin, 1976), p. 276. For other descriptions of works of art see *Frr.* 100, 101 and 114.

40. Fraser, *Ptolemaic Alexandria*, p. 664; cf. vol. ii, p. 931, n. 373.

41. So e.g. C. M. Bowra, 'The Meaning of a Heroic Age' (Earl Grey Memorial Lecture, Newcastle, 1957), in G. S. Kirk (ed.), *The Language and Background of Homer: Some Recent Studies and Controversies* (Cambridge, 1964), 22–47.

42. For the reduction of the heroes of epic, like Jason, to human proportions see below, pp. 201–4.

43. 1.524–7 and 4.580–3.

44. A reference to the ὑπόζωμα (the ropes bracing the hull of trireme); cf. H. de la Ville de Mirmont, 'Le navire Argo et la science nautique d'Apollonios de Rhodes', *R.I.E.* 30 (1895), 230–85, esp. 243–50. On the ὑπόζωμα see J. S. Morrison and R. T. Williams, *Greek Oared Ships: 900–322 B.C.* (Cambridge, 1968), pp. 294–8 and V. Foley and W. Soedel, 'Ancient Oared Warships', *Scientific American* 244 (1981), 117.

45. Cf. Morrison and Williams, ibid., p. 310, who think that Apollonius is concerned here only with oar-storage; but it is plain that the Argonauts are actually pushing against the protruding oar-handles (τῶν at line 380 going with ἐπαμοιβαδίς, ἐνέσταϑεν and ἐπήλασαν). See further de Mirmont, ibid., 249f.

46. Cf. *Il.* 1.480–3, *Od.* 4.780–4; 8.50–5; 9.471–2, 561–4; 11.1–5, 636–8; 12.144–7; 13.76–7; 15.287–91. The scene of the Argo setting sail and Apollonius' use of Homer in his description of it are discussed by de Mirmont, ibid., 250–9, 268–74.

47. 4.815–17, 865–79.

48. Ship-launching and sail-setting are not the only Homeric motifs reworked by Apollonius: for example, a comparison of the description of the sacrifice at 1.425–36 with Homeric models, like *Il.* 1.458–61, shows how much more Apollonius was concerned with visual detail.

49. Apollonius' account of Jason's contest (3.1278–404) is similarly pictorial: see above, n. 36.
50. See e.g. M. M. Willcock, *A Companion to the Iliad* (Chicago and London, 1976), pp. 209–14 and H. A. Gärtner, 'Beobachtungen zum Schild des Achilleus', in H. Görgemanns and E. A. Schmidt (eds.), *Studien zum antiken Epos, Beiträge zur klassischen Philologie* 72 (Meisenheim am Glan, 1976), 46–65.
51. At lines 730, 735, 742, 747, 752, 759, 763.
52. This is noted by J. Palm, 'Bemerkungen zur Ekphrase in der griechischen Literatur', *Kungl. Humanistika Vetenskapssamfundet i Uppsala, Årsbok* 1965–1966, 139f.
53. E.g. the picture of the city at war (*Il.* 18.509–40) and the herd attacked by a lion (573–86).
54. Apollonius stresses the lifelike quality of the final scene with an insistence foreign to Homer and Ps.-Hesiod; cf. *Il.* 18.548f., 561ff., *Sc.* 189, 194, 206, 211, 215, 228, 244, 300. On the relationship of Jason's cloak to earlier and contemporary illusionistic and naturalistic Greek art see further H. A. Shapiro, 'Jason's Cloak', *T.A.P.A.* 110 (1980), 263–86.
55. So e.g. Couat, 'La Póesie alexandrine sous les trois premiers Ptolémées', p. 306; G. W. Mooney, *The Argonautica of Apollonius Rhodius* (Dublin, 1912), p. 34 and his n. on 3.51; Wilamowitz, *H.D.* vol. ii, p. 182; Huber, *Lebensschilderung und Kleinmalerei im hellenistischen Epos*, p. 53f.; M. M. Gillies, *The Argonautica of Apollonius: Book 3* (Cambridge, 1928) on 45–110; D. M. Gaunt, 'Argo and the Gods in Apollonius Rhodius', *G. & R.* 2nd Ser. 19 (1972), 124.
56. There is no need to postulate direct influence from fine art on the passage as is done e.g. by F. Vian, *Apollonios de Rhodes: Argonautiques Chant III* (Paris, 1961) on 117, and F. Vian and É. Delage, *Apollonios de Rhodes: Argonautiques*, vol. ii: *Chant III* (Paris, 1980), p. 114f.: see above, p. 49f. Of course, knucklebones are part of Eros' iconography in poetry (e.g. Asclepiades 15 *H.E.* and Meleager 15 *H.E.*) and art (see Webster, *Hellenistic Poetry and Art*, p. 48; we think especially of Polyclitus' *Astragalizontes*, described by Pliny at *N.H.* 34.55) and Apollonius' use of the motif is traditional rather than motivated by any specific work of art.
57. Cf. the nymphs gazing at the sight of the fleece at 4.1141–8.
58. See further the interesting study of cave temperatures by A. J. Legge, 'Cave Climates', in E. S. Higgs (ed.), *Papers in Economic Prehistory* (Cambridge, 1972), 97–103.
59. Σ ad 2.729–35a; cf. Fraser, *Ptolemaic Alexandria*, vol. ii, p. 887 n. 83 and p. 892 n. 111.
60. See especially F. K. Dörner and W. Hoepfner, 'Vorläufiger Bericht über eine Reise in Bithynien 1961', *A.A.* 1962, 590–3 and Fraser, ibid., vol. ii, p. 892 n. 111.
61. E.g. Paus. 5.26.6 and Pliny *N.H.* 6.1, who calls the River Acheron 'Sonautes'.
62. H. Erbse, 'Homerscholien und hellenistische Glossare bei Apollonios Rhodios', *H.* 81 (1953), 186f.; he is followed by Fraser, *Ptomemaic Alexandria*, p. 634.
63. Erbse, ibid., 186f. and 187 n. 1.
64. Pollux 4.184, quoted by Erbse, ibid., 187.
65. The discussions of this episode by Händel and Köhnken are detailed above, p. 53 n. 47.
66. P. Händel, *Beobachtungen zur epischen Technik des Apollonios Rhodios*, *Zetemata* 8 (Munich, 1954), p. 31 notes that the reference to Hylas' training (1211– 20) motivates the water-search as well.
67. Above, p. 48 A. Köhnken, *Apollonios Rhodios und Theokrit: die Hylas-*

106 The Practice of Pictorial Realism

und die Amykosgeschichten beider Dichter und die Frage der Priorität, Hypomnemata 12 (Göttingen, 1965), p. 63 observes that the motif of the moonlight makes the irresistibility of Hylas' beauty the more believable.

68. See above, p. 48.
69. Händel, Beobachtungen, p. 31.
70. It is thus a visual motif which Apollonius chooses to motivate the departure of the Argonauts. For the lack of such motivation in Theocritus' account see below, pp. 85f.
71. In fact, the earlier rhetors, including Theon, Hermogenes and Aphthonius, had difficulty in distinguishing between mere narrative and 'ekphrasis of actions': see Palm, 'Bemerkungen zur Ekphrase in der griechischen Literatur', 110ff. It was Nicolaus who first, as far as we can tell, formulated a solution, by seeing in enargeia the factor separating ecphrastic from ordinary narration.
72. The rhetors recognised appeal to hearing as a source of pleasure in ekphrasis: Hermogenes Id. 2.4 (p. 331 Rabe), for example, praises Sappho's ekphrasis at Fr. 2.5f., 7f. Lobel-Page.
73. For wish-fulfilment as the origin of dreams see the Hippocratic treatise περὶ διαίτης 4.87 and 93 (dated by W. W. Jaeger, Paideia: The Ideals of Greek Culture, vol. iii (Eng. trans. G. Highet) (Oxford, 1945), pp. 33ff. to about the middle of the fourth century BC) and Herophilus ap. Aet. Placita 5.2.3.
74. So e.g. P. Friedländer, Johannes von Gaza und Paulus Silentiarius (Leipzig, 1912), p. 11f.; Huber, Lebensschilderung und Kleinmalerei im hellenistischen Epos, p. 83; G. Lawall, 'Apollonius' Argonautica: Jason as Anti-Hero', Y.C.S. 19 (1966), 158; C. R. Beye, 'Jason as Love-Hero in Apollonios' Argonautika', G.R.B.S. 10 (1969), 43 and Epic and Romance in the Argonautica of Apollonius (Carbondale and Edwardsville, 1982), p. 91f.
75. See especially Gärtner, 'Beobachtungen zum Schild des Achilleus'.
76. See further my article, 'The Love Theme in Apollonius Rhodius' Argonautica', W.S. N.F. 13 (1979), 54.
77. Cf. the wedding at Il. 18.491–6.
78. So Beye, 'Jason as Love-Hero', 31–55 and Epic and Romance, pp. 91f., 93, 171; cf. Zanker, 'The Love Theme in A.R.', 54, 72ff.
79. See e.g. J. F. Carspecken, 'Apollonius Rhodius and the Homeric Epic', Y.C.S. 13 (1952), 58–99; L. Gil Fernández, 'La epica helenística', Estudios sobre el mundo helenístico (Seville, 1971), 104–8.
80. So Palm, 'Bemerkungen zur Ekphrase in der griechischen Literatur', 119.
81. For the text see M. M. Campbell, Studies in the Third Book of Apollonius Rhodius' Argonautica (Hildesheim, Zurich, New York, 1982), p. 28f.
82. It is, however, exploited in the simile at 4.1062–5; there mention of the widow's children is entirely apposite, for it expresses Medea's disillusioned anguish on Phaeacia.
83. Thus Wilamowitz, H.D. vol. ii, p. 225f.
84. So e.g. the simile of the wayfarer at 2.541–6 goes far beyond its model at Il. 15.80–3: n.b. H. Fränkel, Noten zu den Argonautika des Apollonios (Munich, 1968), p. 200. See also e.g. the simile of the sunbeam which is reflected from water in a bucket on to a wall (3.755–9). This simile renders 'concrete', as it were, the intangible emotion of love; cf. H. Fränkel, 'Das Argonautenepos des Apollonios', M.H. 14 (1957), 17f. It also demonstrates Apollonius' eye for light-effects.
85. See A. S. F. Gow, Theocritus vol. i (Cambridge, 1952), pp. xvii, xxiii, xxvf.; Fraser, Ptolemaic Alexandria, pp. 309, 623.
86. The contrast of the bucolic description with its sublime predecessors is underlined, perhaps with gentle irony, at line 56 where the cup is called an αἰπολικὸν θάημα, 'a goatherd's marvel', recalling the phraseology of Il. 18.466f., 549 and Sc. 140, 224. See further D. M. Halperin, Before Pastoral: Theocritus and the Ancient Tradition of Bucolic Poetry (New Haven and London, 1983), pp. 161–89, 242–4.

87. See above, p. 50 and p. 53 n. 55.
88. Alexander Pope, 'A Discourse on Pastoral Poetry', (1709), in H. Davis (ed.), *Pope: Poetical Works* (Oxford, 1966), p. 11.
89. The motion implied here and at lines 33–5 probably means that Theocritus is not describing a real cup; cf. Palm, 'Bemerkungen zur Ekphrase in der griechischen Literatur', 144f.
90. Theocritus shows a similar interest in musculature at *Id.* 22.48ff.: see below, p. 86. Cf. *Pap. Vindob. Rainer* 29801 (= *G.L.P.* 123.42ff., Gow, *Buc. Gr.*, 170, lines 72ff.): Pan is blowing his pipe with such effort that his neck-muscles stand out.
91. The fisherman motif is also found in the simile at *Il.* 16. 406–8, where the treatment is even balder than that in Ps.-Hesiod and at *Od.* 12.251–4.
92. There is also the anonymous fragment of a fisherman simile quoted by Pow., p. 251.
93. So e.g. Gow on 27–56; Friedländer, *Johannes von Gaza*, p. 13; G. Lawall, *Theocritus' Coan Pastorals: a Poetry Book* (Cambridge, Mass., 1967), p. 30; U. Ott, *Die Kunst des Gegensatzes in Theokrits Hirtengedichten*, Spudasmata 22 (Hildesheim and New York, 1969), p. 132.
94. Cf. e.g. Lawall, ibid., pp. 27ff.; Ott, ibid., pp. 132ff.; T. G. Rosenmeyer, *The Green Cabinet: Theocritus and the European Pastoral Lyric* (Berkeley and Los Angeles, 1969), pp. 91, 191f.; C. Segal, '"Since Daphnis Dies": the Meaning of Theocritus' First *Idyll*', *M.H.* 31 (1974), 5, 10, 13, 18.
95. See further below, pp. 172–4.
96. Its graphic quality is such that it has prompted the conjecture that it is inspired by satyr-statues: see Lawall, *Theocritus' Coan Pastorals*, pp. 80–2.
97. There is a full bibliography on the subject in W. G. Arnott, 'The Mound of Brasilas and Theocritus' Seventh *Idyll*', *Q.U.C.C.* N.S. 3 (1979), 99 n. 1, to which now add E. L. Brown, 'The Lycidas of Theocritus' *Idyll* 7', *H.S.C.P.* 85 (1981), 59–100 and E. L. Bowie, 'Theocritus' Seventh *Idyll*, Philetas and Longus', *C.Q.* N.S. 35 (1985), 68–80.
98. F. Williams, 'A Theophany in Theocritus', *C.Q.* N.S. 21 (1971), 137ff.; cf. Bowie 'Theocritus' Seventh *Idyll*'.
99. See the literature cited in my 'Simichidas' Walk and the Locality of Bourina in Theocritus, *Id.* 7', *C.Q.* N.S. 30 (1980), 375 and 377, to which add Arnott, 'The Mound of Brasilas', 102f.; my article attacks the identification, and its thesis has been accepted e.g. by Bowie, ibid., 77 n. 47.
100. This is perhaps a reason for the repetition of the phrase αἴγειροι πτελέαι τε at lines 18 and 136.
101. So Ott, *Die Kunst des Gegensatzes*, p. 173 n. 478. H. White, *Studies in Theocritus and Other Hellenistic Poets*, London Studies in Classical Philology 3 (Amsterdam, 1979), 9–16 argues that the ὀλολυγών of 139 is not a tree-frog (as Gow *ad loc.* proposes) but a nightingale; cf. S. Hatzikosta, *A Stylistic Commentary on Theocritus' Idyll VII*, Classical and Byzantine Monographs 9 (Amsterdam, 1982) *ad loc.*
102. So e.g. Rosenmeyer, *The Green Cabinet*, pp. 187f.
103. So e.g. Lawall, *Theocritus' Coan Pastorals*, pp. 17f. See also *Id.* 6.3f.
104. When Virgil in *E.* 7.45–52 makes Corydon and Thyrsis tempt their mistress to their respective dwellings, a contrast emerges between Corydon's 'muscosi fontes' and Thyrsis' 'adsidua postes fuligine nigrae' which aids the characterisation of the two contestants. The pictorial emphasis on lowly detail in Thyrsis' responses surely in part explains his failure in the singing-match (69–70).
105. See above, p. 53 n. 53. The motif of a thorn is, however, also found at Call. *Fr.* 24.1, and there is the curious appearance of a cow called Lepargus in both passages; but nothing is known of their relative chronology, Callimachus' lines do not contain a description of thorn-pulling and the person with the thorn is no rustic.

108 The Practice of Pictorial Realism

106. See I. M. Le M. Du Quesnay, 'From Polyphemus to Corydon: Virgil *Eclogue* 2 and the *Idylls* of Theocritus', in D. A. West and A. J. Woodman (eds.), *Creative Imitation and Latin Literature* (Cambridge, 1979), 66.

107. In his eagerness he catalogues the flowers he might have brought her and makes his notorious slip over the seasons in which each flower grows, but he has still sufficient objectivity to recognise his gaffe, a fine mixture of irony and pathos on Theocritus' part (56-9).

108. Cf. e.g. *Idd*. 3 and 10; [Theoc.] *Id*. 20 is slightly different, for the neatherd may in fact be as handsome as he describes himself (19-31), although his city girlfriend does not think so; cf. too [Theoc.] *Id*. 21, where the fisherman's dream is dismissed by his companion's gruff comment ἴσα δ' ἦν ψεύδεσιν ὄψις (64).

109. See below, p. 192.

110. See Fraser, *Ptolemaic Alexandria*, vol. ii, p. 933f. n. 388 for the historical significance of the passage.

111. The picture of Ptolemy surrounded by his cavalry and shielded infantry in their flashing bronze armour (93-4) is a solitary instance.

112. Fraser, *Ptolemaic Alexandria*, p. 640 and n. 193 (vol. ii, p. 902), following Wilamowitz, *H.D.* vol. i, pp. 117-19, uses the term 'eidyllion' to denote short narrative poems like those of Theocritus or Moschus' *Europa*: he quotes with approval the derivation of the term from words denoting sight and argues that 'These poems probably owe something to representational art' (cf. ibid., p. 649). As I have argued, it is simply unnecessary to attribute pictorialism in Alexandrian poetry to direct influence from fine art since *enargeia* was already an aim within literature itself; as we shall see in the following section, moreover, epyllia, as I should prefer to call these miniature epics to distinguish them from pastoral *Idylls*, exhibit a pictorial realism which is demonstrably literary in inspiration; this will also be seen to be true of Moschus' *Europa*.

113. See Köhnken, *Apollonios Rhodios und Theokrit*, pp. 17-83. He argues that Theocritus *Idd*. 13 and 22 were written prior to Apollonius' Hylas and Amycus episodes; however, among other things, he ignores the important differences in the types of epic in which the two poets were working, and his ultimate criterion for posterity, to ascertain which is the better version, is sometimes merely subjective; cf. Fraser, ibid., vol. ii, p. 909 n. 229.

114. See Gow on 52 for this ancient belief.

115. Cf. *Il*. 4.75-9.

116. The Homeric motif is thus deliberately inverted, for the simile no longer refers to the heroic warrior, but to the love-smitten Heracles. Theocritus seems thereby to suggest that the old-style heroic attitudes are now outmoded, a stance also adopted by Apollonius, as we shall see below, pp. 201-4.

117. We are reminded of Orpheus' severed head at Virgil *G*. 4.523-7. Moreover, there was a tradition that Hylas was turned into an echo: see Nicander *Het. Fr.* 48 Schneider (= Antonin. Liberal. 26).

118. So Köhnken, *Apollonios Rhodios und Theokrit*, p. 63.

119. Cf. Gow on 68f. and Köhnken, ibid., p. 79f.

120. See below, pp. 201f.

121. U. von Wilamowitz-Moellendorff, *Die Textgeschichte der griechischen Bukoliker, Philologische Untersuchungen* 18 (Berlin, 1906), pp. 197ff. and Gow, *Theocritus*, vol. ii, p. 382f., followed by Fraser, *Ptolemaic Alexandria*, p. 645, regard it as certain that Theocritus was writing after Apollonius; cf. Köhnken, *Apollonios Rhodios und Theokrit*, pp. 84-121; with n. 113 above. The vastly more extensive pictorialism of *Id*. 22 should be considered as a further argument for the posteriority of Theocritus' account.

122. Lines 19ff. seem indebted to Aratus *Phaen*. 898ff. B. Effe, 'Die Destruktion der Tradition: Theokrits mythologische Gedichte', *Rh. M.* N.F. 121 (1978), 65 n. 32 argues that in *Id*. 22 the Dioscuri are presented as forces of evil

(especially in the latter half of the hymn), so that comparison with Aratus' Zeus, who in his beneficence to men sends the constellations and weather-signs, is intended as ironical. Effe's general thesis is challenged below, esp. p. 220 n. 80.

123. E.g. Gow, *Theocritus*, vol. ii, p. 390.

124. N.b. lines 54–60, 64–72; F. Williams, '῏Ω in Theocritus', *Eranos* 71 (1973), 54f.; F. Cairns, *Tibullus: A Hellenistic Poet at Rome* (Cambridge, 1979), p. 31. Apollonius' genre precludes this vivid form of interchange.

125. See e.g. K. T. Frost, 'Greek Boxing', *J.H.S.* 26 (1906), 217; Fraser, *Ptolemaic Alexandria*, p. 646.

126. Gow on 112 remarks: 'The picture of Amycus reduced by sweating from a giant to a pygmy is ridiculous', but his paraphrase overstates what Theocritus says and, further, the comment is unfair because the poet is drawing on medical terminology (συνίζανον: Gow on 112 cites Plat. *Tim.* 72d, Arist. *de Resp.* 479^a 27, 480^b 2 and Galen VIII.325.500 Kühn) to describe the constriction of the blood vessels from which Amycus would be suffering after taking a steady beating, a fact which Gow himself acknowledges. This is a realistic piece of observation, *pace* Gow, and the phenomenon can be seen in any situation where there is strenuous physical labour.

127. However, A. S. F. Gow, 'The Methods of Theocritus and some Problems in his Poems', *C.Q.* 24 (1930), 146f. points out that there is no room left for the γυμναὶ μάχαιραι in the hands of the Dioscuri (146) who are already carrying shields and spears (143). Similarly, as we saw above, p. 85, Theocritus has not bothered to supply a motive for the Argonauts' departure in *Id.* 13.68f. See, too, Gow on *Id.* 2.144 and 'The Methods of Theocritus' for further examples of this insouciance, which contrasts with the precision of observation we have noted in his descriptive passages. Perhaps these are 'the external matters' that Ps.-Longinus finds fault with (*Subl.* 33.4); see G. B. Ruckh, '"Longinus'" Criticism of Theocritus (Περὶ ὕψους 33.4)', *C.P.* 38 (1943), 256–9.

128. Effe, 'Destruktion der Tradition', 64ff. interprets *Id.* 22 as an 'Entlarvung' of the moral hollowness of traditional myth. Whether or not this is true for *Id.* 22, Effe's thesis that *all* Theocritus' mythological poems are likewise motivated seems untenable: see esp. below, p. 220 n. 80.

129. See especially Ph.-E. Legrand, *Étude sur Théocrite* (Paris, 1898), pp. 184ff.; Huber, *Lebensschilderung und Kleinmalerei im hellenistischen Epos*, pp. 22ff.; H. Hunger, 'Zur realistischen Kunst Theokrits', *W.S.* 60 (1942), 23–7; G. K. Galinsky, *The Herakles Theme: The Adaptations of the Hero in Literature from Homer to the Twentieth Century* (Oxford, 1972), p. 117; J. Stern, 'Theocritus' Idyll 24', *A.J.P.* 95 (1974), 348–61; A. E.-A. Horstmann, *Ironie und Humor bei Theokrit, Beiträge zur klassischen Philologie* 67 (Meisenhem am Glan, 1976), pp. 57–71; Effe, 'Destruktion der Tradition', 53ff.; F. T. Griffiths, *Theocritus at Court, Mnem. Suppl.* 55 (Leiden, 1979), pp. 91–8; B. Effe, 'Held und Literatur: Der Funktionswandel des Herakles-Mythos in der griechischen Literatur', *Poetica* 12 (1980), 145–66.

130. H. Herter, 'Ein neues Türwunder', *Rh.M.* N.F. 89 (1940), 153 points out that Heracles in Theocritus is at a more interesting stage of development than in Pindar, where the brothers are just born when Hera sends the snakes (*N.* 1.35–40).

131. Snakes do not normally spit. Moreover, as is pointed out by A. H. Griffiths, 'Notes on the Text of Theocritus', *C.Q.* N.S. 22 (1972), 107, commenting on line 14 (κυανέαις φρίσσοντας ὑπὸ σπείραισι δράκοντας), 'snakes do not bristle with coils' and his conjecture ὑποσπείραισι (the 'beard' of snakes) and his translation 'dragon snakes, with bristling deep blue beards' would make the description even more minutely observed. Cf. G. Giangrande, 'Two Theocritean Notes', *C.R.* N.S. 23 (1973), 7f.

132. *N.* 1 has 28 lines of dimeters and trimeters; *Id.* 24 has 63 hexameters. Moreover, *Paean* 20 Snell has little more pictorialism than the adjective 'gaily coloured' (ποικίλον: 11) describing Heracles' swaddling-clothes.

133. Cf. Effe, 'Destruktion der Tradition', 53ff. and below, pp. 174–81 with p. 220 n. 80.

110   The Practice of Pictorial Realism

134. Gow, *Theocritus*, vol. ii, p. 439f.
135. We remember the detail of the sinews on the fisherman's neck at *Id.* 1.43, discussed above, p. 80; see Gow on 148f., and G. Chrysaffis, *A Textual and Stylistic Commentary on Theocritus' Idyll XXV*, London Studies in Classical Philology 1 (Amsterdam, 1981), p. 169f.
136. Further evidence of the poet's care over visual detail is seen in his 'stage-directions' concerning the relative position of Phyleus and Heracles as they walk along: their path, which leads through a vineyard, is described as narrow (156), and Phyleus has to walk in front; at the point at which they reach the highway, Phyleus turns his head over his right shoulder to address his companion (159–61); when Heracles consents to tell the story of his struggle with the Nemean lion, Phyleus moves from the middle of the road so that they can walk side-by-side and the story can be heard more easily, and Heracles catches up to walk abreast of him (189–92); cf. Gow on 189.
137. There has been no lack of conjectures about possible models in fine art for the descriptive passages of the poem: cf. e.g. H. Herter, 'Den Arm im Gewande: eine Studie zu Herakles dem Löwentöter', in *Misc. Rostagni* (Turin, 1963), 322–37. See Gow, *Theocritus*, vol. ii, p. 441f.
138. N.b. the simile of the chariot-maker at 247–51.
139. This gives the poem the formal unity of a triptych: see I. M. Linforth, 'Theocritus XXV', *T.A.P.A.* 78 (1947), 77–87.
140. So e.g. Gow, *Theocritus*, vol. ii, p. 440.
141. Cf. too the *Epyllium Diomedis* quoted in Pow., pp. 72–6; there we find a lengthy description of Pheidon's dogs (3–18) and of Pheidon sewing and the son of Iphis being greeted by the dogs with wagging tails (29–40). The poem thus bears striking resemblances to Callimachus' *Molorchus* and *Hecale* and *Id.* 25.
142. G. Mastromarco, *Il pubblico di Eronda*, *Proagones* 15 (Padua, 1979) (Eng. trans. *The Public of Herondas*, London Studies in Classical Philology II (Amsterdam, 1984)), pp. 43–105 (= Eng. trans., pp. 21–63) argues forcefully and convincingly for the view that the *Mimiambi* were presented on the stage by actors and with stage-scenery. Of course, a special place was reserved for pictorialism in drama in the messenger-speeches of tragedy, though Euripides also admitted it into the monody of his *Ion* (82–183).
143. So e.g. W. Headlam, and (edited by A.D. Knox), *Herodas: the Mimes and Fragments* (Cambridge, 1922), p. xliiif.; Palm, 'Bemerkungen zur Ekphrase in der griechischen Literatur', 149; see also Mastromarco, ibid., p. 103f. (= Eng. trans., p. 61f.).
144. See Fraser, *Ptolemaic Alexandria*, vol. ii, p. 1050 n. 247; I. C. Cunningham, *Herodas: Mimiambi* (Oxford, 1971), p. 194; Mastromarco, ibid., pp. 115–23 (= Eng. trans., pp. 70–80).
145. B. A. van Groningen, *Euphorion* (Amsterdam, 1977), p. 249f. dates Euphorion's birth to 272–68, following the *Suda*, and attempts to trace his career down to 223, when he accepted Antiochus the Great's invitation to Syria to take charge of the royal library.
146. So van Groningen, ibid., p. 91.
147. Ibid., p. 90: see in general pp. 254, 256, 265f., 267.
148. = *Fr.* 51 Pow., *G.L.P.* 121 (a) (1).
149. Lipara: cf. Call. *H.* 3.47f.
150. J. U. Powell, in *New Chapters*, 1st series (Oxford, 1921), 110.
151. Mention should here be made of the description of Atē by Rhianus (*Fr.* 1.17–21 Pow.), though he was not an Alexandrian in the sense in which I am using the term in this book (see K. Ziegler, *Das hellenistische Epos: ein vergessenes Kapitel griechischer Dichtung* (2nd edn) (Leipzig, 1966), pp. 19ff.). His model is *Il.* 19.91–4. The picture there is mainly intended to illustrate how Atē affects men's minds: this it does by the graphic image of Atē's walking not on the ground but on

men's heads. The same idea is present in Rhianus, but he adds significant details. The phrases 'delicate feet' and 'on the tops of men's heads' are retained; new, however, are her invisibility and unnoticed approach, the way she sometimes appears as a young transgression among older ones, at others an old transgression among younger, and her service to Zeus and Dikē. The allegorical content has been increased through the addition of such details as Atē's standing amongst other sins and bringing gifts to her masters. The Homeric passage has been expanded and new details of a vivid, if rather fussy nature have been added. See further M. M. Kokolakis, "Ῥιανὸς ὁ Κρής, ἐπικὸς τοῦ 3ου π.Χ. αἰῶνος', in M. M. Kokolakis, Φιλολογικὰ μελετήματα εἰς τὴν ἀρχαίαν ἑλληνικὴν γραμματείαν (Athens, 1976), 137-9.

152. For his date see above, p. 31 n. 14.
153. The literary forbears of Europa's dream are well discussed by W. Bühler, *Die Europa des Moschos, Hermes Einzelschr.* 13 (Wiesbaden, 1960) on 1-71, 8-15, 16-27; he argues (ibid., p. 47) that it was Moschus himself who introduced the dream into the Europa story. For Medea's dream, see above, p. 75; for Moschus' debts to Apollonius' account of it, see Bühler on 2-5, 8-15, 16-27, 17, 20, 21-7, 22-3, 25-6, 25.
154. So Bühler on 1-71.
155. Bühler on 37 lists extant artistic representations of Europa and her basket and discusses the literary descriptions of metal baskets (e.g. Helen's silver spinning-basket at *Od.* 4. 125-35); he concludes that Moschus was indebted to the literary sources in the tradition of the Iliadic shield rather than to artistic representations or models that he may have seen.
156. Friedländer, *Johannes von Gaza*, p. 15.
157. So loc. cit., followed by Bühler on 37-62.
158. So Friedländer loc. cit., who points out the parallelism of lines 46 and 114; he is followed by Palm, 'Bemerkungen zur Ekphrase in der griechischen Literatur', 147f. and Bühler on 37-62.
159. So Friedländer loc. cit., and Bühler on 37-62.
160. So Friedländer loc. cit.; Bühler on 37-62 and p. 207; Palm, 'Bemerkungen zur Ekphrase in der griechischen Literatur', 147f.
161. See Friedländer, ibid., p. 16f.; Bühler on 37-62; Palm, ibid., 171ff.
162. Friedländer, ibid., pp. 19-21.
163. E.g. Fraser, *Ptolemaic Alexandria*, pp. 640 and 648f., vol. ii, p. 911 n. 248; cf. Bühler on 115-24.
164. So Bühler on 115-24. The motif of Europa drawing up the folds of her dress at 126ff., moreover, is probably modelled on *H.H.Dem.* 176: see Bühler *ad loc.* and N. J. Richardson, *The Homeric Hymn to Demeter* (Oxford, 1974) on *H.H.Dem.* 176.
165. Bühler, *Die Europa des Moschos*, pp. 25, 157 n. 8, and 207.
166. Fraser, *Ptolemaic Alexandria*, p. 649.
167. See also Moschus *Fr.* 1 Gow, describing the relative beauties of land and sea, and Ps.-Moschus *Megara* 91-125, which relates Megara's dream in great pictorial detail. Cf. too the pictures in Ps.-Bion's *Lament for Adonis*, e.g. that of the *putti*-like Erotes busied about the dead Adonis at 79-85.
168. E.g. Friedländer, *Johannes von Gaza*, p. 55 and Palm, 'Bemerkungen Ekphrase in der griechischen Literatur', 150.
169. So Friedländer, ibid., p. 57 and Palm, ibid., 150f.
170. Cf. Leonidas' poem on Theris, 20 *H.E.* There is also the anonymous epigram on the dog Tauron, whose death as he fought a wild boar and saved his master is related in graphic detail (*G.L.P.* 109 (1)). These poems, which celebrate ordinary and low life, will be discussed in a more appropriate place (below, pp. 162f.).
171. See also e.g. Call. 12 and 13 *H.E.*, Dioscorides 5 *H.E.*
172. *G.L.P.* 105(a), discussed by Fraser, *Ptolemaic Alexandria*, p. 609f. and vol. ii, p. 860f. n. 412.
173. See too Anyte 14 *H.E.*
174. Cf. Leonidas 90 *H.E.* and Theocritus 15 *H.E.*

112 The Practice of Pictorial Realism

175. E.g. Friedländer, *Johannes von Gaza*, p. 57 and Palm, 'Bemerkungen zur Ekphrase in der griechischen Literatur', 152.
176. Cf. the fragments of the *Niobe* attributed to Sophocles (*Tr. G.F.* 441a–451 Radt) and discussed by W. S. Barrett, 'Niobe', in R. Carden, *The Papyrus Fragments of Sophocles, Texte und Kommentare* 7 (Berlin and New York, 1974), 171–235.
177. So Fraser, *Ptolemaic Alexandria*, p. 623f. and 759f.: Eratosthenes' comment is recorded by Strabo 7 *init.*; cf. ibid., 16–17 and 25. For his scorn of Homeric geography see Strabo 24, discussed by Fraser, ibid., p. 527 and vol. ii, p. 757 n. 59.
178. On Aratus' and Nicander's pursuit of entertainment rather than instruction see B. Effe, *Dichtung und Lehre: Untersuchungen zur Typologie des antiken Lehrgedichts, Zetemata* 69 (Munich, 1977), pp. 22–5, 40–65.
179. H. Fränkel, *Early Greek Poetry and Philosophy: A History of Greek Epic, Lyric and Prose to the Middle of the Fifth Century* (Eng. trans. M. Hadas and J. Willis) (Oxford, 1975), p. 125 n. 25.
180. See Effe, *Dichtung und Lehre*, pp. 40–56 with lines 1–18, 408–12, 732, 741–3, 768–72, 1101–3.
181. *Od.* 5.313–32, 12.403–19; cf. the storm in Theocritus *Id.* 22, discussed above, p. 86.
182. *Subl.* 10.5–6.
183. *Subl.* 26.1.
184. See J. Martin, *Arati Phaenomena, Biblioteca di Studi Superiori: Filologia greca e papirologia* 25 (Florence, 1956) *ad loc.* for the difficulties in the text and construction of this passage.
185. See also 942–72 (birds' and animals' reactions to coming rain) and 1113–31 (cattle and wolf at the approach of a storm). But Aratus' pictorialism is nowhere near as extensive as that of Hesiod, as in the winter and summer passages.
186. Likewise Virgil gently parodies the bees at *G.* 4.67–87.
187. Virgil's heightened sensitivity over sound and visual detail will be revealed by a comparison of e.g. *G.* 1.356–60 with its model, *Phaen.* 409–12. See in general L.P. Wilkinson, *The Georgics of Virgil: A Critical Survey* (Cambridge, 1969), pp. 60–2, 84, 186–7.
188. Cf. Eratosthenes' poem on the duplication of the cube (*Fr.* 35 Pow.), though it is in no sense pictorial. For recent fragments of the *Hermes* see *Frr.* 397–8 *S.H.*
189. A. S. F. Gow and A. F. Scholfield, *Nicander* (Cambridge, 1953), pp. 5–8. For his debt to Callimachus and his membership of the Alexandrian movement, see above, p. 2 and p. 31 n. 15.
190. Gow and Scholfield, ibid., on 187ff. cite Philum. 16.3.
191. See e.g. *Th.* 145–56 (the seps), 190–208 (the ichneumon), 258–81 (the cerastes), 448–57 (the battle of the dragon and the eagle), 565–71 (the hippopotamus trampling fields) and *Al.* 186–94 (the symptoms of taking hemlock).
192. See Gow and Scholfield, *Nicander*, pp. 18, 20 and 24.
193. See ibid., p. 18.
194. Lines 48–50 contain a vignette from the life of country folk like Thracian shepherds who 'follow their leisurely flocks'.
195. See e.g. *Th.* 268–70 (a simile depicting the dinghy of a merchantman tacking to windward), 422–3 (a simile from the work of tanners), 472–3 (shepherds cooling themselves), *Al.* 167–70 (fishermen's children trapping birds), *G. Frr.* 80 (children eating the heart of a date-palm), 81.4 (greedy youths at a feast), 85.5–6 (a simile from the trade of the cobbler).
196. Effe, *Dichtung und Lehre*, pp. 56–65.
197. *G.L.P.* 124.
198. At line 15 (ὅτ' ἐγγύθεν ὄρνυται ὕδωρ) ὕδωρ presumably refers to the Nile flood (as ὄμβρος frequently does in Egyptian contexts); cf. Page's 'when rain rushes near'.

4 The Appeal to Science

It has become a cliché in modern discussions of the Alexandrian period to call it a 'bookish' age. The 'bookishness' of its poets is in turn often alternatively condemned as mere indulgence in the display of erudition or singled out as an especial source of sophisticated wit. Now it is undeniable that the Alexandrian poets do indeed frequently expect specialist erudition of their audiences, that they felt free to refer to fields of scholarship ranging from linguistics and etymology through to the natural sciences, and that in their use of learning they often seem bent upon creating exclusive games for *cognoscenti*. However, I wish to show in this chapter that the taste for erudite *jeux d'esprit* is not the only motivation for the Alexandrians' exploitation of scholarship and science, but that their aim appears on occasion to have been a much more serious one than is generally supposed, namely to confer immediacy and credibility on poetic subject-matter, in particular upon myth, or to define the distance between myth and the present. If that is so, their invocation of science is akin to their pictorial realism in both its intention and effects, but, whereas pictorial realism seeks to achieve its effects by means of the visual precision with which people, objects and events are described, the appeal to scientific knowledge involves the appeal to other fields of the audience's experience which are more indirect, perhaps, but certainly no less engaging, especially given the interest that must have been aroused in Alexandria by contemporary scientific research. We have, then, reached what was called in the first chapter the intellectual approach of realism's perennial mode.[1]

In the Alexandrian movement the appeal to scientific and scholarly knowledge for realistic effect takes four main forms: the use of a wide acquaintance with mythical traditions in order to select the most credible variants; precision in the geographical reconstruction of myth; aetiological evidence to prove the truth of particular myths; and the employment in poetry of science more as we understand the word nowadays, especially medicine. The subject is large enough for a separate work and we shall have to be content with adducing sufficient evidence to demonstrate the importance of this aspect of Alexandrian realism and to suggest lines of approach for further study.

The first topic, then, is the learned, 'informed' choice of variant myths or the reconciliation of divergent traditions, on the assumption that any myth retold in a coherent and well-documented manner — whereby any conflicting variants of it are ironed out — will of necessity be the more credible. The notion is of course already present in Aristotle's dictum that in poetry the impossible but credible is preferable to the possible but incredible,[2] but Callimachus gives explicit evidence on at least three occasions that it was a conscious tenet of his poetic creed. There is an insistent tone to each profession of it. In the *Hymn to Zeus* he claims that even Zeus' elders did not begrudge him Olympus to reign over, since his 'schemes were so perfect' (57); the versions of the ancient poets, that Zeus won Olympus by mere lot, founder on their incredibility, for no one, Callimachus reasons, would cast lots for such unequal prizes as Hades and Olympus;[3] the grounds for his choice of version are expressed in his words about telling fiction that will persuade his audience (65); the poet goes on to follow the Hesiodic account in stating that Zeus came to power by virtue of his might (66f.).[4] His criterion is that of plausibility. Secondly, we have his famous comment 'I sing nothing unattested' (*Fr.* 612). Its precise context is unfortunately unknown, but the thought is found throughout the poet's work; for example, before retelling the story of Teiresias in the *Bath of Pallas*, the narrator denies that he is inventing the tale, claiming that he is following other authorities and is thus recounting an established tradition (56). Now here he does not actually name the source,[5] in line with his common procedure in the *Hymns*.[6] But his practice in the *Aetia* is different, and here we come to a third occasion on which he demonstrates how much he values historical truth and verifiability, for he actually names a source, claiming that it is reliable. Leaving aside the numerous occasions in Books 1 and 2 of the *Aetia* where Clio, Calliope and Erato are depicted as telling the poet the information he requires,[7] we may note that in Book 3, at the close of the story of Acontius and Cydippe, he recapitulates in verse the history of Ceos by the mythographer, Xenomedes, whom he names (*Fr.* 75.53ff.) and calls approvingly 'the old man concerned with truth' (76). The appeal to credibility and to historical research is thus clearly an important element in Callimachus' approach to the recounting of myth.

Apollonius, too, offers striking examples of a desire to give the most credible version possible of a myth, even where he finds a conflicting tradition. The Hylas episode, to take a familiar passage, is a case in point. The variant traditions confronting Apollonius have been analysed by P. Händel and I am fortunate in being able to summarise his discussion here.[8] The strands are these: (1) Hylas' original home was Mysia; (2) the Milesian colonists connected him with the Greek saga; (3) Polyphemus was the founder of Cius; (4) he was erotically involved with Hylas; (5) according to the version of the Heracleotes the lover was Heracles; (6) some sources considered Hylas to be the son of Ceyx; (7) others said Theiodamas the King of the Dryopians was his father. Apollonius combines and reconciles each of these traditions thus: (1) Hylas is lost in Mysia; (2) the people of Cius call on Hylas 'even to this day' because Heracles had threatened to lay waste their land if they did not find Hylas again (1.1348ff.); (3) Polyphemus is destined to be the founder of Cius in Mysia (1321ff. and 1345ff.); (4) Polyphemus reports Hylas' loss to Heracles and shows deep concern for the boy's fate (1240–60); (5) Heracles is made the lover (1211–20); (6) the hostages whom the Cians gave Heracles as their pledge that they would search for Hylas are said to have been settled in Trachis of which Ceyx was king (1354–7); (7) Theiodamas is made the father of Hylas (1211–20). The result of this combination of versions is a freely flowing, unified and plausible narrative, the motivation of which, as we have seen, is notable for its cogency and its dependence on graphically visual detail. All in all, the episode is a remarkable achievement.[9]

The impulse is not so observable in Theocritus, however. To be sure, Gorgo's comment in *Idyll* 15 that the singer 'knows so much' may simply be part of the fun at Gorgo's expense, but it does perhaps show, even if ironically, that the Alexandrian age set great store by erudition in the poetic presentation of myth and that audiences expected it of their poets; it is, moreover, evident that the key poets of the movement apart from Theocritus considered the plausible reconciliation of variants to be an important aspect of erudition in poetry. Euphorion, too, stands outside the general trend: the aim of his erudite, allusive treatment of myth seems, as it has been put, to be *poésie verbale*,[10] and there is no apparent realism in his erudition.

The second method by which the Alexandrian poets tried to render their tales more convincing is the reference to existing and still observable geographical phenomena and landmarks, the history of which was connected with the mythical events being narrated. Such landmarks are described carefully in order to put the heroes of the mythical past into the world as people knew it. The fact that this may properly be termed realistic is demonstrated by the phraseology associated with it. The myth behind the landmark is described, and then the landmark itself, which may be seen 'to this day' (εἰσέτι νῦν γε, ἐξέτι κείνου, ἔνθεν or the like),[11] thus making explicit the connection of mythical past with observable present.

Callimachus yields definite evidence for this kind of realism. An example is to be found in his *Hymn to Zeus*: there the story is told of how, when Rheia had given birth to Zeus and was leaving the Cretan town of Thenae for Cnossus, Zeus' umbilical cord fell away, for which reason (ἔνθεν), Callimachus tells us, the Cretan Cydonians call the plain the Omphalian Plain (42–4).[12] This is not to say that Callimachus' interest in geography and other matters is in each case realistic. Indeed, in the *Hymn to Delos* itself the poet devotes one hundred and thirty lines to the description of Leto's flight; we can only conclude that here he is parading his knowledge of geography.[13] Yet it cannot be denied that on occasion his intention in geographical references is realistic in an important way.

However, by the very nature of his subject, it is Apollonius' *Argonautica* which can be expected most clearly to illustrate the geographical realism under consideration. We have already discussed one example of this in Apollonius: the description of the Acherousian headland (2.728–51). There are also many geographical references in which a landmark is said 'even to this day' to bear witness to the historicity of a mythical occurrence: for example, when the Argonauts have seen Apollo after they have been rowing all night, they set up a temple to Concord which stands εἰσέτι νῦν γε (2.717);[14] a barrow near the Acherousian headland which was dedicated to the Argonaut Idmon killed by a boar is said to 'remain a memorial even for men of a later age to see' (2.842);[15] another barrow is built up in memory of the helmsman, Tiphys, directly after Idmon's death, so that 'two monuments can still be seen' (2.853).

Now there are Homeric ancestors of the device of pointing to a landmark made by men of former days. One instructive instance may be found at *Iliad* 23.326–33, where Nestor tells Antilochus of the turning-point for the chariot-race in Patroclus' funeral games: Nestor conjectures that the marker, a petrified trunk with stones leaning against it, is either a monument (σῆμα) of a man who died long ago or a turning-post made by men of old. But Homer makes no attempt to relate the landmark to the observable present for his audience, and the comparison shows how much more realistic Apollonius' procedure is. The same may be said, for example, of *Iliad* 22.147–56, the description of the springs which Hector and Achilles run past: however poignant the reference to their peacetime functions may be, Homer is in no sense at pains to relate his account to the known physical world. Neither is the Alexandrian use of the device to be descried in the narration of Odysseus' wanderings. Homer, it appears, is too close to myth to need this kind of realism, though the Alexandrians have frequent recourse to it.

Apollonius displays another kind of geographical erudition by mentioning tribes which existed in his own day, for instance the Mossynoeci, and, in order to render his account of the Argonauts' outward journey more vivid and engaging, he gives a few exotic details of their way of life. Phineus tells the Argonauts about the tribe: they build wooden houses and towers on stilts which they call *mossynae*, from which they derive their name (2.379–81[b]). But when the Argonauts actually pass the tribe, Apollonius airs even more knowledge of their *mores*: they do the opposite of what is normal in Greek lands, doing at home all the things the Greeks do openly and 'unshamedly do outside, in the middle of streets' all the things the Greeks do in their homes, even having sexual intercourse in the open air; the king dispenses justice in the tallest of the huts but if he makes any mistaken judgement, they shut him up and starve him (2.1018–29). The two passages present a picture of the tribe like any to be found in Greek historical writings, especially those of Herodotus, who makes a generalisation very similar to that of Apollonius about public and private manners in Greece and Egypt.[16] In fact, the scholiast informs us that the historians Ephorus and Nymphodorus documented the story of the treatment of the judge[17] and Apollonius is probably following them here as he does elsewhere.[18] This is proof of the poet's use of ethnographical scholarship both to lend an atmosphere of romantic remoteness to his narrative and to give an authentic feel to his reconstruction of the Argonaut saga.

It is probable, moreover, that in geographical matters on which

Apollonius is demonstrably wrong his mistakes are the result of his reliance on scholars who he possibly thought could be expected to give the most authoritative information available; indeed, by following them, he may have thought he was being conscientiously realistic. For example, Argus tells the heroes on their return journey that the Danube bifurcates and debouches into the Euxine and the Adriatic (4.288–93). But Apollonius' misconception is not caused by a lack of scientific research, for the scholiast tells us that he is following the geographer Timagetus.[19] Apart from this, he mistakenly assumes the confluence of the Po and the Rhone, for he makes the Argonauts pass into the Po (4.596), then the Rhone (4.627f.) and, after an abortive excursion down the Rhine, back down the Rhone to the Mediterranean (4.634–58). Here, too, he is following Timagetus.[20] He seems to us to be at the mercy of his sources, yet merely by following what he must have considered to be authoritative accounts he probably demonstrates his desire to give his audience an accurate and convincing reconstruction of the Argonauts' return journey with the best information at his disposal.[21] If that is so, his procedure is realistic.

It is interesting in this context to note that the Alexandrian poets had recourse to a less reputable form of scholarship which enjoyed a considerable vogue in the period. It is what we may call the Wonder-Book, which aims to collect and describe bizarre information about purported facts of the natural world. This kind of 'scholarship', which can hardly be called scientific by modern standards, seems to have been a perversion of Aristotelian scientific inquiry.[22] Callimachus himself composed a *Collection of Marvels throughout the World Arranged by Place* (*Fr.* 407), probably under the influence of a desire for recondite knowledge rather than out of a serious historical intent.[23] However, amid much fabulous material, he records recognised natural phenomena, one example being the lethal effects of fumes upon birds flying over areas giving off gases or intense heat; he specifically refers to a marsh in the land of the Sarmatae and two craters in Sicily (*Fr.* 407.24 and 31). This motif occurs in the *Argonautica* (4.601–3) and is culled, no doubt, from quasi-scientific sources like Callimachus' treatise. Now curiosities like this, however incredible they may at times appear to us, were reported to be true and may even have commanded actual belief;[24] the point is, however, that the example just quoted probably does have some basis in nature. It is thus interesting to see Apollonius selecting factual details from a wealth of extraordinary information available in the marvel-treatises of his day. In fact his poem is relatively free of paradoxographical material.

The procedure of Theocritus, however, in those epyllia which deal with mythological themes, differs from that of Callimachus and Apollonius, for he is content merely to indicate in vague terms the dramatic location of his poems and indeed at times to leave that to the audience's general knowledge. *Idyll* 13 is located within the Propontis near Cius (30f.); *Idyll* 18, the *Epithalamium of Helen*, is located in front of Menelaus and Helen's bridal chamber at Sparta (1,3); in *Idyll* 22 the boxing-match takes place in the land of the Bebrycians, of which Amycus is the king, and the fight between the Dioscuri and Apharidae is set without precise location in the Peloponnese (155–8); the geographical vagueness of *Idyll* 24, on the other hand, may be quite deliberate, for the suppression of Thebes as the poem's setting may be intended to facilitate the comparison of Philadelphus with Heracles at Alexandria, a matter which we shall discuss later.[25] Geographical precision in the retelling of myth is therefore generally not of great importance to Theocritus, and, indeed, in the case of *Idyll* 24, may have been something which he consciously avoided.

Similarly, the pastoral poems are on the whole not localised with any great precision.[26] An important exception, however, is *Idyll* 7, which definitely has as its *mise en scène* the Island of Cos. Simichidas, whom I follow the scholia in taking to be Theocritus,[27] walks with friends westwards from Cos-city (2) to the Haleis, probably the deme, but possibly a river or a town which can be located about ten kilometres west of Cos-city on the north coast of the island. As he walks he is joined by Lycidas, a goatherd.[28] During the discussion in which they express their common abhorrence of contemporary poets who persist in emulating Homer, Lycidas claims that their efforts are as futile as those of the builder who tries to build a house as high as Oromedon; this is the ancient name of the highest peak on the mountain-range of Cos plainly visible to wayfarers on their left. After the singing-match, Lycidas turns left and takes the road to Pyxa, located in the foothills west-south-west of Cos-city; Simichidas and his friends turn right to the Haleis (130–2). Moreover, at the beginning of the poem Theocritus mentions an ancient spring with which the family of his hosts at the Haleis have traditionally been associated. Its ancient name was Bourina (and was apparently given its old name again in the early nineteenth century) and it is located about a kilometre south and upland of the Asclepieion, which in imperial times it supplied with water; Theocritus mentions it and describes it at some length (6–9) probably to comment in a complimentary manner on the hallowed antiquity of his hosts' family. He thus describes in precise terms a walk he certainly could have taken while resident on the island and refers to actual landmarks there, like Bourina. This geographical realism is unique in Theocritean and, indeed, Greek pastoral, and we are perhaps entitled to conjecture here why Theocritus has broken with his usual practice. There is, first, the likelihood that he is referring to real people when he mentions folk like his hosts at the festival, the noble Phrasidamus and Antigenes, so a description of a walk to their property is appropriate. On another level, there is the matter of the alleged theophany. We have seen already that Lycidas has been identified with a deity, perhaps Apollo;[29] if that is so, then the meeting will have been fictitious, but Theocritus seems to have wanted to confer immediacy, if not credibility on his account of it, though there are of course elements of irony in the description of the meeting, if only the humorous realism in the representation of Lycidas-Apollo. It is topical in such accounts of theophanies that the time and place of the encounter are specified with considerable precision.

Euphorion, to close this section, incorporates much recondite geographical lore into his poetry. In *Fr.* 80, for example, he refers to the Arganthonian mountain-range in Bithynia. In fact, his knowledge of the geography of Asia Minor is so recondite that it has been suggested that he gained a familiarity with it from his travels there.[30] Once again, however, it is extremely difficult, given the fragmentary nature of our evidence and the poet's own allusiveness, to ascertain what his intention was in such recherché references, but his poetry bears no sign of religious or emotional involvement with myth, and we seem to be left once more with the conclusion that his main interest is *poésie verbale*.

Aetiology is the third branch of scholarly research which, I argue, can be described as the product of a realistic impulse. This statement may at first sight appear rather strange, for modern critics commonly label Hellenistic aetiology as 'preciosity', 'antiquarianism' and the like.[31] But in fact aetiology was capable of being used as a vehicle for providing a much needed sense of cultural continuity for the Greek intelligentsia resident in the newly founded city of Alexandria in the first half of the third century BC. It will have enabled them to see the cult-practices and traditions of the Greek world as rooted in the mythical past and enriched by association with it. Simultaneously, the mythical past will have been 'verified' by the evidence of the still observable cults and institutions, which can be traced back into it: εἰσέτι νῦν περ, ἔνθεν and the like are once again the standard phrases;[32] this too will have helped alleviate the problem of cultural identity experienced by the early Alexandrian Greeks. Thus a two-way process is set up in which realism, bridging the gap between past and present by appeal to tangible evidence, plays an essential role. Interesting also are the instances where we find aitia explaining the recently initiated cults of Alexandria itself. We have discussed the latter-day aition of the festival of Adonis in *Idyll* 15, Callimachus' *Lock* and Apollonius' *Foundation of Alexandria*, and have considered the likelihood of Ptolemaic encouragement for the court-poets to confer on early Alexandria a mythology comparable with that of the old Greek lands, and a culture and identity that could be construed as the city's own and at the same time as authentically Greek.[33]

Of course, the two-way procedure (as I have described it) is already observable in the *Oresteian Trilogy*: we have already seen how in the *Eumenides* Aeschylus is 'building bridges' between the past and present; he is also intent upon ennobling the present by appeal to its grand origins. Now the Alexandrians of the early period employ aetiology for similar ends, though their means are in one regard strikingly different. Whereas Aeschylus had for patriotic reasons emphasised the grandeur of the mythical history of the Areopagus, Callimachus and the other early Alexandrians often seem bent upon stressing the ordinary humanness of men and women of mythical times, as if thereby making them easier to relate to. We have already touched on an example of this when discussing Apollonius' story of the rape of Hylas with its emphasis on human emotion and its reference to cults still practised by the people of Cius.[34]

The shift in emphasis eloquently demonstrates the greater realism of the early Alexandrian poets in their use of aetiology. The middle-man in this development is Euripides, who was notorious, as we shall see, for his insistence on the everyday nature of his characters and subjects, an insistence to be found even in his treatment of aetiology. For example, in the *Iphigenia in Tauris*, which explains the origins of the temples of Artemis at Halae and Brauron in Attica and a cult-practice associated with the latter temple,[35] the tragedian seems keen to underline the common humanity of Orestes and, ultimately, of Iphigenia herself.

Aetiology can be found in Greek poetry from Homer onwards,[36] but it appears that it was Callimachus who invented the idea of collecting aitia into a single poem and he may thus be called the father of the literary genre.[37] A related genre, literature on the foundations of cities, was much older,[38] but Callimachus developed that too, writing a treatise *On the Foundations of Islands and Cities*;[39] his pupil, Apollonius, wrote a series of *Ktiseis*, including the one on Alexandria,[40] and Callimachus appears to have influenced other scholars and poets as well.[41] He is thus the leading figure in this aspect of Alexandrian poetry, as in so much else.[42]

There is no lack of examples of aitia in Callimachus' extant works. The formal point of the *Hecale* is aetiological, to explain how the Attic deme and the cult of Zeus Hecaleios derived their names.[43] The *Aetia* is a collection of cult-origins, of which it will be sufficient here to mention only the stories of how it came about that the people of Paros sacrifice to the Graces without flute-playing (*Frr.* 3–7.14), that wreaths of celery are awarded to victors in the Nemean and Isthmian games (*Frr.* 55–9), and that the constellation of the Lock was located in the sky.[44] The *Hymns* also contain cult-origins, though they are far less frequent than in the *Aetia* and assume a subordinate role in the narrative. The *Hymn to Apollo*, for instance, tells the origins of Apollo's epithet Nomios (47–54) and of his horned altar on Delos (55–64), relates how the cult of Apollo Carneius began in Sparta but was brought by the sixth generation of the sons of Oedipus to Thera and thence to the poet's own Cyrene (65–96), an account most clearly illustrating the realistic manner in which aetiology brings events from the mythical past into relation with the present day, and traces back the cry '*hiē hiē paiēon*' to the shouts of the people of Delphi as the god slew the serpent Pytho with his bow (97–104).[45] Aitia are present in the *Iambi* as well.[46] Aetiology is thus a main preoccupation with Callimachus and is allowed to pervade his poetry. Of course, it cannot be denied that his interest in aetiology is at times apparently due to no more than antiquarianism, but it is clear that an important facet of his interest is, as we saw in his use of geography, the realistic impulse to connect the past with the observable present.

Apollonius' *Argonautica* is hardly less concerned with aetiology than Callimachus' *Aetia*. Apollonius' debts to Callimachus in his use of aitia are considerable,[47] but I suggest that the reasons for his dependence are to be sought in the problem posed by epic which we saw him confronting by means of his pictorialism, and that his debt to Callimachus in this respect is motivated by a real need. The main evidence for Apollonius' dependence on Callimachus is his account of the cult of Anaphe at *Argonautica* 4.1714–30.[48] A consideration of the two versions reveals an important fact about the two poets' methods of narration. Whereas Apollonius tells the aition in a linear manner, Callimachus first asks the Muses to explain the peculiar rite, is then directed by Calliope to call to mind Apollo Aegletes and to start his tale from the point where the Argonauts left Colchis (*Fr.* 7.19ff.) and returns to the aition only after what appears to be a substantial account of the Argonauts' home journey (*Fr.* 21).[49] Callimachus hangs his story of the return of the Argonauts on the cult-origin, thus exploiting the opportunity to insert additional material; for him, aetiological realism is something of a parergon. Apollonius, on the other hand, uses the aition primarily to prove the historicity of his tale. The second and fourth books of the *Argonautica* in particular yield many more examples of aitia. The aim is often to point to observable survivals of the saga in ritual which will bring it into closer relation with the present.[50]

Aitia are not so frequent in Theocritus. It is interesting that in his handling of the Hylas myth the aetiological element is limited to at most an allusive account of the triple cry apparently practised in the cult of Hylas (*Id.* 13.58f.), whereas Apollonius in his version makes quite a prominent feature of it. In the pastorals there is the aition of how the legendary Chalcon brought forth the spring of Bourina on Cos (*Id.* 7.6f.), which is apparently meant to compliment his Coan hosts, Phrasidamas and Antigenes, who claimed descent from Chalcon, and to connect them with the noble mythical antiquity of the island.[51] But most significantly, perhaps, aitia occur with greater frequency in the encomiastic poems, especially *Idylls* 15 and 17, and in reference to the new gods, the deified Ptolemies, where they confer the authenticity and grandeur of Olympian religion on the new cults and give new life to the ancient myths.

Other Alexandrians include aetiological lore in their poems. Aratus, for example, includes the tales of the origins of the constellations, sometimes purely as a variation device, as with the aition of the Crown (*Phaen*. 71–3), sometimes to fit in with the Stoic theme of the *Phaenomena*, as with Virgo, whom Aratus identifies with Dikē (95–136), and sometimes to illustrate the benefits given to men by the gods, as with Pegasus, who brought forth the well of Hippocrene (216–24). But elsewhere he shows he regards these aetiologies as fantasies, for he claims that men in ancient times needed to group the stars into constellations and gave them names for the purpose of identification (373–8). His scientific rationalism has precluded belief in aitia, and his handling of them can, therefore, not be called realistic in the sense I have described. His attitude to aetiology is, however, of considerable interest, for although he disbelieves the truth of aitia, he still employs them to convey other truths which he had inherited from his philosophical system; in this he is a forerunner of Lucretius.[52] It is difficult to ascertain the attitude to aetiology in Eratosthenes' and Euphorion's fragmentary poems, but it seems on the whole quite safe to assume that they aimed at pure entertainment.[53] These two later Alexandrians, together with the earlier Aratus, thus appear not to share Callimachus', Apollonius' or, in certain of his poems, Theocritus' approach to aetiology. The *Europa* of Moschus, moreover, bears no sense of urgency at all on the question of the naming of Europe. With the later generations of the Alexandrian movement, then, aetiology seems to have been exploited simply as a vehicle for erudition or elegant charm, and lacks the urgency often discernible in its use by Callimachus and Apollonius.[54]

We turn, fourthly, to the incorporation of scientific, especially medical knowledge in Alexandrian poetry. Dialogue with scientists and physicians will have been facilitated by the Museum at Alexandria.

Callimachus appears indebted to medicine at a number of points in his poems. A fragment from the third book of the *Aetia* refers to Zeus Epopsius who cannot look upon evil-doers 'with glad eyes' (*Fr.* 35.14f.). The word for 'eyes' here, λογάδες, means the eye-whites, and it is just possible that Herophilus' treatise *On the Eyes* used the term, though confirmation of this is lacking, and that Callimachus has culled it from that work.[55] The same treatise may have been the source of another possible usage of medical terminology in the reference at line 53 of the *Hymn to Artemis* to the single eyes of the Cyclopes as 'like a shield four hide-skins thick' (σάκει ἶσα τετραβοείῳ): Callimachus may have varied the

Homeric epithet for a shield, 'seven hide-skins thick' (ἑπταβόειον) to bring the formula into line with Herophilus' discovery of the four membranes of the pupil.[56] Again, we have noted that in the *Hymn to Delos* he alters Leto's position as she gives birth to Apollo from the traditional one. It has been suggested that the alteration of her pose to a sitting position, leaning against the palm-tree, is inspired by medical research. Herophilus in his treatise *On Midwifery* talks of forward curvature of the spine as a cause of difficult delivery and he would hardly have recommended the position of the Homeric Leto which would have resulted in a curved back; it is thus possible that Callimachus has followed Herophilus in altering Leto's body-position so drastically from the traditional pose.[57] The effect seems to be the ironic 'correction' of Callimachus' model, and to define the distance between the world of myth and contemporary reality, thus again possibly helping the poet's audience to know where they stand in relation to the mythical past.

Apollonius exhibits a more directly realistic interest in medicine. We have already seen how he employs medical technical terms in his description of Phineus' physical state when the Argonauts first meet him;[58] the passage's pictorial realism is made even more effective through Apollonius' use of medical terminology. The death of Mopsus from the bite of an asp at 4.1521–31 is also pertinent, for Apollonius' account of his symptoms is strikingly close to Nicander's description of the death inflicted by the same snake (*Th.* 186–9).[59] Moreover, it has been argued that, when Apollonius says that the asp bites Mopsus between the calf-muscle and the κερκίς, he may be influenced in his terminology by Herophilus, for κερκίς was a medical technical term for the tibia and was apparently first used in that sense by Herophilus.[60] He also appears to be using medical terminology when he says Mopsus 'felt the bleeding wound' (1522), for the verb for 'feeling' here (ἄφασσεν) is found in the medical writers in the sense of examining a wound by touch.[61] The whole passage thus displays precision in its use of medical vocabulary. Finally, there is the fascinating moment when the poet uses his medical knowledge to describe the effects of love on Medea. First he describes, in conventional terms, the effect on her heart, but then that upon her *medulla oblongata* (3.761–5)![62] Again, it appears to be Herophilus who first drew attention to the importance of that part of the brain; he discovered it to be the seat of sensory perception and

126 The Appeal to Science

motivation.⁶³ Now some modern critics have felt this to be too anatomical to do anything but destroy the beauty of the passage,⁶⁴ but it will by now be plain that Apollonius' motive will have been realism: he wanted to describe the effect of love on the legendary princess in the most precise and up-to-date manner possible. An understanding of those aims may help to allay modern feelings of dissatisfaction with his particularism.⁶⁵

Theocritus shows nowhere near as much interest in medical terminology as can be detected in Apollonius, even though he addresses two *Idylls* to the Coan physician Nicias. He sustains the imagery of 'the medicine of the Muses' as a remedy for love which is introduced at the beginning of *Idyll* 11, but uses fairly non-technical terms, like 'remedy', 'unguent' and 'salve' (1f.);⁶⁶ Polyphemus is said to have 'recovered most easily' (ῥάιστα διᾶγ') and 'got better' (ῥᾷον διᾶγ') at lines 7 and 81, the normal terms for convalescence.⁶⁷

Eratosthenes includes in his *Hermes*, as we have seen,⁶⁸ a scientific description for the sake of the poetry of the piece and the sense of awe that an account of the heavens evokes. It is neither certainly didactic, nor does it employ science for realistic effects. Similarly, the poem solving the duplication of the cube (*Fr.* 35 Pow.) is simply a delightful essay in the versification of mathematics. For Euphorion, who for example in the *Mopsopia* discusses perfect numbers (those equal to the sum of their factors), the use of science seems equally unconcerned with realism.⁶⁹

There is, however, a remarkable fragment of an anonymous late second-century lyric⁷⁰ which does use science for realistic description. The fragment begins with a charming picture of dawn in the countryside (1–11), but continues with an account of bees collecting nectar (12–18). Although the poet describes the bees in conventionally picturesque terms as 'snub-nosed', 'nimble-winged', 'summer's reapers who work in swarms' and 'having a low hum', other details are scientifically so precise that the bee can be identified as the *Chalcidoma sicula*.⁷¹ Epithets particularly suitable for the species are πηλουργοί (16), which refers to the collection, preparation, transportation and moulding of their building materials, and ἀσκεπεῖς (17), which denotes wild bees which have no hive; λιπόκεντροι (15) means 'stingless', to which there can be no objection, for the species is not fierce while at work. Certain details may be recollected from scientific treatises; for example, Aristotle's *On the Birth of Animals* refers to bees as 'busy', the ἐργατίδες of line 12, and non-mating, an idea present in δυσέρωτες (16);[72] indeed, the poet who says νέκταρ ἀρύουσιν, 'draw up the nectar' (18), may be even more accurate than the naturalist who says μέλι κομίζειν, 'carry honey'; πιθαναί, 'trustworthy' (12), however, which is echoed by Virgil's *certis sub legibus* ('under fixed laws') at *Georgics* 4.154, is not appropriate to the species since it is not social, a detail which seems the only piece of poetic idealisation in the whole description.

The realism which the Alexandrians aimed to achieve through appeal to scholarship and science is a subject which deserves a much more detailed examination than it has been given here. I trust, however, that in this brief account I have shown that it was widely exploited by the Alexandrians and also that this remarkable but often misunderstood aspect of their poetry is attributable, at least in the early period, to a desire to bring the subject-matter of poetry, in particular mythological material, into a recognisable relation with experience, whether the intention is to point ironically to the rift between myth and the world of the present, as perhaps happens in Callimachus' depiction of Leto's labour, or to help the original audiences find the evocations of myths more compelling.

Notes

1. See my remarks in 'The Nature and Origin of Realism in Alexandrian Poetry', *A.u.A.* 29, (1983) 129–35, from which some of the material in this chapter is drawn.

2. *Poet.* 61^b11f.; cf. *Probl.* 18.10 917^b15. It should be noted, moreover, that in the scholia to Homer credibility (πιθανότης) is a primary aesthetic criterion: see M.-L. von Franz, *Die aesthetischen Anschauungen der Iliasscholien im Codex Ven. B. und Townleianus* (Diss. Zurich, 1943) p. 15f.; for references see J. Baar, *Index zu den Ilias-Scholien: die wichtigeren Ausdrücke der grammatischen, rhetorischen und ästhetischen Textkritik*, Dt. Beitr. zur Altertumswiss. 15 (Baden-Baden, 1961), s.vv. ἀξιοπιστία, ἀξιόπιστος, ἀπίθανος, ἄπιστος, πιθανός, πιθανότης, πίστις, πιστός. The scholia demonstrate the way the idea expressed by Aristotle was taken up in Hellenistic literary criticism.

3. For a discussion of Callimachus' use of 'the old poets' (Homer, *Il.* 15.187ff., Hesiod, *Theog.* 881ff. and Pindar, *Ol.* 7.54ff.) see G. R. McLennan, *Callimachus: Hymn to Zeus, Testi e Commenti* 2 (Rome, 1977) on line 61. But cf. next note.

4. Hesiod *Theog.* 881ff. W. Meincke, *Untersuchungen zu den enkomiastischen Gedichten Theokrits* (Diss. Kiel, 1965), pp. 175ff. gives a judicious account of the historical basis of the passage; he concludes that Callimachus is referring to the accession of Philadelphus over the claims of his elder half-brother, Ceraunus, and is appealing to him to acknowledge Philadelphus' superiority and to renounce his pretensions to the throne. Such an appeal would in my view have come after Soter

128 The Appeal to Science

made Philadelphus his co-regent in 285 BC and before Ceraunus' rebellion and flight which P. M. Fraser, *Ptolemaic Alexandria* vol. ii (Oxford, 1972), p. 915 n. 284 dates to later in 285 BC. McLennan loc. cit., is thus precipitate in dismissing the historical case. For an attempt to relate the poem to Cyrene and Magas, see C. Meillier, *Callimaque et son temps: Recherches sur la carrière et la condition d'un écrivain à l'époque des premiers Lagides* (Lille, 1979) pp. 61–78.

5. The case for Pherecydes is presented e.g. by Wilamowitz, *H.D.* vol. ii, pp. 19–24, K. J. McKay, *The Poet at Play: Kallimachos, The Bath of Pallas, Mnem. Suppl.* 6 (Leiden, 1962), pp. 32–6, and Fraser, *Ptolemaic Alexandria*, p. 657; A. W. Bulloch, *Callimachus: the Fifth Hymn, Cambridge Classical Texts and Commentaries* 26 (Cambridge, 1985), pp. 16f., 19 and on lines 55–6 argues for the *Argolica* of Agias and Dercylus.

6. See Fraser, ibid., p. 661.

7. See e.g. Schol. Flor. 16ff., 29ff. (Clio); *Fr.* 7.22 (Calliope); *Fr.* 43.56 (Clio); *Fr.* 238.8 *S.H.* (Erato).

8. P. Händel, *Beobachtungen zur epischen Technik des Apollonios Rhodios*, Zetemata 8 (Munich, 1954), pp. 30–3.

9. Coherence and credibility of presentation are also the principles by which Apollonius seems to have compiled the catalogue of the Argonauts at 1.23–233: see e.g. Händel, ibid., pp. 15–26 and J. F. Carspecken, 'Apollonius Rhodius and the Homeric Epic', *Y.C.S.* 13 (1952), 38–58. Cf. 4.1381–92, where the poet relates the Argonauts' feat in carrying the Argo overland in Libya for twelve days and nights; he pleads that he is forced to follow poetic tradition (1381–2; cf. e.g. Pindar *P.* 4.25–7) and conjectures that 'the blood of the gods was still in them' (1389). Here he is drawing attention to the rift between myth and experience, but his procedure is, paradoxically perhaps, realistic in the sense in which I have defined the term, for in his teasing way he is relating his saga to his own age's reality. Cf. the remark that describes Jason hurling the stone at the Earthborn Men (above, pp. 65f.).

10. B. A. van Groningen, *Euphorion* (Amsterdam, 1977), p. 269f.; cf. ibid., pp. 257f.

11. See e.g. Call. *H. Jov.* 44, *H. Dian.* 77, 220; A.R. 1.1061, 2.717, 842, 1214, 4.250, 480, 534, 599, 1153.

12. For *H. Dian.* 76–9 see above, p. 60 and p. 103 n. 24.

13. Fraser, *Ptolemaic Alexandria*, p. 658.

14. The conditions under which men might experience such a vision are realistically envisaged: see F. Williams, 'A Theophany in Theocritus', *C.Q.* N.S. 21 (1971), 142 n. 1.

15. καὶ ὀψιγόνοισιν ἰδέσθαι; cf. 1.1062, 4.252, etc. The phrase is modelled after Homer's καὶ ἐσσομένοισι πυθέσθαι ('for men to come to hear of too') at *Il.* 2.119, 22.305, *Od.* 3.204, etc.

16. 'The Egyptians have made their customs and laws for the most part the reverse of those of other people': Herodotus 2.35 (with examples).

17. Σ ad 1029.

18. E.g. at 3.200–9, where he describes the Plain of Circe and the Colchian custom (observable εἰσέτι νῦν: 203) of binding the corpses of dead males to trees and of burying those of females; Σ ad 202–9a tells us that Apollonius is following Nymphodorus, most likely his *Customs of Asia* (so G. W. Mooney, *The Argonautica of Apollonius Rhodius* (Dublin, 1912) on 202). See further Fraser, *Ptolemaic Alexandria*, pp. 626–8, 764.

19. Σ ad 257–62b; cf. Fraser, ibid., p. 627 and vol. ii, p. 885 n. 78 and p. 887 n. 86.

20. Σ ad 282–91b; 17ff. At 4.313 Apollonius makes the Argonauts enter the Danube through the opening called the Narex which, he says, is on the northern side (315) of the Island of Peuce in the mouth of the river; the Colchians are made

to go through the Kalon Stoma which he places on the southern side of the island (313). But he has reversed the true position of the mouths: see Mooney on 313. This may be a mere mistake, for Timagetus had written on the Danube's mouth (Σ ad 303–6b) and may well have got the positions of the channels correct.

21. See further Fraser, *Ptolemaic Alexandria*, pp. 626–33.
22. Ibid., pp. 770–4.
23. So ibid., p. 772.
24. Erathosthenes' sceptical attitude to paradoxography is, however, well known; see Fraser, ibid., pp. 293, 295, 527, 759–60. But we must beware of thinking that his scientific rationalism was typical of the age.
25. See below, pp. 178–81 [Theoc.] *Id.* 25 depends on the audience's general knowledge for its location.
26. See A. S. F. Gow, *Theocritus* vol. i (Cambridge, 1952), p. xixf. below, pp. 164, 168.
27. Cf. Σ ad 21. The poem assumes the author's intimacy with named persons like Phrasidamus and Antigenes who must have been real people living on Cos (the allusions to their mythical forbears at lines 3–9 and the geographical precision with which I argue in 'Simichidas' Walk and the Locality of Bourina in Theocritus, *Id.* 7', *C.Q.* N.S. 30 (1980), 373–7 that their farm is located in the poem would otherwise be pointless); it would seem a strange procedure if Theocritus were to name in the first few lines of the *Idyll* real people, narrate in the first person for twenty lines and then reveal that the narrator is in fact a fictitious character. This does not, however, mean that the poem depicts a real event, or, for that matter, that Lycidas was an actual poet; Theocritus is in my view picturing himself as taking part in an imaginary meeting; cf. E. L. Bowie, 'Theocritus' Seventh *Idyll*, Philetas and Longus', *C.Q.* N.S. 35 (1985), 67f., 77f. See for literature E. A. Schmidt, *Poetische Reflexion: Vergils Bukolik* (Munich, 1972), pp. 55, 231–8.
28. The meeting is said to occur when 'we had not yet finished half our journey and the tomb of Brasilas had not yet come into sight' (10f.). W. G. Arnott, 'The Mound of Brasilas and Theocritus' Seventh *Idyll*', *Q.U.C.C.* N.S. 3 (1979), 99–106 plausibly argues that the landmark is the barrow hill marked 207 m on my map in 'Simichidas' Walk', for it comes into view just less than 4 km outside Cos-city, that is just before the half-way mark on the walk. If correct, Arnott's suggestion would be further proof of the poem's unique geographical precision.
29. Above, pp. 81f., p. 107 n. 98.
30. Van Groningen, *Euphorion*, p. 257.
31. So e.g. G. Codrignani in her seminal article on aetiology, 'L'"aition" nella poesia greca prima di Callimaco', *Convivium* 5th Ser. 26 (1958), 527–45, talks of 'il preziosismo erudito dell' alessandrinismo' (ibid., 545).
32. See e.g. Call. *Frr.* 43.78, 588, *H. Jov.* 11, *H. Apol.* 47, 104, *H. Del.* 275; A.R. 1.1075, 1138, 1354, 2.713, 850, 3.203, 4.990, 1217, 1770. The phrase εἰσέτι καὶ νῦν is already formulaic in Homer (*Il.* 1.445, 9.105, 111, 259, 11.790, 14.234, 16.238, etc.) and is used in the Alexandrian aetiological manner in the *Homeric Hymn to Hermes* 508 (ἔτι νῦν is also thus used at line 125), but it was Callimachus who turned the aition into a literary genre; see below, p. 122.
33. Above, pp. 24–7.
34. Above, pp. 73f., 115.
35. See e.g. Athene's speech at 1446–68.
36. See Codrignani, 'L'"aition"'.
37. So ibid., 545 and Fraser, *Ptolemaic Alexandria*, pp. 761 and 775.
38. Fraser, ibid., p. 775f.
39. *Test.* 1.18, the *Suda*-life.
40. *Frr.*; 4–12 Pow.; see Fraser, *Ptolemaic Alexandria*, p. 632 for a discussion of the works.

130 The Appeal to Science

41. See Fraser, ibid., pp. 513f., 522f., 776ff.
42. However, Eratosthenes was one emulator who avoided this form of inquiry; see ibid., p. 777.
43. *Dieg.* X.18–XI.7.
44. See Fraser, *Ptolemaic Alexandria*, pp. 720–32 for a discussion of further examples.
45. Cf. e.g. *H. Jov.* 10–13, *H. Del.* 249–54.
46. *Iamb.* 7–11 (*Frr.* 197–201).
47. Cf. Fraser, *Ptolemaic Alexandria*, pp. 628–33, 637–40, 749–54.
48. For Apollonius' omission of details in Callimachus' account (*Frr.* 9–21 Pf., with *Frr.* 250, 251 *S.H.*) see R. Pfeiffer Callimachus, vol. i (Oxford, 1949) on *Fr.* 21.8ff.
49. See further Fraser, *Ptolemaic Alexandria*, p. 628 and vol. ii, p. 887 n. 86.
50. For further examples see above, n. 32; for discussions of Apollonius' use of aetiology see H. Fränkel, 'Das Argonautenepos des Apollonios', *M.H.* 14 (1957), 5; L. Gil Fernández, 'La epica helenística', *Estudios sobre el mundo helenístico* (Seville, 1971), 110–12; Fraser, *Ptolemaic Alexandria*, pp. 626–33; and C. R. Beye, *Epic and Romance in the Argonautica of Apollonius* (Carbondale and Edwardsville, 1982), p. 27.
51. Cf. *Id.* 12.27–37.
52. Thus Lucretius can express scepticism over traditional myth (*R.N.* 2.167–81, 600–43, 655–60, 1090–104, 5.14–54, 110–234, 6.379–422) and still use it for polemic purposes, as in his version of the Iphigenia story (1.80–101), or because it provides powerful imagery, as in the proem to Venus (1.1–49). On irony in Aratus' use of myth see B. Effe, *Dichtung und Lehre: Untersuchungen zur Typologie des antiken Lehrgedichts*, Zetemata 69 (Munich, 1977), pp. 51–3; on Nicander's 'Gelehrsamkeit' see ibid., p. 62f.
53. Eratosthenes *Frr.* 2, 14, 22–7, 28b Pow.; Euphorion *Frr.* 9, 20–1, 104, 115, 121, 125, 145 v.Gr. See Fraser, *Ptolemaic Alexandria*, vol. ii, p. 903 n. 202.
54. On the interpretation of A. Momigliano, 'Terra Marique', *J.R.S.* 32 (1942), 53–64 and 'The Locrian Maidens and the Date of Lycophron's *Alexandra*', *C.Q.* 39 (1945), 49–53, the *Alexandra* of Lycophron traces the chain of grievances between Europe and Asia down to the struggle between Pyrrhus and Rome, supposedly referred to at lines 1446–50; this would make the poem link myth and the present in a realistic way. But S. West, 'Lycophron Italicised', *J.H.S.* 104 (1984), 127–51 (with lit.) has argued forcefully that lines 1446–50 are an interpolation.
55. This is suggested by Fraser, *Ptolemaic Alexandria*, p. 356.
56. H. Opperman, 'Herophilos bei Kallimachos', *H.* 60 (1925), 14–32 (= *W.d.F.* 296, 1–20); F. Solmsen, 'Greek Philosophy and the Discovery of the Nerves', *M.H.* 18 (1961), 196 n. 61; F. Bornmann, *Callimachi Hymnus in Dianam*, Biblioteca di Studi Superiori: Filologia greca e papirologia 55 (Florence, 1968) *ad loc.* Cf. F. Williams, *Callimachus: Hymn to Apollo* (Oxford, 1978) on *H*.2.51, 110.
57. G. W. Most, 'Callimachus and Herophilus', *H.* 109 (1981), 188–96, referring to Herophilus *ap.* Soran. *Gynaecia* 4.1.53, p. 131.1f. Ilberg. For further uses of medical terminology see *Fr.* 75. 12–14, *H. Dem.* 103 (ἀφίστημι: cf. Galen XIII. 846 Kühn, quoted by Fraser, *Ptolemaic Alexandria*, vol. ii, p. 526 n. 157), *Ep.* 3 *H.E.* Scientific precision is observable, though drawn from another branch of science, in his epigram on the nautilus (*Ep.* 14 *H.E.*); see Fraser, ibid., p. 587f. on its skilful incorporation of Aristotelian research on the nautilus (at e.g. Arist. *H.A.* 622b 5ff.) into poetry of high quality. For further striking examples see Williams on *H*. 2.51 and 110; cf. also D. Geoghegan, *Anyte: the Epigrams*, Testi e Commenti 4 (Rome, 1979) on Anyte 19.4 *H.E.*
58. Above, pp. 72f.
59. So Gow and Scholfield, *Nicander* (Cambridge, 1953) on *Th.* 187ff. The poets are possibly drawing on the same source, the *On Animals* of an Apollodorus who apparently lived at the beginning of the third century; see ibid., p. 18.

60. Fraser, *Ptolemaic Alexandria*, p. 634; cf. H. Erbse, 'Homerscholien und hellenistische Glossare bei Apollonios Rhodios', *H.* 87 (1953), 189 n. 5.
61. See e.g. Galen XIX. 87 Kühn, cited by Erbse, ibid., 188.
62. See my 'The Love Theme in Apollonius Rhodius' Argonautica', *W.S.* N.F. 13 (1979), 61.
63. See Solmsen, 'Greek Philosophy and the Discovery of Nerves', 184–97.
64. So M. M. Gillies, *The Argonautica of Apollonius Rhodius: Book 3* (Cambridge, 1928) on 3.765; Erbse, 'Homerscholien', 189f.; Fraser, *Ptolemaic Alexandria*, vol. ii, p. 895f. n. 141.
65. Cf. Medea's wish-fulfilment dream at 3.617–31 (above, p. 75). For further examples see Erbse, ibid., 186–90.
66. See Gow on 1 and 2.
67. So Gow on 7. On the constriction of Amycus' blood vessels and flesh see above, p. 109 n. 126.
68. Above, p. 99.
69. Cf. *Frr.* 93, 172, 180–2 v.Gr.
70. Pow., p. 185f., *G.L.P.* 92 (b).
71. J. U. Powell, in *New Chapters in the History of Greek Literature*, 2nd series (Oxford, 1929), 62f.
72. Arist. *G.A.* 759^a 8–61^a 1; cf. Virg. *G.* 198f.

5 The Ancient Theory and Pre-Alexandrian Practice of Everyday and Low Realism

We have already had frequent occasion to note that the Alexandrian poets were most attracted to realistic or, as I have called it, everyday and low material, and we have seen how they often lavished upon it their pictorialist skills and at times even enlisted the aid of science to engage their audiences in their depiction of it. It is now time to analyse this material for its own sake and to examine the Alexandrian poets' precise attitude to it. As we shall see, the distinction between everyday and low material was made by Aristotle; it will prove a convenient one for our purposes.

The important question of the employment of such material in antiquity and of the tones that it can produce has never been thoroughly examined. The only account of it is that by Auerbach in the opening chapters of his *Mimesis*. Auerbach, we remember, denied any nineteenth-century Realist seriousness of tone to ancient Greek poetry, including that of the Alexandrian period. In this chapter I intend to show that Auerbach's generalisation is correct for pre-Alexandrian Greek literary thought and literature, but that it takes no notice of at least two vital exceptions. In the following chapter I shall try to give some idea of the impressively wide tonal range that the Alexandrians achieved by their use of the everyday and the low, including their serious portrayal of it, which represents a significant exception to Auerbach's thesis.

This part of our inquiry leads us directly into the question of genre-crossing in the more general sense. For example, one critic, L. E. Rossi, has concluded that in the archaic period rules pertaining to the different genres were unwritten but respected, that in the classical period they were both written and respected, but that in the Alexandrian period they were rigidly formulated but disregarded, or, as Rossi puts it, that the classification of the literary genres was made 'for the special purpose of violating the rules'.[1] But we are concerned here with only one quite specific aspect of the ancient theory and practice of the genres: I mean the process (and the ancient thinking that lies behind it) whereby subject-matter which is normally depicted in a low genre, especially comedy, is depicted in a grand genre like epic or tragedy. The main genre in Alexandrian poetry in which a crossing of this kind took place was epic, so we shall concentrate on the theory and practice of epic and its appropriate subject-matter. Tragedy, which was associated with epic in subject-matter and tone, sheds light on epic's position in Greek poetic thought, so it must be considered too. Comedy is useful because it dealt with subject-matter which was regarded as low and also, in the case of fourth-century comedy, everyday, and such material was frequently depicted by the Alexandrian poets in the grand genres, that of epic in particular. We shall discuss lyric only when the points of reference are relatively clear[2] and when grand themes related in it are cited by the Alexandrians, for example for comic purposes by means of a juxtaposition with everyday and low matter, as in Theocritus' *Idyll* 24 where the poet wants us to remember Pindar's versions of the infant Heracles and Hera's snakes. We shall find it most convenient to deal with elegy and epigram in the same way.

The comedies of Aristophanes are the first extant sources offering evidence for Greek thought on the question in a literary-critical context. The *Frogs* is especially informative, but much of what is expressed there is adumbrated in earlier plays, in particular the *Acharnians* and the *Wasps*. We are justified in searching in these comic works for at least a kernel of orthodox thinking, for, if that were not present, there would be no comedy: the poet and his audience must be able to count at least to some degree on a set of common perceptions and expectations before a joke which runs contrary to expectations or a caricature, for example, can be amusing.

Most important for our purposes is the agon of the *Frogs* (905–1088). The nub of the matter is expressed at lines 949ff. when Euripides says he gave important roles in his tragedies to what would have been regarded as socially inferior people or people inappropriately domestic in a tragedy, namely women, both young and old, slaves and householders. Aeschylus objects violently to the notion,[3] but Euripides claims that he 'was acting democratically' (952). Certainly the contrast between the two dramatists is comically overstated here, and Aeschylus is a caricature of old-fashioned aristocratic morality more than he is a representative of poetic norms, but Aristophanes must have felt that he was basing the passage on a recognisably common opinion about the two dramatists and their art if he was to make his comic point. The exchange, therefore, leads to the speculation that in the late fifth-century Greek scheme of things ordinary people were not considered suitable for any serious part in tragedy and that Euripides was notorious for his innovations.

This kind of thinking is in fact basic to the humour of the passage in which Euripides defends his deliberate inclusion of banal, everyday domesticities with his famous statement that his aim was to instruct 'by introducing common things which we experience and know' (959). And he is made (absurdly) to state that his aim was to help his audiences with household-management (976f.), which provokes Dionysus' parody of the domestic realism said to result (980–8). This is also, I submit, one of the issues at stake behind the 'lost a little oil-flask' joke at lines 1200ff.: Aeschylus is scoring off Euripides for adopting a grand literary framework, tragedy, and debasing it with trivia.[4] The same line of attack is used by Aeschylus when he parodies Euripides' lyrics (1331–64). The parody consists mainly of the bathos which results from the juxtaposition of the tragic form with ridiculously inappropriate domesticities. Though it is on the whole true that Euripides did not mix grand and lowly subject-matter and diction in his monodies and though Aristophanes is mainly concerned with the comedy of his scene,[5] Aeschylus is in general correct in his claim that Euripides included humble matter in his tragedies and that his diction is as a consequence more colloquial than that of the other tragedians, though we would perhaps wish to add that Euripides' interest in simplicity and clarity may have been a factor here.[6]

Another pertinent issue emerges at lines 1030ff. where Aeschylus says that he followed the example of Homer by depicting characters who were paragons of heroic virtue; for him the tragic stage has a moral and didactic role, just as Homeric epic is conceived to have, and should keep up its 'high tone'. Homeric epic is thus placed on a par with tragedy as regards its grandeur. This probably reflects popular thought, and of course there is the story of the historical Aeschylus' saying that his tragedies were slices from the banquets of Homer (Ath.347e). The idea is explicit in Plato and Aristotle, as we shall see.

Aeschylus' accusation at lines 842 and 1063ff. that Euripides debased the grandeur of tragedy by staging royalty in rags (as he did with his Telephus or, a more ready example, Menelaus in the

Helen) for cheap emotionalism is also based on morality: one should not degrade one's 'betters', for that will corrupt the audience. Clearly, for Aeschylus, costume too should be appropriate to the dignity of the heroes of tragedy. This charge had also been levelled against Euripides at *Acharnians* 393–489 when Dicaeopolis goes to the tragedian as the person best equipped to help him in the art of emotional appeal. He takes so much in the way of stage-wardrobe, Telephus' rags, a beggar's stick and other props, that Euripides expostulates that Dicaeopolis will rob him of his tragedy (464); without them, he says, 'my plays are gone' (470).[7] Again, there must have been at least some element of agreement on this aspect of Euripides' stage-craft for the caricature to have been appreciated.

One final point in the *Frogs* deserves our attention. At lines 1056ff. Euripides is criticised for innovations in *style* which arise directly from his innovations in subject-matter: with the introduction of everyday and low material there has followed a lowering of diction. Euripides and Aeschylus agree on the didactic responsibility of the tragedian, and Euripides charges Aeschylus with bombastic and unclear diction; if one is going to instruct, he says, one should do so 'in a human fashion' (1058), so that the instruction is comprehensible. Aeschylus rejoins by saying that great thoughts produce grand diction and implies that Euripides has disregarded the need for gravity (1058–62). Euripides is once more criticised, again for introducing innovations tending towards realism, this time stylistic. In view of Aeschylus' and Euripides' agreement that the latter was unconventional in this regard, it is possible that Aristophanes himself saw in their diction a crucial distinction between the two tragedians' dramatic approach, though it is not clear whom he favoured on this question: clearly the high-flown language of traditional tragedy was just as good for a laugh as the new style of Euripides.[8]

Perhaps Aristophanes gives us an inkling of what he himself thought the level of comedy was when he makes Xanthias in the *Wasps* tell the audience not to expect anything 'over-grand' from the play (56). And the occasional protests that comedy can be serious (*Wasps* 64, *Acharnians* 500 and *Frogs* 389f.) probably in fact constitute evidence that his audiences perceived the genre as basically non-serious.

It seems, therefore, that Aristophanes, whatever his own views, was catering for an audience which thought that a grand genre like tragedy should for reasons of morality depict grand material and that the separation of genres was disregarded by Euripides.

Further evidence of the separation of genres is to be found in Plato. Not only does he reflect orthodox thinking on the subject through the opinions which he makes the speakers of his dialogues utter, but he shows that he himself, for his own reasons, on occasion passionately upholds the doctrine, as becomes abundantly clear in the *Laws*.

He voices constant criticism of genre-mixing in the broad sense. For example, the idea of blurring the distinctions of lyric poetry is categorically deplored at *Laws* 700aff. There Plato champions the separation of genres on the grounds that the function of art is moral and didactic: the mixture of the different species of lyric is supposed to have led to political anarchy as well. This is a stance discernible in Aristophanes, but Plato develops the thought elsewhere.[9] On the other hand, Socrates in the *Ion* claims that poets are drawn to the different poetic genres through the various types of the Muse's inspiration, not by technical knowledge alone (534c), a claim which provides a purely aesthetic reason for the separation. Not surprisingly, this conservatism is extended to Plato's thinking on the more specific question of the genres and their appropriate subject-matter.

That the genres of tragedy and comedy are viewed as opposed is quite evident from the passage in the *Theaetetus* where Socrates talks of the 'foremost poets in each brand of poetry, Epicharmus in comedy and Homer in tragedy' (152e).[10] (The classification of Homer as a tragedian will be discussed below.) But precisely in what way does Plato consider them to be opposed? The fact that Socrates could talk of comedy as having a 'foremost poet' probably means that Plato did not think that all comedy was bad, and this seems to be borne out by certain traditions about his own literary tastes.[11] But he clearly thought the comedy of his day to be a low genre and saw moral danger in it.[12] As for contemporary tragedy, there is plenty of evidence to show that Plato thought of it as the grand genre, even if it is, like all art-forms, vitiated. At *Laws* 816e–817a the Athenian concludes his account of the conditions for the performance of comedy in the ideal state and begins his analysis of tragedy, characterising the tragic poets as those who are, 'as they say', *spoudaioi*, 'superior'.[13] The use of the word *spoudaios* in connection with tragedy is common in Plato and becomes a key term in Aristotle's *Poetics*. Finally, tragedy is considered to possess a grand style of expression; thus at *Republic* 545d Socrates ironically asks whether he and Glaucon should settle a point by calling on the Muses, as Homer did, and expect an answer from them in the pseudo-serious, grand manner of tragedy.[14]

As is already evident from *Theaetetus* 152e and *Republic* 545d, Homer and epic are placed on the same level as tragedy in Plato's thought. Indeed, the leading position of Homer in tragedy is evidenced quite frequently as, for example, when Socrates in the *Republic* calls Homer 'the first teacher and leader' of all the good tragedians (595b–c).[15] We have already met the idea in Aristophanes' *Frogs*. The view of Homer as a tragic poet *par excellence* seems, then, to have been general in the period. Plato, however, is quite explicit in differentiating Homer and epic from tragedy in connection with the different modes and metres of the genres.[16]

But though contemporary tragedy and epic are universally considered to be grand and to have a higher calling than comedy, Plato regards both of them as open to the objection of being mere entertainment, not anything serious (*paidia, ou spoudē*: *Rep.* 602b). His reasons, that in accordance with the theory of Forms the tragedian, like all artists, is at third remove from the truth (*Rep.* 597e) and that Homer tells falsehoods about the gods (*Rep.* 377d–392c) are too well known to need discussion here.[17] Indeed, the logical consequence in the case of the *Republic* is that the traditional distinction between the high and low genres is ultimately meaningless, especially when we consider his statement that tragic *mimēsis* is not *spoudē*: the choice of words seems to fly in the face of the traditional view of tragic poets as *spoudaioi*.

The picture is different in the *Laws*, however, where Plato allows himself to a greater extent to follow traditional lines of thought about the separation of the genres. In the passage in which the Athenian argues against innovations in lyric music and choristry he deduces that epic is the best art-form because in a poetry-contest old men, the most experienced social group, would award the first prize to the recitations of Homer and Hesiod; educated women and young men would award it to tragedy, whereas boys would opt for comedy. So lyric music and choristry should be judged by the amount of pleasure afforded to the most well-educated and virtuous men (658a–659a). Here again we have evidence of the view that comedy is a low genre and that tragedy and epic are high, epic being 'the best'. And again the basis of the hierarchy is moral. Later, at 816d–817e, it is clear that Plato is prepared to admit comedy and tragedy into the ideal state of the *Laws*, an unthinkable notion in the case of the *Republic*. Comedy is still, however, considered very much a low genre and is put firmly in its place: it involves the movements of ugly bodies and the expression of ugly ideas and, as such, it will be performed only by slaves and foreign hired workers and will never be a matter of *spoudē* or studied by free men and women. As for the tragedians, 'the so-called superior poets', their works must conform with the ideas embodied in the ideal state's constitution, which is 'an imitation of the fairest and best life', which is in turn claimed to be the truest kind of tragedy (817a). The strict control to which comedy and tragedy are subjected in the *Laws* has the effect of making the traditional separation of the genres all the more rigid.

Plato, then, amply illustrates traditional, orthodox thinking about the genres in his day. He also shows that epic as a genre was thought to be on the same level as tragedy in its grandeur, and, indeed, that Homer and Hesiod (though the latter is mentioned less frequently in this connection) were regarded as teachers of the tragedians, a view with which we are familiar from Aristophanes. As for the philosopher's own thought about the separation, it is the logical implication of the *Republic* that for the ideal state described there it is irrelevant in view of the radical criticisms of all forms of *mimēsis*, but it is re-introduced, and even substantiated, in the *Laws*. Basic to the hierarchy of the genres, whether orthodox or Platonic, is the question of morality.

The fullest and most systematic account of the separation of the genres is, however, to be found in the *Poetics* of Aristotle, though the *Rhetoric*, too, sheds valuable light on the subject. Indeed, the *Poetics* is of special importance to our inquiry, for Callimachus and others of his circle appear to have been opponents of the doctrines expressed in it.[18]

That Aristotle upheld the separation is made quite clear from Chapter Thirteen of the *Poetics* (53^a 10ff.), where he states that the proper characters for tragedy are 'those enjoying high repute and prosperity' and *hoi epiphaneis*, the 'men of distinction' from the families of myth like those of Oedipus and Thyestes. For Aristotle, then, tragedy had grand personages as its province and excluded people of lower social status from any principal role.

This restriction is inherent in Aristotle's key distinction of the types of poetry on the basis of whether their objects are *spoudaioi*, *phauloi* or *toioutoi*. The categories are introduced in Chapter Two (48ª 1–5). The *spoudaioi* or the *beltiones ē kath' hēmās* mentioned there can for the moment be called 'superior characters', the *phauloi* or *cheirones* 'inferior characters', and *hoi kath' hēmās, toioutoi, homoioi* or *hoi nȳn* 'the average citizen' or 'people like you or me'. Aristotle differentiates tragedy and comedy on the basis of these categories: tragedy represents 'superior people', comedy 'inferior people' (48ª 16–18).[19] Moreover, he considers *spoudaioi* to be the proper subjects of epic as well as tragedy. In Chapter Three (48ª 25–8), for instance, he observes that Sophocles and Homer differ only because they have chosen different modes of narration;[20] they are identical in another respect, namely that they both represent *spoudaioi*.[21] As we have noticed, Aristophanes and Plato had already seen an affinity between Homer and the tragedians, but in Chapter Four of the *Poetics* (48ᵇ 24–7) Aristotle offers his historical reason for it, that from its first beginnings poetry was divided according to the natural inclinations and character of the different poets, some choosing to represent the deeds of superior characters, others those of 'inferior people'. But Homer in his heroic poetry is said to have developed epic in such a way that it began to foreshadow tragedy, for he represented superior subject-matter and did so in a dramatic manner (48ᵇ 34–6), by which Aristotle means first that Homer let his characters speak in their own person, for which he is admired in Chapter Twenty-Six (60ª 5–11), and secondly that he made his representations structurally more unified and of more generalised significance than those of other epic poets.[22] Thus a historical kinship between heroic epic and tragedy is postulated which explains their similarity in subject-matter. Likewise, in the *Margites*, the burlesque attributed to Homer, the poet is said to have marked out the outlines of comedy, because he did not compose lampoons but gave a dramatic representation of humorous subject-matter (48ᵇ 36–49ª 2).

We can now more closely define the terms *spoudaioi* and *phauloi*, and their equivalents, *beltiones* and *cheirones*.[23] They must all be seen within the traditional aristocratic Greek scale of values. The characteristic trait of the *spoudaios* is his preoccupation with *aretē*.[24] Down to the fifth century this denotes honour-oriented, competitive excellence based on birth, wealth and social position, and the physical and military prowess with which these can be maintained.²⁵ By Aristotle's period co-operative moral qualities have been added to the concept.²⁶ But even for Aristotle the individual's claim to *aretē* is limited by certain factors, and in this respect his thinking remains quite traditional. These factors include ambition and capability. The ambitions of the *spoudaios* are considerable, and those of a *phaulos* negligible. So at *Rhetoric* 2.9.11–16 1387^b 4–15 *phauloi* are set alongside people of servile character and those without ambition as people who do not think they are worth any preferment or honour. The *spoudaioi* are presented as the opposite of these: they have a sense of what is right and are linked with people in a position of power and people of ambition as folk who consider themselves worthy of high status. The second limiting factor in one's aspiration to *aretē* is the capability to acquire it. Here social position and class are important. Certainly, when Aristotle argues in Chapter Fifteen of the *Poetics* (54^a 19–22) that characters should be morally good in order to secure the true tragic effect, he refers to the way a woman, whose standing in society is inferior (*cheiron*), or even a slave, who is at the absolute bottom of the social scale (*phaulon*), may possess a noble character (*ēthos chrēston*). But he shows that he thinks such a phenomenon is an exceptional case when he says that a man's character is 'almost always' conditioned by whether he is in the category of *spoudaioi* or that of the *phauloi* (*Poet.* 48^a 1–4). The general rule is, therefore, that *aretē* is the preserve of people of superior social standing like *hoi epiphaneis* of Chapter Thirteen. Such a social position is consequently a basic component of the *spoudaios*.²⁷ The social connotation of the words *cheirōn* and *phaulos* (and hence of *spoudaios*) is, moreover, clearly brought out by their use in Chapter Fifteen.²⁸

The separate question of idealisation is raised by the quotation of Sophocles' famous comment that he depicted men as they ought to be, and Euripides as they are (60^b 32–5). What Sophocles meant is probably best illustrated by 54^b 8–15, where it is recommended that the tragedian follow the example of the good painters who preserve the likeness of the originals but depict them as finer than they actually are; so the poet should portray his characters, for all their faults (irascibility, laziness and so forth), as finer than is found in real life. Sophocles is saying, then, that while he did not disguise their character-blemishes he idealised his heroes, whereas Euripides idealised his figures to a noticeably lesser degree.²⁹ The comment, incidentally, underlines how aware Euripides' contemporaries were of his realistic tendencies and squares with the evidence of the *Frogs*. The context in which it is quoted makes it likely that Aristotle, too, agreed with Sophocles' assessment of his rival.

We can conclude that when Aristotle refers to *spoudaioi* in his categorisation of characters suitable for representation in tragedy he means those people who are equipped for the pursuit of moral excellence by ambition and capability, the latter being determined principally by social status. Since tragedy and epic in Aristotle's view both represent *spoudaioi*, this conclusion will be true for epic as well. The *phauloi*, the people whose humble aspirations and low social station normally impose severe limits on their sphere of moral self-expression, are not worth serious attention and are therefore suitable for representation in comedy alone.

It follows from Aristotle's statement about tragedy and *hoi epiphaneis* and from his related observations about *spoudaioi* and *phauloi* that, although he asserts that the pleasure proper to art is aesthetic rather than moral (*Poet.* 48^b 4–24) and thus disagrees with the thinking present in the plays of Aristophanes and explicit in Plato, he none the less upholds the separation just as rigidly.

At the root of Aristotle's differentiation of genres on the basis of their objects is the notion of appropriateness, *to prepon*. This can refer to the appropriateness of the words with which emotion, character and subject-matter are expressed in rhetoric (*Rh.* 3.7.1 1408^a 10–16), but also in poetry, for Aristotle claims that it would be inappropriate if, for example, a slave in a play were to speak in high-flown diction, and praises Euripides for his lead in composing with words from everyday language (*Rh.* 3.2.3–5 1404^b 12–25). But, more importantly, the doctrine of *to prepon* is relevant to the question of genres: *hoi epiphaneis* and *spoudaioi* demand representation in an appropriate poetic medium, and the *phauloi* likewise. Though this is never argued in as many words, it is clearly what Aristotle assumes. We have seen his views on the grandeur of the hexameter,[30] but he also remarks that, if anyone composed narrative poetry in any other metre, it would be 'inappropriate' in view of its grand scale and hence its 'dignity' (*Poet.* 59^b 32–4). Thus in the case of epic *hoi epiphaneis* and *spoudaioi* are represented in a medium suited to them. The converse, that the grand poetic media must represent grand people alone, is likewise based on the theory of appropriateness.

Yet there are signs that Aristotle himself was aware that his categories were over-schematic. The main problem was the *Odyssey*. In Chapter Thirteen of the *Poetics* the statement is made that the tragedy with a double plot, in which the good and the bad meet with opposite fates, is in its emotional effect akin to comedy and is preferred by tragedians who court the favour of audiences who enjoy happy endings; the *Odyssey* has this kind of plot (53^a 30–9). In Chapter Twenty-Four (59^b 12–15) Aristotle remarks that the *Iliad* has a simple plot, reiterates his claim that the *Odyssey* has a double plot, and calls the *Iliad* a poem 'productive of emotion' (*pathētikon*) and the *Odyssey* 'expressive of character' (*ēthikē*).[31] In his comment about the double plot of the *Odyssey* and its kinship with comedy he perhaps betrays some uneasiness over his rigid division of the genres.

It is, furthermore, evident that even in Aristotle's day there were critics who would have challenged his rigid ascription of the *Odyssey* to the poetry representing *spoudaioi*. At *Rhetoric* 3.3.4 1406^b 12f. Aristotle quotes Alcidamas the sophist's description of the *Odyssey* as a 'fair mirror of human life'. It is likely that the metaphor was coined by Alcidamas.[32] Anyway, he obviously viewed the *Odyssey* as descriptive of ordinary human life rather than as exclusively concerned with grand material. Significantly, when the mirror metaphor next appears in literary criticism, it is used in reference to comedy: Cicero calls comedy an 'imitation of life, a mirror of ordinary experience, an image of truth' (XXVI.1–3 Koster), a definition which will be examined in a different context below. Moreover, later criticism developed Aristotle's notion of *pathos* and *ēthos* and used it as the basis for distinguishing between comedy and tragedy: thus Quintilian calls *ēthos* 'more similar to comedy, *pathos* to tragedy' (*Inst. Or.* 6.2.20);[33] the method of distinguishing the genres has been traced back to Aristotle's pupil, Theophrastus.[34] As a consequence of this view, critics came to regard the *Odyssey*, because of its preoccupation with *ēthos*, as a comedy. So, for example, Ps.-Longinus claims in *On the Sublime* 9.15 that Homer's description of Odysseus' household makes 'a sort of comedy of manners',[35] which shows that the critic recognised that at least certain sections of the *Odyssey* have an affinity to comedy. The idea is generalised to refer to the whole poem in the Latin comic *Prolegomena* by Euanthius who says that Homer composed the *Iliad* 'according to the pattern of a tragedy', the *Odyssey* 'in the image of a comedy' (XXV.1.25–8 Koster). Thus Aristotle stands, *malgré lui*, perhaps, at the head of an important development in later Homeric criticism, in which the *Odyssey* is considered not to conform strictly to the doctrine of the separation of the genres. Indeed, we shall see how figures like Eumaeus and Eurycleia exerted a vital influence on Alexandrian epic and contributed to the actual breaking of the doctrine there. However, as far as Aristotle himself is concerned, we may conclude that he did not permit any extensive genre-mixing and that for him even the *Odyssey* remained basically a representation of *spoudaioi* (*Poet.* 48^a 11f., 48^b 34–49^a 2).

Again, we have seen that in his categorisation of the objects of *mimēsis* in Chapter Two of the *Poetics* Aristotle mentions the *spoudaioi* and the *phauloi*, but also a third class, the *toioutoi*, or *hoi kath' hēmās*, the 'everyday' people 'like you and me', whom we have not yet examined. Aristotle clearly considered such people to be viable objects of *mimēsis*.[36] Indeed, at 48^a 12 he states that a certain Cleophon portrayed 'people like us'. It is a pity that this group is not discussed anywhere else in the *Poetics*, our only source of knowledge about them.[37] Where did it fit in drama? If Cleophon was the Athenian tragic poet mentioned in the *Suda*,[38] then there were tragedies depicting the *toioutoi* class which must have occupied a position somewhere in the no-man's land between the grand and the low genres. In point of literary history, of course, *toioutoi* characters are claimed for the New Comedy.

Theophrastus appears to have adopted the traditional stance on the question of genres and to have both simplified and extended Aristotelian doctrine on the matter. We are told by the grammarian Diomedes that Theophrastus defined tragedy as a 'crisis in the fate of heroes' (ἡρωϊκῆς τύχης περίστασις:XXIV.2.2 Koster). Tragedy was thus for Theophrastus a sublime genre. Diomedes also cites definitions in Greek for epic, comedy and mime. Epic is said to be defined 'by the Greeks' as a 'crisis in the affairs of gods, heroes and men' (περιοχὴ θείων τε καὶ ἡρωϊκῶν καὶ ἀνθρωπίνων πραγμάτων:1.484.2 Keil), comedy as a 'crisis, involving no harm, in the affairs of private citizens' (ἰδιωτικῶν πραγμάτων ἀκίνδυνος περιοχή:XXIV.2.25f. Koster) and mime as a 'representation of life (*mimēsis biou*) admitting what is permitted and not permitted' (μίμησις βίου τά τε συγκεχωρημένα καὶ ἀσυγχώρητα περιέχων:XXIV.3.16f. Koster). Right at the beginning of this century H. Reich argued that all four definitions are probably Theophrastan.[39] The similarity of approach, which concentrates on the kind of characters involved, together with the simplicity and pithiness of the definitions, and the similarity of phraseology and wording suggest that the four definitions came from the same author and, since Theophrastus is named as the author of one of them, it is in all probability he. Reich's arguments have won general assent.[40] The Peripatetic critic thus appears to have put epic on the same level as tragedy as a grand genre and opposed them to comedy, which he considers a low genre dealing 'harmlessly' with the lives of 'private' individuals.[41] It must be concluded, then, that Theophrastus also upheld the separation of the genres.

Theophrastus' definition of mime as *mimēsis biou* is significant for our inquiry and this is the appropriate place in which to discuss the phrase and its history. Reich argued that the concept of imitating ordinary life must originally have been associated with mime on the grounds that it is not referred to in either Aristotle's or Theophrastus' definitions of comedy. Theophrastus is, moreover, the first critic to whom the phrase can be ascribed and it is probable that he was its inventor.[42] However, though it was first employed in connection with mime, it was soon used in reference to comedy, in particular to the New Comedy which portrayed the lives of people in Aristotle's 'average citizen' category. The first extant occurrence of the term after Theophrastus is Aristophanes of Byzantium's famous comment on Menander, 'Menander and life, which of you imitated the other?'[43] The idea is commonly expressed in literary criticism thereafter. Cicero's description of comedy as an 'imitation of life, a mirror of ordinary experience, an image of truth' is generally accepted as deriving from Peripatetic criticism, if not from Theophrastus himself.[44] As we have seen, moreover, the mirror metaphor was originally applied to the *Odyssey* by Alcidamas, and it is significant that later criticism appropriated it as a term more relevant to comic *mimēsis biou* than to the genre of epic. Quintilian is also familiar with the notion of comedy imitating life, as is clear from his praise of Menander: 'his representation of life is perfect' (*Inst. Or.* 10.1.69). In all of these statements it is evident that *mimēsis biou* is specifically the province of comedy, that comedy is thus opposed to tragedy and, by implication, epic, and that the separation of genres is upheld.[45]

The doctrine of the separation of genres persists into Roman literary criticism, as we have already seen from the passages just quoted as evidence of Roman thinking about *mimēsis biou*. Indeed, the Romans so closely follow the doctrine as enunciated by Aristotle and Theophrastus that we need discuss only a brief selection of representative texts in order to establish the convervatism of the standard Roman line.

There is, for example, the comment in the treatise *ad Herennium* that tragedy takes myth, *fabula*, as its plot while comedy deals with 'realistic narrative', *argumentum*; the two genres are thus contrasted there with regard to grandeur and realism of plot.[46]

Cicero states his position quite clearly in the opening of the *de Optimo Genere Oratorum*, where he says that comic matter is a fault in a tragedy and tragic elements are bad in a comedy.[47] We have seen that he viewed comedy as an imitation of life. He also regards comic diction as more like prose (*Orat.* 20.67). The concept of *to prepon*, *decorum*, is present here as elsewhere in Cicero's works on rhetoric, and the application of it in poetry is repeatedly invoked as an example to the orator.[48]

Horace, too, upholds the separation. In the *Letter to Augustus* he states that 'comedy draws its material from the everday' (*Ep.* 2.2.168f.) and in the *Ars Poetica* he forbids the portrayal of comic themes in tragic metres or style and tragic matter in the comic (*A.P.* 89–92). At the basis of the separation is, again, the concept of appropriateness (*A.P.* 92).[49]

This survey of Greek and Roman texts from the late fifth to the late first century demonstrates that, given the different literary-critical premises of the authors whom we have considered, the separateness of the genres was a remarkably tenacious idea and in fact became the orthodox opinion, although qualifications and refinements were constantly made. Accordingly, the 'standard' literary critics considered that material from everyday and low life should not be depicted in the sublime genres like epic and tragedy but in the low genres like comedy. In the ancient scheme of things this was tantamount to saying that the everyday should never be portrayed seriously.

Broadly speaking, it is fair to say that the rules formulated by literary criticism are a true reflection of poetic practice right down to the end of the fifth century BC. While there are approximations to the Alexandrians' deployment of low matter in grand genres, there are in general few serious breaks with the separation of genres before Euripides. In the *Iliad* and the *Odyssey* lowly, even domestic material may indeed be used as a tool for the most profound pathos in certain passages,[50] but there it is only as a means to an end. And Eumaeus, Philoetius and Eurycleia are taken seriously precisely because they are faithful servants.[51] We have already in our discussion of the *spoudaios* and the *phaulos* seen why this should be so: the *phaulos* was unable to attain to the traditional competitive *aretē*, a thought forcefully enunciated in several key passages in Homer.[52] Eumaeus and Eurycleia are given noble birth:[53] even to go as far as he does in ascribing moral worth to the two *phauloi* Homer seems to have needed to reassure his audience that they were really of noble origin. Such parentage is not given to a Melanthius, for example, or a Thersites. The *Homeric Hymn to Hermes* and to a lesser degree the *Hymn to Demeter* look like counter-instances, with their admission of everyday motifs, but in fact the elements of burlesque in them show just how fixed expectations about the genre of epic were.[54] In pre-Euripidean tragedy, too, figures like the Watchman, the Herald and the Nurse in the *Oresteia* may move us, but their roles are firmly circumscribed.

The only serious rupture in the early period is the *Works and Days* of Hesiod. While the *Theogony* expresses reverence for the kings (84–96), the *Works and Days* styles them as perverters of the law, and they are sternly reminded of their duty as dispensers of justice.[55] The task of the king is to dispense straight judgements, for these are the only form of redress open to the people, who are thus at the kings' mercy.[56] This change in attitude to the kings, together with Hesiod's sense of the age's total moral depravity,[57] has significant consequences, for the poet addresses his poem no longer to the kings but to people who are, like his refractory brother Perses, low on the social scale.[58] Moreover, there is no hint of humour in his depiction of the life of the exemplary commoner. And, even more importantly, at lines 274–92 he makes it quite clear that he regards high position on the social scale (*aretē*) as attainable for the lowly through legally correct relations, toil and the prosperity which results from these.[59] This possibility is inconceivable for Homer, who pictures a social structure which restricts mobility, on the whole limiting it to the movement downwards illustrated by the kidnap and enslavement of Eumaeus (though the sons of slave-women may move upwards if their fathers are princes), and in which a Thersites is put firmly in his place and not even a Eumaeus or Eurycleia can aspire to social independence. It is evident also that Hesiod considered his poem to belong to what we have called the grand genre of epic: witness the proem to Zeus (1–10) and the serious tone which pervades the work. There is, therefore, every justification for calling the *Works and Days* a 'poor man's epic'.[60] As such, it represents a true crossing of the genres. This is an aspect of Hesiod which seems to have made him particularly attractive to the Alexandrians.

But Euripides is the true father of the Alexandrians' crossing of the genres and we must consider him, and in particular his *Electra*, in some detail.[61]

In the *Electra*, the Farmer[62] claims that his family was of Mycenaean nobility (35), but now, though it has a noble lineage, its actual social superiority has collapsed, since it no longer has the money necessary to back its claim to nobility (37–8). The Farmer is, therefore, humble in his situation, and would in traditional Athenian thought have been considered a *kakos*, a synonym of *phaulos*, his chances of possessing moral virtue being non-existent.[63] When Electra tells Orestes that the man has not touched her bed since he did not think it right to affront her parents, does not consider that Aegisthus had the proper authority to give her in marriage and is in addition *sōphrōn*, self-controlled (253–61), Orestes is made to follow traditional thinking and doubt that moral nobility could be attributed to such a lowly creature, but he finally acknowledges the fact (262). After seeing for himself the hospitality of the Farmer (357–63), he expresses full recognition of the man's moral worth. The Farmer, he says, has proven to be *aristos*, though not high on the social scale (380–5). *Aristos* here has a moral force foreign to traditional usage, where it denotes social status and possession of the 'competitive virtues'. Orestes challenges people who judge by superficial appearances to judge men's moral worth 'by their relations in social intercourse'[64] and by their character. The violence of the address seems to indicate that the idea contained in it was new and that Euripides considered it revolutionary and vitally important.[65] True, the poet ascribes noble lineage to the Farmer, but perhaps he is to some extent concerned to explain to his audience the Farmer's goodness in terms of traditional morality, much as Homer did with Eumaeus and Eurycleia. But the essential fact is that the Farmer's situation is now that of a *phaulos*, and, on traditional thinking, it will come as a surprise to see him displaying moral goodness.

The Farmer is unlike Eurycleia and Eumaeus in that his moral nobility is given explicit recognition and is, furthermore, held up as a model to Euripides' audience. Moreover, it is not essential to the play that he should have such a noble character, which suggests that Euripides is going out of his way to make a point. Indeed, Orestes' comment that he has seen 'a great heart in a poor man's body' (372) looks almost like a deliberate answer to those like Aristophanes who criticised Euripides for being a 'beggar-poet'. The tragedian has given an active role in his tragedy to a character who is a *phaulos*. As a result, the separation of the genres is threatened, even though the Farmer is still precluded by the grand genre from being given a *main* role, and Euripides' characterisation of him comes strikingly close to realism in one of its most important senses.

The Middle and the New Comedy are also relevant. First, the main characters come from what Aristotle would have called the *kath' hēmās* section of society, 'people like you and me'. Examples are Sostratus and Cnemon's daughter in the *Dyscolus*. In depicting this 'middle' class and not merely 'inferior people', comedy has taken a step towards mixing the genres. Secondly, persons from the lower classes are frequently portrayed sympathetically and with an emphasis on their moral goodness, just as the Farmer had been in the *Electra*. The comic type which illustrates this best is, perhaps, the 'golden-hearted hetaera'. A good example is Habrotonon in Menander's *Epitrepontes*, but she is only one example of a wide class.[66] The type almost certainly occurred in the Middle Comedy, to judge, for example, by Antiphanes *Fr.* 212, in which mention is made of a hetaera who has a 'character which is golden in its virtue', and by Ephippus *Fr.* 6, which describes a hetaera's genuine and sympathetic concern for her client's well-being.[67] Outside the sphere of hetaerae we have poor, though free, men, such as the noble Daemones in Plautus' *Rudens*. Loyal slaves of high principle are of course common, Daos in Menander's *Aspis* and Lampadio in the *Cistellaria* being good examples. This elevation of the low will have been instrumental in bridging the gap between the genres, though the overall framework remains that of comedy.

From this survey we are entitled to draw certain conclusions. As far as ancient literary criticism is concerned, the doctrine of the separation of genres was never seriously threatened, though the reasons for upholding it may have changed, from the didacticism voiced by Aristophanes' characters to the exclusive concern with proper aesthetic effect in Aristotle and Horace's use of the concept of *decorum*. The practice of pre-Alexandrian poetry in general supports the testimony of literary theory, though the *Odyssey* is less strict in its adherence to the rule (and as a consequence often represented something of a stumbling-block to the literary critics), Hesiod's *Works and Days* is a real exception to it, Euripides appears to have reacted consciously against the traditional separation, and the New Comedy attempts sympathetic portrayal of ordinary and low folk. The trend towards a mixing of the genres gathers momentum from Euripides onwards, but it is only in the Alexandrian period that genre-mixing becomes a widely-used means for deliberate artistic effect, and at times for realistic representation in a sense very close to the modern.

Notes

1. L. E. Rossi, 'I generi letterari e le loro leggi scritte e non scritte nelle letterature classiche', *B.I.C.S.* 18 (1971), 69–94. For sporadic attacks on the notion of 'the crossing of the genres' see e.g. R. K. Hack, 'The Doctrine of Literary Forms', *H.S.C.P.* 27 (1916), 1–65 and M. Lenchantin, 'Sul preteso sincretismo dei generi nella letteratura latina', *R.F.I.C.* N.S. 12 (1934), 433–46. For useful surveys and discussions of the debate see Rossi, ibid., 71ff. and E.-R. Schwinge, 'Griechische Poesie und die Lehre von der Gattungstrinität in der Moderne', *A.u.A.* 27 (1981), 130–62. Rossi, ibid., 82f. has a list of the Greek words for the term 'genre'.

2. It is difficult to ascertain the precise status of lyric's different forms. On the problem see e.g. H. Färber, *Die Lyrik in der Kunsttheorie der Antike* (Munich, 1936); I. Behrens, *Die Lehre von der Einteilung der Dichtkunst* (Halle/Saale, 1940), pp. 3–8; A. E. Harvey, 'The Classification of Greek Lyric Poetry', *C.Q.* N.S. 5 (1955), 157–75; R. Harriott, *Poetry and Criticism before Plato* (London, 1969), p. 140; Rossi, ibid., 78; Schwinge, ibid., 142f.

3. Of course, the historical Aeschylus would hardly have suggested that his own Electra or Sophocles' Antigone were not tragic characters; Aristophanes probably means us to understand Euripides and Aeschylus as referring to women like the Nurse in the *Hippolytus*.

4. Cf. 1202–4, where Aeschylus sarcastically states that even the most commonplace things 'fit in' in Euripides' iambics. The re-appearance of the 'little oilflask' and the similarity of the objects enumerated to those mentioned by Dionysus at 980–1 make it likely that the same point is being made in each passage. Thus a serious criticism is being voiced, even if, as Harriott, *Poetry and Criticism before Plato*, p. 152 says, 'nonsense overcomes reasoned fault-finding' with the continued repetition of the tag. Other issues are at stake, of course: the monotony of Euripides' metre and sentence-structure and his love of commonplace words and diminutives have, among other things, been seen as relevant (see W. B. Stanford, *Aristophanes: The Frogs* (London, 1963) ad loc.). The tag's alleged sexual innuendo has been disputed by D. Bain, 'ΛΗΚΥΘΙΟΝ ΑΠΩΛΕΣΕΝ: Some Reservations', *C.Q.*, N.S. 35 (1985), 31–7 (with lit.).

The Ancient Theory and Pre-Alexandrian Practice 151

5. Cf. Harriott, ibid., p. 154f.; Ion's monody at *Ion* 82–183 contains mundane material: see B.M.W. Knox, 'Euripidean Comedy', in *The Rarer Action: Essays in Honor of Francis Fergusson* (New Brunswick, N.J., 1970), 78f. (=Knox, *Word and Action: Essays on the Ancient Theater* (Baltimore and London, 1979), 259).

6. Cf. *Ach.* 480.

7. φροῦδά μοι τὰ δράματα, a neat joke: φροῦδος ('vanished') was a favourite word of Euripides; Aristophanes pokes further fun at it at *Frogs* 304 (after a quotation of *Orestes* 279), 1344a (φροῦδη Γλύκη, in the parody of Euripidean lyrics) and *Clouds* 718–22.

8. In his own day Aristophanes was criticised for his stylistic dependence on Euripides: Σ ad Pl. *Apol.* 19. Cf. Harriott, *Poetry and Criticism before Plato*, p. 160.

9. See *Laws* 656c–657b, 660b, 669b–670b, 798d.

10. See also *Symp.* 223d, *Rep.* 395a.

11. Plato is said, for example, to have introduced the mimes of Sophron to Athens and to have used them as bedside-reading: *Sophr. Test.* 1 and 3 Kaibel. See in general R. Pfeiffer, *History of Classical Scholarship* vol. i: *From the Beginnings to the End of the Hellenistic Age* (Oxford, 1968), p. 265 and A. S. Riginos, *Platonica: The Anecdotes concerning the Life and Writings of Plato*, Columbia Studies in the Classical Tradition 3 (Leiden, 1976), pp. 44 n. 26, 174–7, 196.

12. See *Rep.* 395c–396e, 606c, *Laws* 935c–e.

13. Cf. *Gorg.* 502b, *Rep.* 568af., *Minos* 320ef., *Laws* 838c.

14. Cf. *Rep.* 413b, *Men.* 76e, *Phaedr.* 237a.

15. Cf. *Rep.* 598d, 605cf., 606ef., *Minos* 318e.

16. See *Rep.* 379d, 392df., 394bf., 602b.

17. See I. Murdoch, *The Fire and the Sun: Why Plato banished the Artists* (Oxford, 1977). For the more favourable assessments of poetry (at e.g. *Laws* 681e–682a, *Phaedr.* 245a, *Ion* 534c–d, *Rep.* 404b, *Symp.* 209d, *Alc.* 2 147bf.,) see especially W. J. Verdenius, *Mimesis: Plato's Doctrine of Artistic Imitation and its Meaning to Us*, Philosophia Antiqua 3 (Leiden, 1949) and H. Gundert, 'Enthusiasmos und Logos bei Platon', *Lexis* 2 (1949), 25–46 (=K. Döring and F. Preisshofen (eds.), *Hermann Gundert: Platonstudien, Studien zur antiken Philosophie* 7 (Amsterdam, 1977), 1–22).

18. See below, pp. 155f.

19. See also 49^b 24, 49^b 32 and D. W. Lucas, *Aristotle: Poetics* (Oxford, 1968) on 48^a 16.

20. Cf. 49^b 9–20.

21. Cf. 48^a 11f., 48^b 34–49^a 2, 49^b 9–20.

22. So Lucas on 48^b 35.

23. Lucas, ibid., has a particularly useful discussion of the terms in his note on 48^a 2.

24. Lucas, ibid., quotes Arist. *Cat.* 10^b 7: 'the *spoudaios* comes from having *aretē*, for he is called *spoudaios* by virtue of his possessing *aretē*.'

25. See especially A. W. H. Adkins, *Merit and Responsibility* (Oxford, 1960), pp. 31–40, 156–63; Adkins, *From the Many to the One* (London, 1970), pp. 28–32, 74–9, 266f.; Adkins, *Moral Values and Political Behaviour in Ancient Greece* (London, 1972), pp. 12–14, 22–57, 60–72, 99–147.

26. Adkins, *Merit and Responsibility*, pp. 172–354, *From the Many to the One*, pp. 143–51, 205–9, *Moral Values*, pp. 112–19.

27. If Aristotle were asked how he reconciled this with the existence of tragic heroines like Electra, Antigone or Alcestis, he could have claimed that, as *epiphaneis*, they had something to lose.

28. I am, therefore, in disagreement with those scholars who have seen in *phaulos* and *spoudaios* in the *Poetics* an exclusively moral sense, a view held by e.g. S. H. Butcher, *Aristotle's Theory of Poetry and Fine Art*[4] (London, 1911), pp.

228ff., G. F. Else, *Aristotle's Poetics: the Argument* (Cambridge, Mass., 1957), pp. 71–8, 455–62, and M. E. Hubbard, in D. A. Russell and M. Winterbottom, *Ancient Literary Criticism* (Oxford, 1972), p. 92, who translates the words at *Poet.* 48^a 2 as 'good' and 'bad'. A. W. H. Adkins, 'Aristotle and the Best Kind of Tragedy', *C.Q.* N.S. 16 (1966), 78–102 argues rightly, I think, that the terms *aretē, dikaiosynē, kakia, mochthēria* and *hamartia* at *Poet.* 53^a 10ff. refer to co-operative values and as such are foreign to their usage in the fifth century where they denote competitive values. But he nowhere considers the terms *hoi epiphaneis, spoudaios* and *phaulos* or the thinking behind their use, which, on my reading of the *Poetics*, are competitive.

29. So Lucas on 60^b 34.
30. Above, p. 11.
31. On these terms see further Lucas on 52^b 10, 56^a 1 and 59^b 15 and, most recently, C. Gill, 'The *Ēthos/Pathos* Distinction in Rhetorical and Literary Criticism', *C.Q.* N.S. 34 (1984), 149–66, esp. 150f.
32. So E. Fraenkel, *Elementi plautini in Plauto* (Florence, 1960), p. 368 n. 2 and Fraenkel, *Aeschylus: Agamemnon*, vol. ii (Oxford, 1950), p. 386 n. 1. On the metaphor, see E. R. Curtius, *Europäische Literatur und lateinisches Mittelalter* (Bern, 1948), p. 339 n. 1 (= Eng. trans. W. R. Trask, *European Literature and the Latin Middle Ages, Bollingen Series* 36 (New York, 1953), p. 336 n. 56) and Pfeiffer, *Hist. Class. Schol.* vol. i, p. 50f.
33. See further D. A. Russell, *'Longinus': On the Sublime* (Oxford, 1964) on *Subl.* 9.15 and Gill, 'The *Ēthos/Pathos* Distinction', 160.
34. E.g. by A. Rostagni, 'Aristotele e l'Aristotelismo nella storia dell' estetica antica', *S.I.F.C.* N.S. 2 (1922), 110–13 (=*Scritti Minori I: 'Aesthetica'* (hereafter *Scr. Min. I.*)) (Turin, 1955), 212ff.)
35. So Russell *ad loc.*; cf. Lucas on *Poet.* 56^a 1 and Gill, 'The *Ēthos/Pathos* Distinction', 163.
36. See e.g. 48^a 5f. where the tripartite division is illustrated from painting. On Dionysius' 'average' subjects see Ael. *V.H.* 4.3, Pliny *N.H.* 35.113 and G. Sörbom, *Mimesis and Art* (Bonniers, 1966), pp. 191f.
37. As Lucas, *ad loc.*, notes, the requirement expressed at 54^a 24, that the characters of the tragedy should be *homoioi*, is of no relevance to this question, for there Aristotle is referring to the need for the audience to be able to identify with tragic characters in order to be moved by their fate (cf. 53^a 5f.).
38. So E. M. Cope, *The Rhetoric of Aristotle*, (revised by J. E. Sandys) (Cambridge, 1877) on *Rh.* 3.7.2 1408^a 15, where a Cleophon is criticised for inappropriate diction; cf. I. Bywater, *Aristotle on the Art of Poetry* (Oxford, 1909) *ad loc.* and Lucas *ad loc.*
39. H. Reich, *Der Mimus: ein litterar-entwickelungsgeschichtlicher Versuch* (Berlin, 1903), pp. 263ff., following U. von Wilamowitz-Moellendorff, *Euripides: Herakles* (Berlin, 1889), vol. i, p. 55 (=Wilamowitz-Moellendorff, *Einleitung in die griechische Tragödie* (Berlin, 1910), p. 56).
40. See especially W. W. Fortenbaugh, 'Theophrast über den komischen Charakter', *Rh.M.* N.F. 124 (1981), 257f. and R. Janko, *Aristotle on Comedy: Towards a Reconstruction of Poetics II* (London, 1984), p. 48f. (with lit.).
41. For Theophrastus' possible use of Aristotelian *pathos* and *ēthos* to distinguish tragedy and epic from comedy see above, p. 143.
42. Reich, *Der Mimus*, pp. 267 and 281ff.
43. Syrian. *Comment. in Hermog.* II.23.6 Rabe (= *Men. test.* 32 Körte); see Janko, *Aristotle on Comedy*, p. 111f. for further literature.
44. So e.g. Wilamowitz, *Einleitung*, p. 56; Reich, *Der Mimus*, p. 265; A. Rostagni, 'Sui "Caratteri" di Teofrasto', *R.F.I.C.* 48 (1920), 429 n. 2 (= *Scr. Min. I,* 339 n. 5); Rostagni, 'Aristotele', 140f, (= *Scr. Min. I,* 230); Rostagni, *Orazio: Arte Poetica* (Turin, 1930) on *A.P.* 317; A. Plebe, *La teoria del comico da*

Aristotele a Plutarco (Turin, 1952), p. 32ff.; C. O. Brink, *Horace on Poetry: Prolegomena to the Literary Epistles* (Cambridge, 1963), p. 98; Pfeiffer, *Hist. Class, Schol.* vol. i, p. 190 n. 9; C.O. Brink, *Horace on Poetry: the 'Ars Poetica'* (Cambridge, 1971) on *A.P.* 90.

45. For further references see Lucil. *Fr.* 1029 Marx (= 1106 Krenkel), *ad Herenn.* 1.8.13, Cic. *Rosc. Am.* 47 (cf. Euanthius *de Com.* XXVI.20–7 Koster), Manil. *Astron.* 5.475f., Mart. 8.3.20, 10.4.10, Gell., *N.A.* 2.23.12, Scholia to Dionysius Thrax XVIII b 1α Koster.

46. For a discussion of the Peripatetic use of the terms 'myth' (μῦθος, *fabula*), 'history' (λόγος, *historia*) and 'realistic narrative' (πλάσμα, *argumentum*) see Janko, *Aristotle on Comedy*, pp. 48ff.

47. Cf. Quint. *Inst. Or.* 10.2.22, Accius *Didascalica Fr.* 8 Funaioli, Hor. *A.P.* 80, 89–92, and Ps.-Longinus *Subl.* 3.1.

48. See especially *Orat.* 21.70–22.74, *Off.* 1.28.97.

49. See further *C.* 1.6, 2.1.37–40, 3.3.69–72, 4.9.25–8, 4.15, *S.* 1.4.39–62, *Ep.* 2.1.245–59.

50. E.g. *Il.* 6.392–502, 9.485–91, 24.599–633, *Od.* 6.48–116, 17.290–327, 19.386–507; n.b. also the similes, e.g. *Il.* 12.433–5, 15.362–4, 20.252–5.

51. E. Auerbach, *Mimesis: Dargestellte Wirklichkeit in der abendländischen Literatur* (Bern, 1946), p. 27 (=Eng. trans. W. R. Trask, *Mimesis: the Representation of Reality in Western Literature* (Princeton, 1953), p. 21).

52. See especially *Il.* 2.188–206, 212–77, *Od.* 17.322–3.

53. *Od.* 1.429–33, 15.403–84.

54. N. J. Richardson, *The Homeric Hymn to Demeter* (Oxford, 1974), pp. 56–8. The same is true of epic parody, as in Hipponax *Fr.* 77 and the *Batrachomyomachia* (dated to the last quarter of the fifth century by L. J. Bliquez, 'Frogs and Mice at Athens', *T.A.P.A.* 107 (1977), 11–25 (with lit.)); cf. the fragment of the *Margites*, *P. Oxy.* 2309 (= *Fr.* 7 West) with Lobel *ad loc.*

55. *W.D.* 35–41, 213–73; on δωροφάγοι ('bribe-eaters') at 39, 221, 264 see M.L. West, *Hesiod: Works and Days* (Oxford, 1978) on 39.

56. So M. Gagarin, '*Dikē* in the *Works and Days*', *C.P.* 68 (1973), 90f. This is, moreover, the import of the hawk and nightingale αἶνος (202–12): see my 'A Hesiodic Reminiscence in Virgil, *E.* 9.11–13', *C.Q.* N.S. 35 (1985), 235f.

57. *W.D.* 174–201.

58. At *W.D.* 213–16 Perses is warned that, as a *deilos*, he should avoid *hybris*, a burden which not even an *esthlos* can bear easily. The sense of *deilos* and *esthlos* is clearly social; so West *ad loc.*

59. For the social, non-moral meaning of *aretē* and *kakotēs* see West on 287–92. For the thought see especially Adkins, *Merit and Responsibility*, pp. 70–3 and *Moral Values*, p. 25, and J. Fontenrose, 'Work, Justice, and Hesiod's Five Ages', *C.P.* 69 (1974), 1–16.

60. So in general M. Puelma, 'Sänger und König: Zum Verständnis von Hesiods Tierfabel', *M.H.* 29 (1972), esp. 108f. For Hesiod's awareness of his low social class in the *Theog.* see W. Stroh, 'Hesiods lügende Musen', in H. Görgemanns and E. A. Schmidt (eds.), *Studien zum antiken Epos. Beiträge zur klassischen Philologie* 72 (Meisenheim am Glan, 1976), 85–112, esp. 101ff. Cf. H. Fränkel, *Early Greek Poetry and Philosophy: A History of Greek Epic, Lyric and Prose to the Middle of the Fifth Century* (Eng. trans. M. Hadas and J. Willis) (Oxford, 1975), p. 108 with n. 29. — The Greeks had no separate category of didactic epic (see Lucas on *Poet.* 47[a] 28–49[b] 2; hence, presumably, Aristotle is not thinking of the *W.D.* when he talks of the φυσιολόγοι at *Poet.* 47[b] 13–20). So at *Frogs* 1032ff. the Hesiod of the *W.D.* is one of the 'useful' and 'able' poets, like Orpheus, Musaeus and Homer; cf. Plato *Laws* 658d. See further Stroh, ibid., 110ff.; B. Effe, *Dichtung und Lehre: Untersuchungen zur Typologie des antiken Lehrgedichts, Zetemata* 69 (Munich, 1977), pp. 9–26; Schwinge, 'Griechische Poesie', 143ff., 150ff., 154ff.

61. See especially Knox, 'Euripidean Comedy'.
62. Discussed by Adkins, *Merit and Responsibility*, pp. 176–8, 195ff., 'Aristotle', 86 and *Moral Values.*, pp. 115–18.
63. See Adkins, loc. cit.
64. For ὁμιλία see Fraenkel on *Agamemnon* 838–40
65. So Adkins, *Merit and Responsibility*, pp. 176f., *Moral Values*, p. 116. On the recipients of the address see D. Bain, 'Audience Address in Greek Tragedy', *C.Q.* N.S. 25 (1975), 20. The thought contained in Orestes' speech is an extension of what Euripides says elsewhere. See e.g. *Suppl.* 403–8, 433–7. The characterisation can be considered as a contribution to the *nomos/physis* debate, for which see e.g. *Andr.* 636–41, *Hec.* 596–602, *Hipp.* 305–10, *Frr.* 142, 166–8, 378. For the view that lines 368–72, 373–9, 383–5, 386–90 are spurious see M.D. Reeve, 'Interpolations in Greek Tragedy, III', *G.R.B.S.* 14 (1973), 151–3 (with lit.).
66. Cf. Thais in Terence's *Eunuch* (from Menander), Chrysis in the *Andria* (also from Menander), and Bacchis in the *Hecyra* (n. b. 763).
67. For a survey of these 'golden-hearted hetaerae' see F. Wehrli, *Motivstudien zur griechischen Komödie* (Zurich and Leipzig, 1936), pp. 40–5.

6 The Everyday and the Low in Alexandrian Poetry

The Alexandrians' literary-critical thinking on the content appropriate to the genres can be reconstructed quite clearly. The movement's central figure, Callimachus, provides us with the most direct evidence. This is found in the proem to the *Aetia*, which is written in elegiacs, but by this time narrative elegiac and hexameter poetry were both viewed as epic, so that the prologue's programme is relevant to Callimachus' thought on hexameter epic as well.[1] Callimachus claims that his poetry is criticised 'because I did not accomplish one continuous poem of many thousands of lines on . . . kings or . . . heroes, but I unroll a tale (ἔπος) for a short time, like a child' (*Fr.* 1.3–6). The comment is valuable to us because it explicitly shows that readers of Callimachus' poetry missed in it the 'kings and heroes' of traditional epic. Nor does the poet reject these charges. Moreover, the statement implies that his interest was perceived to have been fixed on people of another kind.[2] That these are ordinary, everyday folk like Acontius and Cydippe and their non-heroic encounter, or low folk like Molorchus, or heroes in uncharacteristically domestic settings like Heracles, will become evident in the following pages. Callimachus' reply to his critics that Apollo taught him to tread untrodden poetic paths (25–8) is probably in part a defence against their objections to his avoidance of traditional themes and subject-matter. Perhaps the concern with such people is a reason for Callimachus' interest in Hesiod, whom he seems to have taken over as the authority for his literary doctrine when he rejected traditional epic on the scale of Homer's poems and the bombast that he apparently viewed as the standard epic tone.[3] Quite apart from certain stylistic features of Hesiodic poetry, like its comparative shortness, its continual change of subject, its disjointed, seemingly illogical sequence of thought and its personal tone, Hesiod's celebration of the farmer and not the kings in the *Works and Days* may have struck Callimachus as particularly congenial and fruitful.

It appears from the *Aetia*-prologue, then, that Callimachus was consciously subverting traditional expectations of epic subject-matter. Perhaps he was thinking of Aristotelian notions of epic in particular.[4] But Callimachean thinking can be discerned elsewhere in the Alexandrian movement. Apollonius, for example, yields clear evidence in the *Argonautica* that his conception of the material appropriate to epic was untraditional. He makes the seer Phineus prophesy to the Argonauts that the success of their expedition depends on Aphrodite (2.423f.). Now Phineus is like Teiresias who advises Odysseus which deity should be supplicated (*Od.* 11.101–3, 130ff., and with A.R. 2.310 compare *Od.* 10.539f.), but, while Teiresias directs Odysseus' attention to his persecution by Poseidon, Phineus alerts Jason to the special role to be played by the goddess of love. Love is an emotion which post-Euripidean poets and especially the Alexandrians seem to have viewed as a more human and familiar and hence a more compelling motive for action than a desire for glory or the like. Apollonius makes his intention even more plain in his proem to Book 3. There he calls upon Erato, the Muse of love poetry, to tell 'how Jason brought the fleece to Iolcus through the love of Medea', and makes much of the Muse's close connections with Aphrodite (3.1–5). And he shares Callimachus' misgivings over the traditional status of the epic hero, for, as we shall see, in his characterisation of Jason he scales down traditional ideas of heroic grandeur to a more emphatically everyday level.

Theocritus' agreement with Callimachus' programme cannot reasonably be doubted.[5] There is the interesting passage in *Idyll* 16, the *Graces* or *Hiero*, in which he shows very clearly what he really thinks to be the material appropriate to modern epic. At lines 48–57 he cites examples of poetry's power to confer immortality on men, and it is interesting to see what caught his eye. He devotes three lines to heroes connected with the Trojan war, but he devotes no less than seven to the *Odyssey* (51–7), thereby showing a preoccupation with an epic which refused to fit into the neat categorisations of literary criticism as an epic of unequivocal heroic grandeur. But, most interestingly for us, the list of persons and events in the *Odyssey* culminates with the swineherd Eumaeus and the neatherd Philoetius, and with Laertes, whom we most readily picture at work in his orchard. Theocritus, then, is interested in the *phauloi* of the tradition, in particular those of the countryside. Moreover, he expresses this interest in a poem in which he depicts his contemporaries' lack of interest in poetry by making a reluctant patron say 'Who would listen to another?

Homer is enough for everybody' (20). Poetry, Theocritus suggests, is not 'written out' provided that it strikes out in new directions, and, although Homer is certainly pre-eminent, there are aspects of his poetry which are worth closer attention. Figures like Eumaeus, who stand on the periphery of the heroic main narrative, become the literary legitimation of his pastoral poetry, a specimen of which he gives later in the poem (90–7),[6] and it is to such *phauloi* that he wishes to give the centre stage in his new epos. This is tantamount to saying that in his pastorals he crosses the traditional genres, though that observation is true also of the other main branches of his *oeuvre*. The passage became something of a manifesto for later pastoral. The *Lament for Bion*, for an example, claims that while Homer sang of heroic persons Bion eschewed warlike themes and opted instead for Pan, pastoral song and love (70–84).[7]

One of the problems of particular concern to the Alexandrians was clearly, then, the nature of the hero appropriate to contemporary epic. Callimachus, Apollonius, Theocritus, and the author of the *Lament* all show a distaste for traditional concepts of what constitutes a literary hero, and their literary-critical utterances indicate that they were predisposed towards everyday and low heroes in epic and hence towards the violation of generic expectations like those formulated by Aristotle.

Our main field of inquiry in what follows will be epic. It will pay to heed the reminder of Ziegler and others that Alexandrian epic was in fact an isolated branch of the epic written in the Hellenistic period and that the hexameter-poetry of the age continued to deal with grand themes, whether mythological, historical or encomiastic. Evidently, the grand associations of the genre and its metre were still the norm. Further proof of this is provided (if it were still needed) by the fact that later in the third century Ennius chose to introduce the metre into Latin poetry and to employ it in his *Annales*: if its acoustic grandeur had been dissipated, would he have taken such an enormous step? In investigating the Alexandrians' use of the everyday and low in epic, we must place their generic experimentation within the context of contemporary epic as a whole in order to try to appreciate their poetry's impact on people's minds and ears.

One of the chief aims of this chapter will be to establish the tones and effects which the Alexandrians created through their deployment of everyday and low material. Tone is a notoriously labile commodity, and I am aware that many readers may disagree with my judgements. I have, however, at least tried to relate these to the aesthetic, cultural, political and moral sensibilities of the period as I understand them. But in my attempt to ascertain the tone that might have been perceived by an Alexandrian audience I am aware that here too responses were probably multiple. I can only hope that my readings will not contradict what is known of the Alexandrian audiences' tastes and that they will approximate to the responses of a reasonable section of the original readership.

A poet obviously preoccupied with the everyday and the low is Herodas. His bawds, pandars, child-delinquents, sadistic schoolmasters, chattering housewives, jealous mistresses of sexually disobedient slaves, and his dildo-stitching cobblers are realistic enough as subject-matter, but Herodas makes no attempt at an analytical presentation of their circumstances, or, we may add, of their psychology:[8] the characters are designed simply to provoke our laughter. We may, in other words, conclude that in his poems the separation of genres remains intact.

We need examine only one of the *Mimiambi* in order to substantiate these conclusions. The second, *The Pandar*, is as instructive as any. In his legal suit before the Coan jury Battarus, the Pandar, is, for comic effect, repeatedly made to revert to well-worn phrases and arguments in Attic oratory. So, for instance, he solemnly reminds the court of their duty to judge him and the sea-captain, Thales, as equals before the law, despite the latter's superior wealth (1–10), argues that judgement on his suit will determine the security of the state and the rights of non-citizens like him (25–7, 92–4), and appeals to the legendary glories and deeds of the jury's Coan ancestors to stimulate pride of country (95–8). He even offers his own body to be tortured as if he were a slave, provided that Thales places before the court the compensation-money. This is an impudent and avaricious perversion of the law that the accuser had to pay damages to the master of a slave tortured before giving evidence on a charge which proved false (87–91).[9] The Pandar's claptrap rhetoric is a means of characterising him, rather than simply a parody of legal rhetoric.

Another aspect of Battarus' characterisation is his continual use of proverbs, on occasion supremely sordid. Proverbs had long been an integral part of mime and Sophron himself is attested as having used them extensively.[10] So, for example, when the Pandar asks the clerk to stop the clepsydra, he is reminded of a proverb running something like 'lest the anus is incontinent and the bedcovers are stained' (44–5).[11] Again, he complains that he was treated by Thales 'like the mouse in the pitch-pot' (62–3).[12]

The story of how Battarus was wronged is skilfully unfolded detail by detail, from his own mouth, but in such a way that it becomes perfectly plain that his presentation of himself as a poor, law-abiding metic in Cos is a total sham and that his charge, for all its bullying abuse of rhetoric, cannot stand. We do not get a real idea of what has happened until lines 33ff., when we are told that Thales, in what was evidently a rowdy revel, stole one of Battarus' girls from his establishment by night, setting fire to his house with torches. Finally, and almost incidentally, the Pandar lets it out that Thales abducted the girl because he was in love with her (79). He goes on to claim that all Thales has to do is to pay him for Myrtale's services and there the matter will rest. He thereby reveals that his indignation over the sailor's treatment of her is insincere and that he is bringing suit merely because one of his girls is being used free of charge and because he stands to win a fast buck if he is successful or bludgeons Thales into a settlement out of court.

The characterisation of Battarus is achieved by means of what has been called the 'mosaic' technique. It is the method of the New Comedy and Theophrastus: a general type is selected and then individualised by realistic traits and details.[13] Within the bounds of ancient comic character-portrayal, then, we do not have any difficulty in calling the chief character of *Mimiamb* 2 realistic. However, there are other aspects of the poem which are not at all realistic. Battarus' oratory is a perverted imitation of Athenian legal rhetoric, but the scene of the poem is Cos (95–8). Since the scene is Doric-speaking Cos, the dialect in which Battarus speaks is unrealistic, being an imitation of Hipponax' Eastern Ionic[14] and thus obsolete.[15] The metrical form of the poem, a revival of Hipponax' choliambs, makes it much more stylised than the prose of traditional mime. If, as seems probable, Herodas wanted to catch his audience's interest by presenting a scene from contemporary Coan low life in a revived and confessedly archaic form, one which had originally been used for satirical rather than mimic purposes, and in a defunct form of Greek, then *Mimiamb* 2 must to some extent have represented a literary in-joke: the philological learnedness of the piece (and of the collection as a whole)[16] must have been perceived as colliding ironically with the lowness of the subject-matter. Herodas' aim in selecting and portraying low material like the Pandar is the unswerving pursuit of comic effect, and we can now see how absurd it is to try to label the poet a prototype social realist or the like.

Callimachus' *Iambi* have a moral earnestness absent from Herodas. Callimachus, too, revives Hipponax' choliambic metre and, in modified form, his Ionic, but everyday and low material is firmly subordinated to the comparatively contemplative character of the poems.[17] The first *Iambus* will illustrate my point. The Diegete (*Dieg.* VI.1–21) informs us that the purpose of Hipponax' appearance among the living was to forbid the literati of Alexandria from jealous feuding. Thus the poem is moralistic in intention. Hipponax' speech has a colloquial tone. For example, he expostulates in lively terms at the size of the crowd of scholars who have gathered to listen to him: 'Apollo, these people are swarming in droves like flies on a goatherd or wasps from the ground or Delphians from a sacrifice; Hecate, what a crowd! The old baldy over there will burst his lungs trying to keep his measly cloak from being torn off' (26–30). Secondly, he is repeatedly made to resort to common proverbs. His comments on the crowd, for instance, contain a reference to the Delphians who were proverbial for the way they filched meat from other people's sacrifices. Such proverbs are doubtless intended to give a realistic flavour to Hipponax' speech. True, by this period proverbs had become a field of scholarly research and their use was perhaps to some extent a self-conscious literary device, but this need not detract from a realistic effect. Thirdly, it is worth noting how carefully Callimachus sets the scene. He refers to places and personages of topical interest and makes Hipponax call the scholars outside the city walls to the Serapeum dedicated by Parmenio, where 'the old babbler who fabricated the ancient Panchaean Zeus scribbles his impious scriptures' (9–11), referring to Euhemerus. The 'old baldy' clutching at his cloak in the bustle seems meant to be a Cynic philosopher. The realistic setting of the imaginary scene is wittily ironic. Fourthly, the poet appears keen to make his characterisations as dramatically vivid as possible by means of realistic touches. So Hipponax calls his audience to silence and commands them to begin note-taking (31), interrupting his lecture by abusing someone whom he sees turning up his nose at the thought of a long harangue (32–5). The same concern is present in Hipponax' cautionary tale about the Seven Wise Men. There is, for instance, the picturesque, everyday piece of scene-setting when the cup which Bathycles bequeathed to the best of the Wise Men is offered to Thales. The philosopher, who has been discovered characteristically pondering mathematical problems and drawing diagrams on the ground (52–63), apparently scratches the ground with his stick and with his free hand thoughtfully strokes his beard (69f.)[18]

Among the poems on sex (3, 5, 9, 11), the third is an attack on the materialism of the times and the venality of a boy whom Callimachus is inconclusively lusting after, but, in contrast with what Herodas might have done, the poet apparently refrains from the obvious humour that the theme might lend itself to.[19] The other poems, like *Iambus* 13, with Callimachus' defence of his writing in different genres and his dialect-mixing, also demonstrate how much more reflective the choliambic tradition became in Callimachus' hands.

Brief mention may be made here of Machon's *Chriae*. The name of the work is itself ironical, for, while the title of *Chriae* at this period was given to collections of the witty apophthegms of philosophers, Machon uses it to introduce his comic and often scabrous anecdotes about the *demi-monde* of parasites (1–7 Gow), musicians (8 Gow), gourmands (9–11 Gow) and courtesans (13–18 Gow).[20] The style of the *Chriae* is the same as that of the two extant fragments of Machon's comedies (*Frr.* 19 and 20 Gow); it is that of the New Comedy, and has a colloquial, prosaic vocabulary.[21] Accordingly, the low characters, the sexual jokes and their presentation are all comic in intention. There is no real attempt at characterisation except in so far as the characters reveal themselves by their *bons mots*.

Epigram in all its types turned to everyday and low life for material. In the traditional types, the dedicatory and funerary, we can discern very different effects. The poem, preserved by Herodotus (5.77), on the fetters and bronze which the Athenians hung in the Acropolis to commemorate their capture of Boeotian and Chalcidian troops in around 505 BC illustrates the solemnity of the dedicatory type in the classical period. But what a different tone Asclepiades gave to the type in his poem on the dedication to Aphrodite of a golden spur used by Lysidice for her client's titillation in intercourse *à cheval* (6 *H.E.*): it was a spur 'with which she exercised many a supine horse', though it never drew blood from her thigh;[22] in fact, the race was completed without the need of such stimulation (ἀκέντητος τελεοδρόμος), the implication being that she was highly proficient at her profession. The use of the metaphor from horse-racing appears to have some basis in actual dedications, for a fragmentary inscription from Attica, datable to Asclepiades' period, employs it as well.[23] But the word 'needing no spur' is literary, an ironic reminiscence of Pindar's use of it for Hiero's dashing steed, Pherenicus (*O.* 1.20)![24]

On the other hand, funerary epigrams on humble people can invest their death with a pathos in line with traditional practice, even if homely detail is given an unprecedented emphasis. Consider Callimachus' piece on Crethis (37 *H.E.*): she was a humble working-girl from Samos, and presumably resident in Alexandria; her Samian girlfriends kept looking for her, for she was full of stories, knew many a pretty game and was a chatterbox, but now 'she sleeps the sleep that is due to all women'. Many everyday details are briefly mentioned, and we are left with an impression of striking liveliness. This, however, contrasts quite powerfully with the poem's final pronouncement. Leonidas of Tarentum, often called 'the poor man's poet',[25] has an epigram for the humble fisherman, Theris (20 *H.E.*): he swam 'more than a seagull', stole fish, used a dragnet and crept into holes to catch his prey; he was too poor to have had a boat and to have been killed in his old age at sea, but just died in his hut of rushes, 'like a lamp which dies out of its own accord after a long time'; he had no family to put up his tombstone, but a guild of fishermen grouped together to do so. The subject-matter is realistic enough and there is real pathos in the comparison of Theris' death with a lamp dying out. Yet the style is artificial, the poem features many words not found elsewhere,[26] and it is plainly a display-piece, like most of Leonidas' other funerary poems. Leonidas' attitude to the realistic matter of his poems is thus in fact quite distant, for all his occasional success in evoking pathos; indeed, realistic material is seen as one of the principal means of evoking pathos. Inferences from his choice of subject-matter that Leonidas was concerned with the humble life *per se* or as a reflection of his own poverty are accordingly dubious.[27] Other epideictic funerary pieces show with what freedom the Alexandrians could redirect the type. Drunken old women are a common theme in comedy[28] and it is in such a context that we must regard an epigram like Dioscorides' on Silenis the nurse (29 *H.E.*): out of gratitude for his old nurse, who was never one to refuse another cup when she was drinking neat wine, Hiero has buried her on his estate so that even in death the old drunkard might still be near the wine-vats. The joke was taken up by several other writers.[29]

The new categories of epigram, the amatory and sympotic,[30] have a similar breadth of tonal range. Purely comic is the piece by Dioscorides on Doris (5 *H.E.*): 'Stretching Doris with her rosy buttocks over my bed I was immortalised amidst her dewy flowers. She straddled my waist with her marvellous legs and unswervingly completed the course of Cypris, gazing at me with heavy eyes; her red breasts [?] trembled like leaves in the wind as she rocked to and fro until the white strength was poured out for us both and Doris collapsed in a heap, her limbs relaxed.' The imagery of the poem and the position which Doris assumes are inspired by dedicatory poems for hetaerae like that by Asclepiades, but the transfer of the motifs into an epigram on a personal experience affords Dioscorides the opportunity of combining *enargeia* with a scene from low life in a manner quite unparalleled by the other Alexandrians.[31] An altogether different tone is effected by the sympotic poem by Asclepiades (16 *H.E.*) in which the poet urges himself to keep drinking: he asks himself what his tears mean, for he's not the only one to have been assailed by Eros; so let him drink the neat draught of Bacchus; dawn's just a finger's breadth away and there's no sense in waiting for the lantern which will send him to his bed; all too soon he'll have to sleep the long night of death. This rather melancholy piece demonstrates how naturally the two categories of epigram, the amatory and the sympotic, merge into one another. In the poem on Nicagoras (18 *H.E.*), in which the poet notices from his drinking-partner's behaviour at a party that he is in love, the motif of the lover is placed in a sympotic setting, and a vivid picture and a triste atmosphere are deftly created.[32]

Of the remaining epigram-types there are the remarkable miniature mimes, the most lively, perhaps, being one of the two by Asclepiades (25 *H.E.*) in which a master is agitatedly giving orders to a slave for the final preparations for a dinner-party. His expression of financial embarrassment and his claim that his credit is good with a hetaera (he had made love to her five times in a row) are presented with racy humour.[33] The bucolic pieces like Anyte's poems on children playing with a goat (13 and 14 *H.E.*) create idyllic effects.[34] The satirical epigrams rely on low realism for their jarring, abusive tone.[35]

The inclusion of the everyday and the low in epigrams is thus a major way in which the Alexandrians secured for the form an impressive new range of effects. Some of these depend on the technique of genre-crossing. Here again we can discern the movement's desire to confront and redefine a traditional literary form.

Theocritus' *Idylls*, with their rustics, ordinary city-people and humanised or domesticated heroes, present us with another clear instance of genre-crossing. But before we examine that aspect of the poems we may ask just how true to reality is Theocritus' portrayal of the rustics of his pastorals.

First, there is the matter of the language in which they are made to speak. It is commonly said that Theocritus' use of Doric in the pastoral *Idylls* was motivated by a desire to capture the speech of uneducated country peasants. The idea can be traced back to Probus, who says that the Doric dialect was considered rustic and that it was therefore ideally appropriate for the pastoral poet (p. 15.17–20 Wendel).[36] This attributes to Theocritus a desire for linguistic realism. The trouble is that it does not cover all the facts. It has long been accepted that Theocritus' Doric is more like the artificial Doric of Callimachus' fifth and sixth *Hymns* than that of poets writing in a more strictly regional Doric like Alcman and Stesichorus: the Doric that he uses is inconsistent and contaminated by epicisms and Aeolisms.[37] The current opinion is that Theocritus' Doric was intended to distance readers from the acoustic expectations conditioned by the Ionic hexameter and to achieve a 'heightened musicality', and this is likely to have been the case in a period when the dialects were being levelled and supplanted by the *koinē*.[38] But at the same time there must be some truth in the idea that Theocritus' Doric has at least a partially mimetic value in that it points in general terms to the geographical setting of the pastorals, the Doric-speaking Sicily, South Italy and Cos, and injects a degree of local colour. The urban mime *Idyll* 15 is an interesting borderline case. Gorgo and Praxinoa are Syracusans, so the Doric in which they are made to speak seems realistic enough. But they are immigrants to Alexandria where the *koinē* was the official and dominant dialect. So it comes as a surprise to hear the man in the crowd complain about their Doric, voicing his complaint in the same broad dialect (87–8). And why is the Singer's hymn in Doric? Here, it seems to me, Theocritus is making full use of both the mimetic and the literary functions of his dialect, deliberately juxtaposing the two functions in ironic

The Everyday and the Low in Alexandrian Poetry 165

collision.[39] Be that as it may, the Doric of the pastorals does indeed have an element of realism, but concurrently serves other more purely aesthetic ends as well.

Moreover, there is very little in their diction which appears meant to characterise the people of the pastorals as rustics. Colloquialisms, for instance, are not at all common, *Idylls* 4 and 5 perhaps approximating most closely to the speech of rustics. In fact, the impression of rusticity is produced by a generous use of popular proverbs, in which the fifth *Idyll* is particularly rich (21f., 23, 26f., 38), and by the way Theocritus puts into the mouths of his herdsmen the bawdy sort of things that rustics are supposed to say (*Idd.* 1.81–91, 151f., 4.58–63, 5.41–3, 115f., 147–50). As for the harshness of work in the countryside, it is certainly mentioned, but only in passing. Milon's recommendation to the lovelorn Bucaeus that working men should sing work-songs (*Id.* 10.56–8) comes closest to a recognition of the realities of the rustic's life,[40] though we also have the picture of the old fisherman straining to gather in the net for a cast (*Id.* 1.39–44). But in fact work is kept strictly in the background, for the *raison d'être* of Theocritus' herdsmen is song, and that is only possible when work can be suspended or attended to by others. This is the precise opposite of a Hesiodic world. Social status, furthermore, plays only a carefully circumscribed role in the lives of Theocritus' herdsmen. The thought, which originates in the *Prolegomena Latina*, that the herdsmen had a status-hierarchy, neatherds at the top, shepherds in the middle and goatherds on the lowest rung, is totally lacking in evidence in the case of Theocritus.[41] As for factors of social class in the more general sense, *Idyll* 5 is the only piece in which they are clearly defined and have an indisputable part to play,[42] but even there, as we shall see, they act as a mere backdrop against which tensions of a more private nature may be played out. Again, Theocritus shows no great concern over socio-economic matters. For instance, the cup of *Idyll* 1, the 'goatherd's marvel' for which the Goatherd has paid the Calydnian ferryman a goat and a cheese, seems a luxury outside the realm of experience (and pocket) of a humble countryman.[43] But perhaps the most striking aspect of the pastorals in this connection is Theocritus' total suppression of any mention of the historical realities of life in the country at this period. There is not the slightest hint of the devastation that the countryside of Sicily and South Italy suffered in the poet's time at the hands of condottieri like Agathocles and Pyrrhus.[44]

Thus the realism of Theocritus' portrayal of his rustics is highly selective. They are and foremost literary creations. But Theocritus succeeds in giving them the *impression* of being real, lowly folk. In other words, he establishes quite clearly that he wishes us to regard his characters, for all their artificiality, as *phauloi*. It is his extraordinary achievement that he gives these literary creations such an overwhelming appearance of freshness and life.

What are we to make of the hexameters in which Theocritus chooses to represent his *phauloi*? He appears to be the first Greek poet to have used the metre for dramatic dialogues or monologues depicting the lives and concerns of everyday and low folk.[45] What is of particular concern to us is the peculiar feature of the Theocritean hexameter which has been named the 'bucolic caesura'. This term denotes Theocritus' regular practice in the pastorals of ending the fourth foot with a word-break.[46] In fact, however, though the practice is observable mainly in the pastoral poems, it is not confined to them, for the caesura occurs with a high rate of incidence in the urban mimes, *Idylls* 2[47] and 14. Strictly speaking, therefore, the term 'bucolic caesura' is a misnomer, though the inaccuracy is easily understandable, since the phenomenon is primarily associated with the pastorals; it was for that reason, no doubt, that the bucolic poets after Theocritus preserved the caesura as a characteristic of their verse.

The caesura after the fourth foot is a feature of the Greek hexameter which is present in epic of all periods prior to Theocritus. In *Iliad* 1, for instance, the rating is 61 per cent. In Theocritus' pastorals and in *Idylls* 2 and 14 it almost becomes the rule, the incidence in the pastoral *Idylls* 1, 3, 4, 5, 6 and 7 averaging out to 85 per cent, in *Idyll* 2 to 80 per cent and in *Idyll* 14 to 79 per cent. In the pastorals, moreover, there are long passages where it occurs without exception, notably in *Idyll* 5, where the overall rating is 91 per cent. The incidence in Theocritus' other poems is generally much lower. The remaining urban *Idyll*, poem 15, has one of only 53 per cent.[48] The average in the epyllia, *Idylls* 13, 22, 24 and 26, is 54 per cent,[49] and is thus more or less in line with Homeric practice, but the rate of incidence drops to 47 per cent in the encomia, *Idylls* 16 and 17.

We may legitimately ask why Theocritus employed this caesura so frequently in his bucolic *Idylls* and in two urban mimes. It is a phenomenon recurrent in Western literary history that when a new genre comes into existence it brings with it a new poetic form.[50] So it was, I suggest, with Theocritus. When he made a new literary genre out of poems, predominantly pastoral, which dealt with the loves, the singing[51] and the everyday lives of the lowly folk of the country and (in two instances) of the town, he chose an indeed traditional metre but increased the frequency of the caesura after the fourth foot in order to set his new genre apart from traditional hexametric poetry. Perhaps this procedure started accidentally. Theocritus may have written a piece in which the bucolic caesura was a prominent feature, and liked the result, but its remarkably consistent frequency in the low-life country and urban poems suggests that he came to regard it as a 'genre-marker'. Moreover, his adjustment to the metre must have had a striking effect on its feel and cadence. As he handles it, the hexameter-line commonly ends first with a dactylic fourth foot preceding the bucolic caesura, secondly with the caesura itself and finally with the metrical and verbal unit —⌣⌣|—⌣ in the last two feet, where word-division also often coincides with the metrical division. The endings of the first two lines of *Idyll* 1 provide a clear illustration of the pattern: *hā pĭtȳs, | āipŏlĕ,ˈtēnā* and *melîsdĕtăi, | hādȳ dĕˈ kāi tȳ*. It is significant that Theocritus lowers the rate of the caesura and hence of its cadence in his mythological epics, however much everyday material is included in them.[52] But while Theocritus was thus setting off his new genre from other epic, he was still free to claim that his hexameters were in line with those of tradition, precisely because the caesura in this position was not unprecedented in traditional epic.[53] In the bucolic pieces and *Idylls* 2 and 14, therefore, Theocritus' hexameter could still be made to carry the associations of the metre in its traditional form, its acknowledged rhythmic nobility, appropriateness to grand subjects and unsuitability for conveying conversational speech-patterns — or it could be brought into a humorously incongruous clash with the subject-matter of the *Idylls*, by far the more common procedure. The complex relation of Theocritus' hexameter to that of 'normal' epic, I suggest, gave Theocritus an astonishing new range in these poems.

There is further evidence that Theocritus viewed his poems on the lowly folk of the country or the town as a branch of poetry separate from his own and other epic. This is found in his use of the definite article. Avoidance of the definite article was a characteristic of traditional 'high' epic.[54] In the first 20 lines of the *Iliad*, for example, there are no instances; the same is true of the *Argonautica*; there is one instance in Callimachus' *Hymn to Zeus*

1–20. In the first 20 lines of any of Theocritus' 'low-life' poems there are as many as 22 (*Id.* 5), and never fewer than 7 (*Idd.* 7, 14, 15), the average being 13. Contrast the epyllia: 4 in *Idyll* 18, 1 in *Idyll* 22, 2 in *Idyll* 24 and 4 in *Idyll* 26, with an eccentrically high rate of 13 in *Idyll* 13. Contrast, too, the encomia: none in *Idyll* 16, 2 in *Idyll* 17. These statistics, which match those provided by the bucolic caesura, show that Theocritus put the 'low-life' poems on a lower stylistic level than that of traditional epic.

The kind of subject-matter that concerns us is so pervasive in the pastoral poems that a few examples will suffice to illustrate the main uses to which it is put. In *Idyll* 5 Lacon and Comatas are characterised on the linguistic level by their frequent recourse to proverbs. So, for example, Comatas responds to Lacon's challenge to compete in song by saying 'The pig once challenged Athene' (23) and complains that Lacon is 'biting the hand that feeds him' (38). The impression of realism is fostered by their aquaintance with folk-customs, for example when Comatas calls for squills from a hag's grave to act as a calming agent and Lacon calls for cyclamen (120–4), and when Comatas refers to the custom of the χύτρα, kissing while holding the lover's ears (132f.). By the same token, it is hard to imagine how a rustic could have come by a bowl made by the famous Praxiteles, which Comatas ingenuously claims he is keeping for his girlfriend (105). Theocritus could argue that, while Homer makes the heroes attribute their treasures to Hephaestus, he has come half way (if no more) to bringing Comatas' bowl down to earth,[55] but still the poem's apparent realism is eroded. Rustic realities are allowed to intrude on the singing-contest when Comatas invents a couplet warning his kids not to nibble the wild olives, thus forcing Lacon to match the couplet with a similar command to his flock to come away from an oak-tree (100–4), and both herdsmen make reference to animals that threaten the life and happiness of rustics (106, 108, 110f., 112, 114). But otherwise such facts of country life do not have any role to play. Again, the *mise en scène* is South Italy, and is narrowed down to the vicinity of Thurii (72) and, apparently, another town or village called Sybaris (1,73). The geographical setting is thus quite precise (and the literary Doric generally appropriate).[56] Yet there is not a trace of the vicissitudes which the Lucanians, Bruttians and Tarentines inflicted on Thurii during Theocritus' period, a striking index of his indifference to such matters.

I have already remarked that *Idyll* 5 is unique among the

pastoral poems in that the social status of the speakers is made quite explicit and plays an important part in the characterisation of the two interlocutors. The older, Comatas, a goatherd, taunts the younger, Lacon, who is a shepherd, with the title 'Sibyrtas' slave' (5), which elicits from Lacon the ironic 'Sir Freeman' (8) and the reminder that Comatas, too, is a slave, his master being Eumaras (10). But Lacon knows the name of his mother, Calaethis (14f.), and it is reasonable to infer from this that he enjoyed a superior slave-status, that of a home-born slave.[57] He is flushed with the thought that in this he is Comatas' social superior, and challenges him to a singing-match. But when with fatal defiance he asks what benefit he has ever received from Comatas, the latter deftly cuts him down to size by specifying as the occasion of young Lacon's getting of wisdom 'the time when I was screwing you and it hurt you; the she-goats were bleating and the billy kept tupping them' (41f.). True, Lacon makes a valiant comeback by retorting 'May you never be buried deeper than your thrust, you hunchback' (43f.), but the truth is out, and Lacon is plainly embarrassed by his sexual subservience to Comatas. When Morson, a townsman who is a woodcutter, is called in to judge them, Comatas, intent as ever on mischief, states the plain fact that both he and Lacon are slaves, Lacon to Sibyrtas of Thurii, himself to Eumaras of Sybaris (72f.). Again Lacon reveals his social snobbery by his angry outburst at Comatas for passing on this annoying piece of information. During the contest Comatas again brings up the matter of Lacon's former sexual services, this time stressing Lacon's compliance and willing self-abasement (116f.). Lacon denies any knowledge of the incident in question, but claims that he remembers how Eumaras, Comatas' master, beat him; his only means of self-redress is thus the appeal to his dubious social superiority. Comatas points out to Morson how Lacon is losing his temper and shows thereby that Lacon's air of superiority is merely self-assumed and based on the most fragile of foundations.

The exchange is *phaulon* indeed. Yet the rustics speak in the hexameter. There is thus a basic incongruity between what they say and the metre in which they say it. Such an incongruity must have struck Theocritus' audience most forcibly, especially in the outbursts of vulgar abuse, and, if we use our imagination, we can share their response to it. The result is an innovation in comic irony which is unparalleled in earlier Greek poetry. In fact, it is clear that Theocritus means us to contrast the whole tone and theme of his short style of epic with those of the traditional type. A good proportion of the *Idyll*'s humour is therefore literary. The close of the poem proves that. Comatas has threatened his billy-goat with castration if he keeps on mounting the nannies, and now swears 'If I don't castrate you, may I be a Melanthius instead of a Comatas.' The Melanthius of the *Odyssey* was, like Comatas, a goatherd. His punishment by Odysseus for his disloyalty is well known: his nostrils, ears, feet and hands were cut off, together with his genitals, which were thrown to the dogs (*Od.* 22.475–7). Thus, in the poem's last line, Comatas is made to cite the older epic with remarkable appositeness for a mere rustic. Theocritus' aim seems clear enough: the ironic confrontation of the heroic tradition and the pastoral world has been implicit throughout the poem, given its hexameters, but the poet closes his *Idyll* by making the confrontation quite explicit. Thus he tells us that, for all the freshness and vivacity of his new 'heroes', a principal ingredient of his poem is literary incongruity and the humour that results from it. *Arte allusiva* and realistic material work together towards a novel effect. We can see now one of the reasons why Theocritus' rustics are portrayed with such a limited realism. He could never have carried through with a realistic portrayal when he made Comatas *au fait* with sophisticated literary traditions, and he would have forfeited an attractive interplay of liveliness and literary irony.

This is even more obviously the case in *Idylls* 6 and 11, in which Theocritus introduces in humble pastoral guise a figure traditionally associated with heroic epic. Polyphemus the Cyclops is depicted in his pre-Odyssean youth, in love with the Nereid, Galatea. The theme had been handled by Philoxenus in a satirical dithyramb and also by the comedians Nicochares, Alexis and Antiphanes.[58] Thus in these two poems Theocritus indulges in two of his favourite ploys, the treatment of a heroic personage in an off-stage moment and the crossing of comic material with the metre of epic.

Theocritus' Polyphemus shows nothing of his heroic *persona* apart from his single eye: the poet intentionally puts him on an emphatically everyday level, smitten, moreover, by the common human passion of love. In *Idyll* 6 we see him piping on the seashore, like any rustic, and secretly watching Galatea as she pelts his flocks and his dog. Moreover, as we have seen already, Theocritus further explores the theme of the delusion that love can bring to humans, especially the young. His self-delusion about his handsomeness is quite complete, and when he receives what he takes to be evidence of it he spits three times into his breast to avert the evil eye, a piece of superstition by which Theocritus characterises his naïveté, as he does with his other rustics.

In *Idyll* 11 the poet describes Polyphemus as 'of yore' (8), which places him firmly in the heroic age. Yet immediately after this prelude he is said to have been in love with Galatea when the first down was appearing on his face (8f.). Thus at the beginning of the piece a tension is established between the heroic Polyphemus and the green youth distracted from his task as a shepherd and singing from a rock to his love in the sea (7–18). He proceeds to show a modicum of self-knowledge by saying that the reason for the nymph's flight is his ugliness, in particular his one eye. But straightaway he imagines that he will cancel out that deficiency by mentioning the wealth of his farm: Galatea should leave the discomfort of the sea to enjoy the enticements of his pastoral life (30–44). He expresses the fond wish that his mother had born him with gills so that he might have dived down and kissed the nymph, on the hand if she denied her lips, he adds pathetically. By his wish he contradicts what he has just said about the undesirability of living in the sea. Then there is his notorious display of *gaucherie* over the gifts of flowers which he realises bloom in different seasons. He comes to something like good sense when he asks 'Why pursue one who flees you?' and considers the possibility of finding another girlfriend. But his song closes with the confident statement that other women make overtures to him, and it is likely that this is based on a further self-delusion: when he says that all the women titter when he pays them any attention (78), they are, more likely, laughing at him.

The two *Idylls*, therefore, present Polyphemus like any other of Theocritus' rustics. The poet has taken his lead from comedy and ironically reduced the Cyclops to the status of a love-sick *phaulos*, despite placing him in the heroic age and insisting on the motif of his Homeric single eye. There must have been for Theocritus' contemporaries an initial irony in the representation of such a humble creature in hexameters.

Yet there is the added irony of Polyphemus' unconscious foreshadowing of the events from the *Odyssey* with which he is more normally associated. We see this in *Idyll* 6 in the shepherd-Cyclops' oath 'by my one sweet-eye, with which may I see to the end (and may the prophet Telemus, who prattles of an evil doom to befall me, carry his evil home and keep it for his children)' (22–4): the fate of his 'one sweet eye' is only too well known, and in the event Telemus' prophecy proves ruinously correct. In *Idyll* 11 when Polyphemus claims that he is afire with love for Galatea and will therefore be devoted to her, he continues his typically Alexandrian metaphor with a catastrophically grotesque literalness, saying that, if she thinks him too hirsute, he would put up with her burning even his soul — and his one eye, than which nothing is dearer to him (50–3). This can only be taken ironically in the light of *Odyssey* 9. Moreover, there is his statement that he will learn to swim to experience what Galatea finds so attractive about living in the sea, 'if only a stranger arrives here sailing in a ship' (61), again an ironic glance towards the *Odyssey*. Thus the ironic tension between the Theocritean and the Odyssean Polyphemus is made quite explicit by his citation of events to happen latter in his epic career.[59] The hexameter would have reinforced this irony, for in this context it would have been ironically appropriate to the heroic events to which the poems allude and would have reminded audiences of them.

Theocritus' ironical realism in the pastoral poems is therefore most obvious in these two pieces, for, given their theme, the poet can avail himself of the opportunities for ironical *arte allusiva* even more freely than in the other bucolic *Idylls*. Yet, in spite of the grotesqueness and irony present in them, a piquant pathos emerges here and there in the picture which they present of Polyphemus. This is especially so in *Idyll* 11. There the Cyclops is less in control of his passions and is more prepared to admit it, and his unconscious foreshadowings of his fate add, to some degree at least, to our sympathy for his *gaucherie*. In the sixth poem, however, although he is ultimately not in control at all, he is rather too smugly confident, rather too summary in his rejection of Telemus' prophecy (his scorn of seers is expressed in terms reminiscent of Eurymachus insulting Halitherses at *Odyssey* 2.178, which puts him in bad company indeed), and we perhaps feel that the ironic treatment accorded him there is what he deserves. So Theocritus conditions in us a remarkably complex response to his 'realistic', lowly Cyclops.

But he does not manipulate form and content only for varying effects of deflatory incongruity. In certain significant passages he contrives to harmonise the two components and produce an altogether different effect, one of intense seriousness. This is illustrated in Thyrsis' song 'The Sorrows of Daphnis' in *Idyll* 1.

The seriousness of Thyrsis' song is indicated even before it begins. The Goatherd calls it a 'hymn' (61). Such a description might at first sight seem curious in connection with a song called in the refrains a 'bucolic song'. Yet Thyrsis closes the piece with a coda resembling that of a hymn, and shows how seriously he takes it by telling the Muses that he will sing a 'sweeter' song sometime in the future (145). All this despite the fact that the song remains that of a lowly neatherd, the refrains acting as a substitute for interludes on the syrinx, the only means by which the spoken hexameter was able to convey such rural musical effects.[60]

Whatever the precise details of Theocritus' version of the Daphnis story,[61] it tells how the legendary neatherd resisted Aphrodite to the death. We learn from Priapus that a girl is wandering through the countryside in search of Daphnis (82–5). It seems that Aphrodite is trying to make him give in to his love for the girl, and that she has instilled the passion in him to assert her power over him (95–8). That he has not succumbed seems indicated by his claim that he 'will be a bitter grief to Love even in Hades' (103). It is unclear why he resists: he has, Aphrodite reveals (97f.), provoked her anger by vowing that he will conquer Love, and perhaps has sworn an oath of chastity and, rather than break it, prefers to die. If that is so, he bears a generic resemblance to Euripides' Hippolytus. In any case, his end is tragic. Attic tragedy seems to have inspired the motif of the succession of inquirers, in turn Hermes, rustic herdsmen, Priapus and Aphrodite, and perhaps also it has suggested the motif of Daphnis' defiant silence: it has been felt that Theocritus may have the *Prometheus Bound* in mind.[62] So a mere rustic, complete with his pan-pipes, is cast in a recognisably tragic mould, in a song described as a hymn.

This rustic, moreover, cites the epic tradition in a significant way. He contemptuously tells Aphrodite to go back to Mount Ida to Anchises the neatherd (105–7). The attachment is mentioned at *Iliad* 5.313, but there was another story according to which Anchises was punished for his adulterous involvement with the goddess by being blinded or perhaps even killed by bees,[63] and Daphnis, feigning ignorance, with savage irony describes Ida as a place where 'bees sweetly hum by the hives' (107). More strikingly, he bids her go face up to Diomedes again and challenge him (112f.): she can now hope to redress her disastrous encounter with him in heroic combat on the plains of Troy (*Il.* 5.330ff.) — now that she has conquered Daphnis the neatherd. The irony inherent in the notion that by her conquest of a rustic Daphnis Aphrodite is qualified to take on Diomedes again is bitterly patent. The song thus defines another direction in which epic is to go in Theocritus' hands. It is about a rustic, who, for all the idealisation and tragic heroisation with which he is portrayed, is none the less contrasted with a traditional hero like Diomedes. Moreover, the issue over which heroic struggles may rage in the pastorals is love, though no longer love on the universal scale as in the *Hippolytus*, but love on the level of personal erotic passion. The song also demonstrates the skill with which Theocritus combines the metre of traditional epic and his lowly material. He has here elevated his new epic personnel, and the hexameters in which the *Idyll* is composed will have reinforced the poem's tonal and thematic seriousness.[64] Now we can perhaps appreciate more fully the remarkable range of effects which the poet achieves by his genre-crossing in *Idyll* 1 as a whole: humorously ironical clash of form and content in the frame, with its cheerful rusticity; the sense of distance and timelessness in the cup description; and the moving celebration of the new hero and theme in the song, which is thrown into deeper relief by the other sections.

The mythological poems also attest to Theocritus' interest in redefining the epic hero. *Idyll* 13, the *Hylas*, has a significant thematic resemblance to *Idylls* 6 and 11 with its reduction of a heroic figure to a victim of love, and the everyday and low are put to comparable use.[65]

In the *Hylas* the story of Heracles' loss of his beloved boy and his temporary desertion of his heroic duty places the hero in a similar light: as Polyphemus 'considered all things secondary' to his love (*Id.* 11.11), so Heracles 'put Jason's whole quest in second place' (*Id.* 13.67). The worlds of the heroic and the erotic are opposed throughout the poem. Right at the beginning of the narrative Heracles is designated by the portentously epic-sounding phrase 'Amphitryon's iron-hearted son' (5), and his heroic victory over the Nemean lion is explicitly referred to, but, with a matter-of-factness on a very different stylistic level, it is also said that 'he loved a boy, the pretty Hylas' (5–7). Great emphasis is placed on the traditionally epic nature of Jason's quest (16–24), and the poem ends with a striking contrast between Heracles, driven mad with love, and the heroic Argonauts: the latter are called 'heroes' (*hērōes*), jibe at Heracles for being a deserter who jumped the Argo (*ērōēse*, 74, is a pointed pun),[66] and sail on to Phasis while Heracles is forced to rejoin them there on foot (68–75). Theocritus, then, confronts him with the human passion of love and demonstrates the powerlessness of traditional heroism over the condition; Hylas, on the other hand, who has not yet become a 'true man' of Heracles' type (8–15), is quite at home in the world of the erotic (72). The poet does not go so far as Apollonius who in his version of the episode appears to have wanted to undercut traditional heroism altogether: in the *Idyll* Heracles is made to return to the quest, a notion which is entirely absent from the episode as related in the *Argonautica*.[67] Theocritus simply wishes to imagine what a hero from the Argonaut saga would look like if he were viewed in a realistically human light. In this *Idyll* there is an undeniable amount of humour at Heracles' expense, but we are surely also meant to have some sympathy for his plight, more, probably, than for Polyphemus in *Idyll* 11, who we know is to become an arch-villain in his subsequent career in epic.

The contrast between the heroic and the everyday pervades the poem. This is, perhaps, most noticeable in the time-designations and similes. Hylas and Heracles are said never to have been apart, 'neither when white-horsed Dawn runs up to the heavens nor when the cheeping chickens look towards the roost, when their mother flaps her wings on the sooty perch' (11–13).[68] The Argonauts, 'the noble band of heroes', are said to have set sail on their quest when the young lambs pasture on the uplands (25–8). A similar intentional incongruity is observable in the simile describing Hylas' plunge into the nymphs' spring: he is compared in epic style with a falling comet, but the comparison assumes an everyday complexion when the poet adds that the comet is taken by common sailors as a favourable sign for getting the tackle shipshape and for setting sail (50–2).[69] Moreover, the Argonauts are said to bivouac in a humble, pastoral setting within the Propontis, 'where the oxen of the people of Cius plough the broad furrows, wearing away their shares' (30f.). This kind of juxtaposition mirrors the confrontation of the heroic and the more ordinarily human which figures so prominently in the fate of Heracles.[70]

The scaling-down of traditional heroism and the inclusion of everyday material are taken to their extreme in *Idyll* 24, the *Heracliscus*, where Heracles is presented like the other divine or semi-divine precocious children common in Alexandrian poetry. The motif of Alcmena's breast-feeding and rocking the boys to sleep is a superimposition on the Pindaric account of Heracles' feat in the first *Nemean*, as we have seen. There may have been some domestic colour at this point in the version offered by *Paean* 20 Snell, for at line 6 there is possibly a reference to the bogy, Mormo, though the text is insecure and the form of the word otherwise unrecorded; perhaps it described the fright that the snakes were meant to give the baby. Anyway, Theocritus underlines the tension between the heroic and the domestic at the beginning of the poem by introducing as the boys' cradle the shield which Amphitryon took as spoil when he killed Pterelaus on a heroic venture (4f.). The detail seems to be deliberately reminiscent of the weapon-genealogies in Homer. Again, the poet stresses the normality of Iphicles' reaction on seeing the snakes, but here too there is an ironic opposition of the heroic and the familiar, for the phrase which describes his flight, 'desiring to flee', is also an echo of Homer's war-poetry.[71] Interestingly, Pindar's *Paean* has it that Heracles 'threw the gay swaddling-clothes from his body' (11f.), stripping himself for heroic action; in Theocritus the motif of shedding clothes is transferred to Iphicles, who kicks off his blanket in terror (25). So while the *Paean* uses the motif to emphasise Heracles' might (12), the *Idyll* employs it to draw attention to the more ordinary boy's behaviour (which of course in turn highlights his brother's prowess as well). If Theocritus is thinking of the *Paean*, as is probable, his deployment of the everyday motif is significant and clever.

Domestic detail is prominent in the scene in Alcmena and Amphitryon's bedroom, with Alcmena's agitation on seeing the miraculous light, her repeated orders to Amphitryon to get up without putting on his sandals (35f.) and Amphitryon's half-awake ponderousness. Again we appear to have a pointed transference of a humble motif: in both the *Nemean* (50) and the *Paean* (14) it is Alcmena who leaps out of bed without putting on her peplos, and now we have her telling her husband not to bother about his sandals! Neither husband nor wife breathes the same air as their Pindaric counterparts.

The bustling but comparatively unruffled slaves of the next scene, awoken from their snoring sleep, take the place of the

The Everyday and the Low in Alexandrian Poetry 177

Nemean's heroically armed chieftains of Thebes and the *Paean*'s terrified Cephallenian handmaids whose fear throws Heracles' — and Alcmena's — bravery into sharp relief. Theocritus stresses the infant hero's babyhood with two adjectives: he is 'unweaned' (54) and his hands are 'tender' (55), where Pindar had said that Heracles gripped the snakes 'with his two ineluctable hands' (*N.* 1.44f.; cf. *Pae.* 20.10–13). Amphitryon is simply made to tuck Heracles in again and go back to bed while Alcmena comforts Iphicles; there is nothing here of the Pindaric Amphitryon's mixed emotions of awe and joy at his son's extraordinary courage and strength (*N.* 1.56ff.).

There can be no real doubt that Theocritus includes so much everyday and humble matter in an intentional contrast with Pindar and that his audience is meant to view the heroic episode as it would have happened 'in real life'. But Theocritus has in fact cast his net wider than Pindar, and draws in Homer as well. The inspiration for the motif of the miraculous light is the moment in the *Odyssey* when Athene sends Odysseus and Telemachus a light to illuminate their way as they remove the weapons in the banquet-hall under the cover of darkness (*Od.* 19.31ff.). In the *Odyssey* the light is supernatural aid in the plan for the heroic conquest of the suitors and Odysseus' re-instalment as king on Ithaca. In Theocritus' handling of the motif, however, the light is intended to facilitate the pictorial presentation of Iphicles' fright, to motivate Heracles' attack on the snakes, to supply a reason for Alcmena's awakening and to introduce the ensuing scene between husband and wife. Moreover, it goes out when Amphitryon takes down his sword. Again we see Theocritus using a heroic motif and subjecting it to an incongruous *embourgeoisement*. The same thing happens in the case of the Phoenician woman who wakes the slaves. In the *Odyssey*, Odysseus prays for Zeus' thunder as a sign of his approval of his endeavours, together with a sign from humans. Zeus obliges, and a woman working at the corn-mills prays that Zeus will that very day stop the suitors' feasting in Odysseus' halls, so that she might be spared her hard work (*Od.* 20.98ff.). In Homer, the plight of the poor woman is described with considerable pathos and she plays an unwitting part in the heroic action. In Theocritus, however, she simply urges on Amphitryon's servants with the phrase 'Himself's calling', αὐτὸς αὐτεῖ, a humorously ironic blend of comic (αὐτός) and epic (αὐτεῖ) diction. Furthermore, she calls the servants 'stalwart' (ταλασίφρονες), an epithet used exclusively for Odysseus in the *Odyssey*! The use of Homeric motifs in incongruously domestic contexts thus extends to vocabulary, as we saw happening in the description of Iphicles' desire to flee.[72] One of the effects of Theocritus' inclusion of the everyday in this part of the poem is the ironically humorous light cast on the heroic tradition, and Heracles' feat itself is presented with the humour that arises from the incongruous contrast of the heroic and the everyday. Surely, too, the presence of such domestic matter in the hexameter must have added to the humour of the episode. Yet all this does not entirely detract from Heracles' heroism: he still accomplishes his traditional feat. He is a hero in a bourgeois idyll, just as Callimachus presents Artemis as 'any little girl' in the first part of his *Hymn to Artemis*, stressing her potent divinity later in the poem.

In the Teiresias scene the dominant themes are the deification of Heracles after his twelve labours (79f., 82–5) and the purificatory rites to be performed with the corpses of the snakes so that Alcmena's family might always be masters over its enemies (83–100), but domestic detail is still allowed to intrude. Whereas in Pindar Teiresias addresses Amphitryon and the whole group immediately after the grand event (*N*. 1.60ff.), Theocritus postpones the consultation with the prophet till dawn on the following day, designates the break of dawn by the homely detail of the cockerels' crow, and makes Alcmena the anxious inquirer, who with a mother's concern bids Teiresias to tell her the worst (68–71).[73] Moreover, Teiresias calms her with comfortable words which draw the everyday image of Achaean women who will sing of Alcmena as they rub their yarn over their knees late in the evening (76–8). In the passage describing Heracles' tutors and education, the young hero's curriculum is strikingly like that of a Hellenistic prince.[74] True, his heroic status is stressed in the passage's opening words, '[Heracles] was nurtured under the guidance of his mother like a young sapling in an orchard' (103f.), for they recall Thetis' words on how she reared Achilles (*Il*. 18.56f., 437f.). But now Theocritus names writing (105) as the first thing that Heracles is taught. His teacher, Linus, was the most distinguished of Heracles' tutors, but now he is made his grammarian and not, as tradition related, his lyre-teacher; the conclusion seems justified that Theocritus has altered his role because of the prime importance of writing in a Hellenistic gentleman's education, and that Heracles' educational priorities have been updated from those of the heroic age. The impression is reinforced by the fact that Heracles is taught war-craft appropriate to a later period, the ordering of a phalanx, the estimation of an advancing army's forces and the correct way to command cavalry (127f.). This is a far cry from Hector's catalogue of what makes a soldier in the heroic age, parrying blows with the shield on the right and the left, attacking fighters on horseback and 'dancing for grim Ares in the hand to hand fray' (*Il.* 7.238–41). It is notable, too, that Heracles' traditional unruliness is played down: no murder of Linus or Eurytus is mentioned here. And, though his traditional gluttony is alluded to, it is only in order to be made acceptable: Heracles is said to have eaten but little during the day, but to have waited forbearingly till evening to satisfy his hunger, when he ate roast meat and a Dorian loaf of bread in a basket, big enough to satisfy a hard-working garden-digger (137–9). Of the thirty-odd fragmentary lines preserved in the Antinoe papyrus all that need be noticed is that they appear to have dealt with Olympus, and hence possibly with Heracles' deification, and the hero's marriage to Hebe (168, 169, 170).[75]

In the *Heracliscus*, then, there is a great deal of everyday material, but the quotient progressively decreases during the course of the poem, to be replaced by the themes of Heracles' deification and immortality. An examination of Theocritus' possible motives in writing the piece may shed further light on the function of its everyday material, apart from the purely literary aims of humorous and ironical incongruity that the poet is obviously pursuing.

The *Encomium for Ptolemy* provides a clue. The dominant themes of that poem include the deification of Soter, pictured on Olympus in the company of Heracles, his ancestor, and the incestuous marriage of Philadelphus and Arsinoe. It is striking how in the *Heracliscus* Theocritus spends some time on comparable themes, the deification of Heracles, prophesied by Teiresias at lines 79–81, and his marriage to his half-sister, Hebe (84, 170), though here there is a far greater proportion of everyday material. There is in fact a good deal of evidence that in the epyllion Theocritus alludes to various key events in the career of the Ptolemaic dynasty and subtly shapes his version of the Heracles myth to make him a suitable forbear for the royal family.[76] Alcmena's consultation of Teiresias, for instance, has plausibly been interpreted as a prefiguration of Alexander's journey to the oracle at Siwah, which he undertook in emulation of Heracles and on which he learned from the temple that he was the son of Zeus Ammon. Moreover, two snakes are said to have led the king to the oasis and back, just as Hera's snakes in the *Heracliscus* represent Heracles' first achievement on his path to immortality. The oracle of Siwah diagnosed the same parentage for Soter as it did for Alexander, which may be said to mark the dynasty's first step in the ascent to Olympus. Again, the modernisation of Heracles' training seems especially apt for a Hellenistic prince, his athletic education echoing the Ptolemies' interest in athletic festivals and amply qualifying him for his role as presiding deity in the Egyptian gymnasia.

Certain features of the poem seem to have direct bearing on Philadelphus in particular. So the remarkably precise passage designating the time of the year at which the episode with the snakes occurred has been interpreted as implying that Heracles was born in the same month (April) as that in which Philadelphus was born and in which, in 285 BC, he became co-regent with Soter. Moreover, Theocritus seems to be bending aspects of the tradition surrounding Heracles in a manner which makes the greatest sense if he has the Ptolemies in mind. He avoids mentioning the unruly side of Heracles' character, possibly out of deference to his patron's ancestor. More importantly, in regard to Heracles' double paternity, which could cast an unwelcome slur on the Ptolemies' marital fidelity, the poet generally talks of Amphitryon as the hero's father (56, 59, 104, 121, 135), but appears to have hinted at Zeus' fatherhood in the word 'of the same father' (170) in the Antinoe papyrus which must refer to Heracles' marriage with Zeus' daughter, Hebe.[77] Zeus' paternity was, of course, a traditional and unavoidable detail but Theocritus seems to have tried to leave the matter in 'decent obscurity',[78] tilting the balance for the purposes of this poem in favour of Amphitryon. If we accept that in *Idyll* 24 Heracles prefigures his descendants, then there is a political motive behind Theocritus' realism, over and above his literary intentions: in making Heracles' education as a young man so recognisably Hellenistic, the poet may be trying to impart the impression of normality to matters like deification and marriage to one's sister, an approach observable also in the *Encomium for Ptolemy*. Of course, the *Idyll* presupposes considerable erudition on the part of its audience, even if it were recited at one of the public festivals (as is suggested by a marginal note on the Antinoe papyrus),[79] and an erudite Alexandrian audience will have seen, as it was clearly meant to see, the ironical twists that Theocritus was giving to the mythological tradition surrounding Heracles. It is interesting that the Ptolemies did not mind ironical treatment in the myths that their poets were creating for them: they apparently considered it satisfactory if the poets put the new gods and dynastic arrangements in the context of traditional Greek religion and, where possible, in the realm of the familiar and the normal.[80]

Theocritus, therefore, seems to fit well into the picture of the Alexandrian literary scene that I drew in the first chapter. We see him, true to his announcement in the *Graces*, addressing the cultural heritage of Hellas and redefining it and his audience's relation to it, revising the form, subject-matter and ethos of traditional epic. His new, humble epic personnel and themes contrast engagingly with the art of allusion that he practises throughout his poetry.

Callimachus' *Victoria Berenices* (*Frr.* 254–69 *S.H.*) puts lowly material to a different effect.[81] The poor but willing Eumaeus-like peasant, Molorchus, entertains Heracles with a meal disrupted by a hunt for the mice which he hears nibbling and for which he prepares the ancestor of the common mousetrap (*Fr.* 259 *S.H.* = *Fr.* 177 Pf.), and is willing to sacrifice his only ram to Heracles' ghost if the hero is killed by the Nemean lion. Heracles' promise to try to kill the lion seems in part to be motivated by the sight of the disrepair of Molorchus' farmstead and by the general devastation that the lion has wrought on the countryside. Here, then, we have the theme of Heracles, the people's saviour.[82] It seems possible that Callimachus made the episode of Molorchus (a figure whom he seems to have invented) the true centre-piece of the poem, displacing the grand moment of Heracles' conquest of the lion.

The same opposition of grand and humble realistic matter is evident in the parallel and contrasting aitia in the poem: on the one hand we have the heroic origins of the use of parsley in the Nemean games (*Frr.* 264, 265 *S.H.* = *Frr.* 57, 59 Pf.) and on the other the origin of the mousetrap. There is more: the moment when Molorchus' wife starts to prepare the meal and Molorchus hears the mice is heralded in by the epic-sounding time-designation 'when the evening star which comes towards sunset is about to loosen the leather straps from the oxen' (*Fr.* 259.5f. *S.H.*

= *Fr.* 177.5f. Pf.).[83] The same play with contrasts can be observed when the mice are described as using their tails, ἀλκαίαι, to draw off the oil in Molorchus' lamp (*Fr.* 259.23 *S.H.* = *Fr.* 177.23 Pf.). The word ἀλκαία was normally used for a *lion's* tail and Callimachus was taken to task by scholars in antiquity for his impropriety in using it for mice.[84] We would now rather say that the poet by the choice of the word is pointing the contrast between Heracles' and Molorchus' feats with masterly deftness. Similarly, the mice are called 'ravening' (σίνται), a word used by Homer to describe lions (*Fr.* 259.29 *S.H.* = *Fr.* 177.29 Pf.).[85] The result is of course humorous, but the dominant tone is apparently not travesty or even parody. It is that of a type of poetry which has been most aptly described as an 'Idyll der Kleinwelt',[86] a phrase which, we shall find, has a particular appropriateness to Callimachus' poetry. For all this irony, however, the story of Molorchus is encomiastic, celebrating the victory of the horses of Queen Berenice II in the chariot-race at the Nemean games. As with Theocritus in *Idyll* 24, therefore, Callimachus appears to have assumed that the Ptolemies would tolerate humble material and the ironic portrayal of heroes in his poetry for them.[87]

Of the remaining epyllia only two more need be mentioned. In Moschus' *Europa* the everyday touches seem meant to collide humorously with the miraculous framework. There is, for example, the moment when, as she is carried over the sea on the bull's back and escorted by the entourage of sea-creatures, Europa feels constrained to pull up her robe to stop it trailing in the water and getting wet (126–8).[88] There is humour, too, in Zeus' recourse to the disguise of a bull to avoid marital strife with Hera and to hoodwink Europa, a humour encapsulated in the line 'he hid his godhead, changed his form and became a bull' (79). In the pseudo-Moschan *Megara*, by contrast, the familiar, human material in the conversation of Alcmena and Megara, Heracles' wife, lends pathos to their plight as women who now feel helplessly on the periphery of the hero's life. Such details include Megara's sense of isolation and her need for someone to talk with (29–55) and Alcmena's terrifyingly naturalistic nightmare about her son (91–121).

Some of these effects are also achieved in Callimachus' *Hymns*. In our discussion of the pictorialism of the *Hymn to Artemis* we saw much everyday detail in the poem. Here we may consider its extent and the motivation for its inclusion.

The Everyday and the Low in Alexandrian Poetry   183

In the first two lines there is a jarring note for the reader expecting a traditional hymn. In the manner of the *Homeric Hymn to Artemis* (*H. H.* 27) Callimachus begins by saying 'we hymn Artemis'. But, while the older poet mentions the goddess' golden arrows and her attribute of 'stag-hunter' (ἐλαφηβόλος:2) and draws a magnificent picture of her as she hunts, the Alexandrian talks of her love of the bow — and hare-hunting (λαγωβολίαι:2). He has picked out the least of her quarries and established a tone which is deliberately lower than that of the Homeric poem.[89] This tone persists, moreover, for, after a brief mention of her love of dance and sport in the mountains (3), we are immediately led into the scene of Artemis and Zeus' tête-à-tête in which Artemis first asks 'daddy' (ἄππα) for no less than eternal virginity (6). The poet does not specify the goddess' age, though we may assume from her expressed desire for nine-year-old Oceanids as her companions (14) that she is about the same age, perhaps a little older.[90] In any case, her naïve precociousness astounds us. Callimachus has, however, carefully prepared us for the moment with a deliberate shift of emphasis in his depiction of the goddess, displacing traditional sublimity with a homely, domestic detail of a child seated on its father's knee. The altered perspective is all the more striking when we consider the solemnity with which Artemis expresses to Zeus her vow of chastity in the Aeolic hymn (Alcaeus 304 Lobel-Page=Sappho 44A Voigt) which appears to have served as Callimachus' model for his Artemis' request, for he makes her voice her wish with a frankness which is borne of truly childlike innocence. It is matched by her desire for polyonymy, which she wants 'so that Phoebus may not rival her' (7). This sibling-rivalry is also a detail taken straight from life.

When she asks for a bow and arrows, but interrupts her request by saying that she won't ask them of '*you*, father', for the Cyclopes will provide her with them 'immediately' (8–10), this is again humorously realistic, for the little girl assumes with an infant's imperiousness that the Cyclopes will have nothing else to do and will drop tools on any other project just for her. Her request for her hunting-dress (11f.) and for no less than sixty Oceanids to dance with has the specification that all of them should be nine years old and all still virgins, which reminds us of her earlier display of precociousness (13–14). Her demand for twenty nymphs, who are to be her attendants in the hunt and will perform the humdrum task of looking after her boots and hounds after it

(15–17), also juxtaposes the marvellous and the banal. Her request for 'all mountains' as her domain is typically childlike in its hyperbole, but when she says that she'll only visit cities when she is called upon to assist women in childbirth (18–25), we notice once more her precociousness over sex, which she talks about in the most matter-of-fact way.

Artemis' whole speech is, therefore, a masterpiece of comic characterisation. This extends to linguistic features. So, for instance, quite apart from her address to 'daddy' (ἄππα) at line 6, we have the five-fold repetition of the phrase 'give me' (δός μοι: 6, 8, 13, 15, 18) and her reference to herself in the third person when she says 'Artemis will rarely go to town' (19), a trait typical of 'naïve' speech in ancient Greece.[91]

We have already compared the scene of Artemis' supplication of Zeus with one of its models, the passage in the *Iliad* which depicts Artemis being comforted by Zeus after her rough treatment at the hands of Hera (*Il.* 21.505–13). The comparison demonstrated Callimachus' concern to outdo Homer's use of pictorialism and humorously realistic material. (The Aeolic poem by Sappho or Alcaeus is outstripped in this respect by far.) But there is a reference in the scene to another passage of the *Iliad*, that famous moment in which Thetis supplicates Zeus for revenge for Achilles (*Il.* 1.495–532).[92] Thetis sits at Zeus' feet and takes hold of his knee with her right hand and his chin with her left (*Il.* 1.499–502); but Artemis sits on her father's knee and grabs in vain at his beard. Thus Callimachus negates the grandeur of the supplicatory gestures in his second model from the *Iliad*.[93] Moreover, Homer's Zeus refers to the strife that he will have to face with Hera if he accedes to Thetis' request, and this is no doubt meant to lend humour to the characterisation of the grand god. But, whereas Homer makes him express his foreboding 'greatly troubled', Callimachus gives the motif a new complexion by making the god voice his claim that with spirited daughters like Artemis he need have no fear of Hera, and by making him laugh with delight and affectionately caress his little daughter. He has expanded the motif of Zeus and Hera's marital friction and relaxed the element of tension contained in the Homeric Zeus' frustrated anger; the god is characterised like a husband or father in the New Comedy.[94]

But what precisely is Callimachus aiming at with this extraordinary mixture of Homeric citation and everyday matter? In his redeployment of moments in the epic tradition he emphasises everyday detail which is already present in them, thus effectively deheroising them. Simultaneously, he cites more elevated moments in the tradition to give, by contrast, even greater prominence to the domestic elements in his poem, so that they thus become comic. In this way he is subverting his contemporaries' received expectations of the epic and hymnal tradition. The use of the hexameter, with all its associations, will have contributed still further to his design. In short, far from committing mere unconscious lapses of taste in the first part of his hymn as he has been charged with doing,[95] Callimachus is experimenting with his audience's notions of appropriateness in order to produce deliberate artistic effects. The result is not simply travesty or parody of either the Homeric passages or the epic genre in general, but rather an episode to which Herter originally applied the phrase 'Idyll der Kleinwelt', which we have found aptly describes other moments in Callimachus.[96] Thus a totally new tone has been created in epic. Moreover, as we have noticed, the poet gives us a precise mental picture of the whole scene which contributes effectively to its special character.

The scene of Artemis' visit to the Cyclopes is no less a conscious study in contrasts. We have already noted its emphatic pictorialism. It is obviously modelled on the episode in the *Iliad* where Thetis visits Hephaestus to ask for arms for Achilles.[97] Now there is light, everyday matter even in the Iliadic passage: so, for instance, Charis greets Thetis by remarking what a long time it's been since they've seen the goddess; she hasn't visited for ages (*Il.* 18.385–7). But Callimachus goes to infinitely greater trouble to bring out such details. The giants of Lipara are making a horse-trough for Poseidon. This is rather a humble project, one would have thought, for the poet to have called it a 'mighty task'; already the episode is placed in an unexpectedly everyday context (46–50). The nymphs' terror at the sight and sound of the Cyclopes at work is pardoned by the poet when he adduces another homely detail of everyday life on Olympus, the role played by the Cyclopes and Hermes as bogy-men for naughty little goddesses (64–71).[98] Artemis' contrasting boldness is stressed by the reference to her willingness to sit, as a three-year-old, on Brontes' knee when she visited him to collect gifts[99] and pulled out a handful of chest-hair (72–9).[100] So now she has no shyness in framing her request for arrows and a quiver like those of her brother, a detail which again suggests her sibling-rivalry.[101] And, as she has self-confidently assumed, the Cyclopes fulfil her wish immediately, by which we may infer that they do indeed drop their tools on the 'mighty task' for Poseidon!

The impression which the scene leaves upon the reader is the same as that of the preceding. The incongruity of so much homely detail and human characterisation in the framework of a hymn which, moreover, deliberately invites comparison with scenes in Homer, again creates an episode which may be called an 'Idyll der Kleinwelt'. We now see the rules according to which Callimachus is operating: he is 'crossing the genres' to secure a brilliant new literary effect.[102]

Yet even though the Alexandrian evidently enjoys his achievement in humour, he is still concerned in other parts of the hymn to present his subject in its serious aspect. Artemis receives from Pan[103] a pack of hounds, which, incidentally, conform with specifications for the very best hounds as laid down in the hunting-treatises of Callimachus' own day (87-97).[104] Next she captures with her own hands huge hinds to draw her chariot (98-109). The hymn here begins to leave behind the domestic tone of the earlier scenes.[105] She tests her bow, first choosing as her target an elm-tree, then an oak, then a wild animal, but finally turning her arrows on a city of unjust men.[106] Thus the hymn proceeds from the levity of its earlier scenes, via the comparatively non-serious motif of target-practice with the bow, to the grave moment where the goddess exercises her supreme moral oversight over men's actions and is revealed in her traditional grandeur. The picture of the unjust city and of that on which Artemis looks with favour (122-37) is directly modelled on Hesiod's description of the unjust and just cities in the *Works and Days*.[107] Here, of course, the subject-matter is in concord with the traditional expectations of its hymn-frame, and Callimachus shows his mastery of the orthodox conception of *to prepon* just as he has shown in the hymn's opening scenes how brilliantly he can subvert it.

But directly after he has conformed with his audience's expectations he proceeds to undermine them again, once more demonstrating his love of contrasting tones. In his description of Artemis' return to Olympus from the hunt Hermes and Apollo meet her, though the latter's task of collecting the goddess's booty has now been usurped by Heracles since his arrival on Olympus. The 'Tirynthian anvil', as he is heroically styled to contrast with the comic labour in which we are about to see him engaged,[108]

The Everyday and the Low in Alexandrian Poetry   187

now stands before the gates, on the alert, as always, in case she brings meat. He is the laughing-stock of the Olympians, especially his mother-in-law Hera,[109] when he drags some animal, a bull or a wild boar, from Artemis' chariot. He 'cunningly' (152) advises her to shoot at boars and bulls, animals which harm man, not harmless deer or hares; in that way men will call her a helper, even as they do to him. It is, of course, implied that his 'cunning' actually consists of his attempt to get more food.[110] The poet explains that though Heracles is dead he still has the hungry stomach with which he faced Theiodamas ploughing (142–61). The nymphs attend to the hinds which draw her chariot[111] while she goes into Zeus' house to sit next to her brother, even though others ask her to sit next to them (162–9).[112]

It is clear that Heracles is presented here in his role as the comic glutton, and again low detail clashes with grand form. This comic tone seems meant as an ironic foil to an impressive episode in earlier epic, the opening scene of the *Homeric Hymn to Apollo* (2–13), where Apollo enters the house of Zeus, all the other gods jumping up from their seats in welcome, and his mother Leto takes his hunting-weapons and leads him to his seat where Zeus welcomes him.[113] Apart from the comic business with Heracles, Callimachus makes his Phoebus attend on Artemis, so that the theme of sibling-rivalry is continued, even if this becomes apparent only once it is recognised that the welcoming-scene is a literary counterpiece to that in the Homeric hymn and that now Apollo is doing the welcoming. The result is again an 'Idyll der Kleinwelt', especially as regards Apollo and Artemis; in the depiction of Heracles we have outright burlesque. The range of comic effects in the passage is thus extraordinarily wide. Integral to it is the poet's skill in crossing the genres.[114]

In *Hymn* 6, the *Hymn to Demeter*, Callimachus again makes extensive use of everyday matter. In the scene depicting Demeter's punishment of Erysichthon we are presented with a domestic comedy of manners. As a result of the bulimia with which the goddess has punished him, we are told, Erysichthon constantly craves for another meal of the same size as the one he has just consumed; it takes twenty cooks to prepare his food and twelve waiters to draw off his wine (68f.). In his present state he will inevitably be a disgrace at any dinner that he attends, and his parents invent every excuse for his not accepting dinner-invitations. This is simply because they are socially embarrassed (αἰδόμενοι:73). Erysichthon's mother is characterised as worried not so much about her son as about her family's reputation. Her bourgeois concerns are matched by the excuses which she fabricates: her son is said to be involved in all the sorts of activities that any son of a well-to-do family might be expected to (72–86). Her embarrassment would be entirely appropriate in a scene from the New Comedy.[115] Likewise, when Triopas prays to his father, Poseidon, it is far from obvious that his words are motivated by pity for Erysichthon's plight, because he concludes the prayer with the wish that Poseidon either get rid of Erysichthon's disease or feed him himself, for the cooks have emptied Triopas' tables, folds and byres. His real feelings are thus ones of pique at the impoverishment of his household. This is made even clearer in the remainder of his speech: the cooks have slaughtered the wagon-mules and Erysichthon has eaten the heifer which his mother was fattening for Hestia, the prize race-horse, the war-horse and even the ancient equivalent of the cat at which the mice trembled (96–110). We are also told how as long as Triopas' provisions held out only the household knew of the scandalous business, but when Erysichthon had got through them, the scandal was a secret no longer: 'the son of the king' sat in the very crossways begging for crusts and scraps (111–15).[116] This, then, is the 'bourgeois dénouement to the story';[117] the parents' shame is complete and so is the comedy. The humour of this part of the story (Callimachus, we note in passing, has kept his version of the tale as light as possible by toning down the more gruesome elements in the legend)[118] will have been increased by the clash of the domestic material with the hymnal form and metre.

The poet's aim in incorporating so much comical domesticity in the hymn seems once again to lie in his love of contrasts. The description of Erysichthon's punishment and his parents' reaction to it is immediately preceded by the episode of his crime. There the tone is anything but comic, and the crime is presented as a very serious affair indeed. Erysichthon is depicted as a wilfully wicked man and is characterised as such by his ruthlessness in the attack on the sacred grove and by his angry and arrogant defiance of the gentle admonitions of Demeter who has disguised herself as one of her own priestesses, Nicippe. Demeter, on the other hand, is both patient and reasonable.[119] When her request that he stop his tree-felling is refused, she assumes her divine form, her feet touching the earth, her head Olympus. She mercifully exempts from her wrath Erysichthon's attendants, who had been acting under their master's orders,[120] but curses Erysichthon, ominously proclaiming that he will indeed have many banquets in future, picking up his hot-headed retort to her that he intended to use the wood from the grove to make a dining-hall for banquets. The narrator tells us that the aim of the cautionary tale is 'so that one may avoid transgression' (22), and Erysichthon's crime is an indisputable instance of transgression. The story is one of crime and punishment and Callimachus couches the crime in serious terms. The scene of punishment, therefore, stands in stark tonal contrast with it. It is unthinkable that such a contrast could be unintentional, and we may conclude that the poet has intended his comedy of manners to act as a foil to the scene with Demeter. Nor do the everyday elements necessarily undermine the seriousness of the narrator's moral or the prayer 'May he be no friend or neighbour of mine who is hated by you, Demeter; I hate evil neighbours' (116f.): Callimachus' approach resembles that of *spoudaiogeloion*-literature like certain of his own *Iambi*.[121]

Finally, there is the *Hymn to Delos*. Apart from the pictorial and scientific elements in the scene of Leto's parturition, consider Leto's cry to Apollo to come forth. It is realistically representative of how a woman sounds in labour, for she speaks in short gasps; each word in the line that she utters, *geineo, geineo, koure, kai ēpios exithi kolpou* (214), corresponds with the metrical divisions, and a strong sense-break occurs at the caesura.[122] This is *mimēsis biou* indeed, and is in stark contrast with the traditional grandeur of the episode which we find in the *Homeric Hymn to Apollo* (89–139). It contributes impressively to the pathos of the scene. But what is such everyday detail doing in a poem in which, among other things, an unborn god prophesies from his mother's womb (88–98, 162–95), an island turns into gold (260–3) and, apparently metamorphosing into a nymph, nurses the baby god (264–74)?

The exuterine prophecies are the basic problem. Callimachus is evidently building on the moment in the Homeric hymn where the god, just born, pronounces to the goddesses in attendance on Leto that music, archery and prophecy will be his particular care (131f.). This is greeted by the goddesses' wonder (135). I suggest that the poet is putting the motif of the god's precociousness, which is a teasing mixture of the everyday and the miraculous, back one stage further, and is thus, as with the birth-scene, trying to outdo his model, with the result that the everyday motif of a child's precocity is put on a miraculous plane indeed, as is underlined by the words 'in his mother's womb' (86) and 'the prophet still in the belly' (189). There may have been a special piquancy for an Alexandrian audience in all this, for they would have been familiar with prophets who made their voice come from the bellies of other people,[123] the point here being that Apollo is presented as a god performing the human practice, from within his own mother's belly! But having got the prophecies into the realm of the truly miraculous, he proceeds to place them in a strikingly immediate relation with his audience's experience. The forward reference to the event of the god's slaughter of Niobe's children is hardly especially immediate, though its accuracy does vindicate the god's exemplary prophetic powers. But when he makes Apollo prophesy the birth of Philadelphus on Cos, the victory over the Gauls in 279 BC, in which the god himself was supposed to have taken part, and Philadelphus' punishment of the Gallic mercenaries in around 274–2 BC (160–95), he touches on matters of direct, even sensational interest to an audience at Alexandria.[124] Thus actual history and the world of myth and miracle are tantalisingly presented as compatible, just as in the birth-scene of Apollo the everyday and the scientific, and the mythical and miraculous are brought into a piquant unison. This is clearly part of the thinking behind Apollo's statement that in their dealings with the Celts he and Philadelphus will be united in a 'common struggle' (171). This, I further suggest, is the rationale of Callimachus' deployment of everyday and topical material in *Hymn* 4: it establishes a relationship between the world of myth and contemporary life, and in the process confers authenticity on Philadelphus' claim to a special and direct link with the Olympians.

Thus in the *Hymns* of Callimachus the incorporation of everyday, realistic detail is an important means of subverting generic expectations, which is evidently one of the poet's special preoccupations and one over which he shows a sure mastery. It also helps the poet to put the grand personages and events of myth into a new perspective. Topical matter is employed to bring the mythical past and the present into close relation with one another, to the enrichment of historical and contemporary people and events. Common to each of these functions is the poet's desire to put a new perspective on the Alexandrians' cultural heritage.[125]

Mention of the *Hymn to Delos* has raised the question of encomiastic poetry again, and we may now inquire into the Alexandrian inclusion of realistic material in the poems written in praise of the Ptolemies. Theocritus' *Heracliscus* and Callimachus' *Victoria Berenices* have taught us that the Ptolemies were quite happy to be celebrated even where everyday and low material created an ironical effect. This is also true of *Idyll* 15, but the effect is striking in *Idyll* 14, where Thyonicus recommends that Aeschinas join Ptolemy's army to get over his shattered love-life.[126] So too with Herodas' first *Mimiamb*, where Gyllis the go-between paints a picture of the pleasures of Ptolemaic Egypt (23–36) designed to convince Metriche that her Mandris is not going to come back to her and that she had better accept Gyllis' proposal of a substitute. Machon felt at liberty to refer to Soter and Philadelphus in the company of parasites and courtesans (*Frr.* 1,5,18 Gow). Sotades' fatal expression of revulsion at Philadelphus' incestuous marriage (*Fr.* 1 Pow.), however, shows that there was a line beyond which you could not go when commenting on the Ptolemies' personal lives.[127] More restrained is the use of everyday matter in Callimachus' *Lock of Berenice* (*Fr.* 110), where the lock deprecates the frosty honour of catasterism since it will never again touch Berenice's head and enjoy the creature comforts of oils and myrrh.[128]

The approach is adopted in the formal encomium, Theocritus' *Idyll* 17. Irony must have been perceived in passages like that on the Ptolemies' ancestor, Heracles (13–33), or in that on the personified Cos (58–71), which is comparable with the motif in Callimachus' *Hymn to Delos*.[129] We may infer that such treatment was to the regents' taste and was actively encouraged by them, if only because they wanted to show they were 'with it' in their appreciation of realistic material in poetry.[130] In any case, the savants of the Alexandrian court for whom these poems were meant would have been diverted by the sophisticated allusiveness of an *Encomium for Ptolemy*.[131] The Ptolemies knew that the masses wanted a Pompe, but they were clearly happy to let their poets indulge in a modicum of irony to amuse the intelligentsia. When Theocritus turns in *Idyll* 16 to another Hellenistic monarch, Hiero II of Syracuse, his approach is perhaps significantly different. To be sure, he parades the *phauloi* of the *Odyssey*, arguably as an announcement of his pastoral poetry, but Hiero himself is portrayed in exclusively heroic terms, indeed as 'the like of the heroes of old' (80).[132] The vignette of the peace in the countryside that will follow Hiero's expulsion of the Carthaginians from Sicily (90–7) is motivated by the belief that peace in the day-to-day life of the ordinary man reflects the prowess of the ruler.[133] And the humour in the scene of the Graces' empty-handed return (8–12)[134] is at Theocritus' expense alone. His failure to 'humanise' Hiero contrasts with his strategy with the Ptolemies. Perhaps this is further evidence of the uniqueness of the Egyptian monarchs' taste for the humorous realism of their court-poets.

But humour is not the only result of the Alexandrians' deployment of humble material in their encomia. In the fragments of Callimachus' *Apotheosis of Arsinoe* (*Fr.* 228), which laments in the unusual iambo-lyric archeboulean metre the death of Queen Arsinoe in 270 BC and celebrates her deification,[135] the Queen's younger sister, Philotera, who apparently predeceased her, is depicted in congenial human terms. When she sees the smoke rolling over the Aegean from Arsinoe's pyre (40–5), she sends Charis to find out the cause and expresses anxiety whether 'her Libya', Egypt, is being harmed (45–51). Charis, too, is very human in her grief when she sees that the smoke is coming from Alexandria (52–5) and in the sympathetic way she assures Philotera that her country is safe and gently breaks the news about Arsinoe, 'her only sister' (66–75). Here the poet is exploring the more serious side of the humanity that Charis exhibits when she welcomes Thetis at *Iliad* 18.382ff. These touches invest the two new deities with real pathos and humanity.

Another lament whose poignancy derives in large part from the inclusion of much domestic, everyday detail is the *Distaff* of Erinna (*Fr.* 401 *S.H.*). We have already examined the pictorial (and psychological) realism with which Erinna recalls two pictures which haunt her from her girlhood with Baucis, whose death she is now lamenting: their game of Tortoise and their fear of the bogy, Mormo, whom Erinna's mother threatens to call in to hurry them along. But there is much else besides. The girls' dolls are mentioned (21). Erinna recollects how they rose early in the morning and how her mother was already busy with the wool-workers (22–5); whether Mormo is invoked to wake the girls up or to get them to start work quickly at the loom with the other wool-workers, the scene is equally realistic. Her memories of their childhood are cut short by her mention of Baucis' marriage, which, she says, made her friend forget all the things she heard as a child in the house of Erinna's mother (28–30). The poetess seems for some reason to be prevented from viewing Baucis' corpse, most probably because of the Greek custom of not allowing unmarried women of childbearing age to visit houses where a dead person was lying or to attend funerals of any but closest relatives.[136] There is mention of the distaff (39).

The first observation we may make about the *Distaff* is that in it the poetess expresses her personal feelings. Yet the poem is in hexameters, and the use of the metre for the personal expression of grief is unparalleled in earlier Greek poetry: traditionally, dirges were composed in choral metres.[137] True, before Erinna there were the laments of Andromache, Hecuba and Helen in the *Iliad* (*Il.* 22.477–514, 24.748–75), but, though these may have eased the way for her, they are not laments in the poet's own person; moreover, they are the human outcries of women who have had to stand by helplessly as Hector pursued his heroic career, whereas in the *Distaff* we have a lowly girl nostalgically recalling her ties to a simple girlfriend. Erinna crosses the personal mode of lament with the metre ordinarily reserved for objective representation.[138] This would have appeared a striking innovation in itself, especially in the recurrent cries of grief (18, 30, 47f., 54) and when she says that her childhood games with Baucis 'remain hot in her heart' (19f.); we may conjecture that the crossing will have made Erinna's audience see the expression of grief in a striking new perspective, greatly intensifying the pathos of the poem. The second point to note is that Erinna's audience must surely have felt a clash between form and content in her poem, given what people in the fourth century had come to expect of the hexameter, as we have seen. We may perhaps assume that the grand associations of the metre helped make them alive to the poem's poignancy. In this as in much else the *Distaff* is a poem of enormous sophistication and beauty.[139] Finally, as we have seen, the domestic details of the life of the girls are given an evocatively picturesque description; this, too, is integral to the poem's pathos.

Pathos seems to be one of the aims of the inclusion of the everyday and low in some Alexandrian didactic epic, especially in Aratus' *Phaenomena*, but the effect is hardly as intense as that in Erinna. As a Stoic, Aratus believes that Zeus is ultimately provident and thus gradually imparts his knowledge of the heavens to man.[140] As a Stoic, too, he feels the moral obligation to share his knowledge of the heavens and meteorology with others, as he shows when he tells us that the man who carefully watches the weather-signs 'is, firstly, himself the safer and also aids other men by his advice when a storm is brewing nearby' (763f.). He repeatedly states his sympathy for suffering humanity, as, for example, when he exclaims 'Thus do we poor, wandering men keep ourselves alive, each in his own way, and we are all ready to recognise the signs displayed before us and take note of them for the future' (1101–3).[141] The targets of his poem are thus ostensibly the people who are most exposed to the elements, sailors and farming folk, whose lives inspire the poet's economical but effective pictorialism. In two set pieces, already discussed, he vividly describes the terror of being at sea in a storm (291–9, 422–9), though the motif of the perils of the sailor's life is recurrent.[142] He relates elsewhere that the migration of birds from the islands to the mainland causes dread for the farmer, for whose harvest it presages ruinous drought, but joy for the goatherd, because his animals will give plentiful milk that season (1094–100).[143] However, the lot of such people is described only incidentally to his main theme, and at least in part simply as a means of giving it colour and life. Pathos there may on occasion be, but we may suspect that in the *Phaenomena*, which is after all primarily a translation into verse of Eudoxus' prose treatise, the poet's interest in humble folk is in fact rather academic.[144] Certainly, they do not play the central role that their counterparts do in the *Works and Days*, nor are they observed from so close a distance. The *Phaenomena*, therefore, can hardly lay claim to being a 'poor man's epic', nor, it appears, was that ever the poet's intention.

Such a claim would be even less true of Nicander's *Theriaca* and *Alexipharmaca*. We have seen several instances of material drawn from the lives of ordinary people which are presented with impressive *enargeia*.[145] The picture of the teething toddler who tries to relieve the itching of his gums is a good example (*Al.* 417–22), yet even here the poet affects an erudite and elevated style: there is an extraordinary combination of homely subject-matter and artificial and high-flown language.[146] The reason for Nicander's choice of such unpoetic material seems to have been to create as great a distance as possible between its triviality and the artistry expended on its presentation — to emphasise the *artistry*. The poet does not appear to be really interested in the subject-matter *per se* or for that matter, despite his protestations (*Al.* 1–7), in the alleged beneficiaries of his advice, country people. This is demonstrated by the medical uselessness of his descriptions and prescriptions.[147] It is interesting, then, to see how far removed from Hesiod the Alexandrian didactic poets are in this respect; in a genre pre-eminently and even avowedly directed to the little man, the everyday is turned into a means towards an end.

In Apollonius' *Argonautica* we can see another Alexandrian poet who makes extensive use of familiar, everyday material and experiments with the traditional genres and the expectations entertained of them. His prime aim in this is, I suggest, to update and make the Argonaut saga of traditional myth more compelling to his post-Euripidean audiences. This is particularly evident in his treatment of love.[148] The idea that love can be used for realistic purposes is a matter that I raised in Chapter 1. Apollonius seems to have viewed love as an experience in which all humans can have a share. If, therefore, he depicted Medea's love for Jason in unprecedented detail, emphasising its human quality, and, if he made love the key to the success of the Argonauts' expedition, could he not thereby make the grand characters of traditional epic more recognisably human and hence more immediate for his contemporaries? We cannot say that he is by this means crossing the genre of epic with the subject-matter of a low genre, as we can see happening in Callimachus' *Hecale*, for it is clear that the love of a Deianeira, for example, was evidently considered to be a quite appropriate subject for representation in a high genre like tragedy. He has, rather, 'contaminated' the genre by his thoroughgoing *mimēsis biou*, in which he is in stark contrast with Homer and perhaps even surpasses a Euripides.

He himself announces in the clearest possible terms the importance of love in his epic. Phineus' advice to the Argonauts that they enlist the 'cunning aid of Cypris since the success of their venture depends upon her' is plainly of vital importance to how the epic should be read and it is surprising that its full significance has been neglected in modern criticism. It would, I submit, have struck the audience as innovative: even though, as we shall see, Aphrodite was Jason's special ally in the tradition which Apollonius had inherited, Phineus' tone is emphatic and his statement absolute, and yet this counterpart of Teiresias in the *Odyssey* is advocating the aid of the love-goddess in an epic purporting to deal with 'the famous deeds of men of old' (1.1), a phrase modelled on Homer's 'famous deeds of heroes' (*Il.* 9.189, *Od.* 8.73; cf. *Il.* 9.524). Indeed, one of the characters in the epic,

Idas, points to the tension when he complains that the Argonauts are wrong to call upon Aphrodite instead of Enyalius, the god of war (3. 555-63) and unsuccessfully tries to obstruct the plan. But Idas is the only Argonaut who does not accept Phineus' advice. When Argus twice suggests getting Medea to help (3.475-63, 521-39), his second speech is followed by a bird-omen sent by the gods which the seer Mopsus interprets as a sign of their approval; Mopsus then reminds his comrades of Phineus' advice and urges them to invoke Aphrodite's aid and adopt Argus' idea (3.540-54, cf. 3.940-3). Thus the love plot is given divine legitimation. Moreover, of course, Phineus' advice proves in the event to be correct.

There are also the proems to Books 3 and 4. In the proem to Book 3 the poet invokes Erato, the Muse of love poetry;[149] she is asked to tell how Jason brought back the fleece 'aided by the love of Medea' (3.3). The invocation to the Muse of love poetry would have been considered by Apollonius' contemporaries to be a remarkable innovation in an epic about 'the famous deeds of men of old' and would have signalised his departure from traditional epic procedure. Certainly the centrality of the character and the love of Medea is here given explicit recognition. In the proem to Book 4 the poet invokes the Muse to tell him of the trials and cunning of Medea and expresses his dilemma over whether it was the 'lovesick grief of a mad passion' or 'shameless flight' which made her leave Colchis (4.1-5); she and her love are thus clearly stated to be central to the fourth book.

A third indication which Apollonius gives of his intentions is found in the scene in which Hera asks Aphrodite to help Jason. When Aphrodite expresses doubt that her 'weak hands' could do any good in a venture like Jason's, Hera claims that she is not asking for a show of might or strength: it is Eros who will, if Aphrodite can persuade him to help, save the day by making Medea fall in love with Jason, for she has the necessary cunning (3.84-9, cf. 3.75). Here, too, love is proclaimed as essential for the mission's success by a goddess known from the *Iliad* as a deity who favours traditional valour and prowess. In this way Apollonius makes reliance on love supplant traditional heroism as the means of attaining the goal of a heroic venture.

In the light of these passages there can be no doubt that Apollonius wishes us to view love as indispensable to the Argonauts' mission. In making Aphrodite important for Jason's quest he is following the traditional stories. Her patronage of Jason is, for example, evidenced in what remains of the early Corinthian epic, the *Naupactia*, which, Pausanias 10.38.11 tells us, was composed about women, apparently after the manner of the Hesiodic *Catalogue of Women*. Again, Pindar in his fourth *Pythian* makes Aphrodite instruct Jason how to win over Medea's heart and obtain her magic aid (213–23). However, as far as we can tell, Apollonius was the first epic poet to treat of the love theme in epic with such foregrounding and in such depth. This seems to be true with regard both to the poems which dealt with the Argonaut saga itself and to early epic in general.[150]

If we wish to find instances in earlier poetry of love being treated in a grand genre, we have to look to Attic tragedy. Sophocles had depicted the love of Deianeira in the *Trachiniae*, but Euripides was to dwell upon the emotion with an interest in its pathology which became notorious. We can see this in his representation of Phaedra in the second version of the *Hippolytus*, though it seems to have been the Phaedra of the first version which earned the dramatist his special notoriety in this regard.[151] Moreover, Apollonius' innovation is paralleled in Euripides' love-tragedy, the *Andromeda*. All this makes Euripides the true forerunner of Apollonius, and, as I shall argue, Apollonius has his Medea very much in mind as the figure into which he wishes us to see his young Colchian princess evolve in the course of his epic. Moreover, I think that we shall agree that Apollonius' characterisation of Medea depends on *mimēsis biou* to a greater extent than is found in Euripides.

It is harder to determine Apollonius' stance vis-à-vis his closer contemporaries, of whose work we possess such fragmentary remains, notably Philetas,[152] Hermesianax and Phanocles, except to say that they give us further evidence of the growth of interest in the poetic representation of love. One thing stands out in all this, however. On present evidence it seems highly likely that it was Apollonius' original innovation to have fused the theme of love with the grand framework of epic and its 'famous deeds of men of old' and to have dealt with it in thoroughgoing and analytical detail in an epic poem. I suggest, then, that the prominence given to love in Apollonius' epic was not motivated merely by the age's penchant for love poetry, but over and above that by a desire to put the heroes of traditional epic in a more familiar, human light than that in which those grand figures, with their reliance on heroic virtues such as manliness and martial prowess, had ever before appeared. In this sense, therefore, it may be said that the poet's handling of the love theme has a realistic intention.

The famous scenes depicting the awakening of Medea's love for Jason provide clear evidence of Apollonius' procedure. By his careful motivation of her every decision and act under the sway of love he humanises the mythical princess. By using her love as a means of accounting for why she helps the Argonauts he brings the grand world of myth into the realm of ordinary human experience.[153]

The realistic detail in the description of the first moments of Medea's love is extensive and brought in the foreground in a way in which it is not in the Nausicaa episode of *Odyssey* 6, Apollonius' main model. Such motifs as Medea's speechlessness at her first sight of Jason (284), her repeated glances at him (287–90), the alternating pallor and blushing of her cheeks as her love glows like the poor hireling-woman's fire (291–8), her stolen sidelong glances at Jason as he leaves, her veil held aside from her face (444f.), her recollection when he is gone of his appearance and voice which still rings in her ears (453–8) — all this emphasises Medea's humanness.

The same is true in the next scene in which she appears, where she is in an agony of indecision whether to help Jason (616–824). We have already noticed the pictorial and psychological realism of the description of her dream (617–32). The wish-fulfilment dream reveals a struggle between what we could call the heroine's id and superego, such is its psychological precision. Further realism of this kind can be seen when she tries to get her sister Chalciope to help her (633–743): there is the picture of her struggling with her conscience, but, more interestingly, there is the detail of her subterfuge in telling Chalciope that her sons are in danger, and in her quickness to take up Chalciope's anxious question whether she has some stratagem to help Jason and thus save her sons. Quite apart from the psychological credibility of the emotional state and motivation of the two women in this scene, the passage sets in motion Medea's tragically inevitable transition from the innocent young princess in the excitement of her first love into the bitter woman of vindictive cunning as we know her from Euripides. Her first exercise in guile is understandable and credible enough, even forgivable, for she is in an anguish of love (686f.). But from this relatively harmless deception there is a terrible progression to the revolt against her parents, to the murder of her brother and ultimately, outside the epic itself, to her awful revenge on Jason. The kernel of Euripides' Medea is present.

Apollonius' realism is evident in his portrayal of every stage of Medea's love. Thus when Chalciope has departed, Medea is pictured alone with her conscience, ashamed and afraid at having gone against her father's will (740–824). While other mortals are described as taking their rest, she is in a turmoil, her heart fluttering like the sunbeam from a bucket of water on to a wall, a simile in which pictorialism drawn from an everyday scene graphically illustrates the familiar symptoms of the emotion. The anatomical realism of the accompanying reference to the effect of love on Medea's *medulla oblongata* gives her feelings a similar 'tangibility', as I have suggested. Again, the poet depicts Medea's changes of mood, her anguish and the interplay of id and superego with extraordinary insight, making her momentarily throw over all guilt-feelings and decide to save Jason and then commit suicide, only to be stayed by the thought of the taunts of the Colchian women after her death, which prompts her to want to end it all then and there with poison, though that idea is in turn aborted when she remembers life's pleasures and her playmates, 'as a maiden does'.[154] Moreover, the poet again wishes us to compare his Medea with the Euripidean. This is made quite clear by the fact that he has modelled Medea's monologue (771–801) on the famous monologue in Euripides' tragedy (*Med.* 1021–80) where the heroine debates whether or not to kill her children, another occasion when her passion, this time for revenge on Jason, overrides her sense of duty to her family.[155]

Apollonius continues to trace Medea's development into the Medea of tragedy in his remark that Medea is in no state of mind to take any heed of her immediate dangers 'and the others which were destined to gather later' (836f.), which refers to the events to happen to the couple in Greece.[156] Moreover, the proem to the fourth book emphasises the destructive side of Medea's love where the prologue to the third book has stressed its gentleness. The two proems therefore signpost Medea's development as a victim of love from an innocent maiden into a desperate and treacherous woman like the Medea of Euripides. The poet's dilemma over whether it was Medea's passion or simple fear that drove her from Colchis is in fact only an apparent one, for both emotions determine her action.[157] Hera prompts her fear that Aeetes has found out about her aiding Jason (11–25) and she steals away in a torment of guilt (26–53). Moreover, the moon-goddess, Selene, espying her flight, says that Medea now shares with her 'a similar mad passion' to hers for Endymion and that 'some god of pain' has given Jason to her to be a 'grievous bane'; Medea must now, for all her cunning, brace herself to take 'her burden of pain, which will cause many groans' (57–65). Selene thus emphasises what the proem has told us, that Book 4 is going to describe the darker side of Medea's love and its desperate consequences. Again, therefore, the poet tells us that the motivation for the plot of his epic is on a more recognisably human level than is traditional, despite the contrasting fairytale motif by which he expresses the thought.

The human quality of Medea's love is indeed emphasised in Book 4, but so is the more sinister complexion hinted at in the proem. When the Argonauts decide to hand over Medea to the pursuing Colchians and to leave her fate to the arbitration of a neutral king, she very naturally flares up in anger. In her frenzy at being treated as the dupe of the very person for whom she has given up so much — she now calls her agency in Jason's success her 'folly' — she wavers between pleas and curses (355–90). Apollonius plainly wants us to view the murder of Apsyrtus, in which Medea guiltily acquiesces (395–420), as an act of vicious cruelty and one inspired by love, for he makes an arresting apostrophe to love in which he claims that it is the origin of much human suffering and has instilled in Medea a 'hateful infatuation' (445–9). Such an apostrophe is all the more striking in an author not given to statements *in propria persona*.[158] This emotional progression is motivated with entirely credible psychological precision and Medea is realistically set forth on her path to becoming the woman that Euripides portrays: first the deception of her sister, then the flouting of her parents' will, and now the murder of her brother, a preparation for the murder of her children at Corinth.[159] And already her lot is conceived in tragic terms, for, as her reflection on the necessity of further wicked action shows, she is conscious that she can either remain passive and be destroyed or reap the evil consequences of action.[160]

The same forces are at work in the episode on Phaeacia. The marriage-ceremony is arranged hastily and the marriage consummated in an atmosphere of terrified uncertainty over whether Alcinous will stand by his edict to let Medea go with Jason if she is already married. Apollonius makes a second authorial judgement at this point, a crushing comment on the grief that always attends upon human happiness. This concept of the human lot and, more specifically, of the nature of love, convincingly explains how Medea could change from an innocent princess into the dark and terrifying figure in Euripides.[161]

It is, therefore, abundantly evident that Apollonius has taken extraordinary trouble to make his mythical heroine alive for his contemporaries. At every stage her thoughts and actions are convincingly motivated. His chief aims in this, it appears, were first to give a realistic motivation for her assistance of Jason in capturing the fleece, a feature of the saga which was firmly established in the traditional accounts, but of which Pindar, for example, had given only the briefest outline. Secondly, he harmonises the two sides of Medea's character, a problem posed for him by Euripides' characterisation of her, which no poet after the tragedian could possibly ignore.

Moreover, as we have seen, Medea's love for Jason is clearly stated on several significant occasions to be the only means by which the venture will succeed. Thus a force which is more familiar to the everyday experience of life, and is hence more realistic than traditional might, is proposed as the key to a heroic deed. Reference is repeatedly made to her indispensability not only in the passages which we have already discussed but throughout the main narrative.[162]

Medea's central role in the *Argonautica* as a poem and in the success of the heroes' venture has most important consequences for Apollonius' conception of what constitutes an epic hero. This is a question which is vitally relevant to us, for I suggest that in his characterisation of Jason Apollonius is modernising notions of heroism in epic and trying to create a type of hero which will be in accord with the experience of the everyday life of his times and will thus be credible and realistic. As Aristotle might have put it, Jason is a hero who is 'like you and me'.

The heroes of the old stamp, Heracles, Telamon and Idas, are all in their several ways found unequal to the task at hand and discredited, especially in their attitudes to love and the idea of enlisting the aid of a woman. In short, they have neither the inclination nor the qualifications to make Aphrodite their champion, though her aid is essential to the expedition's success.[163]

Heracles, the natural choice for the leadership of the expedition

(1.331–49), sneers at the Argonauts for their unheroic love-making on Lemnos (1.865–74), but is hoist on his own petard later when he is so grief-stricken at the loss of Hylas that he deserts the mission (1.1153ff.).[164] In the embassy to Aeetes, when the king receives Jason's request for the fleece with insulting hostility, Telamon is on the point of answering in kind and has to be restrained by Jason (3.382–5); there can be no doubt that Telamon's heroic defiance would have been disastrous where Jason's diplomacy proves ultimately effective. Idas is presented as an arrogant hot-head.[165] His opposition to the idea of using a woman's help is discredited once and for all in the scene where the heroes try out Jason's enchanted weapons; Idas loses his temper and hacks ineffectually at the spear with his sword. At this the other heroes shout for joy (3.1252–5; cf. 3.1170). Idas is made to look ridiculous in the last scene in which he appears in the epic, and that immediately after Jason is said to have acted 'at Medea's injunction' (3.1246). His kind of heroism is shown up as outmoded, and is replaced by a more human, though not necessarily a more gentle code.

Jason, who supplants the old-style heroism,[166] continually exhibits a concern for diplomacy, rather than recourse to brute 'manly prowess' (ἠνορέη), as a means of gaining his ends. This is particularly clear from the way in which he sees the leadership. For him it is a diplomatic post. At the election he talks of the leader of the expedition as one 'who will take care over each thing and will take upon himself quarrels and treaties with other peoples' (1.339f.). He repeatedly shows restraint and tact. For example, he helps in settling the quarrel between Idas and Idmon, though Idas has insulted him (1.462–95), and explicitly renounces 'manly prowess' as embodied in a hero like Idas, recommending in its place 'talk which smooths the way in a fitting manner' (3.188–90).[167] The passages which invite comparison with Homeric views on leadership are also instructive. So, before entering the Symplegades, Jason feigns dismay to the rest of the crew in a trial of their feelings (2.619–49), and his test, far from backfiring as Agamemnon's does in the *Iliad*, is admirably successful; as Fränkel says, Jason shows himself here to be a master at handling people.[168] Again, he is democratic in council and insists that he is merely *primus inter pares*. The Argonauts should choose their leader together, he says at the elections, 'for our journey back to Hellas is a common concern, and common to us all is the journey to the land of Aeetes' (1.336f.). His suggestion of an embassy to Aeetes he leaves to the general vote 'for we share a common need, and freedom of speech is common to all alike: let him who in silence withholds his thoughts and advice know that it is he alone who is robbing this expedition of its journey home' (3.173–5). When the Argo gets lost in sandy lakes and Libyan nymphs give Jason the puzzling advice to save the heroes by paying their mother recompense for carrying them in her womb, he determines to call the heroes to an assembly: 'the counsel of many is better' (4.1336). This emphatic espousal of collective wisdom and strength stands in deliberate contrast with Odysseus' attitude that 'lordship of many' is a bad thing and that there should be only one ruler (*Il.* 2.198–206). And yet Jason's *modus operandi* is justified by the success with which it meets in each case; another heroic attitude is consciously refuted.

In addition to his qualities as a diplomat he possesses a characteristic of vital importance to an expedition which depends upon love for its successful outcome — physical handsomeness, which is emphasised throughout the epic and is frequently the subject of similes.[169] It is evident from the Lemnian episode, for example, that beauty is a special virtue of this unconventional 'hero', as he is called as he walks towards the Lemnians' city (1.781). The whole picture of Jason at this juncture, cloak and all, stands in particularly stark contrast with *Iliad* 3.43–5, 54f. where Hector, attacking the 'woman crazy' Paris, sets physical beauty and the gifts of Aphrodite against the manly virtues of 'force' and 'prowess', βίη and ἀλκή; Apollonius is turning the values of traditional heroism upside down. It is on Medea, of course, that Jason brings to bear both of his cardinal qualities. We have already seen the effect that his physical presence has on the princess, and his extraordinary beauty is dwelt upon just before the rendezvous-scene (3.919–26), but he also has just the right word for each occasion with her and his speeches to her are frequently characterised by the word ὑποσσαίνων, 'fawning', or the like (3.974, 4.394, 410). Typical is his quotation to Medea of the Ariadne myth which leaves out the tale of her abandonment by Theseus on Dia (3.997–1007). He is quick to soothe her grief at leaving Colchis (4.107f.) and tactfully makes public his intention to marry her (4.194f.).

Yet Apollonius seems to go out of his way to impute a third characteristic to him which would hardly be expected in a traditional hero. This is his 'helplessness'. On the eve of the Argo's departure he is said to be 'without resource' (ἀμήχανος: 1.460), and epithets like it occur throughout the epic.[170] This quality sets him off from Odysseus whom in other respects he superficially resembles.[171] Apollonius seems to want to make it perfectly clear that his new hero has all too human failings, and that he confronts his trials more as an average man than Odysseus, on one occasion even expressing misgivings over Medea's aid, when Phineus can have left him in no doubt about her value for his quest (3.487f.).

But, while stressing Jason's ordinariness, so to speak, the poet tries to make convincing the manner by which such a hero could succeed in a venture that is to become one of the 'famous deeds of men of old'. Jason's success is achieved by means of his other qualities, which are positive but totally within the range of ordinary human experience. Through winning Medea's heart he wins her aid, and it is this which enables him to succeed in his trials. It was, therefore, a desire for realism which motivated Apollonius' revision of the nature of an epic hero and his creation of a 'love-hero'.

But the realism of the characterisation of Jason does not end there. When he is in a tight spot, all of his qualities can take a vicious turn. In Book 4 he is diplomatic with Medea to the point of deviousness and downright treachery. Having planned to give her up when he is cornered by her brother Apsyrtus (4.338–49), he is frightened by her rage and hints that his real plan is to lure Apsyrtus to his doom (4.395–410), thereby both assuaging her anger and securing an escape. His deed is called 'murder by treachery', δολοκτασία (4.479), and we may see in the whole episode the beginning of his transition into the Jason of Euripides,[172] just as Apollonius explains Medea's development into the figure of Attic tragedy. By assigning to his Jason the qualities that we have noted, Apollonius has 'set the scene' for Euripides. This is in perfect accord with the tragic conception of love which he presents in the *Argonautica*. We can, therefore, again see the Alexandrian harmonising variant traditions about his material in a way which will be realistic.

But there are other peculiarities of the *Argonautica* which can be explained in terms of the poet's fascination with realistic material and the effects which he can produce from it. In particular, the purpose of the scene in which Hera, Athene and Aphrodite discuss how they are to help Jason (3.6–166) can best be accounted for if we accept that in it Apollonius is crossing genres both by incorporating much comically realistic matter and by continuing his exploration of love. There is, first, the detail of Hera and Athene's retirement to a room on Olympus where they can plot in secret, away from Zeus and the other immortals (3.6–10). The *Argonautica* knows of the traditional domestic friction between Hera and Zeus, as is clear from the passage in which Hera tells Thetis that she has favoured her from childhood because she rejected Zeus' advances, 'for sleeping with immortal and mortal women is always on his mind' (4.790–804). There is, therefore, a human, domestic motive for the goddesses' withdrawal[173] and Apollonius pictures their intrigue in terms appropriate to important women scheming at a modern court, like that of the Ptolemies, as is often remarked. Secondly, both goddesses, who are acknowledged in the Homeric poems as inveterate proponents of cunning, are presented as surprisingly bankrupt of ideas in the present situation (10–21),[174] until Hera hits on the idea that they go to Aphrodite and get her to persuade her boy, Eros, to make Medea fall in love with Jason with his arrow — 'if he will obey', a phrase which is the first hint of the troublesome fact he is a wickedly disobedient child (22–9).[175] Thirdly, there is the matter of Athene's embarrassment. She approves of Hera's plan, but is comically coy about it: Zeus had begotten her to be a virgin goddess who would know nothing of love, let alone how to instil it (we are meant to remember that she was not even born of woman), yet here she is, invoking the aid of no less than Aphrodite; Hera must therefore do the talking (30–5)! It is amusing to see the Athene of the Homeric poems now suffering such social discomfort; it is, moreover, significant that Apollonius once again represents heroic prowess as no longer what the situation requires.

We meet with further comic realism when the two goddesses arrive at Aphrodite's palace. Her husband, Hephaestus, is already working at his forge, so we remain in an exclusively female preserve. When she sees Hera and Athene, she stops toying with her coiffure, calls them in and greets them 'with cunning words' (52–4). The greeting reminds us of Charis' welcome to Thetis at *Il.* 18.385f.[176] We may justifiably feel that at least part of its 'cunning', aside from the obvious irony with which Hera and Athene are twitted, is brought out by his 'forward citation' of Charis, Hephaestus' later spouse: as we know from the lay of Demodocus in the *Odyssey*, Aphrodite has a taste for extramarital relationships and, as we know from *Iliad* 18, she is later to be supplanted as Hephaestus' wife by Charis.[177] Indeed, we have a clear hint about her affair with Ares within the *Argonautica*, for, in the picture of her preening herself on Jason's cloak, she is using Ares' shield as a mirror: the affair is therefore at least beginning in the epic. Thus here she greets sexually more 'straight' goddesses (how Athene must be squirming!) with all the self-assuredness of a beautiful woman confident in her sexual charm, of which we are given a gorgeous picture as she combs her hair. But there is even more background to the relationship between the three goddesses. Though the judgement of Paris and the subsequent souring of Hera and Athene's relations with Aphrodite have not occurred by the time of the Argonauts' expedition, they are of course well known, one source again being the *Iliad* (24.22–30), and there can be no real doubt that we are meant to discern in the present scene the latent psychological dynamics of the famous rivalry. Once more, then, we see Apollonius using a forward reference to events which are chronologically posterior to the action of his epic to enrich the dramatic interplay between the characters, though here everyday elements are highlighted for the purposes of ironic humour.

Accordingly, the words with which Aphrodite greets Hera and Athene are indeed 'cunning' and fraught with devastating irony: ἡδεῖαι has perhaps a needingly familiar tone to it. Aphrodite is suspicious of the goddesses' motives in coming after so long and she comes close to downright sarcasm when she wonders what can have brought them 'since they are pre-eminent among goddesses'. Her pointedly ironical expression of surprise lends deliberate emphasis to the remarkable fact that the traditionally heroic goddesses are indeed powerless and asking the goddess of love for aid.[178] The realistic, human touches thus contrast with and complement the poet's art of allusion. There is more humour of the kind that is derived from putting the goddesses in an incongruously domestic light in Aphrodite's expostulation over her problem-child (90–110) and in the scene with Eros (111–55).

The resultant picture of everyday life on Olympus is similar to that painted by Callimachus in the *Hymn to Artemis*.[179] But, just as we saw Callimachus gradually introducing a more serious tone into his hymn, so we may observe a shift of tone in Apollonius' handling of Aphrodite and Eros. First of all, the involvement of the goddess, whom we know to have been the traditional

The Everyday and the Low in Alexandrian Poetry   207

champion of Jason in the quest, is presented in comically human terms. Later, however, the effects of her involvement on the human protagonists are to prove all too painful. The scene which forms a bridge between the two presentations of love's role in the plot is that in which Eros fires his arrow at Medea (3.275-98). After he has furtively done his work, he quickly withdraws from the room, but the arrow had lodged in Medea's heart and her pain has begun. The gods' indifference to the pain which they inflict on humans is emphasised in the most sinister way. The capricious and self-willed god of love is said to retreat laughing, καγχαλόων (286), while Medea is already suffering. That is bad enough, but we remember that Apollonius has already used the word καγχαλάω to describe Eros' malicious laughter when Ganymedes loses his knucklebones in their game (124): his reaction to human agony is the same as his expression of pleasure when he wins a children's game. Thus the poet has endowed the gods with a humanness which is more than human, so to speak, but presents them none the less as the arbiters of human destiny. This kind of approach to the Olympians is already present in Homer's depiction of them,[180] but Apollonius, by means of his emphatically everyday presentation of the three goddesses, with the undercurrent of psychological friction which is later to erupt in the judgement of Paris, and his characterisation of Eros, has really twisted the knife in the wound. Humans are represented as prey to forces which are beyond their control and which are quite inconcerned about the pain that they might inflict. Thus in this section of the poem the poet uses everyday realism first for the purposes of the ironical humour that arises from its incongruity in its grand setting but secondly to undercut that superficial humour and make a serious thematic point crucial to the epic. Moreover, he demonstrates the importance of love in his epic in a manner which is quite alien to the rest of the epic tradition. In the Olympus scene and the picture of Eros on earth, therefore, he effects innovations in the conception of an epic which are both subtle and powerful. At the root of his innovations is the technique of genre-crossing.[181]

Apollonius exhibits his facination with realistic scenes at almost every turn in the *Argonautica*. Details from the everyday life of people at all ages are expanded upon to a degree unprecedented in earlier epic. We have seen how the poet uses a baby to powerful emotional effect, when Cheiron the centaur and his wife come down to the shore to give Peleus a last sight of his infant son,

Achilles. Another effective passage of this type is that describing the reaction of the young mothers who hear the hiss of the serpent guarding the fleece: in terror they hug their children to them when they start with fright at the sound (4.136–8).[182] Eros and Ganymede provide the most extended passage depicting older children. The poet's delight in motifs drawn from the everyday life of women surpasses in its intensity and pervasiveness all such interest displayed in earlier epic. We may note here the way in which Chalciope's handmaids drop their sewing when Chalciope's sons appear (3.254–6),[183] Medea tempts her maids out to her rendezvous with Jason by promising songs and flower-plucking (3.897–901) and the nymphs gaze in wonder at the golden fleece before Jason and Medea's marriage (4.1143–8). Apollonius also shows his interest in the ways of family life in the passage in which Alcinous and Arete discuss Medea's case when they are in bed: once Alcinous gives his decision, he immediately falls asleep and Arete gets out of bed and sends a message to Jason and Medea telling them the king's resolve and commanding them to marry (4.1110ff.). Most striking, too, is Apollonius' keenness to depict people in their old age, even where it is not dramatically necessary. We have seen his pictures of Iphias, Polyxo and Phineus and have noted that in the case of the description of Phineus the poet shows an indebtedness to clinical terminology.[184]

This kind of material pervades the similes. We have already noticed the manner in which Apollonius combines in them pictorialism and detail from everyday and low life and how he will often transfer a simile from the warlike context in which he found it in Homer to illustrate the erotic context of the framing narrative. This we found clearly exemplified in his use of the simile subject of the poor hireling spinstress. We shall examine only one more example here. When Jason goes to the city of the Lemnian women, he is compared with the bright star, Hesperus, at which maidens gaze as it rises over the rooftops and shines through the darkness with a red gleam; a maiden, betrothed by her parents to a young man who is abroad, is filled with joy at the sight, but also with yearning for the youth (1.774–80). The pictorial sensuousness of the simile is plain, but equally so is its erotic content. Hesperus, of course, was generally associated with love-making and its appearance signified the commencement of the marriage-ceremony,[185] and the maiden is thus filled with joyful anticipation of the actual day of her wedding. Moreover, the simile aptly

The Everyday and the Low in Alexandrian Poetry   209

illuminates the emotions of the husbandless Lemnian women as they gaze upon him. But it tells us even more than this. Jason's cloak, which Apollonius describes immediately before the Hesperus simile, is meant to be viewed as a counterfoil to Achilles' shield in both decoration and function, and to advertise Jason's status as a love-hero by means of the contrast. Now the simile also seems meant to remind us of the Iliadic Achilles, who, when he approaches Troy, is said to gleam like a star as he rushes over the plain. The star is Sirius, which is the most brilliant but causes much pain for mortals and brings searingly hot weather to them (*Il.* 22.26–31). The Iliadic simile arrestingly captures the menacing doom which Achilles represents for the Trojans. If, as I think likely, Apollonius has the older epic in mind here, he is again using a Homeric motif, transferring its context, and by reflection making it underline a thematic point, in this case, as with the cloak, his adoption of a love-hero. The number of similes in the *Argonautica* that are drawn from the life of ordinary women is in any case far greater than in any earlier epic that we know of, and they are frequently used to illustrate ordinary human emotional states.[186] And, as we have seen, the poet can expand upon the everyday content of his similes to a remarkable extent.

In this extensive incorporation of familiar material, then, we can see a vital aspect of Apollonius' modernisation of epic for his contemporaries: his aim seems to have been to redefine his audiences' relationship to their Hellenic heritage by relating his saga to their experience of life, even where the resultant tone may have been teasingly ironical.

But not even this represents the full range of effects produced by the Alexandrians' deployment of realistic subject-matter. Callimachus' *Hecale* exhibits a realism unprecedented in Greek literature both in its nature and its extent.

The old woman, Hecale, is the figure central to our inquiry. To judge from the fragments, Callimachus described her humble appearance in some detail. She is apparently said to have 'the ever-moving lips of an old woman' (*Fr.* 490).[187] Another fragment describes her broad-rimmed hat, 'the felt headgear of a shepherd' (ποιμενικὸν πίλημα) and her walking-stick (*Fr.* 292). The word for 'hat', πίλημα, which harks back to Hesiod's advice to the farmer to wear a πῖλος 'so as to keep your ears from getting wet', is typically Callimachean in that it is a technically precise word from the life of the peasant-farmer (*W.D.* 545f.).[188] The stick is mentioned again as 'the support of her old age' (*Fr.* 355). Thus Callimachus appears to have used pictorialism to emphasise Hecale's lowly situation.

The old woman's generosity was celebrated right at the poem's opening, for we possess a fragment from there which says that 'all travellers honoured her for her hospitality, for she kept a house which was never closed' (*Fr.* 231). Her generous nature and humble circumstances are prominently displayed throughout the scene in which she receives Theseus in from the storm (the description of which itself contains domestic matter, already noticed, like the simile of the weaving girls laying aside their work for their evening meal: *Fr.* 238. 19f.). The hero casts off his cloak, wet from the storm, Hecale makes him sit down on her pauper's couch, having snatched a small tattered garment from her bed (presumably to spread over the couch), takes down dry wood that she has stored long ago and cuts it (*Frr.* 239–43). Callimachus' model here is the episode in the *Odyssey* in which Eumaeus gives shelter to Odysseus (*Od.* 14.48ff., 418ff.). Next follows the scene in which Hecale washes Theseus' feet. She brings a hollow, boiling pot (*Fr.* 244), empties the bowl and draws another draught (*Fr.* 246).[189] Though the fragments of the foot-washing scene are, to say the least, meagre, it is plain enough that Callimachus' model is this time the moment in the *Odyssey* in which the second great *phaulos* of the epic tradition, Eurycleia, washes Odysseus' feet (*Od.* 19.386ff.). Thus the poet carefully places his heroine in the tradition of paradigmatic *phauloi* of canonical epic. Our fragments give us an idea of the humble meal which Hecale serves, 'olives which grew on the tree, wild olives and white olives which she had laid down in autumn to swim in brine' (*Fr.* 282.4–5 *S.H.* = *Fr.* 248 Pf.), wild vegetables and cabbage (*Frr.* 249, 250), and many bread-loaves 'of the kind which women store up for herdsmen', which Hecale now takes from her bread-basket (*Fr.* 251). Mention is possibly made of her pauper's table (*Fr.* 284 *S.H.* = 252 Pf.).[190]

Her moral goodness and straitened circumstances are further described in the conversation which she and Theseus apparently strike up after the meal. Theseus then asks her why she, an old woman, dwells in such a lonely place. It is likely[191] that she begins by asking Theseus why he wants to 'awaken a sleeping tear' (*Fr.* 682); certainly there is much pathos in what follows. She evidently goes on to tell Theseus of her former life, possibly prefacing her story with the statement 'my poverty is not hereditary, nor am I a pauper from my grandparents' (*Fr.* 254). She mentions men who guarded her threshing-floor which her oxen trod in a circle, an indication of her wealth.[192] She describes the arrival from Aphnidae of what must be her husband. He was godlike in appearance and dressed in a rich mantle (*Fr.* 285.8–12 *S.H.* = *Fr.* 253.8–12 Pf.). Hecale talks about her two sons, whom she reared in an abundantly rich household, with slaves, in all probability, to bathe them in warm baths (*Fr.* 287.1–6 *S.H.*). She says that the two of them grew up like towering poplars beside a river, τώ μοι ἀναδραμέτην ἅτε κερ]κίδες, αἵτε χαράδρης/ . . . π]ουλὺ δὲ μῆκευ/ . . . [ἠ]έξαντο (*Fr.* 287.7–9 *S.H.*). This is a clear reminiscence of Thetis' words about Achilles, doomed to die, at *Iliad* 18.56f.: 'he shot up like a sapling; I nursed him, like a tree in the rising ground of an orchard', ὁ δ' ἀνέδραμεν ἔρνεϊ ἶσος· / τὸν μὲν ἐγὼ θρέψασα, φυτὸν ὡς γουνῷ ἀλωῆς. Hecale is now being compared with one of the noble personages of traditional epic, and the pathos of her situation is greatly enhanced by the comparison. After another gap, we find her bewailing the death of her younger son; the death of the older (*Fr.* 287.12f. *S.H.*) was probably described in the lacuna. Apparently, this son was killed by the robber, Cercyon, in his horrid wrestling-matches (*Fr.* 287.18 *S.H.*). She wishes that she might pierce Cercyon's eyes with thorns while he is still alive and eat his raw flesh (*Fr.* 287.24–6 *S.H.*). There seems to be a connection between the fates of Hecale and Theseus, for Theseus killed Cercyon[193] and presumably told Hecale that her son's death had been avenged. And again Hecale is compared with grand characters from the *Iliad*. Her refusal to die 'when death had been calling for a long time' (*Fr.* 287.12 *S.H.*) recalls Hector's recognition that 'the gods have called me deathward' (*Il.* 22.297) and her threat of cannibalism reminds us of Hecuba's wish to eat Achilles' liver for the death of her son (*Il.* 24.212f.). Thus in her description of the death of her remaining son, on whom she had concentrated all her hopes, the pathos of her characterisation is deepened by association with figures of intense suffering from traditional epic.

It is clear, then, that Callimachus' depiction of Hecale's misfortune is movingly serious, and that in her grief she is raised to the stature of the grand people of the epic tradition. Yet this is the woman whom the poet has evidently wished us to view in terms of a Eumaeus and a Eurycleia. She is, like them, a *phaulos*, despite the fact that she came from a rich family, but her fall from prosperity is described with far greater pathos than Homer depicts those of Eumaeus and Eurycleia (or, for that matter, than

Euripides does in the case of the Farmer). And in this important respect she is markedly different from her earlier counterparts. The New Comedy may have been influential here with its recurrent motif of the kind-hearted slave, menial or prostitute who turns out to be of noble birth. Again, as with Eumaeus, Eurycleia and the Farmer, it seems likely that Callimachus tries to some extent to account for Hecale's generosity by appeal to traditional Greek thought on the matter, but her present position in society, illustrated so amply, remains that of a *phaulos* from whom such nobility was not normally to be expected. In any case, it looks as if the poet is more intent upon extracting the pathos inherent in the motif than in using it to account for his heroine's unexpected moral goodness.

After their conversation, Theseus and Hecale retire, and Hecale says that she will sleep in the corner of the room where there is a bed ready for her (*Fr.* 256). In this way she once more resembles Eumaeus, who prepares a bed for Odysseus near the fire while he himself goes to his usual bed near the pigs to be able to keep guard over them (*Od.* 14.518–33). When Theseus rises she is already awake (*Fr.* 257). Thus Callimachus depicts Hecale in her treatment of Theseus as generous and considerate, while reminding us throughout of her lowly literary antecedents.

Fr. 288 *S.H.* (= *Fr.* 260 Pf.), which relates the puzzling conversation between two birds, probably a crow and an owl,[194] closes with the description of the dawn of Theseus' return to Hecale, in which Callimachus indulges in further *genre*-painting, as we have seen, with his reference to robbers, lanterns being lit, water-carriers singing, wagons with squeaking axles, and blacksmiths or other people fetching fire for the day (*Fr.* 288.64–9 *S.H.*).[195] If, as is likely, the conversation of the birds occurred near Hecale's hut,[196] then the poet is again sketching in the details of her milieu, and using his pictorialist skill for the purpose.

We possess part of the funeral-speech pronounced over her grave by Theseus or her neighbours. The speaker claims that they 'will often remember [her] hospitable hut,[197] for it was a common shelter for everybody' (*Fr.* 263). We know that Theseus fully recognised the old woman's goodness and rewarded her by creating a deme named after her and establishing a shrine to Zeus Hecaleios (*Dieg.* XI.5ff.). Thus the poem began and ended with Hecale and her moral nobility.

Callimachus has indeed given a serious and prominent role to his *phaulos*. But he has not neglected Theseus, a hero who would in traditional thought have been considered a quite appropriate figure in epic. *Frr.* 232 and 233 come from the episode in which Medea attempts to poison Theseus. *Frr.* 234–7 are what remains of the episode in which Theseus unexpectedly appears to Aegeus after being reared in Troezen. *Fr.* 238.1–14 is part of a conversation between the two, Theseus urging his father to let him go out to face adventures; his impetuosity and bravery seem to have been stressed.[198] As we have seen, the victory over the bull of Marathon was described. *Fr.* 288.1–15 *S.H.* (= *Fr.* 260.1–15 Pf.) describes Theseus' triumphal procession, how no one dared to look straight at the 'great hero and the monstrous beast', but eventually greeted him with a ritual shower of leaves. Here we see the commoners' reaction to the conquering hero. Finally, as we have just observed, his slaying of Cercyon is mentioned and appears to have had bearing on his relationship with Hecale. Theseus is, therefore, presented as a traditional epic hero, a true *spoudaios*. Apparently, Callimachus means us to regard him as a foil to Hecale, who is a *phaulos* and yet is elevated to a central role in the epic. Thus, on the one hand, Theseus' gratitude to Hecale and the honours which he posthumously bestows upon her confirm her true moral worth despite her lowly station. On the other, her untraditional status as an epic hero is thrown into sharp relief by juxtaposition with a hero of the traditional type.

Callimachus has brought her and her goodness into remarkable prominence. The seriousness with which he portrays her is striking. In the *Victoria Berenices* he had created a *phaulos*, Molorchus, whose goodly but humble life is set in deliberate contrast with the grand myths and events which frame it, and he had put this contrast to comic effect. But this is not at all the case in his portrayal of Hecale. Certainly, there is a deliberate superficial incongruity in the contrast between her lowly social status and the heroic context in which she is placed, but this is given emphasis only to demonstrate that appearances can be deceptive and that in a deeper ethical sense she is entirely worthy of the world of epic. The poet makes her describe her family's fate and her own emotions with evident pathos and presents her moral goodness as seriously as he does Theseus' traditional heroism. She is, of course, unlike Eumaeus and Eurycleia, with whom we are continually invited to compare her, in that she is portrayed as acting in a way which is spontaneously good. The acceptance of the idea that a *phaulos* might initiate independent moral action had been made possible by developments in Greek thought which we saw evidenced in Euripides' treatment of the Farmer in the *Electra*. But she is significantly unlike that figure as well in the way in which she is presented. Euripides may have defended the integrity and moral worth of low characters like the Farmer, but he was still precluded by the genre in which he was working from giving them a *main* role. Here Callimachus has gone one step further than the tragedian. He has given Hecale the central role in his epic and has made her goodness the poem's real point. Thus for the first time in extant Greek poetry the *spoudaios* has been displaced from the centre stage and is made to share it with a *phaulos*.

We saw at the beginning of this chapter how in the prologue to the *Aetia* Callimachus explicitly rejected the material of traditional epic, 'kings and heroes'. The implication that by removing the *spoudaioi* from their traditional central position in epic Callimachus deliberately intended to leave room for everyday and low heroes is borne out by the poet's practice in the *Hecale* even more strikingly than by that in the *Aetia* or the *Hymns*. The poem represents an instance of genre-crossing which is a significant exception to Auerbach's generalisations about the separation of the genres in ancient literature, and its realism in this respect comes quite close to that of modern literature. Because of this the *Hecale* is one of the poet's most remarkable achievements and one of the most important poems in our inquiry. We should remark, finally, that it is also realistic in a manner that we have come to regard as typical of Callimachus and of the Alexandrian movement as a whole. It attempts to bring the heroic world of myth down to earth and hence help its audiences to relate to their heritage in an arresting new way. But the seriousness of tone with which Hecale is portrayed makes the poem realistic in a sense unique even in Alexandrian poetry.

Notes

1. See E. A. Schmidt, *Poetische Reflexion: Vergils Bukolik* (Munich, 1972), pp. 38, 282 (with lit., to which add E. Reitzenstein, 'Zur Stiltheorie des Kallimachos', in *Festschr. Richard Reitzenstein* (Leipzig and Berlin, 1931), 59). Schmidt is followed by D. M. Halperin, *Before Pastoral: Theocritus and the Ancient Tradition of Bucolic Poetry* (New Haven and London, 1983), p. 18 n. 57. That Callimachus in the *Pr. Aet.* is also expressing his preferences in hexameter-epic is

The Everyday and the Low in Alexandrian Poetry 215

naturally and generally assumed: see e.g. K. O. Brink, 'Callimachus and Aristotle: An Inquiry into Callimachus' ΠΡΟΣ ΠΡΑΞΙΦΑΝΙΙΝ', *C.Q.* 40 (1946), 17.

2. If the prologue was added to the *Aetia* after a hostile reception, figures like Molorchus will have been the sticking-point. On the problem see especially R. Pfeiffer, 'ΒΕΡΕΝΙΚΙΙΣ ΠΛΟΚΑΜΟΣ', *Philol.* 87 (1932), 227f. (= *W.d.F.* 296, 151f.); Pfeiffer, *Callimachus*, vol.i (Oxford, 1949), p. xxxvif.; P. M. Fraser, *Ptolemaic Alexandria* (Oxford, 1972), pp. 719f., with n. 11 (vol.ii, p. 1006), 747, 754; H. Reinsch-Werner, *Callimachus Hesiodicus: die Rezeption der hesiodeischen Dichtung durch Kallimachos von Kyrene* (Berlin, 1976), p. 6; P. J. Parsons, 'Callimachus: Victoria Berenices', *Z.P.E.* 25 (1977), 49f., with bibliographies.

3. See *Pr. Aet.* 7–36, *H. Apol.* 105–13, *Epp.* 2, 55, 56. *Frr.* 2 and 112.4–6 are important instances of homage to Hesiod (*Theog.* 22–34). See in general Reinsch-Werner, ibid., pp. 4–23, following Reitzenstein, 'Zur Stiltheorie des Kallimachos', 41–66. For a discussion of Callimachus' debts to Hesiod in depicting the everyday see Reinsch-Werner, ibid., pp. 134–58, 194–201; for Theocritus', see Halperin, *Before Pastoral*, pp. 245–8.

4. See Brink, 'Callimachus and Aristotle', 16–19.

5. See above, p. 30 n. 12.

6. So F. T. Griffiths, *Theocritus at Court, Mnem. Suppl.* 55 (Leiden, 1979), pp. 7, 16, 44, 49. He is followed by Halperin, *Before Pastoral*, pp. 175f. and 224.

7. See Halperin, ibid., p. 253f. Cf. lines 115–26 and the frog of 106, reminiscent of Theoc. *Id.* 7.41.

8. See e.g. I. C. Cunningham, *Herodas: Mimiambi* (Oxford, 1971), p. 161.

9. For parallels in the orators for the examples quoted see W. Headlam, (edited by A.D. Knox) *Herodas: the Mimes and Fragments* (Cambridge, 1922) and Cunningham ad locc. See also 16–20, 37f., 41–5, 48–55, 68–73 with Headlam and Knox, and Cunningham's notes.

10. Ps.-Demetrius *de Eloc.* 156. For the proverb in the Alexandrian period see R. Pfeiffer, *History of Classical Scholarship*, vol.i: *From the Beginnings to the End of the Hellenistic Age* (Oxford, 1968), p. 83f. For discussions of the proverb in Herodas see e.g. Headlam and Knox, *Herodas*, p. xxixf.; O. Crusius, *Die Mimiamben des Herondas* (revised by R. Herzog) (Leipzig, 1926), pp. 9–12; W. G. Arnott, 'Herodas and the Kitchen Sink', *G. & R.* 2nd Ser. 18 (1971), 130f.

11. So Cunningham, *ad loc.*

12. For further examples in *Mim.* 2 see 73, 80 and 100ff. with Cunningham's notes. For instances in the other poems see 1.41f., 3.10, 21, 61, 66f., 76, 85, 89–91, 5.14, 6.12, 60, 7.49f., 63, 119–21. See further G. Mastromarco, *Il pubblico di Eronda, Proagones* 15 (Padua, 1979), pp. 127f. (= Eng. trans. *The Public of Herondas,* London Studies in Classical Philology II (Amsterdam, 1984), pp. 83f.). See W. G. Arnott, '*Menander, qui uitae ostendit uitam*', *G. & R.* 2nd Ser. 15 (1968), 1–17.

13. The typical nature of Herodas' characters is overstressed by Headlam and Knox, *Herodas*, p.xxxi *et passim*, as Cunningham rightly points out (*Herodas*, p. 15 n.3). Arnott, 'Kitchen Sink', 121–32 discusses the mosaic technique in poems 5 and 6.

14. See Cunningham, *Herodas*, pp. 14f., 211–17; Mastromarco, *Il pubblico di Eronda*, pp. 124–9 (= Eng. trans., pp. 80–5) with bibliography.

15. The sixth and seventh poems, which form a pair, are set in Ionia (Cunningham, ibid., p. 160) and are the only pieces in which Herodas' Ionic is certainly appropriate, though the problem of archaism remains.

16. See Mastromarco, *Il pubblico di Eronda*, pp. 107–42 (= Eng. trans. pp. 65–99).

17. On the comparatively docile nature of the *Iambi* see *Dieg.* VII.23; C. M. Dawson, 'The Iambi of Callimachus. A Hellenistic Poet's Experimental Laboratory', *Y.C.S.* 11 (1950), 22, 139; Fraser, *Ptolemaic Alexandria*

p. 733f.; cf. D. L. Clayman, *Callimachus' Iambi, Mnem. Suppl.* 59 (Leiden, 1980), pp. 55–61. For comparisons of Callimachus with other Hellenistic iambographers like Cercidas and Phoenix see e.g. Fraser loc. cit. and Clayman, ibid., pp. 66–71.

18. Further examples of colloquialisms at *Iamb.* 4.69, 72, 78, 80; of proverbs at 1.2, 3.39, 5.1, and poem 11; of vivid characterisation at 4.22–3, 61–84, 12.27ff.

19. So also, for instance, *Iamb.* 5 attacks a lecherous schoolmaster in an elaborately oblique way that became a model for 'allegory' in antiquity; see Fraser, *Ptolemaic Alexandria*, p. 740 and Clayman, *Callimachus' Iambi*, pp. 29–33, 58f.

20. A. S. F. Gow, *Machon: the Fragments, Cambridge Classical Texts and Commentaries* 1 (Cambridge, 1965), p. 22f.

21. Gow, ibid., p.10f.; cf. Fraser, *Ptolemaic Alexandria*, p. 622 with note 38 (vol.ii, p. 879f.).

22. Gow-Page and Fraser, ibid., p. 564 with n. 98 (vol.ii, p. 805f.) postulate a change of position at this juncture (4f.), Lysidice adopting the more normal supine position and the spur being transferred to the man, who is therefore able to wound her thigh. But this not necessary and misses the point of οὐδέ ποτ' αὐτῆς / μηρὸς ἐφοινίχθη ('nor was her thigh ever bloodied'). The description of Lysidice's *tour-de-force* moves with ironic intent from the racing-metaphors to the physical reality of the moment, when she, the 'jockey', with her heel (and hence the spur) beneath her thighs, could easily cut herself as she gesticulates (αὐτῆς / . . .κοῦφα τιναασομένης). This is the precise reverse of what normally happens to a horse and, possibly, its jockey. Thus Asclepiades scores a 'point' and emphasises Lysidice's skill in her use of the spur. Arguments from the change of position in Dioscorides 5 *H.E.*, an imitation of Asclepiades' poem, are unconvincing.

23. Fraser, ibid., p. 564f. with n. 102 (vol.ii, p. 806).

24. Plato, if the ascription at *A.P.* 6.1 is correct (see Fraser, ibid., vol.ii, p. 832 n. 251), is a literary forerunner. The dedicatory epigrams include the tool-lists; see e.g. Callimachus 14, 16, 26, 27, 28 *H.E.*, Hedylus 3 *H.E.*, Leonidas 7, 8, 41, 42, 43, 45, 47, 52, 56, 80, 82 *H.E.*

25. Cf. e.g. E. Bevan (tr.), *The Poems of Leonidas of Tarentum* (Oxford, 1931), p.xxiii. This view of Leonidas is refuted by Mastromarco, *Il pubblico di Eronda*, p. 135f. (= Eng. trans., p. 90f.) (with bibliography).

26. So ἰχθυσιληιστῆρα, χηραμοδύτην (3), πολυσκάλμου πλώτορα ναυτιλίης (4), σχοινίτιδι (7), συνεργατίνης (10); see Gow and Page ad loc.

27. Cf. also e.g. Callimachus 34, 48, 49 *H.E.*, Hedylus 10 *H.E.*, Theocritus 11 *H.E.*

28. Gow and Page cite Men. *Fr.* 521 Kock (= 454 Körte) for an example. The subject is common in sculpture, too: see e.g. M. Bieber, *The Sculpture of the Hellenistic Age* (rev. edn) (New York, 1961), pp. 81, 141 with figs. 284, 586.

29. E.g. Leonidas 68 *H.E.*, Antipater 27 *H.E.*, Ariston 2 *H.E.* and *A.P.* 7.329 (anon.).

30. For the development of these types from earlier poetry see especially G. Giangrande, 'Sympotic Literature and Epigram', in *L'Épigramme grecque, Entretiens sur l'antiquité classique* 14 (Vandoeuvres-Geneva, 1968), 93–174.

31. Cf. Dioscorides 1, 7, 9, 13 *H.E.*; Fraser, *Ptolemaic Alexandria*, p. 598 raises doubts about the authenticity of 1, 5 and 7, but his grounds are inconclusive.

32. See also for varying effects Callimachus 13 *H.E.*, Hedylus 6 *H.E.*, Posidippus 1, 9 *H.E.*, Anon. 57 *H.E.* (perhaps by Asclepiades: see Fraser, ibid., vol.ii, p. 806f. n. 106).

33. Gow and Page, *H.E.* vol.ii, p. 132, cite as derived from this 'thumb-nail mime' Meleager 71, 72 *H.E.*, Anon. 7. *H.F.*; cf. Phanias 6 *H.E.* Similar food-lists are to be found in the New Comedy, e.g. Alexis *Fr.* 15 and *G.L.P.* 49 and 59 (b), Theocritus' mime, *Id.* 14.14–17, and Machon's *Chriae, Frr.* 5.33ff. and 16.266ff. Gow.

34. See further e.g. Anyte 16–19 H.E., Leonidas 29, 32, 85–7 H.E. with the rustic dedications and funerary pieces, 3–6, 19, 26, 27, 46–53, 80–4, 94, 96, 97 H.E., Theocritus 5, 6, 19–22 H.E., Anon. 73–81 in D. L. Page, *Further Greek Epigrams* (Cambridge, 1981). Cf. the funerary inscriptions for pets, Anyte 9–12, 20 H.E. and G.L.P. 109(1); Gow and Page, H.E. vol.ii, p. 90f. have a list of these epigrams.

35. E.g. Asclepiades 7 H.E., Dioscorides 13, 37 H.E., Hedylus 7–9 H.E.

36. Cf. the *Anecdoton Estense*, pp. 7.8–10, 12.4–18 Wendel.

37. Ph.-E. Legrand, *Étude sur Théocrite* (Paris, 1898), pp. 234–48; T. G. Rosenmeyer, *The Green Cabinet: Theocritus and the European Pastoral Lyric* (Berkeley and Los Angeles, 1969), p. 50f.; G. Fabiano, 'Fluctuation in Theocritus' Style', *G.R.B.S.* 12 (1971), 529; Schmidt, *Poetische Reflexion*, p. 27f.; Halperin, *Before Pastoral*, p. 151f. Moreover, the manuscript and papyrus support for Doric forms in certain of the epyllia, which one might have expected to have been composed uniformly in epic Ionic, is so great as to suggest that editors who restore Ionic and epic forms on generic grounds may well be begging the question: see Halperin, ibid., pp. 154–60.

38. Halperin, ibid., p. 152f., but cf. already A. S. F. Gow, *Theocritus*, (Cambridge, 1952), vol.i, p.lxxvii. Cf. C. J. Ruijgh, 'Le dorien de Théocrite: dialecte cyrénien d'Alexandrie et d'Égypte', *Mnem.* 4th Ser. 37 (1984), 56–88.

39. Cf. A. S. F. Gow, 'The Methods of Theocritus and some Problems in his Poems', *C.Q.* 24 (1930), 151 and on line 88; Fabiano, 'Fluctuation in Theocritus' Style', 521f.; A. E.-A. Horstmann, *Ironie und Humor bei Theokrit, Beiträge zur klassischen Philologie* 67 (Meisenheim am Glan, 1976), pp. 36–8; Ruijgh, ibid., 79f.

40. Cf. F. Cairns, 'Theocritus Idyll 10', *H.* 98 (1970), 38–44 and Cairns, *Generic Composition in Greek and Roman Poetry* (Edinburgh, 1972), pp. 173, 175.

41. Donatus p. 17.21–8 Wendel; Philargyrius p. 19.14–18 Wendel; see E. A. Schmidt, 'Hirtenhierarchie in der antiken Bukolik?', *Philol.* 113 (1969), 183–200 (with bibliography).

42. G. Giangrande, 'Theocritus' Twelfth and Fourth Idylls: A Study in Hellenistic Irony', *Q.U.C.C.* 12 (1971), 106f. sees social tension in *Id.* 4, Battus being a *propriétaire campagnard*, Corydon his inferior.

43. For Comatas' attribution of his bowl to what must be the famous Praxiteles at *Id.* 5.105 see below, p. 168.

44. See Gow, *Theocritus*, vol.ii, pp. 76f. and 94f.; K. J. Dover, *Theocritus: Select Poems* (Basingstoke and London, 1971), p.lvi. On the 'realism' of Theocritus see also e.g. W. Asmus, 'Zu den historischen Grenzen des Begriffs "Realismus"', *Probleme des Realismus in der Weltliteratur* (Berlin, 1962), 497ff.; Schmidt, *Poetische Reflexion*, p. 24 (with lit.).

45. His closest predecessor is Rhinthon of Syracuse who seems to have been the first to have written comedies in hexameters, but his 'hilarotragedies' appear to have been burlesques on tragic and heroic themes; see F. Susemihl, *Geschichte der griechischen Litteratur in der Alexandrinerzeit*, vol.i (Leipzig, 1891), pp. 239ff.; Legrand, *Théocrite*, p. 421f.; Fraser, *Ptolemaic Alexandria*, p. 620 with n. 15 (vol.ii, p. 875) for literature.

46. Probus, p. 15.13–16 Wendel; Donatus, p. 18.28–19.2 Wendel; Servius, p. 21.12–19 Wendel. Useful discussions include Legrand, ibid., pp. 420–7; E. G. O'Neill, 'The Localization of Metrical Word-Types in the Greek Hexameter: Homer, Hesiod, and the Alexandrians', *Y.C.S.* 8 (1942), 165ff.; K. Rupprecht, *Einführung in die griechische Metrik*[3] (Munich, 1950), p. 16.; P. Maas, *Greek Metre* (Eng. trans. H. Lloyd-Jones) (Oxford, 1962), p. 94f.; Schmidt, *Poetische Reflexion*, pp. 38–45; W. S. Allen, *Accent and Rhythm: Prosodic Features of Latin and Greek: A Study in Theory and Reconstruction* (Cambridge, 1973), pp. 286f., 336.; J. P. Poe, *Caesurae in the Hexameter Line of Latin Elegiac Verse, Hermes Einzelschr.* 29 (Wiesbaden, 1974), pp. 11–13, 23ff., 74–7, 78–81; W. Moskalew, *Formular*

218 The Everyday and the Low in Alexandrian Poetry

Language and Poetic Design in the Aeneid, Mnem. Suppl. 73 (Leiden, 1982), p. 52f.; M. L. West, *Greek Metre* (Oxford, 1982), pp. 154, 192; West, 'Three Topics in Greek Metre', *C.Q.* N.S. 32 (1982), 292–4; Halperin, *Before Pastoral*, pp. 209–11, 259–66; further literature will be found in these works. I am not concerned here with Donatus' demands for additional caesurae after a dactylic first foot and after the trochee of a dactylic third: that his requirements are unfounded is demonstrated by Theocritus' practice, for which see Schmidt's table, *Poetische Reflexion*, p. 45 n. 137. The absurdity of demanding a sense-pause at the bucolic caesura is shown by Poe, ibid., pp. 23ff., 78ff. In the figures given below I include instances of the bucolic caesura preceded by both spondaic and dactylic fourth feet; on spondaic fourth feet see Gow on *Id.* 1.130; cf. Maas loc. cit.

47. G. Lawall, *Theocritus' Coan Pastorals: a Poetry Book* (Cambridge, Mass., 1967), pp. 14–33 tries unconvincingly to redeem the *Idyll* to the 'pastoral collection'; cf. Gow, *Theocritus*, vol. i, p.lxix and Halperin, *Before Pastoral*, pp. 126–9, 136, 145, 158–60 (with lit.).

48. Why is *Id.* 15 so different from the other urban mimes in this respect? The encomiastic element in the *Adoniazusae* is so pervasive (22ff., 46ff., 78ff., 100–44) that we may perhaps infer that Theocritus viewed the poem essentially as an encomium (more so than even *Idyll* 14) and brought the incidence of the bucolic caesura in it into something approaching that in the encomia proper where the incidence is very low. It seems at any rate certain that Theocritus is concerned in *Id.* 15 with stylistic levels, marking off the solemnity of the hymn from the low tone of the framing mime by an effort not to violate the bucolic bridge in the hymn (see Maas, *Greek Metre*, p. 94f. and Griffiths, *Theocritus at Court*, p. 83); his treatment of the bridge may provide an analogy to the way in which I regard his practice with the caesura in the poem as a whole.

49. The average in the pseudo-Theocritean *Id.* 25 is 64 per cent. Cf. West, *Greek Metre*, p. 154 for parallel but lower figures for the epic, mimic and bucolic 'groups', which he seems, however, to have partitioned differently.

50. See e.g. R. Poggioli, 'Poetics and Metrics', in *Proceedings of the Second Congress of the International Comparative Literature Association*, vol.i, W. P. Friederich (ed.) (Chapel Hill, 1959), 196 (= R. Poggioli, *The Spirit of the Letter: Essays in European Literature* (Cambridge, Mass., 1965), 346f.) and H. Dubrow, *Genre* (London and New York, 1982), p. 85f.

51. For a convincing critique of the notion that the bucolic caesura was meant to convey the rhythm of actual country singing see Legrand, *Théocrite*, pp. 422–7. The use of a refrain as a means of imitating folk-song in spoken hexameters is another matter; see U. von Wilamowitz-Moellendorff, *Die Textgeschichte der griechischen Bukoliker*, Philologische Untersuchungen 18 (Berlin, 1906), pp. 137–51; Gow, *Theocritus*, vol.ii, p. 16; Dover, *Theocritus: Select Poems*, p.lxii.

52. Moreover, Moskalew, *Formular Language*, p. 52f., notes the frequency of anaphora at the bucolic caesura, as exemplified in *Id.* 1.67, and rightly concludes that 'these repetitions . . . retain much of the refrain's lilting cadence.' Halperin, *Before Pastoral*, pp. 209–11, 259–66, discounts the value of the bucolic caesura 'as a reliable determinant of genre' for pastoral. I agree with this in part, but argue that the caesura is indeed a genre-marker for the new poems dealing with everyday and low folk. Halperin doubts (ibid., p. 210) that an increase of 15 per cent in the rate of incidence in the first seven *Idd.* over that in Homer would make the caesura 'a distinguishing characteristic of bucolic poetry'; but the overall figures with which he operates obscure the fact that there are long passages where the caesura occurs without exception (e.g. *Id.* 5.20–45, 59–76, 78–96 in a poem totalling 150 lines; Maas, *Greek Metre*, p. 94f). and these would assuredly have struck listeners as exhibiting a mannerism, and have reinforced the impression gained from passages where the feature occurs less frequently; contrast Homer's practice in *Iliad* 1 where in the book's 611 lines the longest stretch is 14 lines long, lines 356–69, followed by the

The Everyday and the Low in Alexandrian Poetry 219

10 lines at lines 23–32 and the nine-line passage at 236–44. Moreover, though Halperin notes in passing (ibid., p. 264) that the 'epic' *Idd.* have a much lower rate of incidence of the caesura than the bucolic poems, he attaches no significance to the fact, whereas it is surely a sign that Theocritus distinguished between his everyday and low-life, urban and rustic *Idd.* and his epyllia (where the incidence is decidedly *lower* than in Homeric practice).

53. The ancient literary critics, furthermore, have no compunction about discussing Theocritus' pastorals under the category of epic: see e.g. Quint. *Inst. Or.* 10.1.46–55, Ps.-Longin. *Subl.* 33.4 and, for, further references, Halperin, *Before Pastoral*, pp. 212–16.

54. See F. Schwyzer, *Griechische Grammatik, I. von Müllers Handbuch der Altertumswissenschaft*, Section 2 Pt. 1, vol.ii (Munich, 1950), p. 23, and in general, A. Svensson, *Der Gebrauch des bestimmten Artikels in der nachklassischen griechischen Epik* (Lund, 1937), esp. pp. 65–76.

55. See Gow *ad loc.* and on 1.32.

56. On the possible slip in the introduction of a River Haleis (123), not otherwise attested for this region, see Gow *ad loc.*; for details of the scene see Gow, *Theocritus*, vol.ii, p. 94f.

57. See Gow, *Theocritus*, vol.ii, p. 92 and on lines 1 and 15.

58. See Gow, ibid., vol.ii, p. 118 and on 11.7.

59. There is perhaps even 'prefiguration' on a linguistic level: when the Cyclops asks Galatea why she visits him 'when sweet sleep possesses me' (ὄκκα γλυκὺς ὕπνος ἔχῃ με:22) and flees 'when sweet sleep leaves me' (ὄκκα γλυκὺς ὕπνος ἀνῇ με: 23), he is unwittingly citing Odysseus' order to drill out the giant's eye 'when sweet sleep overtakes him' (ὅτε τὸν γλυκὺς ὕπνος ἱκάνοι: *Od.* 9.333). See further Halperin, *Before Pastoral*, p. 233f.

60. See above, n. 51.

61. Discussion and literature in U. Ott, *Die Kunst des Gegensatzes in Theokrits Hirtengedichten, Spudasmata* 22 (Hildesheim and New York, 1969), pp. 110ff. (especially p. 111 n. 316) and S. F. Walker, *Theocritus, T.W.A.S.* 609 (Boston, 1980), pp. 38ff.

62. See e.g. Gow, *Theocritus*, vol.ii, p. 2; Lawall, *Theocritus' Coan Pastorals*, pp. 19–22; Halperin, *Before Pastoral*, p. 220f. Cf. Halperin, 'The Forbears of Daphnis', *T.A.P.A.* 113 (1983), 183f., 192.

63. *H.H.* 5.286–8: see Gow on 1.106f.

64. There is indeed discord in Priapus' bawdiness and mistaken charge that Daphnis is frigid (81–91: for δύσερως at 85 see Ott, *Die Kunst des Gegensatzes*, p. 123 n. 355), but the god's misplaced banter only adds to the stature of the defiantly contemptuous Daphnis. On Daphnis and epos see further Halperin, *Before Pastoral*, pp. 219–22.

65. See especially D. J. Mastronarde, 'Theocritus' *Idyll* 13: Love and the Hero', *P.P.* 23 (1968), 5–18 (also printed in *T.A.P.A.* 99 (1968), 273–90); G. K. Galinsky, *The Herakles Theme: The Adaptations of the Hero in Literature from Homer to the Twentieth Century* (Oxford, 1972), pp. 117–19; K. Gutzwiller, *Studies in the Hellenistic Epyllion, Beiträge zur klassischen Philologie* 114 (Königstein / Ts., 1981), pp. 19–24.

66. Mastronarde, ibid., 16.

67. Mastronarde, ibid., 16f.; cf. B. Effe, 'Die Destruktion der Tradition: Theokrits mythologische Gedichte', *Rh.M.* N.F. 121 (1978), 64; Galinsky, *The Herakles Theme*, pp. 118f.

68. For the chariot of Dawn see in particular *Od.* 23.246. The simile is well discussed by Mastronarde, ibid., 10f. and Gutzwiller, *Studies*, p. 21; cf. Gow on 13.

69. N.b. the sailor's direct speech at 52. See Mastronarde, ibid., 11; Effe, 'Destruktion der Tradition', 62f.; cf. Gow on 52. On the epic lion simile at 62f., which stands in intentional contrast with Heracles' anguish, see Mastronarde, ibid.,

9; Effe, ibid., 63. On ταλαεργός (19), used of Heracles by Theocritus, but only of mules in Homer and Hesiod, which is evidence of 'scaling down heroic subjects to fit the social environment of the Hellenistic reader', see Halperin, *Before Pastoral*, p. 231f., following Fabiano, 'Fluctuation in Theocritus' Style', 535; see also Halperin, ibid., p. 234f.

70. For a similar opposition see Ps.-Bion *Id*. 2 Gow, *Buc. Gr*., the *Epithalamium of Achilles and Deidameia*, with Gutzwiller, *Studies*, pp. 73–6.

71. *Il*. 8.511; Horstmann, *Ironie und Humor*, p. 63.

72. See also e.g. line 49 citing *Il*. 12.454 and *Od*. 21.46, line 61, modelled on *Il*. 10.376, 15.4 and line 63, taken from *Od*. 7.138, 16.481. See further Fabiano, 'Fluctuation in Theocritus' Style', 535 and Halperin, *Before Pastoral*, p. 231.

73. There are Homeric echoes in her speech (with 68f. cf. *Od*. 3.96f.; with 71 cf. *Il*. 1.365), and these, together with the inverted reference to *Il*. 18.54 in 'mother of noble children' (ἀριστοτόκεια: 73), go some way to elevating the tone of Alcmena's characterisation here.

74. See Gow on 105; Griffiths, *Theocritus at Court*, p. 92.

75. See Gow on 141ff.; Griffiths, ibid., p. 95.

76. See Gow, *Theocritus*, vol.ii, p. 415 and on 4 and 11f.; Griffiths, ibid., pp. 91–8.

77. On the surface, γαμβρὸς δ' ἀθανάτων κεκλήσεται (84) preserves Amphitryon's role as father, but must have struck Alexandrian audiences as an amusing understatement, given the tradition about Hebe (present, of course, in Theocritus himself at *Id*. 17.32), especially if ὁμοπάτ[ριον (170) does refer to her; see further Griffiths, ibid., p. 94f.

78. Griffiths, ibid., p. 97.

79. See Gow on 141ff.; Griffiths, ibid., p. 57f.

80. See in general Griffiths, ibid., pp. 51–71. We are now in a position to assess the thesis of Effe, 'Destruktion der Tradition' that in the mythological poems Theocritus is throughout bent on destroying the traditions of Greek myth. If we accept the political interpretation of a poem like the *Heracliscus*, then we must reject Effe's conclusions at least as far as *Id*. 24 is concerned (for *Idd*. 18 and 26 see Griffiths, ibid., pp. 86–91, 98–106). Perhaps his approach is more convincing when applied, for example, to *Id*. 22, where there is doubt that there is any link with the new Ptolemaic mythology (see Griffiths, ibid., p. 54 n. 5); see in general Halperin, *Before Pastoral*, pp. 236–42.

81. In what follows I make particular use of Parsons, 'Callimachus', 1–50; E. Livrea, 'Nota al nuovo Callimaco di Lille', *Z.P.E*. 32 (1978), 7–10; Livrea, 'Der Liller Kallimachos und die Mausefallen', *Z.P.E*. 34 (1979), 37–42; Livrea, 'Polittico Callimacheo: contributi al testo della Victoria Berenices', *Z.P.E*. 40 (1980), 21–6; *Frr*. 254–69 *S.H*. (where further literature is cited).

82. The theme is important in the *Heracles Leontophonos* as well. The common folk of the countryside are there repeatedly referred to as the people who suffered most from the Nemean lion's depredations: the traveller from Argos called the beast 'a monster that was bad for country-folk' (168), and Heracles describes their suffering (201–3), tells how he had to track down the lion alone since the common people had fled their work in the fields (218–20), and ends his account of the fight with the words 'This was the way the beast of Nemea was killed, my friend, having caused many sufferings for cattle and men' (280f.). In the last two lines of the poem, then, we are reminded that it was the ordinary people who benefited from Heracles' labour. Cf. J. Duchemin, 'A propos de l'*Héraclès Tueur de Lion*', *Misc. Rostagni* (Turin, 1963), 311–21; Gutzwiller, *Studies*, pp. 30–8.

83. Cf. *Il*. 16.779. Hesiod also has inspired the passage, μέσσαβα, 'leather straps', for instance, being a reminiscence of *W.D*. 469; see Reinsch-Werner, *Callimachus Hesiodicus*, pp. 143–6. A similar contrast is present at *Fr*. 259.9–11 *S.H*. = *Fr*. 117.9–11 Pf., with which compare *Il*. 11.113–19.

84. Σ ad *A.R.* 4.1613–16bc.
85. *Il.* 11.481, 20.165. Compare also Callimachus' διχθαδίους . . . φονέας (32) with Achilles' 'twofold dooms', διχθαδίας κῆρας, at *Il.* 9.411, and 'in the two traps he placed a fatal bait' (ἐν δ' ἐτίθει παγίδεσσι ὀλέθρια δείλατα δοιαῖς: 17) with Homer's 'in it he placed two fates of grievous death' (ἐν δὲ τίθει δύο κῆρε τανηλεγέος θανάτοιο: *Il.* 8.70 and 22.210), which constitutes a travesty indeed. Small wonder that the passage has affinities with *Batrachomyomachia* (see Pfeiffer on 17, 22, 28, 31).
86. H. Herter, 'Kallimachos und Homer: Ein Beitrag zur Interpretation des Hymnos auf Artemis', *Xenia Bonnensia* (Bonn, 1929), 73 (= *W.d.F.* 296, 372).
87. For other descendants of Eumaeus and Eurycleia see also Iambe in Philicus' hymn to Demeter (*Fr.* 676–80 *S.H.* = *G.L.P.* 90), discussed by e.g. J.U. Powell, *New Chapters in the History of Greek Literature*, 3rd series (Oxford, 1933), 195–200, Fraser, *Ptolemaic Alexandria*, pp. 650–2 and *S.H. ad loc*; the introduction of the old woman is explicitly humorous, for it is prefaced with the question 'Is the funny story without value on solemn occasions?' (*Fr.* 680. 55 *S.H.*). See also the moving depiction of Diomedes' faithful old retainer, Pheidon (Pow., p. 78f. = *G.L.P.* 122), and Eratosthenes' Erigone in *Frr.* 22–7 Pow. (for the *Erigone*'s resemblance to the *Hecale* see Fraser, ibid., p. 641 with n. 202 (vol.ii, p. 903f.)). For the rustic of the *Heracles Leontophonos* see above, pp. 89f., and for Callimachus' Hecale, see below, pp. 209–14.
88. See Gutzwiller, *Studies*, pp. 63–73 on the ambiguity of Europa's naïveté.
89. So Herter, 'Kallimachos und Homer', 57–9 (= *W.d.F.* 296, 354–6). Herter's study is vital to our subject and my discussion of the everyday in *H.* 3 is indebted to it.
90. So e.g. Wilamowitz, *H.D.* vol.ii, p. 52 n. 1; Herter, ibid., 68 (= *W.d.F.* 296, 366); F. Bornmann, *Callimachi Hymnus in Dianam, Biblioteca di Studi Superiori: Filologia greca e papirologia* 55 (Florence, 1968), p.xxiii and on 14.
91. Herter, ibid., 65f. (= *W.d.F.* 296, 363f.).
92. Herter, ibid., 71–3 (= *W.d.F.* 296, 370–2); see also e.g. Bornmann, *Hymnus in Dianam*, pp.xviii, xxviii and on 30–2.
93. Similarly, while the Homeric Zeus' nod makes Olympus shake (*Il* 1.528–30), Callimachus introduces nothing out of the ordinary when his Zeus nods to Artemis: see Herter, ibid., 72f. (= *W.d.F.* 296, 371).
94. So Bornmann, *Hymnus in Dianam*, pp. xviii, xxviii and on 30–2. See further Herter, ibid., 76f.
95. So A. Couat, *La Poésie alexandrine sous les trois premiers Ptolémées (324–222 av. J.-C.)* (Paris, 1882), p. 278 and other critics cited by Herter, ibid., 61 n. 2 (= *W.d.F.* 296, 359 n. 17).
96. Herter, ibid., 73–5 (= *W.d.F.* 296, 372–4); cf. (as far as he goes) Fraser, *Ptolemaic Alexandria*, p. 664 with nn. 376 and 377 (vol.ii, p. 932), where further literature is detailed.
97. *Il.* 18.396ff. See the excellent discussion by Herter, ibid., 87ff.
98. See Herter, ibid., 82 for Callimachus' allusion to *Il.* 6.467f., where the baby Astyanax screams at the sight of Hector's helmet, and to *Il.* 18.271f., where Teucer, who ducks under Ajax' shield after firing his arrows, is compared with a child who rushes to his mother's arms; the poet implies that Artemis is far braver than her Homeric counterparts.
99. Another human custom transferred to Olympus: Herter, ibid., 83.
100. Cf. *Fr.* 24.3, where the motif has a moving bitter-sweetness.
101. Herter, 'Kallimachos und Homer', 84.; Bornmann on 83: cf. 'me too' (κἤμοί:81). Note too her bribe, that she will provide the Cyclopes with game-meat if they comply with her demands (84f.); Herter, ibid.
102. Cf. Couat, 'La Poésie alexandrine', pp. 249, 272, 278, 282f.
103. Herter, 'Kallimachos und Homer', 84f. observes that the goddess comes across Pan while he is at the banausic task of cutting up meat for the dogs (88f.) and

that, while Homeric animals are fed with ambrosia if divine (*Il.* 5.777) or, if mortal, with wheat and wine (*Il.* 8.188ff.), Pan's hounds are here given a more everyday diet.

104. See Couat, 'La Poésie alexandrine', p. 277; Bornmann on 87, 88–9, 90, 95, 197.

105. On the transition see the useful remarks of Herter, 'Kallimachos und Homer', 86–93.

106. Cf. K. J. McKay, 'Mischief in Kallimachos' *Hymn to Artemis*', *Mnem.* 4th Ser. 16 (1963), 249ff., refuted by Bornmann on 120–2.

107. *W.D.* 225–47. Cf. Herter, 'Kallimachos und Homer', 96–100; Bornmann on 122–3, 125, 128, 129–35, 129, 130–1, 133–5; Reinsch-Werner, *Callimachus Hesiodicus*, pp. 74–86.

108. Cf. 'Alcides', Ἀλκεΐδην, at 145 with Bornmann *ad loc.*

109. For comparisons of lines 148–9 with their model, *Il.* 1.595–60, see Herter 'Kallimachos und Homer', 100f. and Bornmann on 149.

110. See Herter, ibid., 101, following Σ ad 154: cf. 'swift' (ταχινός:158) and 'gluttony' (ἀδηφαγίης:160).

111. The hinds are fed clover (165), which is fodder for mortal horses in Homer (*Il.* 2.776; cf. *H.H. Herm.* 107), whereas the horses of the Homeric gods feed on ambrosia (cf. above, n. 103). Again the poet puts such matters on a more earthly plane; see Herter, ibid., 101f.; Bornmann on 165.

112. Bornmann on 168–9 aptly calls the words 'you sit beside Apollo' (169) 'il coronamento del motivo dell' emulazione di Apollo'.

113. Comparisons of the two welcoming-scenes in e.g. Couat 'La Poésie alexandrine', p. 271f.; Wilamowitz, *H.D.* vol.ii, p. 56f.; G. Th. Huber, *Lebensschilderung und Kleinmalerei im hellenistischen Epos: Darstellung des menschlichen Lebens und der Affekte* (Diss. Solothurn, 1926), p. 67; Herter, 'Kallimachos und Homer', 102; Bornmann on 141.

114. The goddess' grandeur is reasserted in the rest of the hymn: so, for instance, the reader is warned in the coda not to compete with her in stag-hunting (262), which 'corrects' the statement at the poem's inception that mere hare-hunting was her concern (2). See in general Herter, ibid., 102–5. For the Hesiodic realism of 170–82 see Reinsch-Werner, *Callimachus Hesiodicus*, pp. 87–93. For a contrastingly everyday self-portrait of the poet at lines 170–82 see P. Bing, 'Callimachus' Cows: a Riddling Recusatio', *Z.P.E.* 54 (1984), 1–8.

115. If K. J. McKay, *Erysichthon: a Callimachean Comedy, Mnem. Suppl.* 7 (Leiden, 1962), p. 113 is right in saying that the people who issue the invitations are all related to Erysichthon's family, there is further domestic realism.

116. A. W. Bulloch, 'Callimachus' *Erysichthon*, Homer and Apollonius Rhodius', *A.J.P.* 98 (1977), 108f. discusses Callimachus' debt here to *Od.* 17.222 where Melanthius derides Odysseus 'the beggar'; Bulloch correctly sees irony in the reminiscence, 'for Erysichthon is indeed exactly what Melantheus (mistakenly) accuses Odysseus of being'. Cf. Reinsch-Werner, *Callimachus Hesiodicus*, p. 228f. for the possible ironical allusion to Hesiod's command that the farmer be self-sufficient (*W.D.* 229–301, 307f., 364–9).

117. So, happily, McKay, *Erysichthon*, p. 71. See also McKay, *The Poet at Play: Kallimachos, The Bath of Pallas, Mnem. Suppl.* 6 (Leiden, 1962), p. 99f.; Huber, *Lebensschilderung*, p. 67; Wilamowitz, *H.D.* vol.ii, p. 32f.; Reinsch-Werner, ibid., p. 228f.

118. The grizzly alternatives are represented by the version of Ovid at *Met.* 8.738–873 and the modern Coan folk-tale derived from the Erysichthon story, for which see McKay, *Erysichthon*, pp. 33–60 and N. Hopkinson, *Callimachus: Hymn to Demeter, Cambridge Classical Texts and Commentaries* 27 (Cambridge, 1984), pp. 20–30.

119. See lines 31–7, 50–6, with McKay, *Poet at Play*, pp. 115–17; McKay, *Erysichthon*, pp. 88–90; Reinsch-Werner, *Callimachus Hesiodicus*, p. 218f.

120. 61f.: *pace* Bulloch, 'Callimachus' *Erysichthon*', 100f., therefore, Callimachus emphasises Demeter's rationality and justice.
121. Cf. McKay, *Poet at Play*, pp. 50f., 119f.; McKay, *Erysichthon*, pp. 123–5; Reinsch-Werner, *Callimachus Hesiodicus*, pp. 216–19, 229; Gutzwiller, *Studies*, pp. 39–48; A. W. Bulloch in P. E. Easterling and B. M. W. Knox (eds.), *The Cambridge History of Classical Literature*. vol.i: *Greek Literature* (Cambridge, 1985), p. 564f.
122. So McKay, *Erysichthon*, p.181f. W. Meincke, *Untersuchungen zu den enkomiastischen Gedichten Theokrits* (Diss. Kiel, 1965), pp. 116–24 compares the birth-scenes in *H.H. Apol.*, Call. *H.* 4 and Theoc. *Id.* 17 (arguing for the priority of Theocritus to Callimachus) and discusses the use of realistic details in each, e.g. showing (ibid., p. 119f.) how Callimachus handles the motif of the island suckling the baby more realistically than Theocritus.
123. See D. M. MacDowell, *Aristophanes: Wasps* (Oxford, 1971) on *Wasps* 1019. I owe this idea to a suggestion of Dr R. L. Hunter's.
124. See e.g. Wilamowitz, *H.D.* vol.ii, pp. 70–2; Fraser, *Ptolemaic Alexandria*, p. 659f.; G. Nachtergael, *Les Galates en Grèce et les Sôtéria de Delphes. Recherches d'histoire et d'épigraphie hellénistiques* (Brussels, 1977), esp. pp. 150–64. Moreover, the River Inopus beside which Leto gives birth was supposed to be connected to the Nile by a subterranean channel: see lines 206–8 and *H.* 3.171.
125. For other examples of the everyday in the *Hymns* see also *H.* 1.15–17, 55–6, 2.58–64, 4.1–6, 11–15, 316–24, 5.5–12, 13–32, 57–67, 70–4. For a different explanation of Callimachus' interest in such material see A. W. Bulloch's stimulating essay, 'The Future of a Hellenistic Illusion: Some observations on Callimachus and religion', *M.H.* 41 (1984), 209–30.
126. See the discussions by J. Stern, 'Theocritus' *Idyll* 14', *G.R.B.S.* 16 (1975), 51–8 and Griffiths, *Theocritus at Court*, pp. 107–16.
127. On the incident see Fraser, *Ptolemaic Alexandria*, p. 117f.
128. See H. Herter, 'Die Haaröle der Berenike', in *Festgabe für Edith Heischkel und Walter Artelt* (Stuttgart, 1971), 54–68 (= *W.d.F.* 296, 186–206). Cf. lines 13/14, possibly on how Euergetes showed signs of stress after the newly-weds' love-making the night before, and line 51 on the lock's sisters' mourning the loss of its company. Parsons, 'Callimachus', 49 aptly calls the *Lock* a 'sister poem' to the *Victoria Berenices*.
129. For a comparison of the two poems see Meincke, *Untersuchungen zu den enkomiastischen Gedichten Theokrits*, pp. 111–24, 159, 189f.
130. See further Meincke, ibid., pp. 99–101; Griffiths, *Theocritus at Court*, pp. 56f., 71–82.
131. E.g. the inversion of a Homeric model at 24, where, instead of Homer's 'lifted life from [my] limbs' (μελέων ἐξείλετο θύμον: *Od.* 11.201), we have 'lifted old age from [their] limbs' (μελέων ἐξείλετο γῆρας), describing Alexander and Soter's immortalisation.
132. Lines 73–81 remind us of Achilles arming with his men at *Il.* 19.351ff.
133. Cf. lines 34–9. See Griffiths, *Theocritus at Court*, pp. 41f.
134. For Theocritus' use of Simonides here see Meincke, *Untersuchungen zu den enkomiastischen Gedichten Theokrits*, pp. 38–41; Griffiths, ibid., pp. 22f., 26f., 30–2.
135. See Fraser, *Ptolemaic Alexandria*, p. 668f.
136. So M. L. West, 'Erinna', *Z.P.E.* 25 (1977), 108f. against C. M. Bowra, 'Erinna's Lament for Baucis', in *Greek Poetry and Life: Essays presented to Gilbert Murray* (Oxford, 1936), 333f., who thought Erinna must be a priestess forbidden to look on the dead.
137. Bowra, ibid., 337, 341f.
138. See e.g. Aristotle *Poet.* 59^{b}31–4.
139. West, 'Erinna', 117 argues that the Doric elements of the poem are meant to give local colour and the impression of the speech of 'a homely little Telian maid', and that the Aeolic forms are designed to put the poem into the literary

context of Sappho. In that case, the Doric forms in part represent an additional attempt at realism.

140. Cf. 5–14, 668–72, 732, 741–3.
141. Cf. 408–19, 1072–4.
142. Cf. 744, 758–68, 935f.
143. Cf. 7–9, 1072–4, 1104–12, 1113–17.
144. See B. Effe, *Dichtung und Lehre: Untersuchungen zur Typologie des antiken Lehrgedichts*, Zetemata 69 (Munich, 1977), pp. 55f.
145. See above, p. 100; less pictorial are *Th.* 57ff., 74f., 541–9, 554, 666–75, 793, 829–31, *Al.* 175f., 473, *Frr.* 16, 72, 74.66–72, 75, 81.4, 90.
146. Epic forms: παρασφαλέες, ἠέ, κομάων, σμυγεροῖο, κακανθήεντας, γναθμοῖσιν, ἐνοιδέα; epic vocabulary: κομάων, ὀλοήν, σμυγεροῖο, βρωτῆρας, δάμναται; neologisms: παρασφαλέες, σπείρημα (for σπάργανον), κακανθήεντας.
147. See Effe, *Dichtung und Lehre*, pp. 56–65.
148. Several of the issues raised in what follows have been discussed at greater length in my 'The Love Theme in Apollonius Rhodius' Argonautica', *W.S.* N.F. 13 (1979), 52–75.
149. Plato *Phaedr.* 259d. That Apollonius viewed her as such is proven by his play on the words Ἐρατώ, ἔρως and ἐπήρατον, by what he says at 3.1–5 and by the way in which his imitators (Virg. *A.* 7.37 and Ov. *A.A.* 2.15f., *F.* 4.195f.) understood the passage; cf. Σ ad 1–5a.
150. See Zanker, 'The Love Theme in A.R.', 69f., to which it should be added that the fragments of Antimachus' elegiac *Lyde*, which influenced Apollonius (*Frr.* 3.3, 34, 35, 39, 53.2 Wyss), have nothing in them to suggest that the poet is exceptional in this regard, but they are notoriously sparse.
151. *Frogs* 850, 1043, 1050f., 1078–82; *Arg. Hipp.* 29f.; W. S. Barrett, *Euripides: Hippolytus* (Oxford, 1964), pp. 10–15, 30f.
152. His *Hermes* (*Fr.* 5 Pow.) told of Odysseus' love for Polymele: see above, pp. 55f. In lyric we have the *Fragmentum Grenfellianum* (Pow., p. 177–80).
153. Hera's inspiration of love in Medea is not to ancient thinking unrealistic: on the Greek gods as 'psychic interventions' see E. R. Dodds, *The Greeks and the Irrational* (Berkeley and Los Angeles, 1951), pp. 1–27. On Apollonius' gods in general see especially L. Klein, 'Die Göttertechnik in den Argonautika des Apollonios Rhodios', *Philol.* 86 (1931), 215–54; P. Händel, *Beobachtungen zur epischen Technik des Apollonios Rhodios*, Zetemata 8 (Munich, 1954), pp. 102f., 114–16 and 'Die Götter des Apollonios als Personen', in *Misc. Rostagni*, 363–81; H. Fränkel, *Noten zu den Argonautika des Apollonios* (Munich, 1968), on 3.179–93, 3.275–87, 818, 4.1199f.
154. For Hera's intervention at 818 cf. Klein, 'Göttertechnik', 222–5; Händel, *Beobachtungen*, p. 110 and 'Die Göttertechnik', 368f.; Fränkel, *ad loc.*: the realism of Medea's characterisation here is in no way undermined, given the traditional Greek scheme of things.
155. Comparable realism can be observed in the scene in which Jason and Medea meet (948–1162).
156. So Couat, *La Poésie alexandrine*, p. 311. Further foreshadowing of Medea's tragic fate is to be found in Apollonius' use of the Ariadne myth. In wooing Medea to his purpose, Jason compares her future with that of Ariadne, who, he misleadingly relates, was rewarded for helping Theseus by being turned into a star (3.997–1007); he brushes aside Medea's questions about Ariadne, which would force him to disclose facts hardly conducive to persuasion (3.1077–86, 1096–1101). But Apollonius knows these facts and so does Jason: in the episode of the murder of Apsyrtus Jason sends gifts to lure him to his doom and among them is a cloak given to Jason by Hypsipyle; it is that on which Dionysus made love to Ariadne when she had been deserted by Theseus on Dia (4.423–34). The more ominous side of the myth is now revealed and Medea's tragedy is prefigured just at

the moment when she irrevocably alienates herself from her family. There is, then, tragic irony in Medea's statement 'nor do I liken myself to Ariadne' (3.1107f.). Cf. J. W. Mackail, *Lectures on Greek Poetry* (London, 1926), p. 263f.; Händel, *Beobachtungen*, p. 113; A. Körte, *Die hellenistische Dichtung*, revised by P. Händel (Stuttgart, 1960), p. 168; Fränkel on 4.423–34.

157. Against H. Fränkel, 'Das Argonautenepos des Apollonios', *M.H.* 14 (1957), 10; cf. C. R. Beye, *Epic and Romance in the Argonautica of Apollonius* (Carbondale and Edwardsville, 1982), p. 144f.

158. See H. Fränkel, 'Ein Don Quijote unter den Argonauten des Apollonios', *M.H.* 17 (1960), 5 and *Noten* on 4.445–9.

159. Körte, *Die hellenistische Dichtung*, p. 197.

160. So Fränkel, 'Das Argonautenepos', 9.

161. Lines 1165–7 of the judgement recall *Od.* 23.52f. where Eurycleia encourages Penelope to meet Odysseus who has now discarded his disguise as a beggar (Fränkel *ad loc.* notes the echo). Apollonius seems to be contrasting the happy meeting of Odysseus and Penelope with the rather sordid circumstances and tragic outcome of Jason and Medea's marriage, thus again pointing to Corinth. The scholars who deny the unity of Medea's character and give her two unsuccessfully integrated characters, one of a lovesick girl and one of a violent murderess, include Wilamowitz, *H.D.*, vol.ii, pp. 196f., 202 and 214; Händel, *Beobachtungen*, p. 116f.; C. Collard, 'Medea and Dido', *Prometheus* 1 (1975), 137ff.; cf. Beye, *Epic and Romance*, pp. 158–66.

162. 3.988f., 1026–62, 1069–71, 1111–17, 1191–224, 1246–67, 1305, 1363f., 4.163, 193, 195f., 1031–57, 1638–88.

163. See Zanker, 'The Love Theme in A.R.', 57f., 59f., 72 n. 68; Beye, *Epic and Romance*, pp. 77–99.

164. See C. R. Beye, 'Jason as Love-Hero in Apollonios' *Argonautika*', *G.R.B.S.* 10 (1969), 39–48; Galinsky, *The Herakles Theme:* pp. 108–16; Zanker, 'The Love Theme in A.R.', 55f.; B. Effe, 'Held und Literatur: Der Funktionswandel des Herakles- Mythos in der griechischen Literatur', *Poetica* 12 (1980), 164; Beye, *Epic and Romance*, pp. 93–8.

165. See especially Fränkel, 'Ein Don Quijote', 5–12, 19f.

166. For discussions of Jason see e.g. Couat, *La Poésie alexandrine*, pp. 319ff.; G.W. Mooney, *The Argonautica of Apollonius Rhodius* (Dublin, 1912), p. 37; Wilamowitz, *H.D.* vol. ii, p. 214f.; Mackail, *Lectures on Greek Poetry*, pp. 262ff.; M.M. Gillies, *The Argonautica of Apollonius Rhodius: Book 3* (Cambridge, 1928), p. 40; J.F. Carspecken, 'Apollonius Rhodius, and the Homeric Epic', *Y.C.S.* 13 (1952), 99–125; Händel, *Beobachtungen*, pp. 101ff., 117; D.A. van Krevelen, 'Bemerkungen zur Charakteristik der in den Argonautika des Apollonios auftretenden Personen', *Rh.M.* N.F. 99 (1956), 3–8; Fränkel, 'Ein Don Quijote', 3f., 17ff.; Körte, *Die hellenistische Dichtung*, p.195ff.; G. Lawall, 'Apollonius' *Argonautica*: Jason as Anti-Hero', *Y.C.S.* 19 (1966), 121–69; Beye, 'Jason as Love-Hero'; Collard, 'Medea and Dido', 136f.; F. Vian, 'ΙΙΙΣΩΝ ΑΜΙΙΧΑΝΕΩΝ', in E. Livrea and G.A. Privitera (eds.), *Studi in onore di Anthos Ardizzoni*, vol.ii (Rome, 1978), 1025–41; Zanker, 'The Love Theme in A.R.',72–4; Beye, *Epic and Romance*, pp. 77–99, 114f., 128–42, 148f.; H. Lloyd-Jones, 'A Hellenistic Miscellany', *S.I.F.C.* 3rd Ser.2 (1984), 70f.

167. See also 1.1289–344, 3.171–95, 372–96.

168. Fränkel, 'Ein Don Quijote', 17f.

169. 1.307–10, 774–81, 3.919–23, 956–61.

170. 1.1286–9, 2.410, 885, 3.432f., 4.1318. Fränkel, 'Ein Don Quijote', 6 is wrong to argue from 'like a man downcast' (1.461) that at 1.460ff. Jason is feigning depression: n.b. 1.460f., 'helpless, he brooded within himself.' Cf. Vian, 'ΙΙΙΣΩΝ ΑΜΙΙΧΑΝΕΩΝ'.

171. Indeed, it is Medea who is given one of Odysseus' most important virtues, cunning; we have seen many examples of this in action and she is called 'cunning' by Hera at 3.89; Phineus uses the same word to describe the aid of Aphrodite at 2.423, but is ultimately referring to Medea.

226 The Everyday and the Low in Alexandrian Poetry

172. See Couat, *La Poésie alexandrine*, p. 311; Wilamowitz, *H.D.* vol.ii, p. 203; Mackail, *Lectures on Greek Poetry*, p. 263f. The Euripidean Jason's gift for smooth-talk is exemplified at *Med.* 522ff. and is acknowledged by the heroine herself at lines 800ff.

173. The gods of the *Argonautica* are notable for their lack of friction over their human protégés, a matter in which the poem differs markedly from the Homeric epics (see Klein, 'Göttertechnik', 247–54); the divine friction hinted at here, therefore, stands out as purely domestic. Cf. P. G. Lennox, 'Apollonius, Argonautica 3, 1ff. and Homer', *H.* 108 (1980), 47f.

174. F. Vian, *Apollonios de Rhodes: Argonautiques Chant III* (Paris, 1961) on 3.22 notes that the phraseology recalls Antenor's description of Odysseus at *Il.* 3.217; Apollonius is drawing a humorous contrast between his nonplussed deities and Homer's arresting and resourceful orator; cf. Lennox, ibid., 48.

175. Cf. Lennox, ibid., who makes Aphrodite the subject of αἴ κε πίθηται; his reasons are unconvincing.

176. Cf. *Il.* 18.424f., *Od.* 5.82f. The citation of this episode in *Il.* 18 points to the fundamental difference between a Homeric hero like Achilles and the new hero, Jason: Achilles is provided with arms for combat, Jason with the love of a woman. The same contrast is present in the description of Jason's cloak: see above, pp. 75f and cf. p. 203.

177. Cf. Lennox, 'Apollonius, Argonautica 3', 49f.

178. Of course, Hera gets aid from Aphrodite in *Il.* 14: it is significant, however, that what is a motif in an episode of the *Iliad* gains central importance in the main plot of the *Argonautica*.

179. Critics have also seen parallels with Theoc. *Id.* 15 and Herodas *Mim.* 3 (e.g. Vian, *Argonautiques Chant III*, p. 7; cf. Lennox, 'Apollonius, Argonautica 3', 69).

180. See e.g. J. Griffin, *Homer on Life and Death* (Oxford, 1980), pp. 179–204.

181. For other interpretations of the scene see Huber, *Lebensschilderung*, p. 40f.; Klein, 'Göttertechnik', 35; Vian, *Argonautiques Chant III*, p. 7; D. M. Gaunt, 'Argo and the Gods in Apollonius Rhodius', *G. & R.* 2nd Ser. 19 (1972), 124f.; Lennox, 'Apollonius, Argonautica 3', 70. For further humanisation of deities at the very moment of their exercise of power see 4.922–81.

182. See also 3.732–5, 4.811–15; cf. Huber, *Lebensschilderung*, p. 25f.

183. Huber, ibid., p. 49 discusses the model for this motif, *Il.* 22.448, where Andromache drops her shuttle when she hears the Trojans mourning Hector's death: in Apollonius' hands the motif accompanies a far less significant moment, and we might justifiably be tempted to talk of its trivialisation.

184. Cf. also his use of the motif of the mourning father at 1.97–100, 165–7, 260–4, discussed by Huber, *Lebensschilderung*, p. 71f.

185. See Fränkel *ad loc.* and D. A. Kidd, 'Hesperus and Catullus LXII', *Latomus* 33 (1974), 22–33.

186. Further striking examples include 1.269–75, 3.656–63, 4.35–9, 167–70, 948–52, 1062–5.

187. Cf. A. S. Hollis, 'Notes on Callimachus, *Hecale*', *C.Q.* N.S. 32 (1982), 472f.

188. See Reinsch-Werner, *Callimachus Hesiodicus*, pp. 150–2, who also discusses the πίλημα of *Fr.* 304.2, probably worn by Theseus.

189. The foot-washing scene has been reconstituted, not always convincingly, by e.g. A. S. Hollis, 'Some Fragments of Callimachus' *Hecale*', *C.R.* N.S. 15 (1965), 259f. who suggests that the pot of *Fr.* 244 contains a vegetable as well as water and that in *Fr.* 245 Theseus is relating how he spoke to Sciron the robber; and *Fr.* 247 has been located elsewhere by *P. Oxy.* 2376, at *Fr.* 287.5 *S.H.*

190. Perhaps *Frr.* 268, 341 and 344, mentioning domestic pottery utensils, 286, referring to a ladle, and 270, describing the warming of food(?), belong to the description of the meal. Cf. Gutzwiller, *Studies*, pp. 54–8 for a comparison of the welcome-scene with Homeric predecessors.

191. For her reply (*P. Oxy.* 2376 and 2377) see A. Barigazzi, 'Il dolore materno di

The Everyday and the Low in Alexandrian Poetry 227

Ecale (P. Oxy. 2376 e 2377)', *H.* 86 (1958), 453–71; F. Krafft, 'Die neuen Funde zur Hekale des Kallimachos', *H.* 86 (1958), 471–80; V. Bartoletti, 'Un verso di Callimaco', *S.I.F.C.* N.S. 31 (1959), 179–81 and 'Sui frammenti dell' Ecale di Callimaco nei P. Oxy. 2376 e 2377', in *Misc. Rostagni*, 263–72 (= *W.d.F.* 296, 176–85); Hollis, 'Notes', 472. See the preface to *Frr.* 286–7 *S.H.* for further literature.

192. Reinsch-Werner, *Callimachus Hesiodicus*, p. 136f. demonstrates that δινομένην ('trod in a circle') at *Fr.* 285.7 *S.H.* (= *Fr.* 255 Pf.) recalls Hesiod *W.D.* 597–9, and argues that the reminiscence adds to the realism of the depiction of Hecale.

193. *Fr.* 287.9f. *S.H.* (= *Fr.* 294 Pf.); cf. *Fr.* 328 Pf.

194. So H. Lloyd-Jones and J. Rea, 'Callimachus, Fragments 260–261', *H.S.C.P.* 72 (1968), 140 (with lit.). There is humorous realism in the characterisation of the birds: the crow exhibits its species' proverbial garrulity (e.g. *Fr.* 288.42f. *S.H.*) and omnivorousness (*Fr.* 288.43B–46 *S.H.*: see Lloyd-Jones and Rea, ibid., 141; cf. ibid., 142 on the possibility that Hecale used to feed the crow) and perhaps swears an oath by her withered skin (*Fr.* 288.51f. *S.H.*: Lloyd-Jones and Rea, ibid., 142–4; the irony in the words' reminiscence of Agamemon's great oath at *Il.* 1.234f. is discussed by Herter, 'Kallimachos und Homer', 56), and the two birds abruptly fall asleep, an action described in words ironically recalling *Od.* 15.493–5 when Odysseus and Eumaeus go to sleep (see Pfeiffer on 62f. and 'Morgendämmerung', in *Thesaurismata: Festschr. Ida Kapp* (Munich, 1954), 95–104 (= *W.d.F.* 296, 160–6)).

195. The *Hecale* mentions other humble professions at *Frr.* 272, 287, 290, 295, 301, and other moments from everyday life at *Frr.* 276 and 291.

196. Lloyd-Jones and Rea, 'Callimachus, Fragments 260–261', 145.

197. On καλία, 'hut', see Reinsch-Werner, *Callimachus Hesiodicus*, p. 149f.: it appears to have been a colloquial word elevated to poetic usage by Hesiod, to whom Callimachus appears to be alluding, again with the intention of lending a realistic feel to his description of Hecale's milieu.

198. Cf. especially A. Barigazzi, 'Sull' Ecale di Callimaco', *H.* 82 (1954), 308–17; K. Nickau, 'Zu Kallimachos' Hekale (fr. 238, 4)', *Philol.* 111 (1967), 126–9; Hollis, 'Notes', 469f. N.b. *Fr.* 281 *S.H.* (supplementing *Fr.* 238.4 Pf.).

Conclusion

We can now summarise the Alexandrians' use of realism, whether that of style, intellectual approach or subject-matter. Realism in all its major forms seems often intended in one way or another to put the original audiences in Alexandria in a new and creative relation with the Hellenic past. This can include both the mainstream culture or mythology of Hellas and the literary forms that gave expression to it: Herodas' or Callimachus' revival of Hipponactean verse can bring the latter into a strikingly novel relation with the present in much the same way as Apollonius' evocation of the Argonaut legend does, and Theocritus' modifications of the hexameter go hand in hand with his revisions of what sort of character should populate modern epic. The effects range tonally from the downright humour and burlesque that result from the collision of traditional form and modern subject-matter, to teasing irony when realism actually draws attention to the cultural rift between then and now, to the heightened poignancy perceived in the life of ordinary people and experience, or to the elevation of such material to a position of unprecedented grandeur. Even when the effect is humorous or ironical we can still discern the desire to come to terms with the cultural heritage of Hellas.

The original recipients of such poetry, the court-audiences in Alexandria under its first three regents, had good reason to feel that their links with traditional Hellenic culture were weakened by residence in a land as alien as they apparently found Egypt to be. Presumably, the poets themselves, like Theocritus and Callimachus, who emphasise their origins in Hellenic cities, felt this culture shock as well. It is significant that basic to the Alexandrian poets' redeployment of Hellenic culture and traditional Greek literary forms is their recognisable continuity with it. Theocritus, for example, simultaneously asserts the Hellenic provenance of his poetry and the independence and individuality of his poetic aims. Thus it was at least to some extent the needs of the elite classes of Alexandria, which the early Ptolemies tried to cater for through their poets as well as through their cultural, dynastic and religious programmes, that helped condition the nature of the Alexandrian movement's poetry. The variety of their response to their greater or lesser sense of cultural malaise helped contribute to one of Alexandrian poetry's most characteristic and impressive features, its mercuriality, or *poikilia*.

Naturally, once the realism of the early Alexandrian movement had been conditioned and given shape in this way, it remained a characteristic of the poetry written by members of the later movement, though the sense of urgency often discernible in the earlier Alexandrians' recuperation of Hellenic culture seems to have abated somewhat. True, the *Europa* of Moschus may be said to represent a confrontation of the miraculous and mythical with ordinary experience, but the resultant tone is hardly one of any cultural urgency. In other social and political circumstances, however, when, for example, Virgil takes over the Alexandrian techniques of *enargeia*, aetiology and the incorporation of the lowly in *Aeneid* Book Eight, the result is different again. The pictorialism of the passages on the rustic site of the Rome to come, a site already filled with a feeling of a high religious destiny (306–69), or on the shield of Aeneas (626–731) is now turned to patriotic ends. Aetiology is handled likewise, whether it is meant to show what honest, rustic stock originally inhabited the locality of the future Rome as ancestors of the Roman people (314ff., 337ff.) or whether it is held up as a moral lesson for Virgil's audience, including Augustus (184–279, 351–69). That the original inhabitants of the site of Rome were lowly, but also possessed of an exemplary high moral standing, is emphatically brought home by Evander's words to Aeneas as he enters his humble abode: 'Be brave enough, my guest, to despise riches, and make yourself too [like Heracles] worthy of divinity, and come not disdainful to my poor realm' (364f.).

I have tried to stress throughout this book that realism is only one aspect of Alexandrian poetry. The Alexandrians' non-realistic pursuit of variation and imitation of traditional poetic vocabulary, their fascination with 'glosses' and rare forms, words and expressions from the different dialects of Greek, their passionate attempt to retrieve the texts of the canonical geniuses like Homer, can be set over and against their experiments with realism in its different manifestations. But are its non-realistic preoccupations not also the products of a sense of cultural rift? They are surely just as much an attempt to recuperate Greek culture as the poets' in their updating of it. So the two apparently contrary impulses turn out to be reactions to the same stimulus and to have a common intention: in short, they are aspects of a colonial literature. This perhaps helps us to see a new unity in the variety of Alexandrian poetry.

Bibliography

1. Texts, commentaries and translations

Allen, T. W., Halliday, W. R. and Sikes, E. E., *The Homeric Hymns*² (Oxford, 1936)
Barrett, W. S., *Euripides: Hippolytus* (Oxford, 1964)
Bevan, E. (tr.), *The Poems of Leonidas of Tarentum* (Oxford, 1931)
Bornmann, F., *Callimachi Hymnus in Dianam*, Biblioteca di Studi Superiori: Filologia greca e papirologia 55 (Florence, 1968)
Brink, C. O., *Horace on Poetry: Prolegomena to the Literary Epistles* (Cambridge, 1963)
—— *Horace on Poetry: the 'Ars Poetica'* (Cambridge, 1971)
Bühler, W., *Die Europa des Moschos*, Hermes Einzelschr. 13 (Wiesbaden, 1960)
Bulloch, A. W., *Callimachus: The Fifth Hymn*, Cambridge Classical Texts and Commentaries 26 (Cambridge, 1985)
Butcher, S. H., *Aristotle's Theory of Poetry and Fine Art*⁴ (London, 1911)
Bywater, I., *Aristotle on the Art of Poetry* (Oxford, 1909)
Chrysaffis, G., *A Textual and Stylistic Commentary on Theocritus' Idyll XXV*, London Studies in Classical Philology 1 (Amsterdam, 1981)
Clayman, D. L., *Callimachus' Iambi*, Mnem. Suppl. 59 (Leiden, 1980)
Cope, E. M., *The Rhetoric of Aristotle*, 3 vols. (revised by J. E. Sandys) (Cambridge, 1877)
Crusius, O., *Die Mimiamben des Herondas* (revised by R. Herzog) (Leipzig, 1926)
Cunningham, I. C., *Herodas: Mimiambi* (Oxford, 1971)
Dawson, C. M., 'The Iambi of Callimachus. A Hellenistic Poet's Experimental Laboratory', *Y.C.S.* 11 (1950), 3–168
Denniston, J. D., *Euripides: Electra* (Oxford, 1939)
Diels, H., *Die Fragmente der Vorsokratiker*⁸, 3 vols. (edited by W. Kranz) (Berlin, 1956)
Dover, K. J., *Theocritus: Select Poems* (Basingstoke and London, 1971)
Else, G. F., *Aristotle's Poetics: the Argument* (Cambridge, Mass., 1957)
Fraenkel, E., *Aeschylus: Agamemnon*, 3 vols. (Oxford, 1950)
Fränkel, H., *Noten zu den Argonautika des Apollonios* (Munich, 1968)
Friedländer, P., *Johannes von Gaza und Paulus Silentiarius* (Leipzig, 1912)
Geoghegan, D., *Anyte: the Epigrams*, Testi e Commenti 4 (Rome, 1979)
Gillies, M. M., *The Argonautica of Apollonius Rhodius: Book 3* (Cambridge, 1928)
Gow, A. S. F., *Theocritus*, 2 vols (Cambridge, 1952)
—— *Bucolici Graeci* (Oxford, 1958)
—— *Machon: the Fragments*, Cambridge Classical Texts and Commentaries 1 (Cambridge, 1965)
Gow, A. S. F. and Page, D. L., *The Greek Anthology: Hellenistic Epigrams*, 2 vols. (Cambridge, 1965)
Gow, A. S. F. and Scholfield, A. F., *Nicander* (Cambridge, 1953)
Groningen, B. A. van, *Euphorion* (Amsterdam, 1977)
Hatzikosta, S., *A Stylistic Commentary on Theocritus' Idyll VII*, Classical and Byzantine Monographs 9 (Amsterdam, 1982)
Headlam, W., *Herodas: the Mimes and Fragments* (edited by A.D. Knox) (Cambridge, 1922)
Hopkinson, N., *Callimachus: Hymn to Demeter*, Cambridge Classical Texts and Commentaries 27 (Cambridge, 1984)

Jacoby, F., *Die Fragmente der griechischen Historiker* (Berlin, 1923–30 and Leiden, 1940–58)
Lloyd, A. B., *Herodotus Book II*, 2 vols. to date, *E.P.R.O.* 43 (Leiden, 1975 and 1976)
Lloyd-Jones, H. and Parsons, P., *Supplementum Hellenisticum, Texte und Kommentare* 11 (Berlin and New York, 1983)
Lucas, D. W., *Aristotle: Poetics* (Oxford, 1968)
MacDowell, D. M., *Aristophanes: Wasps* (Oxford, 1971)
McLennan, G. R., *Callimachus: Hymn to Zeus, Testi e Commenti* 2 (Rome, 1977)
Martin, J., *Arati Phaenomena, Biblioteca di Studi Superiori: Filologia greca e papirologia* 25 (Florence, 1956)
Mooney, G. W., *The Argonautica of Apollonius Rhodius* (Dublin, 1912)
Page, D. L., *Select Papyri III: Literary Papyri, Poetry* (London and Cambridge, Mass., 1941)
—— *Further Greek Epigrams* (Cambridge, 1981)
Papathomopoulos, M., *Antoninus Liberalis: Les Métamorphoses* (Paris, 1968)
Pfeiffer, R., *Callimachus*, 2 vols. (Oxford, 1949 and 1953)
Powell, J. U., *Collectanea Alexandrina: Reliquiae minores Poetarum Graecorum Aetatis Ptolemaicae 323–146 A.C. Epicorum, Elegiacorum, Lyricorum, Ethicorum* (Oxford, 1925)
Richardson, N. J., *The Homeric Hymn to Demeter* (Oxford, 1974)
Rostagni, A., *Orazio: Arte Poetica* (Turin, 1930)
Russell, D. A., *'Longinus': on the Sublime* (Oxford, 1964)
Russell, D. A. and Winterbottom, M., *Ancient Literary Criticism* (Oxford, 1972)
Stanford, W. B., *Aristophanes: The Frogs* (London, 1963)
Trypanis, C. A., *Callimachus: Aetia, Iambi, Lyric Poems, Hecale, Minor Epic and Elegiac Poems, Fragments of Epigrams, Fragments of Uncertain Location* (Cambridge, Mass. and London, 1958)
Vian, F., *Apollonios de Rhodes: Argonautiques Chant III* (Paris, 1961)
Vian, F. and Delage, É., *Apollonios de Rhodes: Argonautiques*, 3 vols (Paris, 1976–81)
Wendel, C., *Scholia in Theocritum vetera* (Leipzig, 1914)
—— *Scholia in Apollonium Rhodium vetera* (Berlin, 1935)
West, M. L., *Hesiod: Works and Days* (Oxford, 1978)
Wilamowitz-Moellendorff, U. von, *Euripides: Herakles*, 2 vols. (Berlin, 1889)
Willcock, M. M., *A Companion to the Iliad* (Chicago and London, 1976)
Williams, F., *Callimachus: Hymn to Apollo* (Oxford, 1978)

2. Books, monographs and articles

Adkins, A. W. H. *Merit and Responsibility* (Oxford, 1960)
—— 'Aristotle and the Best Kind of Tragedy', *C.Q.* N.S. 16 (1966), 78–102
—— *From the Many to the One* (London, 1970)
—— *Moral Values and Political Behaviour in Ancient Greece* (London, 1972)
Allen, W. S., *Accent and Rhythm: Prosodic Features of Latin and Greek: A Study in Theory and Reconstruction* (Cambridge, 1973)
Arnott, W. G., *'Menander, qui uitae ostendit uitam'*, *G. & R.* 2nd Ser. 15 (1968), 1–17
—— 'Herodas and the Kitchen Sink', *G. & R.* 2nd Ser. 18 (1971), 121–32
—— 'The Mound of Brasilas and Theocritus' Seventh *Idyll*', *Q.U.C.C.* N.S. 3 (1979), 99–106
Asmus, W., 'Zu den historischen Grenzen des Begriffs "Realismus"', in *Probleme des Realismus in der Weltliteratur* (Berlin, 1962), 495–504
Auerbach, E., *Mimesis: Dargestellte Wirklichkeit in der abendländischen Literatur*

(Bern, 1946) (Eng. trans. W. R. Trask, *Mimesis: the Representation of Reality in Western Literature* (Princeton, 1953))
Baar, J., *Index zu den Ilias-Scholien: die wichtigeren Ausdrücke der grammatischen, rhetorischen und ästhetischen Textkritik, Dt. Beitr. zur Altertumswiss.* 15 (Baden-Baden, 1961)
Bain, D., 'Audience Address in Greek Tragedy', *C.Q.* N.S. 25 (1975), 13–25
—— 'ΛΗΚΥΘΙΟΝ ΑΠΩΛΕΣΕΝ: Some Reservations', *C.Q.* N.S. 35 (1985), 31–7
Barigazzi, A., 'Sull' Ecale di Callimaco', *H.* 82 (1954), 308–30
—— 'Il dolore materno di Ecale (P. Oxy. 2376 e 2377)', *H.* 86 (1958), 453–71
Barrett, W. S., 'Niobe', in R. Carden, *The Papyrus Fragments of Sophocles, Texte und Kommentare* 7 (Berlin and New York, 1974), 171–235
Bartoletti, V., 'Un verso di Callimaco', *S.I.F.C.* N.S. 31 (1959), 179–81
—— 'Sui frammenti dell' Ecale di Callimaco nei P. Oxy. 2376 e 2377', in *Miscellanea di studi alessandrini in memoria di Augusto Rostagni* (Turin, 1963) 263–72 (= A. D. Skiadas (ed.), *Kallimachos, Wege der Forschung* 296 (Darmstadt, 1975), 176–85)
Becatti, G., *The Art of Ancient Greece and Rome* (London, 1968)
Behrens, I., *Die Lehre von der Einteilung der Dichtkunst* (Halle/Saale, 1940)
Bell, H. I., *Egypt from Alexander the Great to the Arab Conquest* (Oxford, 1948)
Benndorf, O., *De Anthologiae Graecae Epigrammatis quae ad Artes spectant* (Diss. Bonn, 1862)
Bernard, P., 'An Ancient Greek City in Central Asia', *Scientific American* 246 (1982), 126–35
Bevan, E., *The House of Ptolemy: a History of Egypt under the Ptolemaic Dynasty* (Chicago, 1968)
Beye, C. R., 'Jason as Love-Hero in Apollonios' Argonautika', *G.R.B.S.* 10 (1969), 31–55
—— *Epic and Romance in the Argonautica of Apollonius* (Carbondale and Edwardsville, 1982)
Bieber, M., *The Sculpture of the Hellenistic Age* (rev. edn) (New York, 1961)
Bing, P., 'Callimachus' Cows: a Riddling Recusatio', *Z.P.E.* 54 (1984), 1–8
Bliquez, L. J., 'Frogs and Mice at Athens', *T.A.P.A.* 107 (1977), 11–25
Bouché-Leclerq, A., *Histoire des Lagides* (Paris, 1903)
Bowie, E. L., 'Theocritus' Seventh *Idyll*, Philetas and Longus', *C.Q.* N.S. 35 (1985), 67–91
Bowra, C. M., 'Erinna's Lament for Baucis', in *Greek Poetry and Life: Essays presented to Gilbert Murray* (Oxford, 1936), 325–42
—— *Problems in Greek Poetry* (Oxford, 1953)
—— 'The Meaning of a Heroic Age' (Earl Grey Memorial Lecture, Newcastle, 1957) in G. S. Kirk (ed.), *The Language and Background of Homer: Some Recent Studies and Controversies* (Cambridge, 1964)
Brink, K. O., 'Callimachus and Aristotle: An Inquiry into Callimachus' ΠΡΟΣ ΠΡΑΞΙΦΑΝΙΙΝ', *C.Q.* 40 (1946), 11–26
Brown, E. L., 'The Lycidas of Theocritus' *Idyll* 7', *H.S.C.P.* 85 (1981), 59–100
Brunn, H., 'Die griechischen Bukoliker und die bildende Kunst', *S.B.A.W.* 1879 (2), 1ff. (= *Kl. Schr.*, vol. iii (Leipzig, 1906), 217–28)
Bulloch, A. W., 'Callimachus' Erysichthon, Homer and Apollonius Rhodius', *A.J.P.* 98 (1977), 97–123
—— 'The Future of a Hellenistic Illusion: Some observations on Callimachus and religion', *M.H.* 41 (1984), 209–30
Cairns, F., 'Theocritus Idyll 10', *H.* 98 (1970), 38–44
—— *Generic Composition in Greek and Roman Poetry* (Edinburgh, 1972)
—— *Tibullus: A Hellenistic Poet at Rome* (Cambridge, 1979)
Campbell, M. M., *Studies in the Third Book of Apollonius Rhodius' Argonautica* (Hildesheim, Zurich, New York, 1982)

Carspecken, J. F., 'Apollonius Rhodius and the Homeric Epic', *Y.C.S.* 13 (1952), 35–143
Champfleury (J.-F.-F. Husson), *Le Réalisme* (Paris, 1857)
Codrignani, G., '"L' "aition" nella poesia greca prima di Callimaco', *Convivium* 5th Ser. 26 (1958), 527–45
Cohen, G. M., *The Seleucid Colonies: Studies in Founding, Administration and Organization*, Historia Einzelschr. 30 (Wiesbaden, 1978)
Collard, C., 'Medea and Dido', *Prometheus* 1 (1975), 131–51
Couat, A., *La Poésie alexandrine sous les trois premiers Ptolémées (324–222 av. J.-C.)* (Paris, 1882)
Curtius, E. R., *Europäische Literatur und lateinisches Mittelalter*, (Bern, 1948) (Eng. trans. W. R. Trask, *European Literature and the Latin Middle Ages*, Bollingen Series 36 (New York, 1953))
Deubner, L., 'Ein Stilprinzip hellenistischer Dichtkunst', *N.Jb.* 47 (1921), 361–78
Diderot, D., *Oeuvres Esthétiques* (ed. P. Vernière) (Paris, 1965)
Dodds, E. R., *The Greeks and the Irrational* (Berkeley and Los Angeles, 1951)
Dörner, F. K. and Hoepfner, W., 'Vorläufiger Bericht über eine Reise in Bithynien 1961', *A.A.* 1962, 564–93
Dubrow, H., *Genre* (London and New York, 1982)
Duchemin, J., 'A propos de l'*Héraclès Tueur de Lion*', in *Miscellanea di studi alessandrini in memoria di Augusto Rostagni* (Turin, 1963), 311–21
Dunand, F., *Le Culte d'Isis dans le bassin oriental de la Méditerranée I: le culte d'Isis et les Ptolémées*, E.P.R.O. 26 (Leiden, 1973)
Du Quesnay, I. M. Le M., 'From Polyphemus to Corydon: Virgil *Eclogue* 2 and the *Idylls* of Theocritus', in D. A. West and A. J. Woodman (eds.), *Creative Imitation and Latin Literature* (Cambridge, 1979), 35–69
Easterling, P. E. and Knox, B. M. W. (eds.), *The Cambridge History of Classical Literature*. vol. i: *Greek Literature* (Cambridge, 1985)
Effe, B., *Dichtung und Lehre: Untersuchungen zur Typologie des antiken Lehrgedichts*, Zetemata 69 (Munich, 1977)
—— 'Die Destruktion der Tradition; Theokrits mythologische Gedichte', *Rh.M.* N.F. 121 (1978), 48–77
—— 'Held und Literatur: Der Funktionswandel des Herakles-Mythos in der griechischen Literatur', *Poetica* 12 (1980), 145–66
Erbse, H., 'Homerscholien und hellenistische Glossare bei Apollonios Rhodios', *H.* 81 (1953), 163–96
Fabiano, G., 'Fluctuation in Theocritus' Style', *G.R.B.S.* 12 (1971), 517–37
Färber, H., *Die Lyrik in der Kunsttheorie der Antike* (Munich, 1936)
Fittschen, K., 'Der Schild des Achilleus', in F. Matz and H.-G. Buchholz (eds.), *Archaeologia Homerica: Die Denkmäler und das frühgriechische Epos*, vol. ii (Göttingen, 1973), Ch. N. Pt. 1
Foley, V. and Soedel, W., 'Ancient Oared Warships', *Scientific American* 244 (1981), 116–29
Fontenrose, J., 'Work, Justice, and Hesiod's Five Ages', *C.P.* 69 (1974), 1–16
Fortenbaugh, W. W., 'Theophrast über den komischen Charakter', *Rh. M.* N.F. 124 (1981), 245–60
Fraenkel, E., *Elementi plautini in Plauto* (Florence, 1960)
Fränkel, H., 'Das Argonautenepos des Apollonios', *M.H.* 14 (1957), 1–19
—— 'Ein Don Quijote unter den Argonauten des Apollonios', *M.H.* 17 (1960), 1–20
—— *Early Greek Poetry and Philosophy: A History of Greek Epic, Lyric and Prose to the Middle of the Fifth Century* (Eng. trans. M. Hadas and J. Willis) (Oxford, 1975)
Franz, M.-L. von, *Die aesthetischen Anschauungen der Iliasscholien im Codex Ven. B. und Townleianus* (Diss. Zurich, 1943)

Fraser, P. M., *Ptolemaic Alexandria*, 3 vols. (Oxford, 1972)
Frost, K. T., 'Greek Boxing', *J.H.S.* 26 (1906), 213–25
Gagarin, M., '*Dikē* in the *Works and Days*', *C.P.*, 68 (1973), 81–94
Galinsky, G. K., *The Herakles Theme: The Adaptations of the Hero in Literature from Homer to the Twentieth Century* (Oxford, 1972)
Gärtner, H. A., 'Beobachtungen zum Schild des Achilleus', in H. Görgemanns and E. A. Schmidt (eds.), *Studien zum antiken Epos, Beiträge zur klassischen Philologie* 72 (Meisenheim am Glan, 1976), 46–65
Gaunt, D. M., 'Argo and the Gods in Apollonius Rhodius', *G. & R.* 2nd Ser. 19 (1972), 117–26
Giangrande, G., '"Arte Allusiva" and Alexandrian Epic Poetry', *C.Q.* N.S. 17 (1967), 85–97
—— 'Sympotic Literature and Epigram', in *L'Épigramme grecque, Entretiens sur l'antiquité classique* 14 (Vandoeuvres-Geneva, 1968), 93–174
—— 'Théocrite, Simichidas et les *Thalysies*', *A.C.* 37 (1968), 491–533
—— 'Hellenistic Poetry and Homer', *A.C.* 39 (1970), 46–77
—— 'Theocritus' Twelfth and Fourth Idylls: A Study in Hellenistic Irony', *Q.U.C.C.* 12 (1971), 95–113
—— 'Two Theocritean Notes', *C.R.* N.S. 23 (1973), 7f.
Gil Fernández, L., 'La epica helenística', in *Estudios sobre el mundo helenístico* (Seville, 1971), 91–120
Gill, C., 'The *Ēthos/Pathos* Distinction in Rhetorical and Literary Criticism', *C.Q.* N.S. 34 (1984), 149–66
Gombrich, E. H., *Art and Illusion*[4] (London, 1972)
Gow, A. S. F., 'The Methods of Theocritus and some Problems in his Poems', *C.Q.* 24 (1930), 146–53
Greenwood, E. B., 'Reflections on Professor Wellek's Concept of Realism', *Neophilologus* 46 (1962), 89–97
Griffin, J., *Homer on Life and Death* (Oxford, 1980)
Griffiths, A. H., 'Six Passages in Callimachus and the Anthology', *B.I.C.S.* 17 (1970), 32–43
—— 'Notes on the Text of Theocritus', *C.Q.* N.S. 22 (1972), 103–9
Griffiths, F. T., *Theocritus at Court*, *Mnem. Suppl.* 55 (Leiden, 1979)
Gundert, H., 'Enthusiasmos und Logos bei Platon', *Lexis* 2 (1949), 25–46 (= K. Döring and F. Preisshofen (eds.), *Hermann Gundert: Platonstudien, Studien zur antiken Philosophie* 7 (Amsterdam, 1977), 1–22)
Gutzwiller, K. *Studies in the Hellenistic Epyllion, Beiträge zur klassischen Philologie* 114 (Königstein/Ts., 1981)
Habicht, C., 'Die herrschende Gesellschaft in den hellenistischen Monarchien', *V.S.W.G.* 45 (1958), 1–16
Hack, R. K., 'The Doctrine of Literary Forms', *H.S.C.P.* 27 (1916), 1–65
Hagstrum, J. H., *The Sister Arts: the Tradition of Pictorialism and English Poetry from Dryden to Gray* (Chicago, 1958)
Halperin, D. M., *Before Pastoral: Theocritus and the Ancient Tradition of Bucolic Poetry* (New Haven and London, 1983)
—— 'The Forbears of Daphnis', *T.A.P.A.* 113 (1983), 183–200
Händel, P., *Beobachtungen zur epischen Technik des Apollonios Rhodios*, *Zetemata* 8 (Munich, 1954)
—— 'Die Götter des Apollonios als Personen', in *Miscellanea di studi alessandrini in memoria di Augusto Rostagni* (Turin, 1963), 363–81
Harriott, R., *Poetry and Criticism before Plato* (London, 1969)
Harvey, A. E., 'The Classification of Greek Lyric Poetry', *C.Q.* N.S. 5 (1955), 157–75
Heichelheim, F., *Die auswärtige Bevölkerung im Ptolemäerreich*, *Klio Beiheft* 18 (N.F. 5) (Leipzig, 1925)

Herter, H., 'Kallimachos und Homer: Ein Beitrag zur Interpretation des Hymnos auf Artemis', in *Xenia Bonnensia* (Bonn, 1929), 50–105 (pp. 57–76 are reprinted in A. D. Skiadas (ed.), *Kallimachos, Wege der Forschung* 296 (Darmstadt, 1975), 354–75)
—— 'Ein neues Türwunder', *Rh.M.* N.F. 89 (1940), 152–7
—— 'Bericht über die Literatur zur hellenistischen Dichtung seit dem Jahre 1921, II: Apollonios von Rhodos', *Bursians Jahresbericht* 285 (1944–55), 213–410
—— 'Den Arm im Gewande: eine Studie zu Herakles dem Löwentöter', in *Miscellanea di studi alessandrini in memoria di Augusto Rostagni* (Turin, 1963), 322–37
—— 'Die Haaröle der Berenike', in *Festgabe für Edith Heischkel und Walter Artelt* (Stuttgart, 1971), 54–68 (= A. D. Skiadas (ed.), *Kallimachos, Wege der Forschung* 296 (Darmstadt, 1975), 186–206)
Hollis, A. S., 'Some Fragments of Callimachus' *Hecale*', *C.R.* N.S. 15 (1965), 259f.
—— 'Callimachus, *Aetia* Fr. 1.9–12', *C.Q.* N.S. 28 (1978), 402–6
—— 'Notes on Callimachus, *Hecale*', *C.Q.* N.S. 32 (1982), 469–73
Horstmann, A. E.-A., *Ironie und Humor bei Theokrit, Beiträge zur klassischen Philologie* 67 (Meisenheim am Glan, 1976)
Huber, G. Th., *Lebensschilderung und Kleinmalerei im hellenistischen Epos: Darstellung des menschlichen Lebens und der Affekte* (Diss. Solothurn, 1926)
Hunger, H., 'Zur realistischen Kunst Theokrits', *W.S.* 60 (1942), 23–7
Hunter, R. L., *A Study of Daphnis and Chloe* (Cambridge, 1983)
Imbert, C., 'Stoic Logic and Alexandrian Poetics', in M. Schofield, M. Burnyeat and J. Barnes (eds.), *Doubt and Dogmatism: Studies in Hellenistic Epistemology* (Oxford, 1980), 182–216
Jaeger, W. W., *Paideia: The Ideals of Greek Culture*, 3 vols. (Eng. trans. G. Highet) (Oxford, 1939–45)
Janko, R., *Aristotle on Comedy: Towards a Reconstruction of Poetics II* (London, 1984)
Jones, A. H. M., 'The Hellenistic Age', *Past and Present* 27 (1964), 3–22
Kakridis, J. T., 'Erdichtete Ekphrasen: ein Beitrag zur homerischen Schildbeschreibung', *W.S.* 76 (1963), 7–26
Kebric, R. B., *In the Shadow of Macedon: Duris of Samos, Historia Einzelschr.* 29 (Wiesbaden, 1977)
Kidd, D. A., 'Hesperus and Catullus LXII', *Latomus* 33 (1974), 22–33
Klein, L., 'Die Göttertechnik in den Argonautika des Apollonios Rhodios', *Philol.* 86 (1931), 18–51, 215–57
Klein, T. M., 'Callimachus, Apollonius Rhodius, and the Concept of the "Big Book"', *Eranos* 73 (1975), 16–25
Knox, B. M. W., 'Euripidean Comedy', in *The Rarer Action: Essays in Honor of Francis Fergusson* (New Brunswick, N.J., 1970), 68–96 (= B.M.W. Knox, *Word and Action: Essays on the Ancient Theater* (Baltimore and London, 1979), 250–74)
Köhnken, A., *Apollonios Rhodios und Theokrit: die Hylas-und die Amykosgeschichten beider Dichter und die Frage der Priorität, Hypomnemata* 12 (Göttingen, 1965)
Kokolakis, M. M., 'Ριανὸς ὁ Κρής, ἐπικὸς τοῦ 3ου π.Χ. αἰῶνος', in M. M. Kokolakis, Φιλολογικὰ μελετήματα εἰς τὴν ἀρχαίαν ἑλληνικὴν γραμματείαν (Athens, 1976), 129–62
Körte, A., *Die hellenistische Dichtung* (revised by P. Händel) (Stuttgart, 1960)
Krafft, F. 'Die neuen Funde zur Hekale des Kallimachos', *H.* 86 (1958), 471–80
Krevelen, D. A. van, 'Bemerkungen zur Charakteristik der in den Argonautika des Apollonios auftretenden Personen', *Rh.M.* N.F. 99 (1956), 3–8
Kroll, W., *Studien zum Verständnis der römischen Literatur* (Stuttgart, 1924)

Kurman, G., 'Ecphrasis in Epic Poetry', *C.L.* 26 (1974), 1–13
Latte, K., 'Erinna', *Gött. Nachr.* 1953, 79–94 (= *Kl. Schr.* (Munich, 1968), 508–25)
Lawall, G., 'Apollonius' *Argonautica*: Jason as Anti-Hero', *Y.C.S.* 19 (1966), 121–69
—— *Theocritus' Coan Pastorals: a Poetry Book* (Cambridge, Mass., 1967)
Lefkowitz, M. R., 'The Quarrel between Callimachus and Apollonius', *Z.P.E.* 40 (1980), 1–19
—— *The Lives of the Greek Poets* (Baltimore, 1981)
Legge, A. J., 'Cave Climates', in E. S. Higgs (ed.), *Papers in Economic Prehistory* (Cambridge, 1972), 97–103
Legrand, Ph.-E., *Étude sur Théocrite* (Paris, 1898)
—— *La Poésie alexandrine* (Paris, 1924)
Lenchantin, M., 'Sul preteso sincretismo dei generi nella letteratura latina', *R.F.I.C.* N.S. 12 (1934), 433–46
Lennox, P. G., 'Apollonius, Argonautica 3, 1ff. and Homer', *H.* 108 (1980), 45–73
Levin, D. N., 'Quaestiones Erinneanae', *H.S.C.P.* 66 (1962), 193–204
Linforth, I. M., 'Theocritus XXV', *T.A.P.A.* 78 (1947), 77–87
Livrea, E., 'Nota al nuovo Callimaco di Lille', *Z.P.E.* 32 (1978), 7–10
—— 'Der Liller Kallimachos und die Mausefallen', *Z.P.E.* 34 (1979), 37–42
—— 'Polittico Callimacheo: contributi al testo della Victoria Berenices', *Z.P.E.* 40 (1980), 21–6
Lloyd-Jones, H., 'A Hellenistic Miscellany', *S.I.F.C.* 3rd Ser. 2 (1984), 52–72
Lloyd-Jones, H. and Rea, J., 'Callimachus, Fragments 260–261, *H.S.C.P.* 72 (1968), 125–45
Lohse, G., 'Die Kunstauffassung im VII. Idyll Theokrits und das Programm des Kallimachos', *H.* 94 (1966), 413–25
Luria, S., 'Herondas' Kampf für die veristische Kunst', in *Miscellanea di studi alessandrini in memoria di Augusto Rostagni* (Turin, 1963), 394–415
Mackail, J. W., *Lectures on Greek Poetry* (London, 1926)
McKay, K. J., *The Poet at Play: Kallimachos, The Bath of Pallas*, Mnem. Suppl. 6 (Leiden, 1962)
—— *Erysichthon: a Callimachean Comedy*, Mnem. Suppl. 7 (Leiden, 1962)
—— 'Mischief in Kallimachos' *Hymn to Artemis*', *Mnem.* 4th Ser. 16 (1963), 243–56
Macurdy, G. H., *Hellenistic Queens* (Baltimore, 1932)
Maas, P., *Greek Metre* (Eng. trans. H. Lloyd-Jones) (Oxford, 1962)
Mastromarco, G., *Il pubblico di Eronda*, Proagones 15 (Padua, 1979) (Eng. trans. *The Public of Herondas*, London Studies in Classical Philology 11 (Amsterdam, 1984))
Mastronarde, D. J., 'Theocritus' *Idyll* 13: Love and the Hero', *P.P.* 23 (1968), 5–18 (also printed in *T.A.P.A.* 99 (1968), 273–90)
Meillier, C., *Callimaque et son temps: Recherches sur la carrière et la condition d'un écrivain à l'époque des premiers Lagides* (Lille, 1979)
Meincke, W., *Untersuchungen zu den enkomiastischen Gedichten Theokrits* (Diss. Kiel, 1965)
Michelazzo Magrini, M., 'Una nuova linea interpretativa della Connocchia di Erinna', *Prometheus* 1 (1975), 225–36
Mirmont, H. de la Ville de, 'Le navire Argo et la science nautique d'Apollonios de Rhodes', *R.I.E.* 30 (1895), 230–85
Momigliano, A., 'Terra Marique', *J.R.S.* 32 (1942), 53–64
—— 'The Locrian Maidens and the Date of Lycophron's *Alexandra*', *C.Q.* 39 (1945), 49–53
Morrison, J. S. and Williams, R. T., *Greek Oared Ships: 900–322 B.C.* (Cambridge, 1968)

Moskalew, W., *Formular Language and Poetic Design in the Aeneid*, Mnem. Suppl. 73 (Leiden, 1982)
Most, G. W., 'Callimachus and Herophilus', *H.* 109 (1981), 188–96
Murdoch, I., *The Fire and the Sun: Why Plato banished the Artists* (Oxford, 1977)
Mylne, V. G., *The Eighteenth-Century French Novel: Techniques of Illusion* (Cambridge, 1981)
Nachtergael, G., *Les Galates en Grèce et les Sôtéria de Delphes. Recherches d'histoire et d'épigraphie hellénistiques* (Brussels, 1977)
Nickau, K., 'Zu Kallimachos' Hekale (fr. 238, 4)', *Philol.* 111 (1967), 126–9
—— *Untersuchungen zur textkritischen Methode des Zenodotos von Ephesos*, Unters. zur ant. Lit. u. Gesch. 16 (Berlin and New York, 1977)
Nochlin, L., *Realism* (Harmondsworth, 1971)
Oates, J. F., 'The Status Designation: ΠΕΡΣΗΣ, ΤΗΣ ΕΠΙΓΟΝΗΣ', *Y.C.S.* 18 (1963), 1–129
O'Neill, E. G., 'The Localization of Metrical Word-Types in the Greek Hexameter: Homer, Hesiod, and the Alexandrians', *Y.C.S.* 8 (1942), 105–78
Onians, J., *Art and Thought in the Hellenistic Age: the Greek World View 350–50 B.C.* (London, 1979)
Oppermann, H., 'Herophilos bei Kallimachos', *H.* 60 (1925), 14–32 (= A. D. Skiadas (ed.), *Kallimachos*, Wege der Forschung 296 (Darmstadt, 1975), 1–20)
Ott, U., *Die Kunst des Gegensatzes in Theokrits Hirtengedichten*, Spudasmata 22 (Hildesheim and New York, 1969)
Palm, J., 'Bemerkungen zur Ekphrase in der griechischen Literatur', *Kungl. Humanistiska Vetenskapssamfundet i Uppsala, Årsbok* 1965–6, 108–211
Parsons, P. J., 'Callimachus: Victoria Berenices', *Z.P.E.* 25 (1977), 1–50
Peremans, W., 'Égyptiens et étrangers dans l'Égypte ptolémaïque', in *Grecs et barbares, Entretiens sur l'antiquité classique* 8 (Vandoeuvres-Geneva, 1962), 121–66
Peremans, W., Dack, E. van 't, Mooren, L. and Swinnen, W., *Prosopographia Ptolemaica 6, La cour, les relations internationales et les possessions extérieures, la vie culturelle*, Studia Hellenistica 17 (Louvain, 1968)
Pfeiffer, R., 'ΒΕΡΕΝΙΚΗΣ ΠΛΟΚΑΜΟΣ', *Philol.* 87 (1932), 179–228 (= A. D. Skiadas (ed.). *Kallimachos*, Wege der Forschung 296 (Darmstadt, 1975), 100–52)
—— 'Morgendämmerung', in *Thesaurismata: Festschr. Ida Kapp* (Munich, 1954), 95–104 (= A. D. Skiadas (ed.), *Kallimachos*, Wege der Forschung 296) (Darmstadt, 1975), 160–6)
—— *History of Classical Scholarship*. vol. i: *From the Beginnings to the End of the Hellenistic Age* (Oxford, 1968)
Plebe, A., *La teoria del comico da Aristotele a Plutarco* (Turin, 1952)
Poe, J. P., *Caesurae in the Hexameter Line of Latin Elegiac Verse*, Hermes Einzelschr. 29 (Wiesbaden, 1974)
Poggioli, R., 'Poetics and Metrics', in W.P. Friederich (ed.), *Proceedings of the Second Congress of the International Comparative Literature Association*, vol. i (Chapel Hill, 1959), 192–204 (= R. Poggioli, *The Spirit of the Letter: Essays in European Literature* (Cambridge, Mass., 1965), 342–54)
Pomeroy, S. B., 'Supplementary Notes on Erinna', *Z.P.E.* 32 (1978), 17–22
Pope, A., 'A Discourse on Pastoral Poetry' (1709), in H. Davis (ed.), *Pope: Poetical Works* (Oxford, 1966)
Powell, J. U. and Barber, E. A. (eds.), *New Chapters in the History of Greek Literature*, 3 series (Oxford, 1921–33)
Puelma, M., 'Sänger und König: Zum Verständnis von Hesiods Tierfabel', *M.H.* 29 (1972), 86–109
Reeve, M. D., 'Interpolations in Greek Tragedy, III', *G.R.B.S.* 14 (1973), 145–71
Reich, H., *Der Mimus: ein litterar-entwickelungsgeschichtlicher Versuch* (Berlin, 1903)

Reinsch-Werner, H., *Callimachus Hesiodicus: die Rezeption der hesiodeischen Dichtung durch Kallimachos von Kyrene* (Berlin, 1976)
Reitzenstein, E., 'Zur Stiltheorie des Kallimachos', in *Festschr. Richard Reitzenstein* (Leipzig and Berlin, 1931), 23–69
Rice, E. E., *The Grand Procession of Ptolemy Philadelphus* (Oxford, 1983)
Richter, G. M. A., *The Sculpture and Sculptors of the Greeks*[4] (New Haven, 1970)
Riginos, A. S., *Platonica: The Anecdotes concerning the Life and Writings of Plato*, Columbia Studies in the Classical Tradition 3 (Leiden, 1976)
Roberts, C. H., 'Literature and Society in the Papyri', *M.H.* 10 (1953), 264–79
Rosenmeyer, T. G., *The Green Cabinet: Theocritus and the European Pastoral Lyric* (Berkeley and Los Angeles, 1969)
Rossi, L. E., 'I generi letterari e le loro leggi scritte e non scritte nelle letterature classiche', *B.I.C.S.* 18 (1971), 69–94
Rostagni, A., 'Sui "Caratteri" di Teofrasto', *R.F.I.C.* 48 (1920), 417–43 (= *Scritti Minori I: 'Aesthetica'* (Turin, 1955), 327–55)
—— 'Aristotele e l'Aristotelismo nella storia dell' estetica antica', *S.I.F.C.* N.S. 2 (1922), 1–147 (= *Scritti Minori I: 'Aesthetica'* (Turin, 1955), 76–254)
Ruckh, G. B., '"Longinus"' Criticism of Theocritus (Περὶ ὕψους 33.4)', *C.P.* 38 (1943), 256–9
Ruijgh, C. J., 'Le dorien de Théocrite: dialecte cyrénien d'Alexandrie et d'Égypte', *Mnem.* 4th Ser. 37 (1984), 56–88
Rupprecht, K., *Einführung in die griechische Metrik*[3] (Munich, 1950)
Sandbach, F. H., 'Ennoia and Prolepsis in the Stoic Theory of Knowledge', in A. A. Long (ed.), *Problems in Stoicism* (London, 1971), 22–37
Scheidweiler, F., 'Erinnas Klage um Baukis', *Philol.* 100 (1956), 40–51
Schlunk, R. R., *The Homeric Scholia and the Aeneid: A Study of the Influence of Ancient Homeric Literary Criticism on Vergil* (Ann Arbor, 1974)
Schmidt, E. A., 'Hirtenhierarchie in der antiken Bukolik?', *Philol.* 113 (1969), 183–200
—— *Poetische Reflexion: Vergils Bukolik* (Munich, 1972)
Schwinge, E.-R. 'Griechische Poesie und die Lehre von der Gattungstrinität in der Moderne', *A.u.A.* 27 (1981), 130–62
Schwyzer, F., *Griechische Grammatik*, I. von Müllers Handbuch der Altertumswissenschaft, Section 2 Pt. 1, 4 vols. (Munich, 1934–71)
Segal, C., '"Since Daphnis Dies": the Meaning of Theocritus' First *Idyll*', *M.H.* 31 (1974), 1–22
Shapiro, H. A., 'Jason's Cloak', *T.A.P.A.* 110 (1980), 263–86
Sherwin-White, S. M., *Ancient Cos: an historical study from the Dorian settlement to the Imperial Period*, Hypomnemata 51 (Göttingen, 1978)
Solmsen, F., 'Greek Philosophy and the Discovery of the Nerves', *M.H.* 18 (1961), 150–97
Sörbom, G., *Mimesis and Art* (Bonniers, 1966)
Stern, J., 'Theocritus' *Idyll* 24', *A.J.P.* 95 (1974), 348–61
—— 'Theocritus' *Idyll* 14', *G.R.B.S.* 16 (1975), 51–8
Stern, J. P., *On Realism* (London and Boston, 1973)
Stroh, W., 'Hesiods lügende Musen', in H. Görgemanns and E. A. Schmidt (eds.), *Studien zum antiken Epos*, Beiträge zur klassischen Philologie 72 (Meisenheim am Glan, 1976), 85–112
Susemihl, F., *Geschichte der griechischen Litteratur in der Alexandrinerzeit*, 2 vols. (Leipzig, 1891 and 1892)
Svensson, A., *Der Gebrauch des bestimmten Artikels in der nachklassischen griechischen Epik* (Lund, 1937)
Thompson, D. B., *Ptolemaic Oinochoai and Portraits in Faience: Aspects of the Ruler-Cult* (Oxford, 1973)
Vatin, C., *Recherches sur le mariage et la condition de la femme mariée a l'époque hellénistique*, *B.E.F.A.R.* 216 (Paris, 1970)

Verdenius, W. J., *Mimesis: Plato's Doctrine of Artistic Imitation and its Meaning to Us*, Philosophia Antiqua 3 (Leiden, 1949)
Vian, F., 'ΙΙΙΣΩΝ ΑΜΙΙΧΑΝΕΩΝ', in E. Livrea and G. A. Privitera (eds.), *Studi in onore di Anthos Ardizzoni*, vol. ii (Rome, 1978), 1025–41
Vollgraff, C. W., 'χρυσῷ παίζοισ᾽ Ἀφροδίτα', *Mélanges d'archéologie et d'histoire offerts à Ch. Picard* (Paris, 1949), 1075–87
Walker, S. F., *Theocritus*, T.W.A.S. 609 (Boston, 1980)
Webster, T. B. L., *Hellenistic Poetry and Art* (London, 1964)
Wehrli, F., *Motivstudien zur griechischen Komödie* (Zurich and Leipzig, 1936)
Welcker, F. G., 'Entbindung', *Kl. Schr.*, vol. iii (Bonn, 1850), 185–208
Wellek, R., 'The Concept of Realism in Literary Scholarship', *Neophilologus* 45 (1961), 1–20 (= Wellek, R., *Concepts of Criticism* (New Haven and London, 1963), pp. 225–55)
—— 'A Reply to E. B. Greenwood's Reflections', *Neophilologus* 46 (1962), 194–6
West, M. L., 'Erinna', *Z.P.E.* 25 (1977), 95–119
—— *Greek Metre* (Oxford, 1982)
—— 'Three Topics in Greek Metre', *C.Q.* N.S. 32 (1982), 281–97
West, S., 'Lycophron Italicised', *J.H.S.* 104 (1984), 127–51
White, H., *Studies in Theocritus and Other Hellenistic Poets*, London Studies in Classical Philology 3 (Amsterdam, 1979)
Wilamowitz-Moellendorff, U. von, *Die Textgeschichte der griechischen Bukoliker*, Philologische Untersuchungen 18 (Berlin, 1906)
—— *Einleitung in die griechische Tragödie* (Berlin, 1910)
—— *Hellenistische Dichtung in der Zeit des Kallimachos*, 2 vols. (Berlin, 1924)
Wilkinson, L. P., 'The Baroque Spirit in Ancient Art and Literature', *T.R.S.L.* 25 (1950), 2–11
—— *The Georgics of Virgil: A Critical Survey* (Cambridge, 1969)
Williams, F., 'A Theophany in Theocritus', *C.Q.* N.S. 21 (1971), 137–45
—— ' Ὦ in Theocritus', *Eranos* 71 (1973), 52–67
Zanker, G., 'Callimachus' Hecale: A New Kind of Epic Hero?', *Antichthon* 11 (1977), 68–77
—— 'The Love Theme in Apollonius Rhodius' Argonautica', *W.S.* N.F. 13 (1979), 52–75
—— 'Simichidas' Walk and the Locality of Bourina in Theocritus, *Id.* 7', *C.Q.* N.S. 30 (1980), 373–7
—— 'Enargeia in the Ancient Criticism of Poetry', *Rh.M.* N.F. 124 (1981), 297–311
—— 'The Nature and Origin of Realism in Alexandrian Poetry', *A.u.A.* 29 (1983), 125–45
—— 'A Hesiodic Reminiscence in Virgil, *E.* 9.11–13', *C.Q.* N.S. 35 (1985), 235–7
Ziegler, K., *Das hellenistische Epos: ein vergessenes Kapitel griechischer Dichtung*^{2} (Leipzig, 1966)

Index

Acherousian headland 71–2, 116
Achilles 67, 184, 185, 209, 211;
    shield 3, 69, 75–6, 79
Acontius 114, 155
Adonis; and the Ptolemies 12, 14,
    16–17, 24–5; and Theocritus'
    hymn (*Id.* 15.100–44) 12–18,
    24–5; festival at Alexandria 9, 12,
    13, 24–5
Aeschylus; caricatured by
    Aristophanes 134–7; *Eumenides*
    as an aition 6–7, 16, 17, 121;
    Prometheus Bound 173;
    separating the genres 147;
    Theoroi (*Isthmiastai*) and realistic
    likenesses 39
aitia; realistic 6–7, 16–17, 60, 120–4,
    181–2; recent 16–17
Alcaeus (or Sappho) 59, 183–4
Alcidamas; on the *Odyssey* 143, 145
Alcmena 88, 176–8, 182
Alexander the Great 1, 84, 179–80
Alexandrian poetry; a colonial
    literature 231; and the bizarre 6,
    16, 28–9, 118–19, *see also*
    fantastic, the; and *trompe l'oeil* in
    fine art 42–50 *passim*; distinct
    from wider Hellenistic poetry 1,
    18, 157, 191–2; membership
    defined 1–3; non-realistic
    elements 3, 6, 16, 28–9, 113,
    118–19, 230, a response to same
    cultural stimulus as realism
    230–1; realism *see* realism,
    Alexandrian
Alexis 170
Amphitryon 88, 176–7, 180–1
Amycus 68, 86–7
Anchises 173
anon. *see* epigram on a Nymphaeum
    (*G.L.P.* 105 (a)), *Epyllium
    Diomedis* (Pow., pp. 72–6),
    Georgic (*G.L.P.* 124), lyric poem
    on bees (Pow., 185f., *G.L.P.* 92
    (b))
Antipater of Sidon; and *trompe
    l'oeil* 45, 94
Antiphanes 149, 170
antiquarianism 6–7, 16, 120, 122,
    230–1
Anyte; everyday and low 163;
    pictorial realism 95–6

apatē in art 46
Apelles 42–4, 94
Aphrodite; and Argonauts 76, 156,
    195–7, 201, 203, 204–7; and
    Daphnis 81, 173–4; and Eros 70,
    205, 206–7; and Europa 92; and
    Hera 70, 204–7; and Jason's cloak
    47, 69, 75–6, 206; and Ptolemaic
    cult 12–17; beauty 45, 47, 69–70,
    203, 205–6
Apollo 57, 67, 116, 122–3, 155; and
    Artemis 183, 185, 187; and
    Lycidas 81–2, 120; miraculous
    birth 60–1, 125, 189–90
Apollonius; and Homer 65–9, 74–8,
    156, 195–209 *passim*; and
    Pindar 197, 201; and *trompe l'oeil*
    in fine art 44, 69–70; conforming
    with Ptolemaic cultural
    programme 25, 121; everyday and
    low (including love) 66–71, 74–8,
    195–209 *passim*; everyday and low
    in similes 76–8, 199, 208–9;
    everyday portrayal of Aphrodite
    and Eros for serio-comic
    purposes 70–1, 206–7; everyday
    portrayal of Aphrodite, Athene
    and Hera for comic purposes 70,
    204–6 *Foundation of Alexandria*
    25, 121–2 indispensability of
    Medea 156, 195–6, 201; Jason a
    'love-hero' 70–1, 76, 156, 201–4,
    208–9; Jason's cloak 44, 47–8, 50,
    69–70, 75–6, 203; Jason's
    development into Euripidean 204;
    Jason's unheroic diplomacy
    202–4; Jason's unheroic
    handsomeness 203; Jason's
    unheroic 'helplessness' 203–4;
    love as key to heroic success 156,
    195–6, 201; love used for
    realism 14, 28, 156, 195–204
    passim; Medea's development
    into Euripidean 197, 198–201;
    membership of Alexandrian
    movement 2; pictorial realism
    44, 47–8, 50, 65–79 *passim*, 203,
    scientific realism in 70, 71–3, 75,
    125–6, use in psychological
    motivation 48; realism in
    portrayal of Medea's love 75,
    125–6, 198–201; redefinition of the

243

epic hero and subject-matter 75–6, 156, 157, 195–8, 201–4, 208–9; rejection of traditional epic heroism 195–6, 201–4; scientific realism, aetiological 122–3, geographical 116–19; in retelling myth 6, 15, 17, 71–2, 115, 128n9, 198–201, 204, medical 72–3, 75, 125–6, 'relating' 23, 25, 65–79 *passim*, 115–19, 122–3, 125–6, 195–8, 201–4, 209
Apsyrtus 200, 204
Aratus; aetiology 123–4; everyday and low 193–4; membership of Alexandrian movement 2; pictorial realism 97–9; Stoicism 97–8, 193–4
aretē; and *phauloi* and *spoudaioi* 140–1, 147, 151n28; in Hesiod 147
Argo 66–8, 203
Ariadne 203, 224n156
Aristophanes; and Euripides 134–7, 141–2; and Homer 135; and morality in poetry 135–6, 150; and the diction of tragedy 136; and the status of the genres 134–7
Aristophanes of Byzantium; on Menander 145
aristos 148; see also *spoudaioi*
Aristotle; and Callimachus 139, 156, 157; and differentiation of tragedy and comedy on the basis of subject-matter 139–40; and division of subjects of *mimēsis* 11, 46, 139–42; and *energeia* 41, 51n22; and *epiphaneis* ('men of distinction') 139, 141, 142; and *ēthos* 143–4; and fine art 39, 46; and *mimēsis* 39, 144; and *pathos* 143–4; and *prepon* ('appropriateness') 142; on bees 126–7; on credibility in poetry 114; on *phauloi* (*cheirones*) ('inferior characters'), defined 140–2, represented in low genres 140–2; on *spoudaioi* (*beltiones*) ('superior characters'), defined 140–2, represented in grand genres 11, 140–4; on the hexameter 11, 142; on the *Odyssey*'s affinity to comedy 143–4; on the status of the genres 139–44; on *toioutoi* (*hoi kath' hēmās, homoioi, hoi nȳn*) ('average characters'), as objects of *mimēsis* 140, 144, in tragedy (?) 144
Arsinoe II 9, 12, 16–17, 25, 95, 192; incestuous marriage to Philadelphus 34n73, 179–80

Artemis 8, 57–60, 122, 182–7
Asclepiades; and Pindar 162; and *trompe l'oeil* 94; everyday and low (including love) 161–2, 163, for comic effects 161–2, 163, for serious effects 163; membership of Alexandrian movement 2; pictorial realism 95
Athene 66, 68, 204–6
audience, Greek Alexandrian; and the Egyptians 20–2, 229, cultural needs 19–22, 65, 229; Alexandrian realism as a response to 22–7, 65–79 *passim*, 89, 101–2, 121–7, 156, 178–81, 189–90, 195–8, 201–4, 209, 229–30; nature 18–22; population 35n80
Auerbach, E. 7–8, 133, 214

Battarus 158–9
Battus 83
belly-prophets 190
Berenice I 12, 14, 16, 17, 25
Berenice II 25, 182
Bion; membership of Alexandrian movement 2 (*see also* Ps.-Moschus, *Lament for Bion*; Ps.-Moschus, *Megara*)
Bourina 56, 82, 119–20, 123
Bowra, C.M. 56

Cairns, F. 16
Callimachus; and Aristotle 139, 156, 157; and Homer 58–59, 60–1, 124–5, 182, 183–7, 192, 210–14; and Pindar 61–2; central figure of Alexandrian movement 2; conforming with Ptolemaic cultural and religious programme 25, 189–92; crossing grand genres with everyday and low subject-matter, for comic effect 58–9, 160–1, 181–9 *passim*, for serious effect 60, 162, 192, for serious effect in *Hecale* 5, 8, 63, 209–14, in *Aetia* 181–2, 191, in *Epigrams* 162, in *Hecale* 5, 8, 63, 209–14, in *Hymns* 58–60, 182–90, in *Lyric* 192; dialect 160, 161; everyday and low (including love), in *Iambi* 160–1; first to collect aitia into one poem 122; irony in encomiastic poetry 25, 181–2, 189–91; 'kings and heroes' 155, 214; 'mimetic' hymns 62; pictorial realism, in *Aetia* 57, in *Epigrams* 96, in *Hecale* 62–4, in *Hymns* 57–62, in *Iambi* 64–5; redefinition of the epic hero and subject-matter 155–7, 181–90, 209–14;

scientific realism, aetiological 122, geographical 116, 118, in retelling myth 6, 15, 17, 114, medical 124–5, 189–90; tone in *Hecale* 5, 8, 63, 209–14, in *Hymns* 8, 59, 60, 182–90
Castor 86–8
Catullus 93
Celts 190
Cephisodotus 44
Ceraunus 127n4
Cercyon 211, 213
Champfleury (J.-F.-F. Husson) 5
characterisation, 'mosaic technique' 159 *(see also phauloi* ('inferior characters'); *spoudaioi* ('superior characters'); *toioutoi* ('average characters'); *individual characters*)
Charis 185, 192, 205–6
Cicero; on description 40, 100; on *mimēsis biou* 143, 145; on the status of the genres 143, 145, 146
Cleophon; and *toioutoi* ('average characters') 144
Coccale 43, 91
Comatas 82–3, 168–70
comedy; a low genre 133–50 *passim*
Corydon 83
Cos 43, 82, 119–20, 190, 191
Courbet, G. 5
Cydippe 114, 155
Cynno 43, 91

Danube 118, 128n20
Daphnis 81, 172–4
deilos 147, 153n58
Demeter 187–9
Dercylus 128n5
dialect *see* Callimachus, dialect; Erinna, dialect; Herodas, dialect; Theocritus, dialect
Dicaeopolis 136
didactic poetry; aims 96–101 *passim*, 193–5; everyday and low 193–5; no separate category of in Greek literary criticism 153n60; pictorial realism 96–101
Diderot, D. 5
Diomedes 173–4
Diomedes the grammarian 144
Dionysius of Halicarnassus; on *enargeia* 39
Dionysius the painter 46
Dioscorides; everyday and low (including love) 162–3; not of Alexandrian movement (?) 3
Dissoi Logoi 46
Duris 50n4

Egyptians; and Alexandrian Greeks 9, 10, 20–2, 229

ekphrasis ('pictorial description') 39–40; denoting description of works of art 50n7; ecphrastic narration 74
enargeia ('pictorial vividness'); and particularism 42; as an aim of poetry 40, 42–50 *passim*; combined with *mimēsis biou* 55–102 *passim*, 189–90, 209–10; defined 39–41; history of term 41–2; in historiography 40–2; in rhetoric 39–40; origins of, in Alexandrian poetry 42–50 *passim*; *see also individual authors*, pictorial realism
encomiastic poetry 1, 9–18, *passim*, 22–7, 84, 119, 121–3, 179–82, 189–92; an index of Ptolemaic literary taste 24–7, 102, 179–82, 189–92
Ennius 157
Ephippus 149
Ephorus 50n4, 117
epic; and elegiacs 155; cultural function 26, 65, 76, 123, 157; development of hexameter by Theocritus 34n70, 166–7; genre-crossing in Alexandrian *see individual authors*, crossing grand genres with everyday and low subject-matter *individual authors*, everyday and low, (including love), genre-crossing in, pre-Alexandrian 134, 143–4, 147–8, 150; hero of in Alexandrian poetry 75–6, 155–7, 161–90 *passim*, 195–8, 201–4, 209–14 *(see also* Daphnis; Erigone; Hecale; Hecale; Heracles; Iambe; Idas; Jason; Medea; Molorchus; Pheidon; Polyphemus the Cyclops; Telamon); hero of traditional 141–2, 155–7, 173–4, 179, 195–8, 201–4, 206, 209–14; non-Alexandrian Hellenistic 1, 157; separation of genres in 135, 138–50 *passim*; traditional tone 11, 135, 137–50 *passim*, 155–7, 167–8, 183–7, 209–14; *see also* metre, hexameter
epigram; and *trompe l'oeil* 44–6, 94–5; everyday and low (including love) 161–4; pictorial realism 94–6
epigram on a Nymphaeum (*G.L.P.* 105 (a)) 95
Epyllium Diomedis (Pow., pp. 72–6); pictorial realism 110n141; resemblance to Callimachus' *Hecale* 110n141, 221n87
Erato 156, 196

Eratosthenes; aetiology 124; *Erigone* 221n87; *Hermes* 99, 126; membership of Alexandrian movement 2; pictorial realism 99; science in poetry 96, 99, 126

Erigone 221n87

Erinna; and *trompe l'oeil* 94; crossing a grand genre with realistic subject-matter 192–3; dialect 223n139; everyday 56–7, 192–3; membership of Alexandrian movement 2, 56; pictorial realism 56–7; use of hexameter for expression of personal emotion 56, 193

Eros 70–1, 205–7

erudition *see* science; Libraries and Museum

Erysichthon 187–9

ēthos; and comedy and the *Odyssey* 143–4

Euanthius 143–4

Euhemerus 21–2, 160

Eumaeus 90, 144, 147–9, 156–7, 181, 210–14, 221n87; influence on Alexandrian poetry 90, 144, 156–7, 181, 210–14, 221n87

Euphorion 15, 26, 29; membership of Alexandrian movement 2; pictorial realism 91–2; scientific realism, aetiological 124, geographical 120, in retelling myth 115, medical 126

Euripides; and Apollonius' Jason 204; and Apollonius' Medea 197, 198–201; and love in tragedy 197; and the everyday in aetiology 121–2; and the Farmer in the *Electra* 148–50, 211–14; crossing a grand genre with everyday and low subject-matter 134–7, 141–2, 148–50; Farmer and Hecale 211–14; Hippolytus and Daphnis 173, realistic character-portrayal 141–2, realistic diction 136, 142

Europa 92–4, 182

Eurycleia 144, 147–9, 210–14, 221n87; influence on Alexandrian poetry 144, 210–14, 221n87

everyday and low (including love); crossed with grand genres for comic effect 7–8, 9–12, 161–92 *passim* (*see also individual authors*); crossed with grand genres for serious effect 7–8, 14, 17, 162, 172–4, 192–214 *passim* (*see also individual authors*); crossed with grand genres in Alexandrian poetry 155–214 *passim,* (*see also individual) authors*; distinguished by Aristotle 133, 139–40, 144; in grand genres, pre-Alexandrian theory and practice, Euripides 134–7, 142, 148–9, 150, Hesiod 147–8, Homer 143–4, 147; province of low genres in pre-Alexandrian theory and practice 133–50 *passim*

fantastic, the; juxtaposed with the everyday 28, 60–1, 68, 73, 94, 182, 183–4, 189–90, 230

fine art; and Alexandrian poetry 42–50, 94–5; and 'archaic intellectualism' 39, 42; and particularism 42–7; and *trompe l'oeil* 3–4, 39, 42–7, 94–5; parallel to poetry 46–7

Fränkel, H. 97, 202

Fraser, P.M. 19, 21

Ganymede 70–1, 207

genres; crossing of grand genres with everyday and low subject-matter 7–8, 133–4 (*see also individual authors*, crossing grand genres with everyday and low subject-matter; *individual authors*, everyday and low (including love)); separation of 7–8, 133–50 *passim*, aesthetic basis 142, moral basis 135–9, 146

Georgic (*G.L.P.* 124) 101

Gombrich, E.H. 4

Gorgo 9–12, 15, 18, 22, 115, 164

Händel, P. 115

Hebe 179–80

Hecale 5, 63, 209–14; and Eumaeus 210–14; and Euripides' Farmer 211–12, 214; and Eurycleia 210–14; and Hecuba 211; and Molorchus 213; and Theseus the *spoudaios* 213–14; and Thetis 211; a *phaulos* portrayed seriously 5, 8, 209–14; described 209–10; moral goodness 210–14; noble birth 210–12

Hecale 5, 8, 62–4, 90, 122, 209–14; an aition 63, 122, 212; conversation of two birds 212; proximity to modern Realism 5, 8, 209–14

Hedylus; membership of Alexandrian movement 2

Hera 58, 61, 92–3, 184, 196, 204–6

Heracles; and Hylas 48, 73–4, 85–6, 115, 174–5, 201–2; and Molorchus 25, 155, 181–2; and

Nemean lion 89–90, 220n82; and
    Ptolemies 23–5, 84, 178–82, 191;
    as a baby 88–9, 134, 175–81;
    gluttony 84, 179, 186–7;
    paternity 180
Herennium, auctor ad; on
    description 40; on the status of
    the genres 146
Hermesianax 197
Hermogenes 40
Herodas; dialect 159; erudition
    159–60; everyday and low 158–60;
    irony in encomiastic poetry 25,
    191; membership of Alexandrian
    movement 2; on *trompe l'oeil* in
    fine art 43–4; pictorial realism
    90–1; tone 8, 158–60
Herodotus 22, 117
heroism, traditional 141–2, 155–7,
    173–4, 179, 195–8, 201–4, 206,
    209–14; Alexandrian redefinitions
    75–6, 155–7, 161–90 *passim*,
    195–8, 201–4, 209–14 (*see also*
    Daphnis; Erigone; Hecale;
    Hecale; Heracles; Iambe; Idas;
    Jason; Medea; Molorchus;
    Pheidon; Polyphemus the
    Cyclops; Telamon)
Herophilus 124–6
Herter, H. 185
Hesiod; and Plato 138–9; and the
    Alexandrians 96–7, 99, 148, 155,
    165, 186, 195, 197, 209;
    genre-crossing in *Works and
    Days* 147–8, 150
hetaerae; 'golden-hearted' 149
Hiero II 84, 191–2
Hipponax 159–60
Homer; admission of everyday and
    low 143–4, 147, 150; affinity with
    tragedians 135, 139–40; *Odyssey*'s
    kinship with comedy 143–4; and
    Alexandrian scholarship 28, 230;
    and Apollonius 65–78 *passim*,
    117, 156, 195, 198, 202–9; and
    Aratus 97–8; and Callimachus
    58–9, 124–5, 181–90 *passim*, 192,
    209–14; and Erinna 193; and
    Theocritus 79, 85–6, 90, 156–7,
    166–79 *passim*; separation of
    genres upheld by 135, 137–40,
    147–8
Homeric hymns 60, 71, 125, 147, 187,
    189
Homeric scholia; not an influence on
    Alexandrian *enargeia* 51n18
Horace; on description 40; on the
    status of the genres 146
Hylas 48, 73–4, 85, 115, 123, 174–5,
    202

Iambe 221n87
Idas 195–6, 201–2
'Idyll der Kleinwelt' 182, 186–7
Iphicles 88, 176
Iris 61–2
irony; and the technique of
    juxtaposition 32n44, 65, 82, 134,
    161–2, 169–74, 176–8, 205–6;
    compatible with realism 7–8, 12,
    22–7, 65–6, 68, 78–9, 89, 102, 125,
    128n9, 209, 229; in Apollonius
    65–6, 68, 78–9, 128n9, 205–6, 209;
    in Aratus 98; in Asclepiades
    161–2; in Callimachus 8, 65, 125,
    181–90 *passim*; in Herodas 159; in
    Machon 161; in Moschus 94; in
    Theocritus 12, 22–4, 32n44, 82–3,
    89, 134, 164–81 *passim* 191–2;
    Ptolemaic tolerance of 24–7, 102,
    181–2, 191–2

Jason 67, 70–1, 76, 195–209 *passim*; a
    'love-hero' 70–1, 76, 156, 201–4,
    208–9; a scaled down epic
    hero 156, 201–4; development
    into Euripidean character 204;
    unheroic diplomacy 202–4;
    unheroic handsomeness 203;
    unheroic 'helplessness' 203–4

kakos 148
ktistic literature 25, 122

Lacon 82–3, 168–9
Laertes 156
Leonidas; everyday and low 162;
    membership of Alexandrian
    movement 2; on *trompe l'oeil*
    44–5, 94; pictorial realism 95, 96
Leto 60, 125, 189–90
Libraries and Museum 21, 24, 124
Linus 178–9
love; non-realistic use 28–9; used for
    realistic purposes 13–18, 28, 76,
    85–6, 156, 170–5, 195–204 *passim*
Lycidas 81–2, 119–20
Lycophron; *Alexandra* 130n54; not of
    Alexandrian movement
lyric poem on bees (Pow., p. 185f.,
    G.L.P. 92 (b)) 126–7
Lysippus 94

Machon; and Ptolemies 191;
    everyday and low 161, 191; not of
    Alexandrian movement (?) 2
marriage 19, 20, 34n73, 179–80, 191
Medea 4, 14, 70–1, 75–7, 125–6,
    195–208 *passim*; development into
    Euripidean character 197,
    198–201; indispensability for

248 Index

Argonauts' mission 156, 195–6, 201; portrayed realistically 75, 125–6, 198–201
Megara 182
Melanthius 147, 170
Meleager; and *trompe l'oeil* 94; pictorial realism 96
Menander; and *mimēsis biou* 145; and *toioutoi* ('average characters') 145, 149
metre; archeboulean 192; choliambs 159–60; elegiacs and hexameters 155; hexameter 11–12, 22–3, 60, 142, 157, 166–7, 185, 193, 'bucolic bridge' 34n70, 218n48, bucolic caesura as a genre-marker in Theocritus 166–7
Middle Comedy 149
Millet, J.F. 5
mime; a low genre 10, 144–5, 158–60
mimēsis; and 'archaic intellectualism' in fine art 39, 42; and fine art 39, 46–7; and particularism in fine art 42–7; and *trompe l'oeil* in fine art 39, 42–3, 47; Aristotle's three categories of subjects of 11, 46, 139–40, 144; in Plato's thought 138–9; paradox of 5–6
mimēsis biou; combined with *enargeia* 55–102 *passim*, 189–90, 209–10; in comedy 145; in Menander 10, 145; in mime 10, 144–5
miraculous, the *see* Alexandrian poetry, and the bizarre; fantastic, the
Molorchus 25, 155, 181–2, 213
Mormo 57, 176, 192
Moschus; aetiology 124; everyday in *Europa* 28, 92–4, 182, 230; membership of Alexandrian movement 2; pictorial realism in *Europa* 28, 92–4; the fantastic in *Europa* 28, 94, 230
Mossynoeci 117
Museum *see* Libraries and Museum
Myron 44–5, 94
myth, Ptolemaic 14, 16–18, 21–7, 121, 178–82, 190–2

Naupactia 197
New Comedy; and the 'mosaic technique' of characterisation 159; and *toioutoi* ('average characters') 144–5, 149–50, 184, 188, 212
Nicander; and Apollonius 99–100, 125; audience 100, 194–5; everyday and low 194–5; membership of Alexandrian movement 2; pictorial realism 99–100, 125
Nicochares 170
Nile 92, 101
noble birth 147–8, 210–12
Nossis; and *trompe l'oeil* 94
Nymphis 71–2
Nymphodorus 117

Odysseus; and Apollonius 68, 74, 203–4; and Callimachus 210; and Philetas 55; and Theocritus 156, 170–2, 177; and verisimilitude 3

paradoxography 118–19
Paris, judgement of 45, 206–7
pathos; and the *Iliad* and tragedy 143–4
Pauson 46
Phanocles 197
phantasia 41
Pharos lighthouse 95
phauloi ('inferior characters'); represented in grand genres 147–9, 156–7, 166–74, for comic purposes 166–72, 181–2, for serious purposes 147–9, 172–4, 209–14; *see* Aristotle, on *phauloi*
Pheidon 110n141, 221n87
Pherecydes 128n5
Phidias 64, 95
Philadelphus 9, 19, 24, 84, 127n4, 179–81, 190; incestuous marriage to Arsinoe II 34n73, 179–80
Philetas; everyday and low (including love) 55–6, 197; membership of Alexandrian movement 2; pictorial realism 55–6
Philicus; *Iambe* 2, 221n87; membership of Alexandrian movement 2
Philodemus 41
Philoetius 147, 156
Philoxenus 170
Phineus 72, 156, 195–6
pictorial realism; Hellenistic literary theory 39–42; in Alexandrian poetry *see* realism, Alexandrian, pictorial; *individual authors*, pictorial realism
Pindar; and Apollonius 197, 201; and Asclepiades 162; and Callimachus 61–2; and Theocritus 88–9, 134, 176–8
Pissarro, C.J. 27
Plato; on comedy 137–9; on fine art 39, 46; on Homer 137–9; on *mimēsis* 39, 138–9; on morality in poetry 137–9; on *spoudaioi, spoudē* 137–9; on the status of the genres 137–9; on tragedy 137–9
Plautus 149

Plutarch 42
Po 118
Polybius 41
Polydeuces 68, 86–8
Polygnotus 46
Polyphemus the Cyclops 83–4, 170–2
Pompe 26, 191
Pope, Alexander 79, 81
Posidippus; and *trompe l'oeil* 94; membership of Alexandrian movement 2; pictorial realism 95
Praxinoa 9–12, 14, 18, 19, 22, 164
Praxiteles 44, 94, 168
prepon, decorum ('appropriateness') 142, 146, 150
proverbs 9, 10, 158–60, 165, 168
Ps.-Dionysius of Halicarnassus *Ars Rhetorica* 40
Ps.-Hesiod 68, 79–80
Ps.-Longinus; on description 41, 98; on the *Odyssey* 143
Ps.-Moschus; *Lament for Bion*, on Homer and Bion 157; *Megara*, everyday 182
Ptolemies; cultural programme 21–7; encouragement of Alexandrian realism 24–7, 121, 180–1, 191–2; incestuous marriage of Arsinoe II and Philadelphus 34n73, 179–80, 191; poetic preferences 24–7, 102, 179–82, 189–92, unique in Hellenistic world 25–6, 191–2; religious programme 14, 16–18, 21–7; tolerance of irony 24–7, 102, 181–2, 191–2

Quintilian; and *mimēsis biou* 145; on *enargeia* 40–1; on *ēthos* and *pathos* 143; on Menander 145; on the status of the genres 143, 145

Raphia, battle of 20–1
realism *see* realism, Alexandrian; realism, Hellenistic; realism, modern Realism; realism, perennial
realism, Alexandrian; a response to cultural needs of Alexandrian Greek audience 22–7, 65–79 *passim*, 89, 101–2, 120–7, 156, 178–81, 189–90, 195–8, 201–4, 209, 229–30, abates in later movement 15, 28–9, 94, 120, 124, 182, 230; common motivation of different forms 8, 18, 22–7; definition 3–18, 229–31; everyday and low (including love) *see individual authors*, everyday and low (including love); everyday and low, in similes 68, 76–8, 85–6, 175, 178, 208–9; limited contemporaneity 27–8; not reformist 27; not stylistically 'flat' 27; pictorial, and contemporary fine art 42–50, 62, 64, 83, 86, 93–4; and contemporary literary theory 39–42, and motivation of narrative 63, 73–4, 85, 87–90, 93, and psychological motivation 48, 73, 74, 85, 93, and structure 81, 89–90, 93, and themes 63, 71, 75–6, 81, 83–4, 87–90, in similes 64, 67, 76–8, 85, not inspired by specific works of art 49–50, 62, 93–4, 105n56, origins of 42–50 *passim* (*see also individual authors*, pictorial realism); Ptolemaic encouragement for 24–7; scientific 113–27, aetiological 6, 16–17, 60, 120–4, geographical 15, 71–2, 115–20, in retelling myth 6, 10, 14–18, 71–2, 114–15, 127n2, medical 15, 72–3, 124–7, 189–90, non-realistic uses of science 113, 116, 118, 120, 122–4, 126, (*see also individual authors*, scientific realism); similes and time-designations, in Apollonius 67–8, 76–8, 199, 208–9, in Callimachus 64, 181–2, in Theocritus 85–6, 175, 178; uniqueness 3, 18, 22, 24–7, 191–2, 229–30
realism, Hellenistic; lifelike quality in fine art 3–4, 10, 42–7
realism, modern Realism 4, 5, 7–8, 27; a subset of the 'perennial mode' 4; common and familiar experience 5; contemporaneity 27; detail 5; 'kitchen sink' 12; plausibility 6; reformism 27; serious tone 7; the 'flat style' 5, 27
realism, perennial; 'a perennial mode' 3–8; common and familiar experience 5, 8; convention 4, 6, 39; detail 5, 8; fidelity to reality 4–6; functions 7–8; paradox of 5–6, 50; plausibility 6, 8; relating its object to observable present 6–7
Reich, H. 145
Rhianus; not of Alexandrian movement 1, 3; visual detail 110n151
Rhinthon; 'hilarotragedies' 217n45; not of Alexandrian movement 2
Rhone 118
Richardson, S. 5, 6
Roman Poetry; and Alexandrian poetry 1–2, 27, 29, 230; *see also* Catullus; Virgil
Rossi, L.E. 133

Sappho (*or* Alcaeus) 59, 183-4
Sarapis 21
scholarship *see* science; Libraries and Museum
science 113-27 *passim*; *see also* Eratosthenes, science in poetry; *individual authors*, scientific realism; Libraries and Museum; realism, Alexandrian, scientific
Selene 200
Simichidas 82, 119, 129n27
Simonides 41, 42, 46
Siwah, oracle at 180
slaves; in comedy 149; in grand genres 134, 141, 147, 176-8
Sophocles; and love in tragedy 197; idealised character-portrayal 141-2
sōphrōn 148
Sotades; and Ptolemies 191
Soter 14, 21-4, 84, 179-80
spoudaioi ('superior characters') *see* Aristotle, on *spoudaioi*; Plato, on *spoudaioi, spoudē*
Stern, J.P. 3, 4, 6, 17
Stoicism 97-8, 193-4

Teiresias 156, 178-9, 195
Telamon 201-2
Telephus 135-6
Theocritus; and Callimachus 30n12, 156; and Homer 79, 85-6, 90, 156, 166-79 *passim*; and Pindar 88-9, 134, 176-8; conforming with Ptolemaic cultural programme 14, 16-18, 22-5, 84, 119, 123, 179-81; crossing a grand genre with everyday and low subject-matter 11-12, 156-7, 164-81 *passim*; definite article as genre-marker 167-8; dialect 10, 12, 164-5, 168; everyday and low (including love), in encomia 14, 23, 25, 84, 179-81, 191-2, in epyllia 134, 174-81, in pastorals 156-7, 164-74, in urban mimes 9-18 *passim*; hexameter 11, 18, 22-3, 166-74 *passim*, bucolic caesura a genre-marker 166-7; irony in encomiastic poetry 25, 179-81, 191-2; membership of Alexandrian movement 2; on incestuous marriage of Arsinoe and Philadelphus 179-80; on *trompe l'oeil* in fine art 44; pictorial realism, in encomia 84, in epigrams 95, in epyllia 85-90, in pastorals 48-50, 79-84, in urban mimes 13, 17, 84; proverbs 9, 10, 165, 168; redefinition of the epic hero and subject-matter 156-7, 166-81 *passim*; refrains 173; rustics and reality 164-6, 168, 170; scientific realism, aetiological 16, 123, geographical 119-20, in retelling myth 14-15, 115, medical 126; social status in pastorals 165, 168-9; tone, ironical 12, 22-4, 32n44, 82-3, 89, 134, 164-81 *passim*, 191-2, serious 81, 172-4
Theon 40
Theophrastus; and 'mosaic technique' of characterisation 159; on the status of the genres 143-5
Theopompus 50n4
Thersites 147-8
Theseus 62-4, 209-14; a traditional *spoudaios* 211, 213-14
Thetis 184-5, 192, 205, 211
Timagetus 118
Timarchus 44
toioutoi (*hoi kath' hēmās, homoioi, hoi nȳn*) ('average characters'); in tragedy (?) 144; in New Comedy 144-5, 149, 150; *see also* Aristotle, on *toioutoi*
tragedy; genre-crossing in 134-7, 148-50; separation of genres in 134-46 *passim*, challenged by Euripides 148-9

Virgil 3, 29, 41, 79, 93, 99, 101, 127, 230

Wellek, R. 7, 27
women; in pre-Alexandrian grand genres 134, 141, 150n3, 151n27; foregrounded in Alexandrian grand genres *see* Erigone; Erinna, crossing a grand genre with realistic subject-matter, everyday; Gorgo; Hecale; Medea; Praxinoa

Xanthias 136
Xenomedes 114
Xenophon; and *mimēsis* 39

Zeus 92-3, 98, 122, 148, 193, 205, 212; and Artemis 57-9, 183-4; and Heracles 88, 177, 180
Ziegler, K. 1-2, 157

For Product Safety Concerns and Information please contact our EU
representative GPSR@taylorandfrancis.com
Taylor & Francis Verlag GmbH, Kaufingerstraße 24, 80331 München, Germany

www.ingramcontent.com/pod-product-compliance
Lightning Source LLC
Chambersburg PA
CBHW061439300426
44114CB00014B/1751